THE LOST SOUL OF HIGHER EDUCATION

Also by Ellen Schrecker

Cold War Triumphalism:
The Misuse of History after the Fall of Communism (editor)

Many Are the Crimes: McCarthyism in America

The Age of McCarthyism: A Brief History with Documents

No Ivory Tower: McCarthyism and the Universities

Regulating the Intellectuals:
Perspectives on Academic Freedom in the 1980s
(co-edited with Craig Kaplan)

The Hired Money:
The French Debt to the United States, 1917–1929

Mrs. Chiang's Szechwan Cookbook

THE LOST SOUL OF HIGHER EDUCATION

Corporatization, the Assault on Academic Freedom, and the End of the American University

Ellen Schrecker

NEW YORK
LONDON

An earlier version of chapter 5 appeared as "Ward Churchill at the Dalton Trumbo Fountain: Academic Freedom in the Aftermath of 9/11" in the *AAUP Journal of Academic Freedom.*

Published in the United States by The New Press, New York, 2010
Distributed by Perseus Distribution

LIBRARY OF CONGRESS CATALOGING-IN-PUBLICATION DATA

Schrecker, Ellen.
The lost soul of higher education : corporatization, the assault on academic freedom, and the end of the American university / Ellen Schrecker.
p. cm.
Includes bibliographical references and index.
ISBN 978-1-59558-400-7 (hc.: alk. paper) 1. Academic freedom—United States. 2. Universities and colleges—United States. 3. Education, Higher—Economic aspects—United States. 4. Business and education—United States. I. Title.
LC72.2.S36 2010
378.1'2130973—dc22 2010008278

The New Press was established in 1990 as a not-for-profit alternative to the large, commercial publishing houses currently dominating the book publishing industry. The New Press operates in the public interest rather than for private gain, and is committed to publishing, in innovative ways, works of educational, cultural, and community value that are often deemed insufficiently profitable.

www.thenewpress.com

Composition by dix!
This book was set in Minion

Printed in the United States of America

10 9 8 7 6 5 4 3 2 1

For Pazit and Ila

CONTENTS

ACKNOWLEDGMENTS

This book began as an essay in the *Chronicle of Higher Education* comparing the academic freedom violations of the McCarthy period with those after 9/11. When The New Press's editorial director, Marc Favreau, contacted me to suggest that I expand it into a larger work, I foolishly agreed. Having already written a number of essays and lectures about the subject, I assumed it would be easy to stitch them together into a book. But, as so often happens, the more I looked at the contemporary state of academic freedom, the more I realized how much more I needed to know before I could make any sense out of it. This book, then, is the product of more research than I had intended to do when I first set out to write it.

I got a lot of help. In fact, the amount of assistance that I received in this project belies my own complaints about the lack of solidarity within the academic profession. Colleagues, friends, and perfect strangers have all been unfailingly openhanded in volunteering information and advice. They are, of course, in no way responsible for anything I have written, but their contributions have greatly enhanced my work.

For more than a decade I have been active in the American Association of University Professors, first as the editor of its magazine, *Academe*, and more recently as a member of its National Council and its Committee on Academic Freedom and Tenure. Accordingly, I have been able to rely on the AAUP's able and dedicated staff members, who have graciously provided documents, answered questions, and pointed me to sources. Everyone has been helpful, especially Ernst Benjamin, John Curtis, Jordan Kurland, Rachel Levinson, and Gary Rhoades.

Many other friends and colleagues have supplied equally valuable materials and suggestions. Evelyn Hu-DeHart and Paul Lauter were particularly generous in offering access to their personal papers. I am also grateful for the assistance of Fred Anderson, Robert Cohen, Elizabeth Hoffman, David Hollinger, Maurice Isserman, Walter LaFeber, Stephen Leberstein, Frinde Maher, John McDermott, Bart Meyers, Michael Parenti, William Rorabaugh, and Malini Johar Schueller. At Yeshiva University, I was blessed by having a truly gifted historian, Elliot Friedman, as my undergraduate research assistant.

Several people took the time to read all or part of the manuscript. Their suggestions, even if I didn't always incorporate them, have been enormously useful. I know the book has been much improved by the thoughtful comments of Ernst Benjamin, Marjorie Heins, Mary and Howard Hurtig, Michael Nash, David Rabban, Gary Rhoades, Leah Rosenberg, Joan Wallach Scott, Carole Silver, and my fellow Deconstructionists: Renate Bridenthal, Barbara Foley, Leonard Gordon, Jack Hammond, Peter Ranis, and Lise Vogel.

I owe a special debt to Michael Nash and Marilyn Young for the opportunity to spend the academic year of 2007–2008 at New York University's Tamiment Library as the recipient of the Frederic Ewen Academic Freedom Fellowship. Michael, in particular, has been a true godfather to this project in every way. Tamiment has been an invaluable resource, and I cannot be too effusive in thanking Michael and his staff, especially Kevyne Baar, Peter Filardo, and Gail Malmgreen.

I have also been fortunate to work with such a patient and insightful editor as Marc Favreau. His wise comments and commitment to the project, as well as the fine editorial work of Sarah Fan and Sue Warga, have eased the sometimes stressful process of turning a manuscript into a book. My literary agent, Ron Goldfarb, has also been a stalwart facilitator and goad.

Finally, there is my husband, Marv Gettleman, without whose loving support this book could never have been written. Not only did he take on far more than his share of household chores, but he also provided all the editorial assistance and encouragement any author could ask for. As for my granddaughters, Pazit and Ila Schrecker, they have done nothing for this book other than to give its author joy.

THE LOST SOUL
OF HIGHER EDUCATION

Introduction

"OFFICIAL DUTIES": JUAN HONG AND THE CRISIS OF THE UNIVERSITY

Juan Hong was a prickly individual. A full professor in the Department of Chemical Engineering and Materials Science at the University of California–Irvine, where he had been teaching since 1987, Hong apparently felt compelled to police his colleagues and alert his superiors to their wrongdoings. In one instance he complained that a fellow faculty member had not only misrepresented her credentials to obtain a merit increase but also obtained state funding for having solicited a donation of software that had actually come from her husband's company. Another complaint involved a colleague who had been awarded a raise on the basis of a falsified CV. Hong also criticized his chairperson and dean for having offered an academic appointment to a candidate without consulting the full department. And, finally, he protested against the overuse of adjuncts, claiming that letting them teach six of the eight courses in the materials undergraduate program was evading "the department's obligation to its students to staff courses with experienced faculty, rather than younger, transient lecturers."[1]

The university, Hong believed, rewarded him for his whistle-blowing by denying him a merit raise. The administrators who dealt with the matter did not, of course, claim that Hong's complaints were responsible for the denial. Rather, as the provost explained in an official letter to Hong in March 2005, it was Hong's inadequate research, especially his failure to get any grants, that had precipitated the unfavorable decision. The administration then also threatened to change Hong's status from full professor to "lecturer with security of employment," demanded that he come up with a written plan of remediation, and doubled his teaching load. After filing an unsuccessful whistle-blower retaliation complaint with the university, Hong turned to the courts. He wanted vindication for having exercised his constitutional freedom of speech.

His timing could not have been worse. The Supreme Court had just rendered a highly controversial decision in the case of *Garcetti v. Ceballos*, involving a Los Angeles assistant district attorney who was punished for complaining about irregularities in the DA's office. As the Court saw it, the First Amendment did not protect a public employee from retaliation against speaking out if that speech was "pursuant to his official duties." The implications of the decision for the nation's college and university teachers, most of whom teach at public institutions, were frightening. So frightening, in fact, that Justice Anthony Kennedy, writing for the Court's majority, noted there might be problems with "expression related to academic scholarship or classroom instruction" and specifically reserved the issue of "whether the analysis we conduct today would apply in the same manner to a case involving speech related to scholarship and teaching." Justice David Souter's dissent was even more explicit: *Garcetti*, he feared, could "imperil First Amendment academic freedom in public colleges and universities, whose teachers necessarily speak and write pursuant to 'official duties.'"[2]

Hong's suit against his superiors and the University of California was one of the first post-*Garcetti* cases involving a university professor to reach the courts. Ignoring Kennedy's disclaimer, the federal district judge who heard the case ruled in September 2007 that Irvine's retaliation against Hong did not violate his First Amendment rights. Because his complaints dealt with the university's business and because participation in that business through the mechanism of faculty governance was one of Hong's "official duties," those complaints had no constitutional protection. Hong, of course, appealed, and as of this writing, the Ninth Circuit has yet to render its decision.

Recognizing how devastating the case could be for the future of academic freedom, the American Association of University Professors (AAUP), along with the Thomas Jefferson Center for the Protection of Free Expression, submitted an amicus brief in support of Hong.[3] As the traditional guardian of faculty rights, the AAUP really had no choice. Since everything a professor publishes or says in class is related to his or her job, allowing the lower court's decision to stand would undermine much of the legal support that exists for academic freedom in the nation's public colleges and universities. While faculty governance is a less clear-cut component of academic freedom than teaching or research, it is equally crucial. Without a say over the conditions of their employment, professors cannot exercise the autonomy they need in order to fulfill their professional obligations. If the educational quality and intellectual integrity of their institutions is to be maintained, faculty members must participate in decisions about the curriculum and the hiring, tenure, and promotion of their colleagues. For that reason, therefore, Juan Hong's e-mails and letters about the internal workings of his department deserve as much protection as any statement he might have made in class or published in a scholarly journal.

As far as the AAUP's amicus brief is concerned, however, the specific content of Hong's complaints, as long as it does not indicate that he is unfit to teach, is essentially irrelevant. But the issues the case raises go beyond the—admittedly critical—realm of traditional academic freedom, with its quasi-legal safeguards against outside interference with the work of college and university teachers. Today the entire enterprise of higher education, not just its dissident professors, is under attack, both internally and externally. The financial challenges are obvious, as are the political ones. Less obvious, however, are the structural changes that have transformed the very nature of American higher education. In reacting to the economic insecurities of the past forty years, the nation's colleges and universities have adopted corporate practices that degrade undergraduate instruction, marginalize faculty members, and threaten the very mission of the academy as an institution devoted to the common good.

Hong's complaints about his colleagues' misbehavior address some of hazards that this transformation presents. Whatever the validity of his charges (and I withhold judgment here), the perception, for example, that scientists are misrepresenting themselves and their work is a recent and disturbing phenomenon. It reflects the increasingly competitive atmosphere within the academy and the escalating pressure on faculty members to do more research, win more grants, and publish more articles. Similarly, Hong's dissatisfaction with his superiors' failure to consult the entire department before making an appointment speaks to the growing tendency of academic administrators to increase their own power at the expense of their faculties. Finally, and most important, Hong's concern about his department's reliance on part-time lecturers points to what is perhaps the most serious threat to American higher education today: the casualization of the academic labor force. More than 70 percent of all college-level instruction in the United States is now in the hands of contingent faculty members—part-time and full-time teachers with temporary contracts. The implications of that revolution (and it is a revolution) in the composition of the faculty—for the quality of its instruction, for the welfare of its students, and for the university's ability to carry out its traditional mission—can only be disastrous.

• • •

Over the years, the United States has become increasingly dependent upon its system of higher education. A college degree is central to the American dream. It offers the main—and often the only—assurance of economic advancement for most men and women without athletic ability or musical talent. Whether it actually fulfills that promise is another question, but the explicitly meritocratic basis upon which it rests supplies the establishment with an ideological buffer against demands from underprivileged groups and individuals for a more egalitarian distribution of the nation's resources. The college campus has, in other words, replaced the frontier as the nation's most important social safety valve. In addition, universities also provide the research and training that make scientific progress (and the technological and economic advances based upon that progress) possible. There are nonmaterial benefits as well. The academy protects the American mind. In a world of sound bites and bullet points, the nation's campuses are among the last few places where it is still possible to deal with complicated ideas or entertain unorthodox opinions. Professors are the nation's main public intellectuals; they raise the questions with which an informed citizenry must deal. They are, therefore, essential to the preservation of the reasoned debate and unfettered expression that our democratic system requires.

And they are in serious danger. The threat to the academic community takes two forms: one is the ramping up of the traditional attacks on academic freedom in the wake of 9/11 and the recent culture wars, and the other is the corporate-style restructuring of American higher education. The academy has always had to fend off external challenges from politicians and others who want to eliminate unpopular professors or censor the curriculum. Those pressures have not abated. But now the nation's colleges and universities are also confronting demands for so-called reforms that would substitute economic considerations of productivity and cost-effectiveness for the traditional educational values of enlightenment and individual growth. In the name of efficiency and accountability, groups and individuals both on and off the campus threaten to transform higher education into a source of vocational training and corporate research. In the process, the nation's faculties, once the main component of American higher education, have been shunted aside. Yet without a vibrant faculty, the university cannot carry out its educational mission. And without academic freedom, the nation's college and university teachers cannot create new knowledge or stretch their students' minds.

In its traditional form, academic freedom belongs above all to the faculty. It is the system of procedures and protections that allows learning and scholarship to take place on the nation's campuses. It makes it possible for members of the academic profession to speak freely inside and outside their classrooms and to publish the results of their research without fearing that they will be dismissed or otherwise punished by the institutions that employ them. And it protects (or should protect) such squeaky wheels as Juan Hong from retaliation if they criticize those institutions. Without academic freedom, a pall of conformity would descend over the nation's colleges and universities. No longer would professors be willing to raise troubling questions that push at the boundaries of accepted wisdom. Nor would they be able to resist the pressures that are currently deforming the academy by turning it into a dog-eat-dog environment that pits institutions, faculty members, and students against one another in an exhausting and unwinnable struggle for resources.

Let us not, however, get too misty-eyed about the plight of the academic community. As an institution, it was never without major flaws—flaws, moreover, that have in part (though only in part) contributed to its present precarious condition. The uniqueness and, some would say, the strength of the American system of higher education is its diversity. It contains more than four thousand institutions, public, private, secular, and religious, that range from major research universities to proprietary trade schools. It is only to be expected, therefore, that the roughly 1.3 million men and women who constitute the nation's faculties would be as diverse as the institutions that house them. Unfortunately, however, that diversity has militated against the ability of the members of the academic profession to form a common front in their own defense and that of higher education as a whole. Political differences, disciplinary loyalties, generational ruptures, as well as the stratification of the nation's institutions of higher learning, divide faculty members within and between those institutions. As a result, it is often the case that, instead of recognizing their common interest in preserving and renewing the university, faculty members have pursued their own private agendas—often at the expense of one another, their students, and ultimately the common good. Yet unless the nation's college and university teachers get their communal act together, academic freedom may well disappear from their campuses and the academic profession as we know it could vanish from the face of the earth.

This book, then, is a plea to and for the faculty. It examines the current plight of American higher education in the hope that understanding the structural and political threats it faces will help the nation's faculties and the broader public mount a successful defense against those threats. I write from the faculty's perspective, not only because I am a faculty member but also because so much of what passes for a discussion of higher education today does not bring professors into the conversation. There are, it is true, many other people who have an interest in what is happening on the nation's campuses; students are a particularly important—and embattled—constituency. But only the faculty can carry out higher education's central mission of creating and disseminating knowledge. If, in other words, the nation's colleges and universities are to continue to educate—not simply train—the millions of men and women who seek that education, the faculty's voice must be not only heard but listened to.

Because I am a historian, I cannot make sense of any situation without putting it into its historical context. This book, although by no means a history of academic freedom and American higher education, nonetheless looks at the current problems of academe through the lens of the past. It offers a somewhat bifurcated view, however, for I am examining the two separate yet related challenges to the academic community. The first part of the book—Chapters 1 through 5—explores the fate of the traditional form of academic freedom, tracking the faculty's essentially political struggle against the external threats to its autonomy and free expression. The second part—Chapters 6 and 7—examines the structural changes within the academy. It looks at the ways in which those changes affected the nation's colleges and universities, undermining the ability of their faculties to protect their own academic freedom, their students' educations, and that all too elusive common good. Though seemingly very different, the political and structural challenges to American higher education are deeply intertwined. Not only do they both threaten the faculty's central position within the academic community, but they also reinforce each other. Political attacks on controversial teachers and ideas make it hard for professors to maintain their traditional authority within and outside the university, while structural transformations undermine the faculty's ability to resist those politically motivated pressures.

More specifically, Chapter 1 offers an overview of the traditional paradigm of academic freedom, looking at its conceptual evolution as well as at the institutional arrangements such as tenure and faculty governance that have been developed to protect it. Chapter 2 examines the way in which the academy handled the attacks on that freedom from the origins of the modern university in the late nineteenth and early twentieth centuries to the end of the McCarthy period in the 1950s. Chapter 3 looks at the 1960s, sketching out the surprisingly uncharted story of the many ways in which faculty members responded to the challenges of those turbulent years. Chapter 4 deals with the backlash against the sixties and the development of the well-orchestrated campaign against the so-called left academy that ultimately produced the culture wars of the late 1980s and 1990s. Chapter 5 brings the story of the traditional attacks on academic freedom up to date by looking at how the university was affected by the post-9/11 crackdown on civil liberties.

The focus changes in Chapter 6 which explores the structural transformation of the academy in the aftermath of the financial troubles of the late 1960s and early 1970s. It examines what many observers have called the corporatization of the university—the adoption of business-related values and practices and the commercialization of faculty research. Chapter 7 deals with how this transformation affected the nation's college and university teachers. In particular, it explores the way in which the increased emphasis on research has put pressure on faculty members at every level. It also looks at how and why the contingent faculty has grown and how its members cope with their marginal status. Finally, the epilogue offers a preliminary assessment of the implications of the current financial meltdown for the academic community and the future of higher education in the United States.

It would be satisfying to produce a happy ending. But at this point in the history of America's colleges and universities, it is hard to come up with one. Straitened resources are intensifying the competition that has so poisoned the American academy. Unless faculty members can overcome their own divisions and make the rest of the country understand how central their interests are to the system of higher education as a whole, the inexorable downgrading of the academic profession will continue. Still, there are some encouraging signs. For all their griping, most Americans recognize the importance of higher education for their own future and that of their children. A few years ago, when the conservative rabble-rouser David Horowitz was peddling an insidious attack on the nation's faculties, just about every state legislature that considered Horowitz's agenda turned it down. Academic freedom and the integrity of American higher education, when properly understood, turns out to be something that this nation still prizes. Let us hope that continues to be the case.

Chapter 1

"SO FRAGILE AND SO INDISPENSABLE": WHAT IS ACADEMIC FREEDOM AND WHY SHOULD WE CARE ABOUT IT?

When Reverend Dennis Holtschneider, the president of DePaul University in Chicago, refused to grant tenure to the controversial Middle East scholar Norman Finkelstein in June 2007, thus effectively ending Finkelstein's academic career, he was, he claimed, simply defending academic freedom, which was, he insisted, "alive and well at DePaul."[1] A month later, the University of Colorado's Board of Regents made a similar declaration, stating that it was "committed to ensuring that the university will promote and respect" academic freedom, even as it capitulated to political pressures by voting to oust Ward Churchill, the school's most notorious professor.[2] Neither the Colorado regents nor DePaul's president was setting a precedent. The American academy has a long-standing tradition of accompanying the dismissal of politically unpopular professors with invocations of respect toward academic freedom. As early as 1895, when the University of Chicago fired the outspoken economist Edward Bemis, its leaders insisted that his " 'freedom of teaching' has never been involved in the case."[3] During the McCarthy years, it was equally common for university authorities to claim that they were simply preserving academic freedom and the integrity of the academic profession by eliminating Communists or people associated with Communism.

In retrospect, it is hard to see how those authorities could square the dismissal of controversial professors with the defense of academic freedom. Yet in just about every case in which such faculty members lost their jobs because they were too outspoken or politically unpopular, the institutions that dismissed them justified that action by invoking the hallowed norms of academe. Not only do such justifications reveal the malleable nature of the concept of academic freedom, but they also show how central that concept was to the legitimacy of, even the identity of, the academic enterprise. In the following chapters, as I trace the development of academic freedom over the years, I will also be looking at how the challenges to that freedom evolved. But first, it is important to understand exactly what academic freedom is—and is not.

Like pornography, we know, or think we know, academic freedom (or the lack of it) when we see it. In its traditional formulation, it is, above all, a special protection for the faculty that shields professors from losing their jobs if they take politically unpopular positions in their writings, classes, and on- or off-campus activities. And so it is. But academic freedom is also a professional perquisite (not always secured by the First Amendment and the courts) that gives college teachers the autonomy they need to fulfill their professional responsibilities. Buttressed by the institution of tenure and the practices of peer review and faculty governance, it ensures that the academy's scholarship and teaching maintain the quality and level of innovation that have made the American system of higher education the envy of the world.

Unfortunately, one person's pornography may be another's high art. And so it is with academic freedom. Characterized in the important recent study by Matthew Finkin and Robert Post as "a warm and vaguely fuzzy privilege," the concept, so seemingly simple to define, is actually a complex set of beliefs, traditions, procedures, and legal rulings that govern many of the relationships between faculties and their employing institutions, the government, students, and the broader public.[4] Our academic forebears may have set us up for today's confusion by labeling that package "academic freedom" rather than something less resounding but more concrete such as "traditional academic privileges and responsibilities" or "code of academic practices."[5] Certainly, free expression is part of the mix. But to treat academic freedom as only, or even primarily, a form of free speech and a subset of the First Amendment is to view it in much too narrow and legalistic a perspective.[6] Over the years, the concept has expanded to cover almost everything that happens on campus, but at its core it is a faculty perquisite, pertaining to the practices and ideas that define the academic profession and govern the work life of college and university teachers.

Perhaps some of the problem comes from the fact that the earliest formulations of the concept came from abroad. The first generation of American scholars, the men who established the modern research university at the end of the nineteenth century, got their professional training in Germany, where a bifurcated notion of academic freedom held sway. One part, *Lernfreiheit* or "freedom to learn," had to do with the freedom that German students then enjoyed to shape their education according to their own desires while swinging from one institution to another, drinking beer, dueling, and attending classes when so inclined. The other half, *Lehrfreiheit* or "freedom to teach," belonged to professors and not only gave them autonomy within their classrooms but also barred external controls on their research. Faculty governance reinforced this professional independence. German academics ran their universities, making all the personnel decisions and electing deans and other administrators from among their number. That autonomy, so it was claimed, was necessary if scholars were to engage in the unfettered pursuit of knowledge that was central to the mission of the German university. At the same time, their freedom from outside control set these academics apart from (and above) their fellow citizens in the rigidly stratified society of nineteenth-century Germany.

Yet for all their freedom and authority within the university, German professors were quite constrained outside of it. The German university system, unlike the American one, was an arm of the state. Academics were civil servants and were thus expected to support the government. They could be—and were—fired for backing opposition parties. And while their colleagues did protest against such dismissals, they did so because the officials who carried them out were infringing on the faculty's collective prerogatives, not because they were upset about the violations of their colleagues' individual rights. In fact, most professors actually endorsed the restrictions on their own off-campus activities; abandoning their supposed political neutrality would, they felt, interfere with their scholarship and pollute their higher calling.[7]

Despite the limited scope of its *Lehrfreiheit,* the prestige of the German professoriate in the late nineteenth century was so high that the faculty members who staffed the first generation of American research universities consciously sought to emulate it. In particular, they sought to incorporate the concept of academic freedom directly into their institutions, believing, as one later historian put it, "that academic freedom, like academic searching, *defined* the true university."[8] The model they thought they were importing—that of a self-governing faculty that brooked no external interference with its core functions of teaching and research—was to become one of the distinctive characteristics of the American professoriate, developing in tandem with the growth of the modern American university.

In actuality, as the academic profession evolved, it embraced a wide variety of practices, of which the Germanic notion of academic freedom was only one. Its most significant characteristic was the codification of its own identity. This process, which we have come to call professionalization, was not unique to the nation's college and university teachers. As American society became increasingly complex in the late nineteenth and early twentieth century, other fields of endeavor—medicine, law, and engineering, for example—also developed rules of professional behavior, designed in large part to maintain their members' privileged status. Whatever the occupation, the same or similar systems and procedures came to characterize its practitioners' emerging identity as professionals. They exercised considerable autonomy within their workplaces; they controlled access to their ranks by means of some kind of specialized educational requirement or examination; and they built institutions such as bar associations, medical licensing boards, and scholarly organizations to serve as gatekeepers and regulators. Finally, they justified these measures in terms of service. Professionals had a higher calling than other workers; their activities benefited the common good of the entire society. As a result, they had to be free from meddling by outsiders who did not share their special knowledge and commitment.[9]

Universities were central to the process, both as a source of the professions' necessary credentialing and as the institutional home of the newly organized academic profession. As it developed and became increasingly professionalized, the professoriate created its own instruments of self-regulation—the PhD, academic disciplines and departments, and scholarly presses and publications. Gluing all these diverse activities and institutions together ideologically was the code of practices and beliefs that would come to be known as academic freedom.

Autonomy was the crucial element here. Academic freedom, if it was to guarantee the respect and professional status that late nineteenth-century college and university teachers coveted, required that faculty members control the main conditions of their work. Yet that autonomy was—and still is—hard to come by. After all, unlike their fellow professionals in the fields of law or medicine, college teachers are not independent operators who can open up a private practice once they gain acceptance by their peers. They are employees, working within institutions officially governed by lay boards of trustees and subject to the authority of university administrators. As a result, faculties, if they were to retain their distinctive status as professionals, had to develop mechanisms that would keep those outsiders from interfering with what they taught and wrote and whom they hired.

The first generation of professionalized American academics recognized the anomalies of their situation. In their 1915 Declaration of Principles on Academic Freedom and Academic Tenure, the founders of the American Association of University Professors strove to codify the distinctive position of college and university teachers, who were, the declaration explained, "appointees, but not in any proper sense the employees" of the people who hired them.[10] Thus, just as judges maintained their independence from the executive officials who appointed them, so too, professors were to be free from external interference. Legally, they might be subject to the authority of trustees and administrators, but if universities were to perform their modern function of creating and disseminating knowledge, and to perform it in accordance with the common good, then faculty members whose work was central to the universities' mission had to exercise almost complete autonomy within the educational sphere. In that sense, therefore, academic freedom was above all a matter of professionalism, a tool that American college and university teachers could use to control their own terms of employment.

That it was (and still is) also a struggle for free expression stems from the nature of academic work, which, as the intellectual degeneration of the universities under the Nazi and Soviet regimes reveals, cannot be performed adequately under conditions of duress.[11] The teaching and research that academics carry out must be free from outside interference. Scholars and scientists cannot merely follow orders. New knowledge can be produced only through the unfettered interplay of these people's trained minds with the data they collect in their libraries and laboratories. Similarly, as teachers, faculty members can only develop their students' powers of rational and independent thought if they are themselves autonomous within their classrooms. There is nothing controversial about this vision of academic freedom; we hear it every May and June in the nation's commencement addresses—an edifying truism no less accurate for being dull.

What this noble and often empty language does not, however, convey is the bifurcated reality of the struggle for academic freedom; it is both a high-minded campaign for free expression as well as a more self-interested one for professional status and respectability. That the latter campaign is almost always swathed in the rhetoric of the former should not surprise us. Because of their indeterminate position as both employees and independent professionals, academics have often been peculiarly sensitive about their own status. After all, in a society where money counts, they are not rich. Isolated in large part from the rest of the middle class by their cultivated lifestyle, they withdraw into what was, at least until a few decades ago, a decorous and inbred collegial world where prestige is the main commodity and no one wants to rock the boat.[12] At the same time—and this, too, matters—their professed concern for and genuine need for intellectual autonomy is real. Thus, we should not let the less sympathetic aspects of the struggle for academic freedom detract from its legitimacy. After all, intellectual freedom does not exist within a vacuum; it operates through its academic constituents. As a result, whatever strengthens the power and autonomy of the academic profession also protects the broader freedom of inquiry and expression that the rest of society allegedly prizes and actually needs. That there may also be some collateral damage in the form of professorial deadwood is the not too hefty price that academic freedom exacts.

Of course, the freedom and autonomy American faculties enjoy are far from unlimited. As the AAUP's founders recognized, the academic profession had to act responsibly. It had to establish and enforce its own regulations if it was to keep trustees and politicians from dictating syllabi or firing instructors. Those regulations were rather straightforward. According to the 1915 declaration, faculty members had to present the conclusions of their research as "the fruits of competent and patient and sincere inquiry . . . set forth with dignity, courtesy, and temperateness of language." Similarly, as teachers, they must not take "unfair advantage of" their students "by indoctrinating" them with their own opinions, but instead must "train them to think for themselves." Finally, in their off-campus activities, professors had the "peculiar obligation to avoid hasty or unverified or exaggerated statements, and to refrain from intemperate or sensational modes of expression." Fulfilling these obligations not only would ensure the quality of the academic community's research and teaching by establishing standards that the whole community could accept but also would keep outsiders at bay. In other words, academia had to police itself. "If this profession," the AAUP's founding document explained,

> should prove itself unwilling to purge its ranks of the incompetent and the unworthy, or to prevent the freedom which it claims in the name of science from being used as a shelter for inefficiency, for superficiality, or for uncritical and intemperate partisanship, it is certain that the task will be performed by others.

And those "others" will almost certainly "lack full competency" to judge "when departures from the requirements of the scientific spirit and method have occurred," not to mention that they may also be motivated by something other "than zeal for the integrity of science." Above all—and here the language of the 1915 declaration is particularly revealing—"it is . . . unsuitable to the dignity of a great profession that the initial responsibility for the maintenance of its professional standards should not be in the hands of its own members."[13]

Creating the mechanisms to develop and enforce those professional standards has been complicated by the multiple loyalties of faculty members—to the colleges and universities that employ them, to their disciplines, and finally to the academic profession as a whole. Tradition has allocated the chief institutional responsibility in the latter sphere to the AAUP, with the result that many schools and associations within each discipline have borrowed freely from the analyses, policies, and recommended procedures that the association has developed in its nearly one hundred years of existence. Particularly ubiquitous in this regard is the AAUP's 1940 Statement of Principles on Academic Freedom and Tenure, a short document that not only summarizes the way in which academic freedom protects college and university teachers in their research, classrooms, and extramural utterances but also contains guidelines for granting and protecting tenure.[14] More than two hundred scholarly and professional associations have officially endorsed this statement, while many colleges and universities have incorporated its language into their own faculty handbooks and union contracts.

Despite the widespread diffusion of the 1940 statement, the academic profession is too diverse for any single code of behavior to suffice. Accordingly, each discipline has had to elaborate its own set of rules. Art historians, for example, must pay attention to the attribution of artworks, anthropologists must treat their informants humanely, and biomedical scientists must avoid conflicts of interest when doing corporate-sponsored research. Surprisingly, though, the differences may be less significant than one might expect. Almost every field, including the natural sciences, has crafted a code of professional ethics that stresses such elements of the researcher's responsibility to the discipline as ensuring the replicability of his or her work and allocating credit to other scholars.

Here, for example, is a recent statement from my own discipline, adopted early in 2005 by the American Historical Association in the wake of some nasty scandals:

> *Historians should practice their craft with integrity. They should honor the historical record. They should document their sources. They should acknowledge their debts to the work of other scholars. They should respect and welcome divergent points of view even as they argue and subject those views to critical scrutiny. They should remember that our collective enterprise depends on mutual trust. And they should never betray that trust.* [Italics in the original]

What is so striking about this passage is its emphasis on the communal aspects of historical scholarship. Historians, the document notes, define themselves "by self-conscious identification with *a community of historians who are collectively engaged in investigating and interpreting the past as a matter of disciplined learned practice.*"[15] The historian's primary responsibility, the statement seems to imply, is to other historians, a professional obligation that, on the surface, seems rather inbred and does not convey the academy's traditional emphasis on the pursuit of truth or its obligation to serve the public. Yet if we realize that other historians are the only people who can judge whether or not one of their colleagues has violated the discipline's professional norms, then making history professors answerable to each other is, in fact, the very essence of the peer review that protects American academic freedom.

Historians are not alone in recognizing the collective nature of their professional responsibilities. The American Physical Society's Guidelines for Professional Conduct for physicists uses almost identical language about "community" and "mutual trust" and its members' shared "responsibility for the welfare of this community."[16] Sociologists, according to the American Sociological Association's Code of Ethics, also "form a community" with a "shared responsibility for ethical behavior."[17] And, in a like vein, the literary scholars who belong to the Modern Language Association (MLA) constitute "a community valuing free inquiry" that "must be able to rely on the integrity and the good judgment of our members."[18] What these formulations reveal, as Joan W. Scott, the former chair of the AAUP's Committee A on Academic Freedom, points out, is that the support provided by the "disciplinary community" not only verifies someone's "technical expertise and qualifications" but provides "that communal self-regulation based in a certain expertise that made academic freedom different from other notions of individual rights."[19] In other words, the maintenance of academic standards is a communal responsibility, requiring the members of each discipline to respect the informed judgment of the collectivity of their peers.

The institutions through which these responsibilities are undertaken vary, but provisions for peer review crop up at every turn. Within their departments, professors admit and train future academics. They also share the responsibility for hiring, promoting, and, if necessary, firing individual faculty members, usually with the concurrence of university-wide committees. Disciplinary associations organize the conferences that enable researchers to present their findings and get criticism from colleagues. Academic presses and learned journals ask reputable scholars in the field to assess the manuscripts they receive, while grant and fellowship applications undergo a similar process of peer review. None of these procedures is unproblematic. Political, personal, and intellectual conflicts can and do emerge as academics disagree among themselves over what constitutes good work in their fields—or even what kind of work belongs in that field.[20]

Still, the system does work—most of the time. Despite the misinformation spread by conservative critics of the university, America's college professors are responsible individuals who set sensible standards and ensure that they and their colleagues do not abuse their classrooms. Naturally, a few bad apples exist, but most academics do not prey on their students, fabricate their scholarship, or recycle their lectures from outdated graduate school notes. Significantly, during the height of the McCarthy era, when at least a hundred college teachers lost their jobs for political reasons, none were ever accused of indoctrinating students or falsifying research results. If the system seems dysfunctional, as so many detractors of higher education like to claim, the fault lies elsewhere.

Actually, despite legitimate concerns about the erosion of academic freedom, we should resist the temptation to view American higher education as a battleground. For the vast majority of college and university teachers who do not try to push the envelope, the campus has usually been a pretty safe place. When skirmishes over academic freedom did break out, they were almost always political in the broadest sense of the term. Professors got into trouble when they became enmeshed in power struggles on campus or else when they took positions that offended powerful interests outside it. Perhaps the most typical violations of academic freedom occurred at those schools where ambitious administrators sought to eliminate all challenges to their authority. When faculty members questioned that authority, they could find themselves without a job. After all, until the practice of tenure gained near-universal recognition in the mid-twentieth century, employment "at will" was the norm throughout the American system of higher education. Accordingly, professors who antagonized their schools' administrators had little protection against the whims of an autocratic president. Most of the time, it is true, these types of conflicts tended to arise at smaller, more vulnerable, and less prestigious institutions that had yet to embrace the professional norms of the modern university—as they still do today.[21]

A more serious challenge came from external attempts to suppress the controversial political activities of individual faculty members. It was, in fact, a number of such incidents involving outspoken social scientists at some of the nation's leading universities that prodded a group of eminent academics to establish the AAUP. The leading scholars in their fields, the organization's founders were not radicals but thoughtful middle-class professionals ensconced within the progressive reform movement of their time. As we have seen, their 1915 declaration of principles elaborated a set of guidelines for their peers' political activities that, they hoped, would keep outsiders from interfering. Central to this formulation was the assertion that professors should not be punished for taking stands on matters of public interest. Nor should they have to restrict their remarks only to their own subjects of expertise or accept more limitations on their political activities than their fellow citizens endured. At the same time, however, they were expected to behave judiciously and, above all, to make it clear that they were speaking as private individuals, not representatives of their institutions. That final injunction, repeated in the 1940 statement as well, creates a mutual obligation that, though often misunderstood, is crucial to academic freedom. It gives faculty members room to operate in the political sphere without having to answer to their employers, just as it enables those employers to distance themselves from whatever unpopular stands their faculty members may take. As long as universities do not censor, and thus become responsible for, their professors' off-campus remarks, those faculty members do not risk their jobs by taking politically unpopular stands. Such, at least, was the ideal.

In reality, the fledgling AAUP could do little to protect a controversial faculty member against a hostile president or board of trustees. The hyperpatriotism of World War I, for example, stimulated a spate of dismissals that revealed the fragility of academic freedom. But once the war ended, the basic conservatism of most professors ensured that that freedom was rarely tested. Even so, American educators continued to develop an informal consensus about the desirability of academic freedom and the tenure that protected it. The AAUP's 1940 Statement on Academic Freedom and Tenure, drawn up in conjunction with the Association of American Colleges (now the Association of American Colleges and Universities), codified that consensus. Over time, the 1940 statement has come to be accepted by most of the nation's leading public and private institutions. Nonetheless, its guidelines are by no means universally embraced—or adhered to. Nor, as Juan Hong learned to his dismay, do they have constitutional protection.

Academic Freedom and the Law

For a nation that relies so heavily on its legal system to handle its political conflicts, it is something of a surprise to discover that academic freedom did not receive much attention in the courts before the mid-1950s. Despite its obvious relationship to the First Amendment's freedom of expression, it was not until 1957 that the Supreme Court officially recognized the concept of academic freedom.[22] When it did so—in the case of Paul Sweezy, a Marxist economist who was fighting a New Hampshire contempt conviction—it produced an eloquent defense of academic freedom. Although Sweezy had answered most of the questions put to him by the Granite State's attorney general, he claimed that those about the content of his lectures at the University of New Hampshire and the identity of his political associates violated his First Amendment rights. The court's majority agreed, and, for the first time, brought higher education under the Bill of Rights. Academic freedom was necessary, so Chief Justice Earl Warren explained, for

> to impose any strait jacket upon the intellectual leaders in our colleges and universities would imperil the future of our Nation. No field of education is so thoroughly comprehended by man that new discoveries cannot yet be made. Particularly is that true in the social sciences, where few, if any, principles are accepted as absolutes. Scholarship cannot flourish in an atmosphere of suspicion and distrust. Teachers and students must always remain free to inquire, to study and to evaluate, to gain new maturity and understanding; otherwise our civilization will stagnate and die.

The concurring opinion by the former Harvard law professor Felix Frankfurter was equally eloquent about "the dependence of a free society on free universities."

> This means the exclusion of governmental intervention in the intellectual life of a university. It matters little whether such intervention occurs avowedly or through action that inevitably tends to check the ardor and fearlessness of scholars, qualities at once so fragile and so indispensable for fruitful academic labor.
>
> It is the business of a university to provide that atmosphere which is most conducive to speculation, experiment and creation. It is an atmosphere in which there prevail "the four essential freedoms" of a university—to determine for itself on academic grounds who may teach, what may be taught, how it shall be taught, and who may be admitted to study.[23]

Ten years later, in a decision voiding a New York State law requiring college teachers to sign an anti-Communist affidavit, Justice William Brennan offered what still remains the Supreme Court's most powerful defense of academic freedom. It was, he said in *Keyishian v. Board of Regents*, "of transcendent value to all of us and not merely to the teachers concerned. That freedom is therefore a special concern of the First Amendment, which does not tolerate laws that cast a pall of orthodoxy over the classroom." Quoting from an earlier decision, Brennan then went on to explain:

> "The vigilant protection of constitutional freedoms is nowhere more vital than in the community of American schools." The classroom is peculiarly the "marketplace of ideas." The Nation's future depends upon leaders trained through wide exposure to that robust exchange of ideas which discovers truth "out of a multitude of tongues, [rather] than through any kind of authoritative selection."[24]

As in the earlier *Sweezy* ruling, Brennan stressed the benefits that academic freedom confers upon the entire society, thus echoing the rationales that the AAUP's founders had elaborated fifty years before. In other words, by 1967, the Supreme Court had decided that the professional autonomy and intellectual freedom of America's college and university teachers was not only necessary for the pursuit of truth, but also, in some nebulous way, for the national welfare.

Unfortunately, the stirring rhetoric of *Sweezy* and *Keyishian* did not specify how academic freedom might be applied in faculty governance, for example, or in cases where individual professors came into conflict with their institutions—an omission that would lead to confusion about whom and what that freedom was supposed to protect. Moreover, that protection was far from universal. To begin with, it only stretched as far as the First Amendment's strictures against governmental interference with freedom of speech and association. As employees of the state, professors at public institutions would be free to speak out on controversial issues, but the men and women who teach at private colleges and universities have no such protection.[25] They must rely on tenure, contracts, and the force of academic custom, rather than the Constitution. Because Yeshiva University, where I teach, is a private institution, I cannot, for example, invoke the First Amendment if the university's administration or my colleagues interfere with my freedom of expression. Even so, it is clear that I do have (or at least should have) academic freedom despite my inability to cite the Bill of Rights in its defense. The language of *Sweezy* and *Keyishian*, by conveying the Supreme Court's imprimatur to the commonly accepted principles of academic freedom, has shored up those principles—even at institutions the First Amendment cannot reach.

The law evolves, however, and what had once seemed such a straightforward conception of academic freedom—that it protects faculty members in their research, teaching, and public activities—is no longer quite so clear. Over the past thirty years, other players, primarily students and administrators, have sought to stake a claim to the privilege. In particular, colleges and universities have begun to insist that they, too, can invoke the protection of academic freedom, claiming that it is an institutional as well as, or even instead of, an individual right. At the same time, the legal system, which, as one scholar has noted, "operates on an impoverished understanding of the unique and complex functions performed by our universities," has managed to muddle the situation with contradictory and often unrealistic rulings, as the case of Juan Hong reveals.[26] Accordingly, ambiguity reigns supreme. The courts have ruled that academic freedom belongs both to individual professors and to the schools they work for.

The Supreme Court first recognized the institutional version of academic freedom in its landmark *Bakke* decision of 1978. While overruling the University of California's policy of setting aside places for minority group applicants, the justices did allow the university to give a preference to such students if its goal was to enrich the overall educational experience by creating a more diversified student body. In buttressing that argument, Justice Lewis Powell cited the key passages from *Sweezy* and *Keyishian* to show that the university's educational functions, including the selection of students, fell under the protection of academic freedom.[27] Although it did not get much attention at the time, that conceptualization transformed the traditional version of academic freedom from its original function of shielding the professional activities of individual instructors from external interference to one that protects the institutions where those activities take place.

One can argue, of course, that whatever fosters the educational mission of the school, whether implemented by the university's administration or by its faculty members, should fall within the penumbra of academic freedom. Such, certainly, are the implications of Frankfurter's reference to the academy's "four essential freedoms" in his *Sweezy* opinion. The political scientist and current president of the University of Pennsylvania, Amy Guttmann, makes a similar argument when she claims that the university's academic freedom protects that of its professors, by creating "an institutional sanctuary against repression" that allows them to speak and write freely.[28] The legal scholar Peter Byrne also distinguishes between the traditional form of academic freedom that protects individual professors and what he calls the corporate right of "constitutional academic freedom," which belongs to institutions of higher learning. Because universities provide "those structures that permit the individual scholar to engage with others in collective scholarship . . . constitutional academic freedom should protect these structures from extramural political distortion."[29] There is, he claims, no need for the law to intervene on behalf of individual professors. As long as universities rely on the traditional academic practices of peer review and faculty governance, their professors' academic freedom will not be violated. In fact, Byrne and his followers believe that submitting academic disputes to litigation threatens academic freedom: it lets judges, who are, after all, state officials—and, therefore, outsiders—decide key educational issues.[30]

Nor, as we have seen in the case of Juan Hong, are those judges eager to take on that responsibility. As long as a college or university can claim that its action relates to its educational work and does not violate basic norms of due process, the nation's judiciary has tried to keep aloof. Occasionally, however, it has intervened when universities invoked academic freedom to fend off legitimate constitutional claims—either because of violations of the First Amendment or, more commonly, because of racial or sexual discrimination.[31] Thus, for example, in a 1982 dispute involving Princeton University in which the school brought a trespassing case against a nonstudent who was distributing leaflets on campus, the courts ruled that the university could not invoke academic freedom to suppress the leafletter's freedom of speech when no educational issues were at stake.[32] The judiciary reached a similar conclusion when the University of Pennsylvania asserted that academic freedom required it to withhold its personnel files from an Equal Employment Opportunity Commission investigation of racial and sexual discrimination.[33] In that case, the Supreme Court unanimously ruled that the public interest in avoiding discrimination trumped the university's interest in preserving the inviolability of its records. Though the AAUP submitted an amicus brief in support of Penn's argument that the confidential process of peer review had to be protected from federal interference, there was considerable debate within the organization about the propriety of that position.[34]

In a sense, both the Princeton and Pennsylvania decisions were atypical in that the courts did not accept the universities' invocation of academic freedom. Recently, however, the judiciary has been conceding more authority to the schools, especially in situations that pit administrations against faculty members. Here, we can see the wisdom of Byrne's argument against taking academic issues to court. Because judges ordinarily assume that the institution's leaders know far better than they do how to run their schools, they tend to defer to them, as in fact District Judge Cormac Carney did to the Irvine authorities with regard to Juan Hong's complaint.[35] Usually such litigation has involved issues such as student grades or admissions standards, where faculty members and administrations are on the same side. But in cases where professors and their institutions disagree, the nation's judges have sometimes revealed a disturbing lack of insight into the nature of higher education. In 1991, for example, a federal appeals court sided with the University of Alabama in a case involving a physiology professor's discussion of his religious beliefs in class, maintaining that "the university must have the final say in such a dispute. . . . The University's conclusions about course content must be allowed to hold sway over an individual professor's judgments."[36]

Perhaps the most distressing such case, because it touched on issues central to both teaching and research, was the litigation surrounding the 1999 Virginia law prohibiting state employees from accessing sexually explicit material on their workplace computers without the permission of their superiors. Soon after the law was passed, six professors sued the state, claiming that the new regulation prevented them from carrying out their academic duties. The lead plaintiff, constitutional scholar Melvyn Urofsky, explained that the measure made it impossible for him to assign a class project on indecency law; an English professor noted that he was prevented from accessing the sexually explicit poems in an online database that he needed for his work on Victorian poetry; and several scientists could not get the information about human sexuality that their AIDS research required. They lost their case. Admittedly, Urofsky and his colleagues were unfortunate in their choice of venues, for the Fourth Circuit Court of Appeals has a notoriously conservative reputation. And in this case, a seriously divided court ruled that, as state employees, Virginia's college and university teachers could invoke their First Amendment rights only if they were dealing with public issues as private citizens. Activities that took place as part of their job had no such protection. To make matters worse, the majority also declared that individual professors had no claim to academic freedom. "To the extent the Constitution recognizes any right of 'academic freedom' above and beyond the First Amendment rights to which every citizen is entitled," the majority opinion proclaimed, "the right inheres in the University, not in individual professors."[37]

Though the *Urofsky* decision ignores numerous legal precedents and contrary opinions in other circuits, the Supreme Court let it stand by denying certiori. Moreover, in the 2006 *Garcetti* case, which involved a Los Angeles deputy district attorney's criticism of his superiors' actions, the court's majority, as we have seen, reinforced *Urofsky*'s limitations on an academic's freedom of teaching and research. It ruled that the First Amendment covers only statements about public issues and does not protect any job-related utterances. Literally applied, this decision, *Garcetti v. Ceballos*, threatens the entire legal scaffolding that supports the faculty's claim to academic freedom. Perhaps alerted by the AAUP's amicus brief in the case, Justice Kennedy for the majority (as well as Justice Souter in dissent) did recognize that threat and explicitly noted that college professors might require more constitutional protection, but did not address the issue.[38] Unfortunately, the district court in California that ruled against Juan Hong ignored the *Garcetti* justices' warning and struck at the very heart of academic freedom. That ruling denied constitutional protection to almost everything a college and university teacher says in or outside the classroom on the grounds that such statements comprise a teacher's professional duties. But since those professional duties—teaching, research, and university governance—are exactly what academic freedom has been formulated to safeguard, the district court's decision seems more than a little absurd.

Tenure, Due Process, and Academic Freedom

And yet, despite its whittling away by such unfortunate decisions as *Urofsky*, *Garcetti*, and *Hong*, the traditional form of academic freedom still exists, misunderstood and imperiled as it may be. It exists by virtue of two practices that protect the job security and institutional authority of college and university teachers: tenure and faculty governance. It exists as well because of the procedural guarantees that surround those practices. "There can be no academic freedom," the First Amendment watchdog Nat Hentoff explained, "without due process."[39] Nor, as we shall see, without tenure. And it is no accident that the AAUP's 1915 founding document was entitled a Declaration of Principles on Academic Freedom *and Academic Tenure*, or that its 1940 update was also a Statement of Principles on Academic Freedom *and Tenure* (italics added). No tenure, no academic freedom—at least as the professoriate's main organization sees it. Faculty governance, while not granted the same emphasis as tenure, also protects academic freedom: it ensures that faculty members participate in the main educational decisions of their institution. To be sure, considerable controversy surrounds both practices. They do not always work as promised. Nor, more importantly, have they been updated to cover the current majority of the academic workforce, the hundreds of thousands of underpaid and insecure part-time and non-tenure-track instructors. Moreover, as we shall see, trustees, politicians, and ordinary citizens, not to mention professors themselves, are now questioning the relevance and desirability of the traditional forms of tenure and faculty governance in the fast-changing world of the twenty-first century.

The classic, and still the strongest, argument for tenure is that it protects academic freedom. Because universities must jump through so many procedural hoops to fire a tenured professor, they rarely do so except in extraordinary situations. Still, as the academic community's dismal record during the McCarthy era reveals, when those extraordinary situations occur and the university faces apparently overwhelming pressures, even people with tenure can lose their jobs. Ward Churchill's recent experiences simply reinforce this observation: tenure cannot protect a controversial professor when an institution wants him out. Yet, tenure is not a total wash. With only one exception that I know of (Clement Markert, an outstanding scientist whom the president of the University of Michigan was planning to drop when his contract expired), every single junior faculty member who tangled with the anti-Communist inquisition during the late 1940s and 1950s lost his or her job. And while many tenured people were also purged, some did outlast the furor.[40]

My own experiences prove tenure's value. As a historian who wants to conform to the highest professional standards while also trying to contribute in some way to the cause of freedom and social justice, I am viewed as a controversial figure in some circles.[41] I would be seriously hampered in my work, however, if I was constantly worrying about losing my job because of something I wrote or said. This is especially the case because I teach at an institution whose political culture is, in some respects, problematical for me. Yeshiva is an Orthodox Jewish university with a strong institutional commitment to a particular brand of Zionism. Even though I have tenure (and had enough publications at the time I was hired not to worry about obtaining it), my academic freedom is limited. I steer away from Israel and the Middle East in my teaching, research, and off-campus political activities—though more because I don't want to antagonize my students than because I fear for my job. The one time I did take a public stance by signing a petition along with nearly two thousand other "Jews Against the Occupation," there was an immediate response on campus, with letters to the school paper headlined "Terminate Schrecker." Because I had tenure (and a thick skin), I did not expect, nor did I experience, any problems. In fact, Yeshiva's administrators went out of their way to reassure me that the school would take no action against me. But I never would have signed such a petition if I did not have tenure—nor would I recommend that a junior colleague do so.

I am, however, somewhat anomalous. There may be, at most, a few thousand radicals or nonconformists among the 1.3 million men and women who teach at U.S. colleges and universities. Most faculty members are not activists, nor does their work lead them into intellectual or political minefields. As a result, they do not feel the need for the kind of academic freedom that tenure protects.[42] But they gain from it nonetheless, for the academic freedom that tenure shores up is a collective benefit that allows all professors to claim the higher status and professional independence that membership in a learned profession conveys. Tenure is also the mechanism through which institutions create a protected space within which college and university teachers can exercise their craft without worrying that an unpopular or unorthodox undertaking might put their careers at risk. More concretely, it creates an economically secure cohort of senior faculty members who can (and sometimes do) defend the quality of American education as well as the ability of all their colleagues to teach, do research, and speak out as citizens without fear of institutional reprisals. Such, at least, is the idealized version of the relationship between tenure and academic freedom.

But tenure benefits the academy in some very material ways as well. Although it is easy to view that practice only from the perspective of the individual professors who enjoy the kind of job security that most other workers can only dream of, there is a strong institutional rationale for the practice. Universities, after all, are not corporations and cannot provide the kinds of financial remuneration that similarly educated individuals in other fields expect. This was especially the case in the early years of the modern university when faculty salaries were so low that professors ironically referred to themselves as "philanthropists."[43] As a result, the AAUP's early leaders recognized that it would be necessary for the academy to provide "the assurance of an honorable and *secure* position" (italics added) if it was to succeed

> in attracting into its ranks men of the highest ability, of sound learning, and of strong and independent character. This is the more essential because the pecuniary emoluments of the profession are not, and doubtless never will be, equal to those open to the more successful members of other professions.[44]

The organization's 1940 statement makes the same point about the need for "a sufficient degree of economic security to make the profession attractive to men and women of ability."[45] Admittedly, there are other rewards that academic professionals seek: status, rank, recognition by their peers, publication, and desirable working conditions, not to mention the pleasures of reading, writing, and teaching about things they want to read, write, and teach about.[46] Nonetheless, tenure is definitely a major draw.

The nature of the academic profession also militates in favor of its unique job security. Academics are not interchangeable parts. As highly trained professionals who have invested years of study in specific, often narrow, areas of their disciplines, they lack the flexibility to move from one job to another the way people within a private company do—a flexibility that, although not formally codified, gave corporate employees considerable job security. It is—or at least was, until the private sector embarked on the past few decades' orgy of downsizing and outsourcing—a common practice for companies to transfer people from sales, say, to personnel and then to marketing with only a little in-house training. Ironically, this practice meant that corporations gave their employees instant tenure, even if not necessarily in the specific job to which they were assigned. Once hired, unless they were truly incompetent, these employees could be promoted, retrained, and switched around until they ended up in positions that accommodated their level of skill and energy. But they were rarely fired; it was economically undesirable to have a lot of turnover in the workforce.[47]

Obviously, the academic workplace lacks that kind of flexibility. A mathematician cannot teach a class on medieval Islam, nor can an art historian run an organic chemistry lab. Moreover, there is no way that the employing institution can provide the kind of retraining that would facilitate such a transformation, nor would a mathematician teach herself Arabic to retain her position or an art historian become a chemist. They would seek jobs at other colleges or universities rather than leave their discipline.[48] From the institution's perspective, therefore, tenure serves, at least in part, to develop the institutional loyalty that will not only keep a valuable faculty member at the school but also encourage that person to engage in its long-term planning.[49]

Moreover, universities, like corporations, cannot afford much turnover. Because of the academic profession's lack of flexibility, its personnel decisions must be carefully weighed. Unlike an employee in the private sector, an unproductive scholar or inadequate teacher cannot be transferred to a less demanding position within the institution. As a result, in order to ensure that universities do not burden their faculties with washouts, the academic community has developed the onerous assessments that characterize the tenure track. Consider, for example, the amount of effort that goes into the hiring process—the hours of reading dossiers and dissertations, the days of interviews and campus visits, and the interminable rounds of meetings. Consider the even more elaborate procedures that go into most tenure decisions—more reading, plus teaching evaluations, outside letters, and multiple layers of committees. But unless the institution does not care about academic standards, it cannot forgo these time-consuming practices. While corporations assess their employees on a regular basis, they can do so in a fairly mechanistic way. Universities cannot; even the largest and most well-endowed institution lacks the resources to reevaluate and replace its medieval Islamicists and algebraic topologists every year. Tenure thus lets the academic community avoid excessive turnover while still ensuring the quality of the institution's faculty. It is structured around two assessments—one at hiring, the other some six years later—that are far more rigorous than those elsewhere in society and give the institution enough confidence in the ability of the successful candidates to retain them on a permanent basis.

The tenure decision is a big deal for everyone involved. It marks the up-or-out moment that, more than any other, shapes an academic's entire career. In order to increase its fairness, the AAUP has sought to standardize the procedure for awarding tenure. Its 1940 statement specified a seven-year period of probation, with a decision on reappointment to be made during the sixth year. Though the rigidity of that timetable has been called into question as women and minority group members enter an institution that had been designed for white men with stay-at-home wives, most schools still try to follow the AAUP's guidelines. The traditional reasoning behind them is that the deadline provides enough time to tell whether the individuals have fulfilled their colleagues' initial expectations and yet comes early enough in people's careers so that it does not foreclose other options if they do not make the grade. The latter rationalization may no longer be appropriate, given the current state of the academic job market and its almost complete lack of lateral mobility. But it is not clear that keeping potentially unsuccessful candidates around much longer than the AAUP recommends actually does them a favor.

Because of the decentralized and variegated nature of American higher education, the routes to tenure vary enormously. Some schools award it almost automatically, while at other, more selective institutions only one out of three or four candidates makes the cut. The requirements vary as well. Usually it's some combination of research, teaching, and service, though again, the weighting of those components depends on the individual school. At most institutions, teaching, though difficult to assess, is the key component of the tenure decision.[50] As we will see, however, because of the increasingly competitive academic environment, many schools are ratcheting up their research requirements. Where once it was enough for an assistant professor of English at a midlevel public university to have published an article or two and be working on a manuscript, now the successful candidate is expected to have a book in hand and another under way.[51]

Attaining tenure can be anywhere from a major turning point in life to a somewhat ho-hum experience. In 1971, for example, a Harvard faculty committee viewed it as intellectually liberating, "one of the major stimuli to experimentation, providing a faculty member, as it does, the freedom to leave his standard arena of endeavor when he feels inspired to do so, without fear for the effect on his saleable professional reputation."[52] For a more opportunistic sort, however, it can be a signal to relax and let everything slide, though it is hard to imagine what kind of careerist would submit to the insecurities of the academic job market and tenure track just for the final prize. And in any event, the rigors of the process probably would have weeded out such a person long before. Still, tenure committees do not necessarily eliminate all the academy's incompetents, nor do they ensure that someone will not encounter problems later in life that make him or her unfit for the classroom.

Contrary to common assumptions, however, tenure does not grant its holders guaranteed lifetime employment. They can still be fired—just not arbitrarily.[53] Dismissal of a tenured faculty member, as the AAUP's policy statements have repeatedly stressed, must be for "adequate cause"—usually for some form of incompetence, neglect of duty, or "moral turpitude" or else because the institution has eliminated a particular program or encounters a situation of "financial exigency" that forces it to shed faculty members in order to survive. Whatever the reason, the termination must take place in accordance with procedures that ensure against violations of academic freedom. At institutions where collective bargaining is in place, the faculty's contract usually contains similar—and legally enforceable—provisions. The school must either show that the professor's misdeeds are serious enough to merit dismissal or else prove that the alleged financial exigencies are genuine and not a cover for illegitimate reprisals. Due process, in other words, backstops tenure.[54]

It protects the untenured as well. In a well-run university, probationary as well as part-time and non-tenure-track faculty members receive the same procedural guarantees as senior professors when they are not reappointed. Theoretically, at least, they should be given adequate notice with a statement of the reasons for their termination and the opportunity to appeal an unfavorable decision. The process for dismissing tenured professors is more elaborate, of course; it requires a quasi-judicial hearing, and it shifts the burden of proof from the individual to the institution.[55] To a large extent, these enhanced procedural guarantees are a recognition of the rigorous process a tenured faculty member has already endured. As the constitutional scholar William van Alstyne explains, once an academic has survived the often excruciating probationary period, that person's college or university has officially recognized his or her "professional excellence" and so must engage in an equally onerous process if it seeks to reverse that decision later on.[56]

Schools rarely do that. Although, as we shall see, junior people, part-timers, and people with off-the-ladder appointments can and do lose their academic positions for all manner of legitimate and illegitimate reasons, few tenured professors have actually been dismissed for cause.[57] Admittedly, most situations involving the dismissal of senior faculty members have been resolved by a quiet deal in which the person in question retires voluntarily rather than undergoing a prolonged and potentially embarrassing investigation. But the rarity of cases in which faculty committees have recommended discharging a tenured professor has, at least in some quarters, raised suspicions that academics have become so self-protective they cannot prune their own deadwood. Such suspicions, coupled with administrative demands for greater flexibility and public hostility toward a profession that has been portrayed as a sinecure for lazy, pampered lefties, have led to questions about tenure. Especially when higher education comes under attack—as it did during the late 1960s and early 1970s and again during the culture wars of the late 1980s and early 1990s, and as it may well do during the current financial meltdown—tenure becomes an easy target. Why not get rid of it? Academic jobs with their flexible hours and long vacations are cushy enough. Moreover, tenure's critics claim, it should be possible to shelter college and university teachers from retaliation for what they say and write without offering them unlimited appointments.

Flexibility is an issue. There is no question that at many schools the presence of large numbers of tenured professors has made it hard for administrations to reorient their institutions' offerings toward new and more popular fields. Tenure, as one critic puts it, creates "curricular inflexibility . . . [T]o tenure a classicist is to tenure classics; and, by extension, the curriculum cannot be altered markedly unless there are some changes of academic personnel." This creates problems for the institution "where a largely tenured faculty offers a curriculum or product mix out of phase with market demands," and "the college's ability to compete for students may suffer and enrollments may decline."[58] Whether or not an academic institution should pay such close attention to the market is something that I address elsewhere (as I will the financial problems that create the demand for flexibility). But the situation is not quite so dire, for administrators have, in fact, managed to increase their institution's flexibility by hiring ever larger numbers of contingent faculty members. Moreover, the related claim that the tenuring of so many faculties makes it hard for people from underrepresented minority groups to gain academic posts seems disingenuous in the mouths of administrators who do not replace the tenure lines of their own retirees—that is, they discontinue a tenured position after its current holder retires.

Still, tenure does limit what an institution can do, and, especially in situations where a financial crisis looms, administrators and trustees look for alternatives. It is rarely possible to eliminate tenure outright. The legal system stands in the way, the courts having ruled that tenure gives its holders a property right in their jobs that cannot be abolished without due process of law.[59] And the AAUP is quick to censure institutions that take unfair advantage of a financial exigency to fire tenured professors. Some schools, facing hard times, find more acceptable ways to prune their faculties. Buyouts are one solution, as was the plan of one small Missouri college to offer its faculty members the choice of tenure or additional sabbaticals and higher salaries.[60] A few other institutions give their professors long-term renewable contracts in place of tenure. However, as one observer noted, "nearly all institutions renew nearly all contracts." As a result, instead of encouraging faculty turnover as its authors hoped, the system of long-term contracts turns out to be the equivalent of instant tenure, with the evaluating committees simply postponing negative decisions and leaving it up to their equally reluctant successors to terminate somebody's contract. Moreover, the constant assessments that a system demands are extremely time-consuming; they would not work at a large school that would have to deal with hundreds of contract renewals every year.[61]

Much more common has been the widespread adoption of systems of post-tenure review. In many respects, such systems are a response to the broader drive for accountability that, as we shall see, is currently surging through the nation's campuses. At the moment, despite the hopes of the politicians and bureaucrats who called for them, these post-tenure reviews have not rooted out much in the way of faculty deadwood, nor, as far as I can tell, have they produced much innovation. Instead, they seem to have created a lot of additional paperwork as well as employment opportunities for so-called consultants in the field. Perhaps I am too cynical. It may well be that a stiff dose of self-assessment will rejuvenate American higher education, though—and this is crucial—it will not do so unless the faculty buys into it.

Faculty Governance and Academic Freedom

Here we come to the other vital prop of academic freedom: faculty governance. In order for academic freedom to flourish, the faculty must participate in the key decisions that concern its professional work. Once again, the AAUP has been quite explicit: "a sound system of institutional governance is a necessary condition for the protection of faculty rights and thereby for the most productive exercise of essential faculty freedoms."[62] It's a matter of democracy. An academic institution that is run in an authoritarian manner cannot readily grant its faculty members the kind of freedom their teaching and research require. But, in an equally important way, it's also a matter of competence. It is obviously in the interest of the institution as a whole to grant the faculty considerable power over its main educational decisions, since that increases the effectiveness of those decisions. Again, we need to view faculty governance through the collective lens of professionalism, as a mechanism that enables academics to do their work.

Naturally, the faculty does not need a say in every decision on campus. Professors do not have to approve schedules for building maintenance or oversee how the trustees invest the school's endowment. But in those areas that are central to the faculty's concerns—teaching and research and the personnel decisions related to them—its members must have a major voice. Moreover, since these are the core activities of every college and university, that voice should have considerable weight. In other words, to use contemporary parlance, college and university professors are, because of their expertise and experience, perhaps the most important "stakeholders" in their institutions and need to be represented as such. Mathematics professors are, after all, more likely to know what sequence of math courses should be offered or what new fields need to be represented in their department than a businessman on the Board of Trustees or even a dean (unless she is a mathematician herself). Significantly, when we look at the violations of academic freedom that the AAUP has investigated, almost all of them are also violations of governance as well. They occur when administrators or trustees go beyond their traditional roles and make decisions about personnel or curricula without consulting their faculties or utilizing the institutional structures provided for such decisions.

Those structures are crucial. Without independent departments, faculty senates, ad hoc and standing committees at every level, and, on those campuses where collective bargaining exists, strong union locals, shared governance cannot exist. These institutions have to have power, however; token representation will not suffice. This is particularly the case with regard to what the AAUP calls "authority over faculty status."[63] Faculty members, thus, need to play a major role in decisions about hiring, promotion, and tenure; when there is the possibility that a professor could be fired for "cause," they must serve on the panel that hears the case. Similarly, when a financial exigency might result in the discontinuance of programs or the dismissal of tenured professors, the faculty should be consulted. These requirements are essential for maintaining academic freedom; they preserve the faculty's status as independent professionals who retain their effectiveness by virtue of their ability to regulate themselves. At the same time, they also sustain the faculty's morale and thus help the university function more effectively.[64]

Faculties gained considerable power during the second half of the twentieth century. Not only had trustees long distanced themselves from academic matters, but administrators, eager to strengthen their institutions, scrambled to acquire ever more illustrious professors whom they then had to keep happy.[65] Faculty senates and all manner of personnel, budget, and other specialized committees proliferated within the governing structures of most colleges and universities. In fact, until financial exigencies and federal regulations triggered bureaucratic growth after the mid-1970s, professors handled most of their institutions' administrative chores and most administrators were themselves academics. Even today, despite considerable grumbling about the unwieldy nature of the beast, faculty decision making usually works. In fact, a 2001 survey revealed that administrators were more positive about shared governance than their faculties.[66]

There's considerable irony here, for critics of faculty governance claim that its traditional procedures are simply too balky and inefficient to be relied upon in today's world of information overload and globalization. As anyone who has sat through the interminable speechifying of a regular faculty meeting well knows, such reservations are not without merit. Yet it is by no means the case that a democratic campus culture cannot adapt to the twenty-first century or that an authoritarian one produces greater innovation. A quick glance at postmortems by former university presidents reveals, among other things, their understanding that a failure to consult the faculty about major academic decisions can only lead to trouble.[67] Such was the backstory of the 2006 resignation of Harvard president Lawrence Summers. Despite his much publicized denigration of female scientists, it was the widespread professorial discontent with his authoritarian style of leadership that eventually forced his departure. Admittedly, Harvard's star-spangled faculty is uniquely powerful, but similar situations at less prominent institutions produce similar outcomes.

Still, it must be noted, faculty governance does not always work. To begin with, it no longer conveys the status it once did. Where administrative duties and committee assignments used to be the province of the academy's most highly respected members, such is no longer the case. The growing demands on professors' time often make those activities seem more of a burden than a benefit, especially when schools reward research rather than service. Moreover, as the percentage of tenured people on the faculty shrinks, there are disproportionately fewer senior professors available to staff the necessary committees and governing bodies. As a result, the work becomes more onerous, making it increasingly more difficult to recruit qualified people to do it. Shared governance can also be undermined by the internal conflicts that afflict many campuses and render committee service uninviting. After all, faculties are far from monolithic and can often be torn apart by infighting and factionalism, especially when it comes to decisions about allocating resources, tenure, and hiring. Sometimes, in fact, this warfare renders departments or faculties so dysfunctional that outside intervention is necessary if the institution is to function. Finally—and this is a serious, though rarely discussed, problem—professors are not always committed to the maintenance of academic freedom or aware of the ways in which it can be undermined. Even where they have power and the desire to use it in the faculty's interest, they may be so swept up by a sense of crisis or so hostile to a transgressive and unpopular colleague such as Ward Churchill that they surrender to the political passions of the moment. In other words, faculty governance is necessary for the protection of academic freedom, but it's not always enough.

When we come to assess the academic community's record in protecting that freedom over the past one hundred years, it will be good to keep in mind the words of the early-twentieth-century Yale president Arthur T. Hadley, whose school was then recognized as having the most powerful faculty in the country. Yet as Hadley noted in 1903, "The fact seems to be that the form of corporate control chosen makes far less difference with the degree of freedom of the teacher than does the general habit or standard of the community concerning toleration."[68] In other words, though a school may have strong institutional protections in place, individual faculty members may still suffer if the institutional culture cannot withstand outside pressures deemed too strong to resist. And, as we shall see in the following few chapters, that is exactly what has happened.

Chapter 2

ACADEMIC FREEDOM UNDER ATTACK: SUBVERSIVES, SQUEAKY WHEELS, AND "SPECIAL OBLIGATIONS"

Tenure did not protect the three professors that the University of Washington fired in the beginning of 1949. Even though there were no complaints about their research or teaching, because of their connections to Communism they were, the university's president explained, "incompetent, intellectually dishonest, and derelict in their duty to find and teach the truth."[1] Two of the men were Communists and had publicly admitted it, but the other, a social psychologist named Ralph Gundlach, was not. He denied it repeatedly and even sued the university's president and won a retraction. He was, however, a political activist who had joined more left-wing organizations than anyone else on the Seattle campus and may just have been too ornery for such a disciplined outfit as the American Communist Party (CP). Ralph Gundlach, in other words, was a squeaky wheel—and had been for years. On the Washington faculty since 1927, he was a prolific scholar and so well respected within his field that he became president of the Western Psychological Association the year he was dismissed. But he had been promoted to associate professor only after the chair of his department wheeled into the president's office a shopping cart full of Gundlach's writings and references to them in the works of other psychologists.[2]

As a scholar-activist, Gundlach believed in applying his psychological knowledge to real-world problems and did not hide his own views in class. That stance did not win him support—either from his colleagues or from his students. Some undergraduates were so outraged by his lectures that they complained to the president about "his ranting and raving for the overthrow of the United States government."[3] He had also gotten into a spat with the administration over his use of what were seen to be improperly partisan questionnaires. One set, which polled members of the press about the area's politicians, was then used by a local congressman in his 1946 reelection campaign; another asked about anti-Semitism; yet a third dealt with labor unions. For the dean of the faculty, Edwin Guthrie, a psychologist himself, these questionnaires were "political," which deprived them "of all possibility of being accepted as a scientific piece of work."[4]

Still, despite his run-ins with the administration, Gundlach would have remained on the Washington faculty had he not been called before the state legislature's Fact-Finding Committee on Un-American Activities in the summer of 1948. The committee's chair, an ambitious former deputy sheriff and first-term legislator named Albert Canwell, was determined to root out all vestiges of radicalism from the state, and since conservatives had long considered the university a nest of subversion, it was clear that Canwell's investigation would reach the campus. Even before the committee's formation, the university's president, Raymond Allen, had warned those professors who were Communists "to get off the faculty . . . before they were smoked out." He promised Canwell his cooperation, and at a special faculty meeting before the hearings began, he told the prospective witnesses to brief him about their political activities. Once Canwell's subpoenas reached the campus—and there were at least a dozen—Allen called in six of the recipients and asked them if they were Communists. Most denied it. Gundlach, however, refused to respond. "No one," he explained, "could prove that I was and I could not prove that I was not."[5]

He was no more accommodating before the Canwell committee, refusing to answer its questions about his political activities. The university responded at once. Publicly insisting that the school would "observe to the letter the due processes that are precious . . . to our academic traditions," President Allen asked a special committee appointed by the faculty senate to authorize action against six faculty members. Three of those professors—Joseph Butterworth, Herbert Phillips, and Gundlach—had defied Canwell; the other three had admitted they had once been in the Communist Party but refused to name names. In formulating the university's charges against these people, Allen and his advisors strove to show that their past and present Communist affiliations constituted academic misconduct. Whether or not the special committee believed that these men were unfit to teach, its members assumed that if they did not act, the regents and legislators would. Accordingly, the committee agreed to press charges, sending the case on to the Faculty Committee on Tenure and Academic Freedom for a formal hearing.[6]

Once again Gundlach refused to cooperate. While all the other professors involved, including Phillips and Butterworth, who were still in the party, agreed to discuss their political activities and beliefs with their faculty colleagues, Gundlach did not. He stood on principle, insisting that his politics were his own business. The Tenure Committee disagreed. Though it opted to retain the more cooperative witnesses, it voted 7–4 to fire Gundlach on the grounds that he had not been sufficiently candid. Thus, despite his denial of party membership, the committee's majority concluded, "If he is not presently a member of the Communist Party, his non-membership is either a deliberate effort to avoid the adverse consequences which he might fear would accompany Party membership or is caused by relatively minor personal ideological differences with the Communist Party." Gundlach's presumably "evasive" behavior before the committee and his previous conflicts with the administration were, these committee members believed, sufficient to warrant his dismissal on the grounds of "neglect of duty," which, they explained, "necessarily also includes . . . a reasonable measure of cooperation with the administrative officers of the University in matters affecting the welfare and reputation of the institution."[7]

President Allen concurred with that finding, insisting that Gundlach's defiant attitude, as well as his political activities, indicated that, if not a Communist, he was at least as culpable as one. Allen also overruled the Tenure Committee by asking the Board of Regents to fire the two admitted Communists as well. Their dismissal was, he explained, an academic matter; they were "unfit for faculty membership" because of "their dishonesty and neglect of duty in maintaining secret membership in the Communist Party."[8] The Board of Regents accepted Allen's recommendation and, on January 22, 1949, brought Ralph Gundlach's academic career to an end. After serving a thirty-day prison sentence for the contempt charge that stemmed from his defiance of the Canwell Committee, Gundlach went onto the job market. Though he was a widely published scholar and had good connections in his field, he was never again to have another regular teaching position. Nor, it must be noted, did either Butterworth or Phillips.[9]

Gundlach's dismissal tells us a lot about academic freedom. To begin with, the case is important in and of itself. It was the first major test of academic freedom during the McCarthy era. Other institutions soon followed, and before the anti-Communist furor abated in the mid-1950s, more than one hundred college teachers lost their jobs or were denied tenure because of their politics. Gundlach's experiences are of interest as well because, unlike most of the academic victims of the time, including his two Communist colleagues, his case was not accompanied by violations of due process and shared governance. His dismissal had been recommended by two faculty committees, and the university gave him ample opportunity to defend himself. Moreover, even though it was obvious that Washington had sacrificed Gundlach, Butterworth, and Phillips because of pressure from conservative politicians, journalists, and regents, the university's leaders justified that action in academic terms. Not only did they claim that Communism was incompatible with academic employment, but they redefined their conceptualization of the faculty's professional responsibilities to include preserving the reputation of the institution. That conceptualization was not unique to the University of Washington. All too often, such a concern for the university's reputation, along with lapses in due process and a stated emphasis on the academic rather than political sins of the individual in question, have come to characterize serious violations of academic freedom.

Gundlach deserves attention for another reason as well. He was a squeaky wheel. And squeaky wheels, especially political activists like Gundlach, who refuse to conform to the expectations of their peers and administrators, often get into trouble. They did during the McCarthy era, they did during earlier episodes of political repression, and, as Juan Hong's experiences show, they do today. I was actually surprised to discover, as I looked back over the academic freedom cases of the late nineteenth and early twentieth centuries, how many of the protagonists were described by contemporaries as prickly or contentious.[10] Temperament does not figure significantly in the kinds of structural analyses that historians feel comfortable with, yet it may well be that someone with an affable and accommodating disposition has more wiggle room than a feistier individual. At the least, colleagues may be more willing to come to that person's defense. Perhaps Gundlach could have kept his job if he had been less outspoken and if he had conceded—as he did not—that the university's investigation was legitimate. But he was simply too ornery, or perhaps too principled, to collaborate with a procedure that he felt violated his rights. Moreover—and this needs to be said—he was on the left.

Gundlach, though unusual, was not unique, even during the McCarthy period. The University of Michigan mathematician Chandler Davis was another squeaky wheel who lost his job and went to prison for contempt. He had refused to cooperate with the House Un-American Activities Committee (HUAC) by taking the First instead of the Fifth Amendment at his 1954 hearing. He then repeated that refusal with the two Michigan faculty committees that were set up to investigate him. Again, as with Gundlach, Davis's refusal to cooperate with what he believed was an illegitimate investigation cost him his job. The same thing happened to Stanley Moore, a tenured full professor of philosophy at Reed College, a supposedly liberal institution that, one might assume, would have protected its faculty members, but did not. Moore, an unfriendly witness like Davis and Gundlach, also like them would not collaborate with his school's investigation and so was ousted.[11]

In none of these cases—and, in fact, in none of the academic freedom cases of the McCarthy era—was anybody's teaching or research at issue. It was the off-campus political activities of these three men and, particularly, their insistence that their institutions' investigations not only violated their academic freedom but also interfered with their First Amendment freedom of speech and association that cost them their jobs. To legitimize what was, in fact, their collaboration with the witch hunt, the nation's leading universities articulated a new requirement for academic employment: people had to be candid about their political affiliations. Even so, those professors who did cooperate with their institutions' investigations did not fare much better than their more obstinate colleagues. We've seen what happened to Joseph Butterworth and Herbert Phillips at the University of Washington, where, despite their candor with the faculty's Tenure Committee, they lost their jobs. The same thing happened at Michigan, where Mark Nickerson, a tenured biology professor who had defied the same HUAC subcommittee as Davis, cooperated fully with the school's investigation but was fired anyhow when the president disregarded the faculty committee's recommendation to retain him.

In retrospect, most observers realize these dismissals were a horrendous mistake and that Gundlach, Davis, and Moore were right: universities had no business inquiring into the political views and activities of their faculty members. And, in fact, all three schools have belatedly tried to make amends in one way or another. Still, these men's stories are instructive. If a university is to maintain its academic freedom, it must protect the teaching, scholarship, and legitimate political activities of *all* its faculty members, including those of its squeakiest wheels. Justice Oliver Wendell Holmes expressed this idea best in 1929 when he stated that "if there is any principle of the Constitution that more imperatively calls for attachment than any other it is the principle of free thought—not free thought for those who agree with us but freedom for the thought that we hate."[12] In a more recent decision specifically about universities, a federal appeals court noted in 1980 that "the possibility . . . that [faculty members punished for criticizing administrative policies] may have been . . . obstinate . . . does not derogate from the status of their expression as speech within the First Amendment."[13] The implications of these admonitions are clear. To mix a few metaphors, academia's squeaky wheels are the canaries in the coal mine, perched at the edge of a slippery slope. To fire or censor such unpopular dissidents is to endanger the academic freedom of everyone on campus. This was a problem in the 1950s, it was a problem at the time the AAUP was formed, and it remains a problem today.

Common Threats to Academic Freedom

To understand how the current threat to the traditional form of academic freedom operates, we need to examine how earlier generations of academics dealt with those members of the professoriate who took unpopular political stands. It would, of course, be satisfying if that history took a positive trajectory and revealed a growing understanding of and commitment to faculty autonomy and free expression both on and off the campus. Instead, the route meanders and even backtracks at times. In addition, as the proportion of college teachers on part-time and temporary appointments continues to grow, the academic profession's traditional protections cover an ever smaller fraction of its members.

Even so, there is real progress. We will not, for example, see the kinds of overt First Amendment violations that precipitated the dismissals of people such as Ralph Gundlach and Chandler Davis. Courts, faculties, and most academic administrators now protect political speech as such, although they sometimes undermine that protection by invoking academic norms like collegiality or scholarly integrity to punish the squeakier wheels on campus. Since few ordinary citizens care strongly about academic freedom, such invocations of professional values are, no doubt, designed to win faculty support. In a sense, then, the fact that academic administrators seek to woo their faculties is actually a sign of progress, for it shows that professors have a stronger voice in their institutions than they once had. It would be hard, but certainly not impossible, for the president of a major research university to overrule the findings of a faculty investigation as Washington's and Michigan's did during the late 1940s and 1950s.

Nonetheless, some things do remain the same. To begin with, except in situations that are institutionally specific—that is, where the cases arise because of a power struggle within the college or university—major violations of academic freedom have almost always involved the most fraught political issues of the moment: industrial unrest, racial discrimination, unpopular wars, or questions of national security. Professors do not lose their jobs over trivial matters. Nor, the record shows, do they lose them because they are conservatives. Again, internal power struggles excepted, the protagonists in the main academic freedom cases of the past one hundred years have almost always (though not entirely) been on the left. There have also been moments when entire fields, not just individuals, come under attack. This usually happens when the subject matter of that discipline becomes enmeshed in broader controversies. Thus, for example, the labor struggles of the late nineteenth century created problems for economists, the Cold War and Chinese Revolution rendered East Asian scholars vulnerable in the 1950s, and the current war on terror is taking its toll on people who study Islam and the Middle East.

Whatever the content, these attacks on academic freedom have almost always come from outside the academy; they are not internally generated. Ever since the academic community underwent professionalization in the late nineteenth century, it has attracted criticism from all sides. Its members are too elitist, too socialistic, too partisan, too atheistic, too out-of-touch. Especially intense during periods of crisis, those assaults on the university have sometimes culminated in demands for the removal of this or that dissenter. In every case, those demands did not originate on campus; they came from trustees, politicians, the Federal Bureau of Investigation, or members of the media. Though there is evidence that during the McCarthy era, for example, some schools took precautions to avoid appointing political undesirables to the faculty, I know of no situation where an institution fired someone for political reasons without pressure from outside.

What makes the history of academic freedom so confusing, however, is that public relations considerations require concealing that pressure. Although, as we have seen, the powers that be demanded candor from those of their professors who tangled with the investigating committees of the 1950s, they did not practice that candor themselves. No university president openly admitted that he had ousted a controversial professor because he feared the state legislature would reduce the school's appropriations for that year. Politically motivated dismissals, therefore, came to be clothed in academic garb. Either they would be described as routine administrative matters or else the professors in question would be charged with some violation of the institution's official code of conduct—incompetence, moral turpitude, or at the very least disloyalty and a failure to maintain their school's reputation with the public. In addition, the institution would try to make these dismissals acceptable to the faculty. And all too often the faculty did not object.

Here due process comes into play. If an administration and board of trustees fired a professor in an arbitrary manner—either by flouting the machinery of shared governance or by overruling a faculty committee's recommendations—it usually indicated that a violation of academic freedom had taken place. That person's colleagues might protest or resign en masse. But what if the majority of the faculty goes along with the action? What if, as happened in the cases of Ralph Gundlach and Chandler Davis, the internal committees themselves recommend the dismissal? All too often, as we shall see, the academic community fails to protect its politically vulnerable members. Especially during moments of stress, when strong outside pressures demand the sacrifice of an institution's squeakiest wheels, many of its leading professors capitulate. The external trappings of due process ease the operation. Faculty members and administrators go through the motions of an official investigation that cloaks their capitulation in the language of academic freedom and claims that the culprit has somehow violated the norms of the scholarly community and is no longer qualified for its membership. Rarely do the victim's colleagues protest. After all, it takes both prescience and courage to recognize how seriously the proposed dismissal threatens academic freedom and then to stand up against it. Such solidarity is as uncommon within the professoriate as it is in the rest of American society.

Early Violations of Academic Freedom

The first violations of academic freedom in the modern sense occurred in the late nineteenth century. There had, it is true, been earlier instances of religious dissenters ousted from denominational colleges and opponents of slavery fired from antebellum southern schools, but neither the protagonists in those dismissals nor their colleagues at other institutions sought to conceptualize those cases as a violation of professional norms. For such a conceptualization to occur, the nation's college and university teachers had first to develop their identity as autonomous professionals by adopting the beliefs and practices that fell within the rubric of academic freedom. The men (few women here) who did this were the leaders of their fields, the pioneering scholars who not only founded the AAUP but also established the disciplinary parameters of the modern American research university. Two tasks confronted these people as they began to grapple with the early violations of academic freedom. First, they had to disseminate the concept of academic freedom widely enough for the rest of the academic community to recognize when it was being violated; second, they had to develop enough confidence in their own professional identity to collectively enforce its norms.

Most early academic freedom cases involved economists. Their field itself was evolving and many of its practitioners were activists who wanted their scholarship to deal with the main social problems of the day. That involvement, especially when it led to support for labor unions, governmental regulation of industry, or the redistribution of wealth, brought criticism, especially from the conservative politicians and businessmen who were funding the nation's new universities and staffing their boards of trustees. Thus it was that in 1894, at the height of a nationwide railway strike, one of the most well-known academics of the day, the University of Wisconsin's Richard T. Ely, found himself in trouble, charged by a member of the university's Board of Regents with encouraging strikes and entertaining a union organizer at his home. Ely, who was a Christian reformer sympathetic to the goals if not the methods of socialism, was also a founder of the American Economic Association and was prominent enough in his field, despite his apparently difficult personality, to enlist an eminent cohort of academics in his cause, including Wisconsin's president. As a result, although conceding that if the charges against him were true they would show him "to be unworthy of the honor of being a professor in a great university," Ely was able to convince Wisconsin's regents of his innocence. The regents then reinstated him with an eloquent reference to the institution's steadfast support for "that continuous and fearless sifting and winnowing by which alone the truth can be found." Ely had saved his job, but at a price. After his vindication, the formerly outspoken economist became, in the words of one historian, "conspicuously silent" and was never again to speak or write about contemporary problems.[14]

Not every controversial academic had Richard T. Ely's luck in having such a sympathetic president and Board of Regents. When Ely's student Edward Bemis lost his job at the University of Chicago the following year for advocating the public ownership of municipal utilities and railroads, he could not resuscitate his career. Instead of resigning quietly, as similarly compromised scholars had done so that they could find a new position, Bemis decided to publicize his dismissal as the violation of academic freedom that it was. Chicago's administration retaliated by persuading the school's senior social scientists to raise questions about Bemis's competence, thus making it impossible for him to find another academic post. John R. Commons, another Ely student, learned from Bemis's mistakes; when he lost two jobs because of his allegedly radical views, he remained silent and was eventually rewarded with an appointment at Wisconsin. Significantly, as these early encounters illustrate, the successful resolution of an academic freedom case required the protagonist to find a new job. For that to happen, however, the individual in question had to win the collective support of his academic peers. He could not be a squeaky wheel, but had to keep his scholarship within the limits of permissible dissent, curry favor with the leaders of the discipline, and, above all, avoid unfavorable publicity.[15]

By the time Stanford University dismissed yet another Ely student, E.A.

Ross, in 1900, the professoriate had more or less reached a consensus about the parameters of academic freedom. Ross, an eminent economist who was also a pioneer in the field of sociology, had been recruited by the new university's founding president, David Starr Jordan. Because some of his positions, like his support for free silver in 1896, were, to say the least, unpopular within the local business community, he was already under a cloud. Jordan tried to protect him, but when Ross hinted at the public ownership of railroads and condemned the importation of Chinese workers, the university's sole trustee, the imperious widow of Leland Stanford, cracked down. The controversial economist, she wrote to Jordan, "literally plays into the hands of the lowest and vilest elements of socialism . . . I must confess I am weary of Professor Ross, and I think he ought not to be retained at Stanford University."[16] Though Jordan tried to defend his provocative faculty member, it was useless. Jane Stanford was determined that Ross should go; believing that his institution's very survival was at stake, Jordan capitulated.

Ross did not leave quietly—or alone. The case was front-page news. Not only did Ross publicly announce that his forced resignation violated academic freedom, but several other faculty members left Palo Alto in protest and many of the nation's most prominent economists came to his support. Because Ross was not a radical, his colleagues viewed his dismissal as, in the words of one of them, "a blow at the position of all professional economists."[17] They circulated a petition and even toyed with the idea of a boycott. Though their mobilization could not restore Ross's Stanford job (and he had to wait a few years before Ely could bring him to Wisconsin), the economists' collective action had reinforced the academic profession's growing commitment to its own autonomy. In order to prevent a recurrence, the professoriate had to gain acceptance of the principle that external interference in key academic decisions was illegitimate and that scholars could only be judged by other people in their field. When, fifteen years later, many of the same academic elites who had led the protest against Stanford established the AAUP to safeguard their professional status, it was no coincidence that A.J. Lovejoy, the key author of the association's founding document, was someone who had resigned from Stanford when Ross was fired.

By then, as the AAUP's 1915 statement made clear, Lovejoy and his associates were willing to defend even fairly radical faculty members as long as they retained the support of their colleagues, did not abuse their classrooms, and behaved in a professional manner outside them. Admittedly, the embrace of the essentially moderate Progressive movement by most reform-minded academics meant that they posed less of a challenge to the system than had been the case fifteen years before. Thus, when the trustees of the University of Pennsylvania suddenly decided to fire the Wharton School economist Scott Nearing in the summer of 1915, the AAUP promptly investigated. Nearing's socialist sympathies and exposés of child labor in the coal industry had brought on the wrath of Penn's conservative alumni and trustees. But his dean and colleagues were firm in their support, describing him as, among other things, "a man of extraordinary ability, of superlative popularity," who "exerted the greatest moral force for good in the University." As was often the case in such situations, the university gave no official reason at the time for Nearing's dismissal. There was, however, a national outcry, leading to an AAUP investigation. Three months later, Penn's trustees finally responded that because Nearing's "efforts—although doubtless perfectly sincere—were so constantly misunderstood by the public and by many parents of students," they felt compelled to let him go "for the good of the university as a whole." Firing a professor because of what people outside the academic profession thought about his work was, the AAUP's investigators believed, a clear violation of academic freedom—all the more so because the trustees not only had ignored the faculty's judgment but had refused to grant Nearing a hearing.[18] The association's condemnation may have had an impact; the university quickly revised its bylaws to ensure that the protagonists of future cases would receive the hearing Nearing had been denied. As for Nearing, he soon found a more congenial position at the University of Toledo, whose board was under labor union control.

He did not keep it for long. A pacifist, Nearing was ousted by Toledo's trustees once his opposition to American participation in World War I became an embarrassment.[19] He was not alone. At least twenty academics also lost their jobs during the war. And it is likely that many more were quietly eased out of their positions or fired from such insignificant or isolated institutions that their dismissals did not reach the historical record. In any event, their colleagues did little to help these wartime casualties. The conflict, as the historian Carol Gruber points out,

> exposed the repressive underside of majority sentiment on the campus; it exposed a lack of commitment to academic freedom within the profession at large and a willingness even of its chief defenders to bend the principle to the pressures of the moment; and it exposed an absence of collective consciousness and solidarity within the American academic profession.[20]

The AAUP was less than helpful here. Just when it would have been crucial for the organization to have taken a strong stand against the wartime hysteria and defended faculty members against attacks on their loyalty, it folded. At a time when the federal government was already criminalizing dissent, the association, in a special report on academic freedom in wartime written by Lovejoy in December 1917, made it clear that the organization would not support anyone who ran afoul of the law. It further stated that professors had "special obligations" to refrain from saying or doing anything that even indirectly encouraged opposition to the war or discouraged people from voluntary activities in support of it. Thus, for example, if a college teacher refused to let a Red Cross recruiter interrupt his class, that act could be considered "dangerous to the public security" and become grounds for dismissal. Academics from Germany or Austria-Hungary had an additional burden: they were warned to avoid all appearance of disloyalty and "refrain from public discussion of the war; and in their private intercourse with neighbors, colleagues, and students . . . avoid all hostile or offensive expressions concerning the United States and its government."[21] As this refusal by the AAUP to protect dissent reveals, the academic community was no more immune from the wartime frenzy than any other sector of society. It may also be the case that its constricted view of the permissible bounds of expression was, at least in part, a reflection of that community's lingering anxiety about its professional status.

That combination of insecurity and patriotism found its most toxic expression in some serious violations of academic freedom. Predictably, the protagonists of those cases tended to be among their institution's squeakiest wheels. The University of Minnesota's William Schaper was a political scientist and a prickly individual who had tangled with the state's corporate elite and alienated his fellow faculty members. Columbia's James McKeen Cattell was an eminent psychologist who had long been critical of the university's hierarchical structure and of his colleagues' allegedly spineless acceptance of it. Although both men had previous run-ins with their administrators and trustees, it was their presumed disloyalty that precipitated their dismissals.

Like many midwesterners, Schaper initially opposed America's entry in the war, but then abandoned that opposition. Minnesota's Board of Regents nonetheless called him to a special meeting where they quizzed him about his apparently equivocal stance on the war and then dismissed him on the grounds that "his attitude of mind . . . and his expressed unwillingness to aid the United States in the present war, render him unfit and unable rightly to discharge the duties of his position." The university, the regents explained, required "unqualified loyalty on the part of all teachers."[22]

Columbia's president, Nicholas Murray Butler, made the same demand. Concerned that faculty and student critics of the war would damage the university's reputation, he announced in his 1917 commencement address:

> What had been tolerated before becomes intolerable now. What had been wrongheadedness was now sedition. What had been folly was now treason. . . . There is and will be no place in Columbia University for any person who opposes or counsels opposition to the effective enforcement of the laws of the United States, or who acts, speaks or writes treason. . . . This is the University's last and only warning to any among us . . . who are not with whole heart and mind and strength committed to fight with us to make the world safe for democracy.

No doubt Cattell was on Butler's mind. Though the unconventional psychologist did not publicly condemn the war, he had asked several congressmen to support a measure against sending draftees to Europe against their will. That petition, as well as the highly publicized antiwar activities of Professor Henry Wadsworth Longfellow Dana, drew so much flak that Butler decided to ask the trustees to fire the two professors, which they promptly did.[23]

Significantly, neither Cattell nor Schaper had been granted the slightest modicum of due process; they received no formal charges, nor were they given the opportunity to appear before a committee of their peers. Such blatant violations of faculty prerogatives presumably should have spawned massive opposition, but on neither campus did these men's colleagues mount an organized protest. At Columbia, there were a few scattered demurrals, the historian Charles Beard resigned in opposition, and a few other eminent scholars made critical statements. But on the whole, the bulk of Columbia's faculty acquiesced in Cattell's dismissal. He had long been a difficult colleague, and his and Dana's supposedly "treasonable conduct" deprived the two men of their fellow faculty members' support. Schaper, too, had a few individual champions, but most Minnesota professors simply ignored the way in which the regents' loyalty test had infringed on his—and their—academic freedom. Both cases went to the AAUP, but its wartime report skirted the issues they raised, ignoring Schaper entirely and referring only in passing to Cattell's dismissal without mentioning the name of either the professor or the institution involved.[24]

Twenty years later, Minnesota's regents formally apologized to Schaper, rescinding the resolution of dismissal and reinstating him as an emeritus professor with $5,000 in back pay.[25] But as the experiences of the McCarthy era revealed—when the University of Minnesota again dismissed a professor for political reasons—it is unclear how much the academic community learned from what had happened during World War I.[26] True, the years between the wars found most campuses fairly placid, with only occasional outbursts of student unrest and faculty radicalism in places like City College of New York (CCNY). And, in fact, outside of New York City there were no major violations of academic freedom. Rather, there was the normal background noise of sanctions against campus mavericks and conflicts between authoritarian administrators and their faculties, but the heavy outside pressure that had ejected people like Bemis, Nearing, and Schaper from academe had let up. With the Cold War, however, that pressure returned. Once again the academic community came under attack. And once again, as we have seen, it sacrificed its squeakiest wheels. But this time, in the most widespread political purge of the nation's faculties in the history of American higher education, most of the professors who lost their jobs were neither campus activists nor cantankerous colleagues.

McCarthyism and Academic Freedom

What distinguishes the violations of academic freedom during the McCarthy period from both earlier and later ones is that the academic community developed such a narrow political test for employment that it was possible to rationalize firing dozens of college and university teachers merely because of what it was assumed they believed. Admittedly, most of the people involved were or had been in or near the Communist Party; but by the time they came under attack, few were still in the party. They lost their academic positions because they opposed the McCarthy era witch hunts and believed it was morally wrong to name names and identify their former comrades. They were, in the jargon of the day, "Fifth Amendment Communists," uncooperative witnesses who had relied on their constitutional privilege before HUAC or some other investigating committee. Though there were a handful of squeaky wheels like Gundlach and Davis, most of the men and women who lost their jobs were hardworking scholars and scientists who had had no previous run-ins with their colleagues or administrations. Even so, the institutions that employed them cut these people little slack, since most schools assumed that having an unfriendly witness on the faculty at the height of the anti-Communist furor would be a public relations disaster. At the same time, however, most of the institutions involved had subscribed to the AAUP's 1940 Statement on

Academic Freedom and Tenure or else had developed other formal or informal rules and procedures designed to protect the security and status of their faculty members. As a result, the often moderate and judicious individuals who ran the nation's colleges and universities could not simply oust a professor because of the damaging publicity he or she attracted; they had to find an academically acceptable rationale for doing so.

The 1949 dismissals at the University of Washington inaugurated the first phase of developing that rationale: the disqualification of Communist Party members. Adopting the argument of Washington's president Allen, the academy's leaders claimed that, because of the party's secrecy, professors who joined it had flagrantly violated their professional obligation to openly search for the truth. This formulation constituted a highly selective vision of American Communism. The CP had, it is true, expected its members to remain secret, in part because of a Soviet requirement that it retain the potential for clandestine revolutionary work. But Communists had also concealed their affiliation because the party was so unpopular that, even during its heyday in the 1930s and early 1940s, belonging to it could destroy someone's career. Even so, it had attracted a small but active cohort of idealistic college students and teachers who were concerned about the rise of fascism, sympathized with the labor movement, and believed that joining the Communist Party was the best way to achieve their social and political goals. They were wrong, but at a time when Communism seemed the most dynamic movement on the American left, they were neither crazy nor malevolent.

The leaders of the nation's institutions of higher learning, however, did not acknowledge that an academic could belong to the CP without surrendering his or her integrity. Instead, these educators embraced the negative stereotypes of American Communism then in vogue: Communists were devious, disloyal, and completely under the thumb of their Soviet masters. Exhibit A was the party's clandestine character, which made it possible to charge its academic members with dishonesty. Even more damning was their adherence to the party line. Communist professors had, in the words of Cornell's president, repudiated the "free and honest inquiry after truth" and were "thereby disqualified . . . from belonging on a university faculty devoted to the search for truth." Stanford's president agreed.

> I doubt very much that a member of the Communist Party is a free agent. If he is not a free agent, then it would seem to follow that he cannot be objective. If he cannot be objective, he is by definition precluded from being an educator.[27]

According to this formulation, excluding Communists from the nation's faculties was not a political issue but simply, as Sidney Hook, the nation's most influential anti-Communist intellectual, put it, "a matter of ethical hygiene . . . the enforcement of proper professional standards."[28] Of course, the advantage of such a formulation was that it seemed to preserve the university's autonomy and thus might keep such external witch hunters as Albert Canwell off the campus. Accordingly, in the months immediately following the Washington dismissals, the nation's leading educators rushed to assure the public that the academic community would police itself. "There will be no witch-hunts at Yale," President Charles Seymour announced in June 1949, "because there will be no witches. We do not intend to hire Communists."[29] There is no reason to question the sincerity of such statements. Most academic leaders embraced the anti-Communist consensus of the early Cold War and found nothing uncongenial in the ban on Communist teachers, even if it had been forced on them by the pressures of the moment.

Within the next few years, however, the problem that faced the nation's colleges and universities was no longer that of excluding Communists from their institutions. Rather, the issue now became how to deal with those former Communists on their faculties who invoked the Fifth Amendment before HUAC and the other anti-Communist investigating committees. By the early 1950s, most of the academics who were to become unfriendly witnesses had become disillusioned with Communism and had dropped out of the party. But they had not repudiated all their earlier beliefs. In particular, they viewed the anti-Communist inquisition as, in the words of one of them, "utterly inconsistent with American traditions of freedom" and thus had no intention of cooperating with it.[30]

For the institutions that employed them, the problem was, once again, one of public relations. As the congressional committees refined their techniques in the late 1940s and 1950s, the only way that witnesses could legally avoid naming names and not go to prison for contempt was to rely on the Fifth Amendment's privilege against self-incrimination. The problem here was that the Supreme Court had ruled that people could not talk about themselves and then refuse to talk about others; they had, the Court explained, waived their privilege. As a result, many former Communists, including many academics, who were willing to tell the committees about their own experiences had to refuse to answer every question about themselves if they were to avoid becoming informers. The committees recognized the dilemma these witnesses faced—and they took advantage of it. Knowing that these people had to remain silent if they were to avoid a contempt citation, the committees purposely asked them embarrassing questions and then trumpeted their failure to respond. "A witness's refusal to answer whether or not he is a Communist on the ground that his answer would tend to incriminate him," Senator Joseph McCarthy explained, "is the most positive proof obtainable that the witness is a Communist."[31] Of course it wasn't, but few members of the general public understood the legal issues involved. And having a "Fifth Amendment Communist" on the faculty could be as potentially damaging to a university's public image as having a real one.

But how was an institution to rid itself of such individuals while still retaining its stated commitment to academic freedom? Here, it is hard to believe that the well-meaning and intelligent gentlemen who ran the nation's colleges and universities really thought that the unfriendly witnesses on their faculties—none of whom, it must be emphasized, were ever accused of indoctrinating their students or distorting their research—were unqualified to teach. They did, however, pose a political threat that had to be confronted. The issue became acute in the beginning of 1953 when the main congressional investigators, who until then had not paid much attention to the academy, announced they would hold hearings on Communism in higher education. At that point, the nation's academic leaders scrambled to find a formula that would allow them to transform the political sins of their prospective unfriendly witnesses into academic ones. They found it by invoking what came to be called an "obligation of candor." According to that formulation, because professors had a special commitment to freedom of speech, they had a corresponding duty to speak out and, in the words of the president of an institution that had just fired two Fifth Amendment witnesses, "render an explanation . . . whenever such an explanation is called for by duly constituted governmental bodies." The most authoritative such conceptualization came from the Association of American Universities (AAU), a group whose membership consisted of the presidents of the nation's thirty-seven leading universities. A professor who was called before a legislative inquiry, the AAU explained, not only had an "obligation to maintain [the university's] reputation," but

> above all, he owes his colleagues in the university complete candor and perfect integrity, precluding any kind of clandestine or conspiratorial activities. He owes equal candor to the public. If he is called upon to answer for his convictions, it is his duty as a citizen to speak out. It is even more definitely his duty as a professor. Refusal to do so, on whatever legal grounds, cannot fail to reflect upon a profession that claims for itself the

> fullest freedom to speak and the maximum protection of that freedom available in our society. In this respect, invocation of the Fifth Amendment places upon a professor a heavy burden of proof of his fitness to hold a teaching position and lays upon his university an obligation to reexamine his qualifications for membership in its society.[32]

Since by 1953 almost everybody (or at least everybody in the circles within which these university presidents traveled) knew that most unfriendly witnesses were just trying not to name names, the hypocrisy of that statement is stunning. Its function, of course, was to urge prospective witnesses to cooperate with the committees.

Some did, though we do not know how many there were, since the testimony of friendly witnesses with nothing newsworthy to say was usually kept secret. Still, with only one exception (a cooperative witness at a denominational institution where even having once been in the Communist Party was unacceptable), all the academics who named names retained their jobs. The fate of the others was less auspicious. Although not all of the unfriendly witnesses were fired, they were all subjected to some kind of internal academic investigation. Not all those investigations granted the accused professor much in the way of procedural due process or respected the autonomy of the faculty. At the municipal colleges of New York, for example, the authorities simply invoked a provision of the city charter originally designed to punish corrupt officials and automatically fired all the unfriendly witnesses on their faculties. At Ohio State, the president suspended a physics professor named Byron Darling as soon as he took the Fifth before HUAC. Formal charges came a few days later and, after a perfunctory hearing before an ad hoc committee composed mainly of administrators, the president then asked the Board of Trustees to fire the physicist. Though he had tenure and had cooperated with the university investigation, Darling's "public refusal to answer pertinent questions" was sufficient grounds for dismissal. There was no appeal, nor, because his behavior supposedly was "gross insubordination" and demonstrated a "lack of candor and moral integrity," did he receive the year's notice that Ohio's bylaws required.[33] (It turns out that, according to recent revelations from the KGB archives, Byron Darling had been a spy during World War II. But there is no way that the Ohio State authorities could have had that information in 1953.[34])

The speed with which Ohio State's president whisked Darling off the faculty was unusual. But the school's administration had displayed little previous regard for academic freedom and was, in any event, under considerable political pressure from a legislature that had its own Un-American Activities Committee. Most other schools with unfriendly witnesses on their faculties adopted more leisurely procedures, though ones that ultimately produced the same results. Temple University, which had also delegated its investigation to an administrator-heavy panel, spent several months examining Barrows Dunham before recommending his dismissal. Dunham had invoked the Fifth Amendment at an exceptionally early point in his HUAC appearance and was under indictment for contempt at the time. Temple's trustees cited that unwillingness to testify as a sign of Dunham's "intellectual arrogance" as well as of his failure to fulfill his "cardinal duty" as an academic to display "complete candor and perfect integrity." Although the Supreme Court ultimately exonerated Dunham, Temple did not. Like Gundlach and the other defrocked Washington professors, he was never to teach again.[35]

At schools where there was more genuine faculty input, the results were mixed. As we have seen in the cases of Ralph Gundlach and Chandler Davis, when campus nonconformists confronted their fellow faculty members, formally correct procedures did not always allow room for dissent. Moreover, as in the case of Davis's colleague Mark Nickerson, administrators and trustees sometimes overruled the favorable findings of a faculty panel. This had happened at Rutgers at the end of 1952, when the president and trustees ignored the recommendations of a special faculty committee and dismissed two Fifth Amendment witnesses. This was the case as well at Reed, where Stanley Moore, although unwilling to testify about his relationship to the Communist Party, was nonetheless cleared by a faculty panel that considered such matters irrelevant to an academic hearing. The president and trustees, however, did not; they believed that membership in the party was such a disqualification for an academic position that Moore's refusal to discuss it was an act of "misconduct" that demanded dismissal. Significantly, the Reed case may have involved the McCarthy era's only unqualified defense of academic freedom by a faculty committee, in that, unlike the panels at such schools as Rutgers and Michigan, Reed's did not question Moore about anything but his teaching and scholarship.[36] At every other institution, faculty panels, whether recommending retention or not, operated under the assumption that someone's political beliefs and activities were somehow relevant to that person's fitness to teach. In other words, even when the individuals in question passed their political tests, simply by administering those tests the McCarthy-era faculty committees had undermined academic freedom in a very significant way.

Not every academic who defied an anti-Communist investigation lost his job. A few tenured professors at schools such as Harvard, Cornell, and the University of Buffalo, as well as Clement Markert at Michigan, were able to convince their administrators and trustees, as well as their fellow faculty members, that they had left the Communist Party and so could be safely retained. Some of these people, including the Cornell biologist Marcus Singer, had opted for the so-called "diminished Fifth" at their congressional hearings: they answered questions about themselves but refused to talk about other people. Though that strategy risked a prison term for contempt, it had the propaganda value of enabling the witness to deny party membership. It was hard to fire someone or send someone to prison for simply refusing to become an informer, and, to my knowledge, most of the people who waived the Fifth and talked about themselves but refused to name names managed to ride out the storm.

Besides the highly publicized academic freedom cases of the 1950s, there were other, less obvious assaults on the academy's political autonomy and freedom of speech. Loyalty oaths were ubiquitous. They had been around since the 1930s and, by the early Cold War, almost every state required them in one form or another. They had the great advantage of allowing their sponsors to boast that they had eliminated the subversive threat from the nation's classrooms without costing a penny. Many of these oaths caused little furor, but the one that was imposed on the University of California in 1949 tore the institution apart. Sensitized to the Communism issue by the firings in Seattle, California's Board of Regents adopted a special "disclaimer oath" that required all faculty members to swear not only that they upheld the Constitution (which they had been doing since 1942) but also that they did not belong to the Communist Party. Though the measure had initially been proposed as a kind of pro forma adherence to the anti-Communist consensus of the times, it quickly escalated into a conflict over the regents' power to impose a political test for employment. Before the controversy subsided, thirty-one nonsigners had been fired. They were soon reinstated by the California Supreme Court, which ruled that the loyalty oath the legislature imposed on all state employees superseded the university's one.[37]

Speaker bans were another mechanism that sought to enforce political orthodoxy on the nation's campuses. Like loyalty oaths, they had been around for years and had been sporadically enforced against controversial individuals or partisan politicking—usually at vulnerable public universities or second-tier institutions. The anti-Communist furor spread those bans to just about every campus. Needless to say, Communists were barred from most colleges and universities, as were, in many cases, such controversial individuals as the physicist J. Robert Oppenheimer and the China scholar Owen Lattimore, who, if they weren't disinvited, were often forced to share the platform with an antagonist. There was also an informal blacklist that lasted until the red scare eased in the early 1960s, making it almost impossible for the men and women who lost their jobs for political reasons to find academic employment. Moreover, because public attention can prove deleterious to one's career, as Edward Bemis learned to his distress, many people tried to keep their troubles to themselves. As a result, we may never know how many other college teachers were quietly eased out of their posts. Nor, for all the contemporary buzz about the chilling effect of McCarthyism, can we know what its intellectual fallout was. There is anecdotal evidence about people abandoning controversial projects or changing the focus of their work, but we will never know what books were not written, what research was abandoned, or what courses were not taught.[38]

Could the academy have done a better job of protecting its members? I'm not sure. It is asking a lot of a politically vulnerable institution for the academic profession to have stood up against such strong forces of repression. Admittedly, it was operating under some unique disadvantages. To begin with, during the 1950s the American Association of University Professors was missing in action. The organization, which might have warded off some of the damage by condemning the purges at the University of Washington and elsewhere, did not issue a report on them until 1956. There were internal organizational reasons for that delay, but political vacillation may also have been a factor.[39] Moreover, the academic profession was only just beginning to expand beyond its narrow social origins to admit Jews and other types of outsiders, and the new cohort of professors may have felt too vulnerable to challenge their institutions' leaders. A final obstacle was the professional culture of the academy, with its emphasis on caution, rationality, and judiciousness. Moreover, since most professors subscribed to the anti-Communist consensus of the era as well as to the prevailing code of civility, mounting a serious protest on behalf of the academy's political pariahs would have risked ostracism, social isolation, or worse.

To what extent the McCarthy-era purges imposed institutional and intellectual damage on American higher education remains unclear. Studies of specific disciplines have uncovered instances of individual and even collective self-censorship, but the life of the mind is so variegated that it would be a mistake to attribute all the scholarly developments in an affected field to McCarthyism's fallout. How it affected people's teaching rather than their research is even less well known, since documenting the Red scare's impact on the nation's classrooms would probably require the intensive examination and comparison of course catalogues and syllabi that, to my knowledge, has yet to be to undertaken. In any event, as the raucous doings of the following decade reveal, the academy's timidity during the McCarthy era certainly did not prevent a new generation of academics from mounting the most radical challenges American higher education would ever face. As a result, it is intriguing to speculate that the apparent paucity of major violations of traditional academic freedom during the 1960s may well indicate that the nation's colleges and universities actually learned a few lessons from the travails of the previous decade. On the other hand, it is just as likely that the massive expansion of the academy at that time simply minimized the damage of the political firings that did take place.

Chapter 3

"PART OF THE STRUGGLE": FACULTIES CONFRONT THE 1960S

The American historian Eugene Genovese had been granted tenure and promoted to associate professor by the Board of Governors of Rutgers University only two weeks before he appeared at the university's first teach-in about the Vietnam War on April 23, 1965. Like similar gatherings on campuses across the nation, the Rutgers event featured lectures by faculty members and others about the background and nature of the escalating conflict in Southeast Asia. Both supporters and opponents of the war addressed the nearly one thousand students at the all-night meeting. Genovese, who had been expelled from the Communist Party in the mid-1950s, was the most radical. "Those of you who know me," he explained, "know that I am a Marxist and a Socialist. Therefore, unlike most of my distinguished colleagues here this morning, I do not fear or regret the impending Viet Cong victory in Vietnam. I welcome it." Picked up by the local papers and then the national press, these remarks were to become the centerpiece of New Jersey's gubernatorial campaign. The Republican candidate called for Genovese's dismissal. "Academic freedom," State Senator Wayne Dumont declared, "does not give a teacher in a state university, supported by taxpayers' money, the right to advocate victory of an enemy at war, in which some of his own students may very well lay down their lives in the cause of freedom." The former vice president and future president Richard Nixon took the same position, asking in a letter to the *New York Times*: "Does the principle of freedom of speech require that the state subsidize those who would destroy the system of government which protects freedom of speech?"[1]

Apparently it did. Though New Jersey's liberal establishment certainly did not endorse Genovese's support for the Viet Cong, its members recognized that his statement at the teach-in was protected by the First Amendment. As Governor Richard Hughes explained, "A free and open discussion—even though involving a controversial subject—is basic to our American democratic tradition." Robert Kennedy, then a senator from New York, reinforced Hughes's position by repeatedly insisting to New Jersey crowds, "I would not be here today if Governor Hughes put any pressure upon the [Rutgers] board of governors to fire Mr. Genovese. This would destroy the whole idea of academic freedom." And the Rutgers trustees, although concerned enough about the political fallout from Genovese's remark to hold several meetings specifically devoted to him, did not dismiss their controversial professor.[2]

Such an outcome would have been unthinkable ten years before (and might well be today). After all, Rutgers had been the first American university to fire faculty members explicitly for taking the Fifth Amendment. However, the school's 1956 censure by the AAUP had been a considerable embarrassment, and both the board and the administration were determined to avoid a repeat. Once the trustees were assured by Genovese's colleagues that he was a serious scholar who did not proselytize in class, they decided to take no action. Rutgers's bylaws did not prevent faculty members from speaking out on political issues as long as they kept to their syllabi and did not bring irrelevant material into the classroom. Thus, when Hughes won reelection by the largest margin in New Jersey's history, it seemed as if academic freedom was more secure than ever.[3]

As for Genovese, his pathbreaking work on slavery and the culture and political economy of the South earned him a successful academic career—but not at Rutgers. Although the university had refused to fire him, the administration, Genovese later recalled, "made clear to me that I was going to be a second class citizen in salary and in promotion possibilities." So he left New Jersey and moved to Sir George Williams University in Canada, the country that had welcomed Chandler Davis and several other academic emigrés during the 1950s.[4]

In many respects, what happened to Eugene Genovese in 1965 exemplified the situation with regard to the traditional form of academic freedom during the turbulent 1960s and early 1970s. The lessons of the previous decade—or at least some of them—had been learned. No longer would mainstream schools like Rutgers perpetrate the outright violations of due process and freedom of expression that had characterized the McCarthy era. Although such academic authoritarianism could still be found at more marginal institutions, faculties had accumulated enough power by the early 1960s to serve as a brake to the more repressive impulses of administrators and trustees. Moreover, the academic community's brush with McCarthyism had alerted its members to the dangers of clamping down on dissent. As a result, when the civil rights movement and the Vietnam War politicized the nation's colleges and universities, faculties were more protective of their students' and each other's rights than they might otherwise have been.

At the University of California, for example, even before the Free Speech Movement tore up the Berkeley campus in 1964, the faculty, which had been thoroughly demoralized by the loyalty oath conflict of 1949–50, was particularly sensitive to academic freedom issues.[5] When early in 1960 the regents tried to interfere with the content of an exam question, the faculty senate blew up and condemned the action as "improper."[6] President Clark Kerr, who had apparently been selected to placate California's professors, saw it as his duty to create more political space on campus as well as to keep the regents from cracking down on dissenting instructors, no matter how distasteful he personally found them. He did so with some success, but his proclivity for behind-the-scenes mediation was to prove inadequate when faced with the hard-core intransigence of radical students and reactionary politicians.[7] Nonetheless, what is significant for us about Berkeley (and many other schools) in the sixties is the willingness of an often bitterly divided faculty to tolerate some rather extreme behavior on the part of their students in order to defend their own autonomy. Unfortunately, while the professoriate's collective support of the right to dissent did help to ensure that the violations of traditional academic freedom that occurred during the 1960s and 1970s did less damage than those of the previous decade, it also aroused the hostility of those elements of the American public who felt threatened by what was happening on campus. But that backlash, although ultimately devastating, did not make itself felt until the halcyon expansion of the 1960s was long over.

In the meantime, the academic community's mood had changed. Gone was the political timidity of the McCarthy era. A new generation of college teachers had come on board, and older ones overcame the fear and shame that had kept them from speaking out only a few years before. Moreover, the issues—Vietnam and the struggle for racial equality—seemed to demand political activity. Faculty members spoke out, organized, and demonstrated, and not always with what the vice chair of Rutgers's Board of Governors called "appropriate restraint."[8] Quite a few lost their jobs, but almost all were men and women without tenure, often at nonelite institutions, who were let go on other pretexts. There were, it is true, some high-profile cases, like the California regents' dismissal of Angela Davis and the expulsions from academe of the radical activists Staughton Lynd and Michael Parenti. Nonetheless, although by 1968 the AAUP reported receiving "an unprecedented number" of complaints, few involved people who were specifically fired because of their political activities, and even fewer of those had tenure.[9] In addition, almost everyone who wanted to could find another academic job—a situation that alleviated the personal problems of the dismissed instructors.

The 1960s were, after all, a period of such rapid expansion within American higher education that academia, where enrollments increased by 120 percent between 1960 and 1970, became a seller's market. New institutions were being founded and older ones were being upgraded. Schools that had been teachers colleges in the 1950s became liberal arts colleges and then added graduate programs and became universities. The professoriate grew accordingly, from 381,000 in 1960 to 551,000 in 1970.[10] Between 1965 and 1970, 150,000 people were added to the nation's faculties. Recruiting them was not always easy. That situation was one reason why Rutgers did not fire Genovese. To have done so, the school's president, Mason Gross, explained, would have been "disastrous" and would have led to "censure and probable loss of accreditation. This in turn would result in loss of faculty and great difficulty in recruiting new faculty."[11] Well-trained academics were in demand. "At meetings of many professional associations in the fifties and sixties," a former president of Princeton recalled, "department chairmen literally stood in line to interview job candidates."[12] And, as Gross understood, these people could be picky about where they taught. In addition, the informal hiring procedures of the time, though perpetuating the injustices associated with the old-boys' network, did allow people to get jobs through word of mouth, with the result that it was relatively easy for people who lost their positions at one school to find another. When, for example, a radical faculty organization decided to set up an academic job file for its unemployed members in early 1970, it advised them: "Come to us if you are trying to find a place where you can be fired from next."[13]

Expansion was only part of the story. By 1965, the political atmosphere had changed as much as the institutional one. The anti-Communist consensus that had facilitated the McCarthy-era political dismissals was seriously fraying. The Cold War Red scare was already running out of steam in 1956 when the AAUP finally caught up with its backlog of academic freedom cases from the previous few years. Pockets of nonconformity had reappeared and peace groups had begun to organize, but it was the pressure from and example of the mobilized African American community that brought politics back onto the nation's campuses. The Supreme Court's 1954 *Brown* decision encouraged African Americans all across the South to press for an end to segregation. Within a few years, students in the region's all-black colleges and universities were openly confronting the Jim Crow system and, in the process, not only gaining their own freedom but also creating models of direct action and opening up space within the rest of society for others to challenge the status quo. As a result, by the time the Vietnam War escalated in early 1965, American colleges and universities were on the verge of becoming politicized in ways that had never before been seen.

Though contemporaries and historians have paid the most attention to the student unrest of the era, professors were also active. Not only did they engage in political protests both on and off the campus, but they also began to challenge their own institutions and the academic profession as a whole. They questioned the intellectual direction of their disciplines as well as the racial and gender composition of the nation's faculties and student bodies. In conjunction with the student movements of the day, they managed to transform the university, but they also divided it. Within a few years, the academic reforms and radical scholarship that these faculty activists embraced inspired a backlash that, as we shall see, was to undermine public support for higher education when the nation's political climate changed.

Although a few of these activists were people who had managed to evade the McCarthy-era purges, most were younger men and women who had been students in the late 1950s and early 1960s. The expansion of American higher education had produced a massive cohort of youthful academics. Fifty-five percent of the men and women teaching in the nation's colleges and universities in 1969 had earned their PhDs after 1959, while 40 percent of all faculty members were under forty years old.[14] Although they lacked tenure (only slightly less than half of all college teachers then had it), some were, nonetheless, conspicuously active on their campuses, serving as advisors to undergraduate organizations, speakers at demonstrations, or intellectual mentors to the student left. Not only did many of these people oppose racial inequality and the Vietnam War, but they also turned their attention to their own campuses and disciplines, calling for intellectual and institutional changes within the world of academe. Many did, it is true, experience harassment and isolation, but others were actually recruited specifically for their politics—either because, like Evergreen State College in Washington or the State University of New York (SUNY) at Old Westbury, the institutions that hired them were themselves experimental or else because the administrators who sought them out wanted to ensure that there would be enough political ferment and educational innovation on their campuses to attract desirable undergraduates.[15]

Academic Freedom and the Civil Rights Movement

A handful of academic freedom violations in the late 1950s and early 1960s formed a bridge between the McCarthy era and the more turbulent times to come. Some of these cases, all of which took place at small black colleges in the South, involved professors, both black and white, whose support for racial equality threatened the tenuous equilibrium that had allowed these institutions to survive under the Jim Crow system. Ironically, a few of the protagonists, like Chandler Davis's mother, Marian, were Communists or former Communists who had found jobs at schools, such as Benedict College in South Carolina, that were so eager for qualified instructors they were willing to hire the political pariahs the mainstream academy was blacklisting. When, however, the rumbling among their previously quiescent charges threatened to alienate the segregationist white politicians and trustees who controlled these institutions, their administrations cracked down on the student activists and their faculty supporters. Red-baiting helped the white supremacists quash dissent. South Carolina's governor, for example, claimed that the six professors he sought to fire from Benedict and its sister school, Allen, were "looking toward an ultimate Communist goal of creating civil and racial disorder."[16] Such sentiments were common throughout the South. Professors who had left-wing ties or supported integration were viewed as "outside agitators," a label that made them vulnerable to dismissal once the civil rights movement washed over their campuses. This was what happened to the important black scholar Lawrence Reddick, who lost his job as chair of the history department at Alabama State College in Montgomery even though he had purposely kept a low profile at the school.[17]

The segregationists struck at civil rights organizations as well as individual activists, using the McCarthy-era tactic of loyalty oaths and membership lists to flush out movement supporters. Here, the National Association for the Advancement of Colored People (NAACP), not the CP, was the intended target, with several states passing laws requiring state employees—including college teachers—to list all the organizations to which they had belonged during the previous five years. In Arkansas, a group of faculty members challenged the measure that Governor Orville Faubus had pushed through a special session of the legislature in the wake of the Little Rock crisis in 1958. Supported by the local and national AAUP, they took their case all the way to the Supreme Court—and won. In a 5–4 decision, the Court's majority threw out the Arkansas law, asserting "that to compel a teacher to disclose his every associational tie is to impair that teacher's right of free association, a right closely allied to freedom of speech and a right which, like free speech, lies at the foundation of a free society." But, since the state authorities dragged their feet about reinstating the plaintiffs and restoring their back pay, it was by no means clear how much the Court's decision had bolstered academic freedom in Arkansas. In fact, Faubus and his segregationist allies actually welcomed the AAUP's censure: it would, they hoped, keep unsympathetic northerners from seeking faculty positions in the state.[18]

The situation was even worse in Mississippi. That state had also enacted a law requiring its teachers to list their memberships, but, unlike in Arkansas, no local professors could be found to challenge it.[19] Things were so bad that the AAUP created a special committee just to assess the status of academic freedom in the state.[20] The way that it was squelched in the one Mississippi institution that supported integration reveals how strong the pressures for conformity were. This was Tougaloo College, a private black institution whose white president, Daniel Beittel, sympathized with the movement and did not crack down on the civil rights activities of his students and faculty members. In response, Mississippi's white supremacists threatened to withdraw accreditation from the school. The threat, which would have denied Tougaloo graduates the right to teach in Mississippi's public schools, was so serious that the college's Board of Trustees forced President Beittel to resign in the spring of 1964. Ironically, the strongest internal pressure for Beittel's ouster came from the North, from the president of Brown University, who had established a paternalistic relationship with Tougaloo and who had apparently threatened to scuttle a crucial Ford Foundation grant unless the president was sacked. Beittel departed, the Ford money came through, and Tougaloo, in the words of historian John Dittmer, "would never again be at the center of civil rights activity."[21]

Student Protests

Campus activism elsewhere intensified after the summer of 1964. The well-publicized Mississippi Summer project drew more than six hundred northern students into the state, radicalized them, and then sent them back to their home institutions—seasoned New Left organizers who would have a powerful impact on the developing student protests.[22] The Berkeley Free Speech Movement's leader, Mario Savio, was only the most well-known of these Mississippi veterans who brought what they learned in the South to their own campuses in the North. But even without any direct involvement with the Mississippi Summer project, the early student movement was deeply influenced by the struggle for racial equality. This was especially the case since so much of the civil rights movement *was* a student movement. It was black students who had, after all, initiated the sit-ins that revitalized the civil rights struggle in 1960, and one of the key organizational components of that struggle, the Student Nonviolent Coordinating Committee (SNCC), was, at least originally, composed of students. Thus, when we assess the student movement, we need to remember that it consisted not only of the long-haired radicals who took over campuses and trashed the Reserve Officers' Training Corps' (ROTC) buildings in the late 1960s and early 1970s, but also the well-groomed undergraduates from North Carolina A & T in Greensboro, Morehouse and Spelman colleges in Atlanta, Fisk University in Nashville, and dozens of other all-black colleges and universities who put their bodies on the line at lunch counters, bus stations, and demonstrations throughout the South.

It was logical, therefore, that when the young northern activists who had watched their peers in the South mount such a powerful challenge to segregation began to mobilize on their own campuses, they would adopt similar forms of direct action—especially since, as their TV screens showed them, those nonviolent confrontations had actually worked. Intellectually as well as tactically, these white New Leftists drew heavily on the civil rights movement's analysis and identification of injustice. They were also influenced by SNCC's creation of a "beloved community," with its rejection of elitism and emphasis on participatory democracy. And, especially after the Vietnam War escalated early in 1965 and opposition to the war became as important a cause as civil rights, they put these ideas and tactics into practice.

It is important to make some distinctions here between graduate students and undergraduates. In the late 1950s, as the educational establishment looked to the future expansion of the nation's colleges and universities, it began to worry about a potential scarcity of faculty members. This concern intensified after the 1957 launch of the Soviet satellite Sputnik seemingly showed up the inadequacies of American higher education. Private foundations and the federal government responded to this perceived crisis by funding fellowships to entice bright undergraduates into the academic profession. As a result, by the 1960s, there was a large cohort of graduate students who had gone into academia under these auspices and who were to serve as a kind of transmission belt between the undergraduates whose world they had just left and the faculty whose world they were about to enter. More mature and politically sophisticated than most undergraduates, these graduate students often took positions of leadership on the campuses where they were being trained. Moreover, by the late 1960s, many of these people had begun to teach.

Their age was only one factor determining how American professors responded to the student movement; their social background, political views, discipline, career path, and type of institution also counted. Humanists and social scientists generally supported the students, while professors in fields like engineering and business tended to resist them.[23] Nor were the men and women who became faculty activists influenced only by what was happening on their campuses. Like many of their fellow citizens outside the academy, they were already caught up in the struggle for racial equality and the antiwar movement, participating as individuals or through local community organizations. Thus, even without pressure from radical students, these people's political commitments might well have pushed them to challenge the academic status quo. They did so in a wide variety of areas, from admissions policies to campus-based military research to the content of their own teaching and writing. The changes that they were able to implement did not always correspond to specific student demands, but it is hard to imagine that they would have occurred without pressures from social movements both on and off the campus.

The Berkeley Free Speech Movement established important patterns. In order to avoid intervention by the state's regents and politicians, the university (like many less-prestigious schools elsewhere) had imposed serious restrictions on its students' political activity. When the issue came to a head over on-campus recruiting for civil rights demonstrations in the fall of 1964, the faculty split. Many of its members, especially in the early stages of the struggle, shrank from antagonizing the administration or supporting the civil disobedience of the student protestors. But as the crisis began to affect the faculty's ability to control the situation, large numbers of professors sided with the students—though not, it must be noted, without some hesitation. Eventually, however, the Berkeley administration behaved in such a repressive manner that even the moderate and uninvolved majority of the faculty was moved to condemn it. At that point, the administration and regents caved in.[24] There was now free speech on the Berkeley campus, but the escalating war in Vietnam ensured that calm would not return. And, as we shall see, a backlash began to build.

The Free Speech Movement had implications far beyond California. To begin with, it was the first highly publicized campus confrontation of the 1960s, establishing precedents that later antiwar and black power activists could take advantage of. Morever, by disrupting the nation's leading public university, it forced thoughtful students and faculty members at the University of California and elsewhere to grapple with preconceived notions about higher education. As the historian David Hollinger, then a Berkeley graduate student, recalled, "Life outside of classes seemed to have become an all-day, half-the-night informal seminar involving everyone I knew discussing the meaning of the university and of the life of the mind in relation to the rest of the world."[25] The academy had become politicized and could no longer remain an enclave unto itself—as if it had ever been. In certain respects, however, the victory of the Free Speech Movement was to prove misleading; the Berkeley protestors had succeeded in large part because of the issue they were pushing. Free speech was, after all, something that—unlike later, more divisive demands—enjoyed support across the entire political spectrum. When students and their on- and off-campus allies began to press for more radical measures, the faculty's unanimity, at Berkeley and elsewhere, disappeared.[26]

Because the nation's system of higher education is still feeling the backwash of the events of the 1960s, we need to clarify exactly how faculty members were involved in those events and how they were affected by them. Only a few college and university teachers became militant activists. In an influential 1969 Carnegie Foundation study of the professoriate, Everett Carll Ladd Jr. and Seymour Martin Lipset found that only 5 percent of the more than sixty thousand professors they surveyed were willing to identify themselves as radicals.[27] Though they may have had more influence than their numbers suggest, that was probably because their moderate and liberal colleagues had moved to the left and were also ready to question the status quo. Reform, not just revolution, was in the air, and if it didn't attract the media's attention the way building takeovers and police busts tended to, it did change the face of higher education. After all, it was hard for faculties to resist their students' reasonable demands for more say in matters that concerned their daily lives such as dress codes and parietal rules. And few at the time questioned the need for eliminating racial and ethnic inequities in undergraduate admissions. There was, it is true, somewhat more resistance to curricular revisions and the creation of programs in African American and women's studies. But, desperate to dampen campus unrest, administrators were often eager to set up such programs.

Faculty Members Speak Out

Of course, not all the faculty activism during the 1960s developed in response to student demands. In the spring of 1965, for example, the professors who organized the national teach-in movement needed no prodding from below. One did not have to be an expert on Southeast Asia to recognize the problematic nature of the U.S. intervention in Vietnam, but those academics who did have that expertise were among the early opponents of the war. Once the United States began bombing North Vietnam in February 1965, they started to organize.

The movement began at the University of Michigan among a group of social scientists who wanted to make their scholarship more relevant. After rejecting a one-day work stoppage as too confrontational, they decided to hold an all-night session of lectures and debates. The idea caught on at once. Within a few days of the Michigan event on March 24, there were teach-ins at more than thirty-five other institutions. By the end of the semester, hundreds of such programs had taken place at schools ranging from Columbia and Berkeley to Marist College and Flint Junior College. There was even a National Teach-In with nationwide media coverage in Washington, D.C. The formats varied; many featured prominent antiwar activists such as Oregon senator Wayne Morse or journalist I.F. Stone, as well as local faculty members with expertise in the area. Organizers usually tried to present all points of view, though pro-war speakers were not always willing to participate. The crowds were enormous. Up to twelve thousand people flocked to a thirty-five-hour marathon at Berkeley; on many campuses, so many students showed up that they had to be seated in overflow auditoriums or else, as at Washington University in St. Louis, accommodated in shifts of two thousand at a time.[28]

Devoted to supplying historical background and an analysis of American foreign policy, these gatherings were intellectually ambitious endeavors as well as protests against the war. As one of the Washington University organizers put it:

> There is nothing improper in what we are doing here. We are just covering up for, or updating a poorly designed curriculum. We forgot to have courses on Southeast Asian politics in the curriculum this year. The academic community failed in Germany during the 1930s. We are not going to let it happen here.[29]

Quintessentially liberal undertakings, the teach-ins operated on the assumption that if only the American people and their leaders really understood the situation in Southeast Asia, they would seek a negotiated settlement and end the war. Students came for the intellectual stimulation, as well as to show their opposition to the war—and, of course, to take part in the most exciting event on campus that year. "You can't duplicate this in a classroom," an Oregon undergraduate explained. "I've learned an awful lot."[30]

There was opposition, to be sure: bomb threats and heckling, but also attacks from conservative faculty members such as the Berkeley political scientist Robert A. Scalapino, who charged that the teach-in he refused to address was "symbolic of the new anti-intellectualism that is gaining strength today." Off-campus conservatives were similarly dismissive. The recently defeated Republican presidential contender Barry Goldwater derided the teach-ins as a "raggle-taggle protest," while the journalist William S. White Red-baited their organizers as "professors and students with observably close ties to undeniably far-left movements who faithfully speak the harsh, twisty jargon that passes for Communist logic" as well as "mere frustrated beatniks and middle-aged show-offs."[31]

Within a year, as the war in Vietnam continued to escalate, the intellectual earnestness that marked the earliest stage of the campus antiwar movement began to give way to a willingness to engage in more direct action. Student protests came to dominate the front pages and nightly news; while many faculty members remained active in the antiwar movement, they often did so in off-campus community groups.[32] The student unrest split the faculty. Again, as at Berkeley, when administrators infringed on faculty prerogatives or seemingly countenanced police brutality, as happened at Columbia in 1968, many moderate as well as radical professors sided with the students. But when the protests became gratuitously destructive or when they interfered with people's teaching and research, most of that faculty support evaporated.[33] Age was an important factor, since most but not all of the students' allies were younger academics. But, it is important to realize that very few professors actually participated in campus protests—only 1 percent, according to the 1969 survey by Ladd and Lipset. Moreover, although they largely agreed with their students on issues such as Vietnam and racial integration, liberal and even radical college teachers were not always willing to give undergraduates a voice in the faculty's traditional academic functions, such as hiring and curricular development.[34]

The 1969 statement by the AAUP's Special Committee on Challenge and Change reflects the discomfort that so many mainstream academics felt. Though neither young nor radical, the statement's authors were admittedly more devoted to and knowledgeable about academic freedom and governance than most of their peers. Even so, they were clearly ambivalent about the turmoil on the nation's campuses. While condemning those protest activities that would interfere with the "proper functions of the academic life," they nonetheless offered a sympathetic exegesis of the students' discontents. Not only did the statement's authors recognize that the Vietnam War, the draft, and the existence of racial discrimination were among the underlying causes of the campus unrest, but they also—surprisingly—mirrored the language of the early New Left with its idealism and disillusionment about

> the disparity between espoused ideals of society and actual practice; the inability of social institutions to move promptly to correct recognized social evils; the limited emphasis on humanistic goals; and the growing inability of the individual to influence the conditions of his own life.

Perhaps most significant, the statement took account of the protestors' critique of the academic system itself. It noted the students' demands for their schools to provide greater access and more sensitivity to the surrounding communities, as well as their opposition to the university's lack of internal democracy, its participation in classified research, and the irrelevance of many of its academic offerings.[35]

Perhaps one reason for the ambivalence that pervaded the AAUP's document was that many faculty members shared their students' conviction that both American society and their own institutions needed a major overhaul. The formerly nonpartisan academic community had begun to take political stands. Opposition to the Vietnam War was widespread.[36] By the fall of 1969, a few faculties, including Harvard's, had passed resolutions against the war, while seventy-nine college presidents signed an open letter calling for a "stepped-up time-table for withdrawal of troops from Vietnam."[37] At the same time, the antiwar movement had pushed certain issues, including the on-campus presence of defense-related research, the draft, and ROTC, onto the faculty's agenda. Student sit-ins and demonstrations against the university's cooperation with the military as well as its facilitation of recruiting by the Central Intelligence Agency (CIA) and corporations that, like Dow Chemical, were producing napalm and other weapons gave urgency to the matter.

For many professors, the academy's collaboration with the draft became an issue of academic freedom. Like their students, they were particularly upset about the Selective Service director's fall 1965 edict making undergraduates with low GPAs eligible for the call-up and requiring the institutions that housed them to provide class rankings to the military.[38] In April 1967, after a four-to-one vote by the undergraduates and a unanimous one by the University Council, Columbia's trustees simply abolished the system of class rankings.[39] There was more ambivalence about the draft at other institutions. The local AAUP chapter at SUNY Buffalo supported a joint student-faculty statement that the Selective Service System was

> undermining the autonomy of the university by establishing for the university the definitive qualities of intellectualism and intellectuals, using the coercive device of the 2-S [student] deferment.
>
> Due to excessive pressures, many students are encouraged to conform academically, to cheat, and to plagiarize. Fear of low grades discourages experimentation in course work and selections. In these instances, the Selective Service System is destroying the idea of the university.[40]

However, when, in the aftermath of a sit-in, there was a campus referendum on the issue, 67 percent of the Buffalo student body still urged cooperation with the draft.[41]

Like the Selective Service system, the ROTC program also attracted opposition at dozens of institutions, its presence a local symbol of the militarism against which the antiwar movement was struggling. Naturally, radicals sought to eliminate the program from their campuses. "We are convinced from our study of American foreign policy," a left-wing faculty group at SUNY Buffalo explained,

> that the uses of ROTC graduates are insupportable on moral and political grounds. We do not wish to continue a program in which students from the University of Buffalo are put in a position where they either subject themselves to court martial or commit murder on the innocent to protect landlords and the wealthy in Vietnam, or perhaps in years to come, in South Africa, South America, Laos, Thailand, Indonesia, or wherever the theory and practice of counter-insurgency may send them.[42]

While few of their colleagues, at Buffalo or elsewhere, shared these people's sense of outrage, because ROTC instructors were not regular faculty members but military officers, it turned out to be possible to treat the issue as a matter of faculty governance and academic freedom. Not only did the armed services determine the substance of the ROTC curriculum, but they also selected the people who taught it, thereby posing a direct challenge to the faculty's control over its core academic functions.

The conflict at Northwestern University was typical. Even before student protests rocked the campus, many professors were questioning the academic value of the school's Naval ROTC program. The faculty senate debated the issue and decided to retain the program "in order that it may provide our country with naval officers who have been educated in an environment with a broad liberal background." But in 1969 the faculty of the College of Arts and Sciences voted 162–123 with 95 abstentions to eliminate credit for the NROTC's courses. Not only was the program designed, staffed, and funded by "outside sources," but its intellectual quality and the academic credentials of its instructors were seen "as being below that of other departments in the college."[43] Similar arguments surfaced at other institutions, and by the end of the 1960s, professors at dozens of schools had voted to either end compulsory ROTC or else to deny it academic credit.[44] Even so, the issue remained controversial; at Northwestern, once the campus calmed down in 1971, a remorseful faculty actually restored credit to the NROTC's offerings.[45]

Faculties were similarly divided over the problem of on-campus recruiting by the CIA, the armed services, and the defense industry. Although radical instructors opposed the university's collaboration with agencies and corporations they considered responsible for wartime atrocities, they did not necessarily support the sometimes unruly student demonstrations that blocked access to military recruiters and representatives from the CIA and the Dow Chemical Company. Their more conservative colleagues were even less supportive, not only backing sanctions against the student demonstrators but also, as a 197–72 vote by SUNY Buffalo's faculty senate revealed, choosing to permit continued access to the campus by such recruiters.[46]

Defense-related research was an equally contentious matter. Although some schools had already banned classified research, mainly on the grounds that the secrecy it required violated the academy's commitment to openness, professors at other institutions were divided about the issue.[47] Thus, for example, while eighty Berkeley faculty members and graduate students pledged not to do weapons or other war-related research, UCLA's faculty voted 514–329 to retain the university's ties to the nuclear weapons facilities at Los Alamos and Livermore.[48] Top-tier institutions like the Massachusetts Institute of Technology (MIT) and the University of Michigan were the main beneficiaries of these military connections. As of 1969, MIT was receiving 80 percent of its income from the Department of Defense.[49] In addition, many of its faculty members consulted for the Institute for Defense Analysis, a consortium of a dozen top research universities that had been established to assess the Pentagon's weapons systems and which became a target for campus demonstrations, including the 1968 confrontation at Columbia.[50] Less prestigious schools also pursued defense-related research. In 1967, for example, Secretary of Defense Robert McNamara developed the THEMIS project to distribute funding to some forty second-tier institutions to encourage the upgrading of their schools' research capabilities—and avoid student disruptions.[51]

Faculty radicals were often at the forefront of the movement to eject that kind of research from their campuses. Like the professors who helped to expose Spicerack and Summit, the chemical and biological warfare projects at the University of Pennsylvania, these individuals usually provided information to document the academy's collaboration with the military.[52] Thus, for example, these antiwar activists discovered that more than fifty schools, from Harvard to the George Peabody College for Teachers, had military contracts for such projects as the "mechanism of action of toxic compounds" and "the explosive dissemination of chemical agents."[53] It was, however, by no means clear how effective the opposition to that research was, since many faculty members, especially the scientists and engineers who benefited directly from the military's largesse, were understandably hostile to any effort that would eject their projects from the campus. In addition, it could be, and was, argued that eliminating that research would interfere with academic freedom in the sense that it would restrict the ability of individual professors to decide what projects to pursue.[54]

Faculty Radicals

The way in which faculty activists handled the issue of military-related research revealed their own political dilemma. Should they undertake the same kind of organizing and direct action that student radicals engaged in, or should they focus their efforts on more academic pursuits—producing scholarship and teaching courses that challenged the status quo?[55] This question was, in fact, never resolved. A few faculty members did turn to physical destruction, such as the young historian who wanted to support the Black Panthers by trying to blow up the New York University (NYU) computer or the California academic who set off a bomb in a piano.[56] More commonly, however, small handfuls of faculty radicals participated in sit-ins and building takeovers, usually as a protest against military research and/or the dismissal and nonreappointment of their colleagues.[57] Others, however, felt they could be more effective doing work that was more closely tied to their professional activities.

In the process, they established a wide variety of formal and informal groups that circulated petitions, published magazines, and organized teach-ins. Not only did these groups protest against the war and the other ills of

American society, but they also sought to make their own academic work more relevant to the problems of the day. Historians, economists, psychologists, sociologists, East Asian scholars, and scientists all had their own radical caucuses or organizations, and all struggled in one way or another to establish a balance between activism and scholarship. Nothing illuminates the nature of that struggle as much as the internal debates that took place within one of the most ambitious radical faculty organizations of the period, the New University Conference (NUC). Established in the beginning of 1968 by a group of academic leftists and Students for a Democratic Society alumni who had aged out of the student movement but who wanted to remain politically active, the NUC saw itself as "one of the first solid adult organizations from the New Left of the 60's" that would become, as one of the group's founders put it, "prologue to the university section of a revolutionary socialist party."[58] More specifically, as an early position paper explained, the NUC's members

> share the basic goals and commitments of the student movement. We share with student activists the aim of constructing a grass-roots movement in this country that can have real effect in stopping American efforts to dominate other peoples, that can win a fundamental reordering of priorities in this country so that genuine equality can become a realistic hope, that can disrupt the drift toward technologically based authoritarianism and a garrison state, that can find new modes of political and social organization which will permit our vast resources to be shared for the benefit of all men and provide the basis for personal liberation.
>
> We have hoped that the university could be a center of work toward these ends. That hope, however, seems increasingly illusory. Desiring the university to be a home for humane and democratic values, we have found, instead, that its proclaimed purposes conceal a deep-going corruption.[59]

Determined to carry out its political work, as the group's oft-quoted slogan put it, "in, around, and in spite of institutions of higher education," the NUC hired a full-time administrator and sought to expand beyond its initial base in the elite colleges and universities. By the spring of 1970 it had about sixty chapters and more than six hundred members, and it fielded an eleven-person staff. Two years later, it had collapsed. Beset by internal struggles, a worsening job market, and reprisals against its members that forced them out of the academy, the New University Conference formally dissolved itself in the summer of 1972 and, as befitting its academic provenance, deposited its files in an archive for future researchers to consult.[60] The group's struggles were representative of those that wracked the rest of the left at that time. At one point, for example, Maoist cadres from the Progressive Labor Party threatened to take over and divert the NUC's anticorporate campaign to the off-campus organizing of workers at the General Electric Company.[61] The role of women turned out to be particularly troublesome. Despite a stated commitment to gender equality, charges of chauvinism split the leadership, with many of the group's most active feminists pulling out to devote themselves to the then-burgeoning women's movement.[62]

Though the organization had a few African American members, it did not try hard to recruit others, since black separatism was then in vogue on the left.[63] Nonetheless, it supported the struggle for racial equality. Chapters pressed their institutions to work with community organizations as well as to admit more minority students and to revise the curriculum to accommodate those students. Connected to that drive for wider access was an interest in pedagogical experimentation, driven by the sense that the current approach to higher education not only alienated undergraduates but also replicated the elitism that deformed the rest of American society. Relevance was the key issue here. Classrooms, these radical teachers insisted, could no longer be isolated from the nation's broader social problems. Not only the content but the structure of their courses had to be changed. Grades, many activists believed, would have to go, since they encouraged the individualism and competitiveness the organization's more egalitarian members hoped to destroy. One NUC stalwart recalls giving a collective final and collective grades in a course on revolutionary literature—and being reprimanded by the dean for doing so.[64]

Self-education flourished, with study groups of NUC members and other radicals reading the Marxist classics as well as the writings of Chairman Mao, Frantz Fanon, and other icons of the left. Drawing on their experiences in the civil rights movement's freedom schools, academic radicals also set up alternative educational ventures. At NYU, the Free University–Liberation School, for example, offered courses entitled Militarism, Women: Checking It Out, Marx and Economic Theory, The Black Panther Party, and Imperialism.[65] Such projects sprouted during the strikes and campus crises that offered opportunities for these activists to put their political and pedagogical ideas into practice. During the 1968 troubles at Columbia, for example, students and faculty members established a Liberation School that taught everything from Balkan dance and karate to Liberated Talmud and Socio-Economic Functions of the University.[66] Similarly, when Northwestern University shut down after the Kent State killings in May 1970, students, professors, and even entire departments organized an alternative institution. Their so-called New University boasted a curriculum of more than eighty new and retooled courses that included, among other subjects,

> Myths and Symbols of Peace and War; Northwestern, Whither Goest Thou?; The Sociology of Math; Application of Engineering Analysis to Social Problems; The Press and the Strike; Physics and Politics; Draft Resistance Seminar; Pacifism; The Role of the Computer in Society; Food Buying Co-ops; Toward a Psychology of Conscious Values; Persuasion and Social Agitation.[67]

Their disdain for academic decorum and support for student protests rarely earned these radicals good relationships with their institutions' administrations or their more conventional colleagues. As a local American Civil Liberties Union report noted, calling his fellow faculty members "bourgeois assholes" did not help an NUC founder keep his teaching position at Michigan State.[68] Nor was he alone, although we know surprisingly little about the fate of academic radicals at this time. At some schools, every untenured radical lost his or her job, while those few with tenure found promotions and pay raises hard to come by.[69] In 1968, for example, the NUC chapter at Penn State had thirty members; in 1973 only one was still on the faculty.[70] At several institutions, firings of well-known campus figures triggered student protests; the University of Chicago's refusal to rehire the feminist sociologist Marlene Dixon, for example, precipitated a two-week sit-in at the school's administration building.[71] The NUC seems to have taken these dismissals in stride, treating the agitation around them as organizing opportunities that served "to smash the myth of the university's apolitical and pristine nature."[72]

Challenging the Curriculum

Had the New University Conference engaged only in campus confrontations, its main historical contribution would have been as the faculty footnote to the larger story of the 1960s New Left. However, because some of the slightly older intellectuals among the organization's founders, including the sociologist Richard Flacks and the literary critics Paul Lauter and Richard Ohmann, wanted to radicalize their academic disciplines or, like the feminist scholar Florence Howe, establish a new field altogether, their activities and those of other left-wing scholars outside the organization were to have a lasting impact on academe. The thrust of these people's ambitions was avowedly academic.

They were out not to destroy the university but to transform it. "You don't shit where you eat" was the way Lauter described their relationship to the institutions that employed them. In a sense, these people were responding to the students' (and their own) complaints about the irrelevance of American higher education. They wanted to revise the curriculum, treat contemporary issues in their classes, and bring a radical perspective into their scholarship. Some of the NUC's hard-liners disparaged such activities, arguing that to focus so intensively on their academic work would dilute these people's commitment to radical change and would suggest, as one NUC report explained, "that 'socialist scholarship' is an adequate response to the needs of our movement and society."[73] While it was obvious that the radical faculty members' efforts to politicize the content of academic life did not bring on the revolution, they did, I would argue, transform American culture in ways that still resonate today.

These activists focused on their disciplines, joining forces with other academics who had already formed radical working groups within their professional associations. Almost every field had such an organization: the Union of Radical Political Economists, the radical caucuses of the American Anthropology Association and the American Philosophical Association, the Sociology Liberation Movement, the Middle Atlantic Radical Historians Organization, Psychologists for a Democratic Society, the Committee of Concerned Asian Scholars, and Scientists for Social and Political Action, to name a few of the often ephemeral, but sometimes still extant, organizations.[74] They held conferences, published newsletters and scholarly journals, and tried to get the learned societies in their fields to take political stands. The issues they pressed were predictable: Vietnam, open access, and the abolition of the draft. But there were also special subjects that varied according to discipline. Scientists sought to ban weapons research; anthropologists decried imperialism and opposed the CIA's appropriation of their fieldwork; historians urged their colleagues to study African Americans, workers, and women. Some scholars demanded a sweeping reorganization of their entire discipline, such as the sociologists who, according to a report Flacks submitted to the NUC newsletter, called for

> a new sociology committed to the abolition of racism, opposition to imperialism, support for national liberation; . . . new research orientations, emphasizing service to the oppressed, and new directions in graduate education, emphasizing intellectual, critical commitments rather than professional ones.[75]

By the late 1960s, the radicals had begun to mount confrontations within their scholarly associations. Though almost every professional organization did cancel plans for meetings in Chicago to protest the police violence at the 1968 Democratic National Convention, many of the leftists' other demands encountered stiff opposition from their more traditional colleagues who did not want to politicize their discipline or undermine its reputation for objectivity. The radicals could be quite disrespectful. Members of the Sociology Liberation Movement, for example, stormed into the 1968 meeting of the American Sociological Association, where they organized their own sessions, distributed leaflets, and disrupted a speech by the secretary of health, education, and welfare. When the NUC's Martin Nicolaus managed to get the microphone, he not only called the field "an exercise in intellectual servility" but attacked his fellow sociologists as spies for the establishment who "report to [their] master on the movements of the occupied populace."[76] The historians made their move at the American Historical Association in the following year. But their attempt to elect the antiwar activist Staughton Lynd as the AHA's president failed as dismally as their resolution against the war.[77]

Radical English professors had more success. Not only did they get the Modern Language Association to pass antiwar and other resolutions at its annual meeting in December 1968, but they also managed to put one of their own people in line for the organization's presidency. Disruptions occurred, including the arrest of the future president, Louis Kampf, for putting up unauthorized posters. But, perhaps because the MLA activists were among the movement's so-called heavies, prolific authors and organizers with established reputations like Ohmann, Kampf, Lauter, and Howe, they could not be ignored. Their activities resulted not only in the creation of a permanent radical caucus within the MLA but also in the transformation of their discipline through the inclusion of previously ignored female and minority group authors in the canon.[78]

Literary scholars were overrepresented among the disenchanted academics of the sixties. According to one study, 73 percent of the English professors it surveyed wanted withdrawal from or deescalation of the Vietnam conflict.[79] Whether this was because of their training in criticism and their cultural (perhaps even high-cultural) disdain for ordinary bourgeois values, as Richard Ohmann has suggested, or because they were among the first college teachers to be hit by the crash of the academic job market and the subsequent proletarianization of much of the profession, their disillusionment with the state of American society in the late 1960s and early 1970s brought them to question their own discipline, its relevance, and its structure. "I found it harder to believe that Humanity was being served well by the academic humanities," Ohmann recalled, "or that the professional apparatus we had invented was a rational structure and not a Rube Goldberg machine."[80]

Expanding the Curriculum: African American Studies

Although they certainly did not turn American higher education into a bastion of revolution, Ohmann and his colleagues did help to bring multiculturalism to the curriculum. Within a few years, the nation's colleges and universities were offering thousands of courses in ecology, women's studies, African American studies, Chicano studies, gay and lesbian studies, cultural studies, and other new and/or neglected fields. In some cases, the transformation came in response to student pressure, while in others faculty members themselves took the initiative. Whatever the reason, the result would change the way humanists and social scientists approached their own teaching and research.

Student protests played a major role in bringing black studies programs onto the nation's campuses. During the 1960s, many largely white colleges and universities responded to the civil rights movement by recruiting thousands of African Americans to their campuses, which until then had had few, if any, black undergraduates. Problems arose, mainly because the institutions that housed these students were unprepared to handle them. They had no experience dealing with racial issues and had hired few African American administrators or faculty members who could serve as mentors and intermediaries. In addition, many of the students at these institutions, as well as those at the traditionally black colleges and universities, got caught up in the black power movement with its emphasis on asserting a militant racial identity that rejected all forms of white authority. Accordingly, even though they constituted less than 6 percent of the nation's student bodies, black undergraduates were involved in 57 percent of all campus protests during the 1967–68 academic year, with at least eighty-five race-related demonstrations the following year. These protests ranged from the trashing of the president's office at the University of Wisconsin–Oshkosh followed by the arrest and expulsion of 90 of the school's 114 African-American undergraduates to the more ladylike building takeover at Vassar that ended with the presentation of a list of demands and several bouquets of yellow daisies.[81]

Black studies programs were—along with calls for increased admissions, separate all-black dormitories and dining halls, and better relations with the local African American communities—these militants' main demands. In many instances, their proponents viewed these programs as contributions to the ongoing struggle for racial justice, not as conventional academic courses of study. Black studies had to be, one student activist explained, "founded on social need and . . . aimed at social action."[82] This was not, it turned out, a new agenda. African American intellectuals, following the example of W.E.B. Du Bois, had a long tradition of social commitment. Not only did their scholarship, according to Columbia's Manning Marable, "use history and culture as tools through which people interpret their collective experience," but it also served "the purpose of transforming their actual conditions and the totality of the society all around them." From the start, therefore, black studies was designed to produce "a critical body of scholarship that sought over time to dismantle powerful racist intellectual categories and white supremacy itself."[83]

There was, however, a separatist element to the late 1960s conceptualization of these programs. Years of segregation and discrimination had sensitized the student activists and their intellectual mentors to what they saw as the underlying paternalism, if not outright racism, of the academic establishment. A position paper from the Washington, D.C., Center for Black Education articulated this antagonism toward traditional higher education:

> The educational process that we are forced to undergo demands a commitment to white standards and values. It insists that we become white of mind if not white of skin, and that our commitment be to the assumptions, practices, and priorities of white supremacy and white nationalism.[84]

The kind of black studies program that such militants were seeking, therefore, would be under black and, often, student control. It would foster the development of an independent black identity, stripped of the submissiveness and stereotypes that centuries of oppression had inculcated. "For us," the poet June Jordan insisted, "there is nothing optional about 'black experience' and/or 'black studies': we must know ourselves."[85] Moreover, because of its reflexive nature, such an intellectual exploration had to be guided by teachers who, in Jordan's words, could convey to a student "the truth about himself: the truth of black experience . . . teachers least likely to lie, least likely to perpetuate the traditions of lying—lies that deface the father from the memory of the child. We request black teachers of black studies."[86]

That request—and the concomitant demand to limit classes to African American students—was controversial, to say the least.[87] Even though they conceded that white students should take black studies, some militants felt that the presence of whites who did not understand the black experience would inhibit open discussion, thus making it harder for African Americans to explore their own identity.[88] Like other symbolic demands, it was also a question of power. As a Cornell undergraduate explained during the crisis provoked by the appearance of firearms in the wake of a building occupation in 1969:

> A black studies program designed by whites for blacks . . . was never going to work. The whole issue was that, as African-American students, we felt very strongly that we should design the program. It was more than we had to be consulted; we should be the principal architects of the program.[89]

Although some administrators, who were hurriedly inserting black studies courses into the curriculum, were willing to grant such demands in order to fend off potential disruptions, and some white professors believed that they lacked the moral authority and cultural understanding to convey the black experience correctly, most faculty members, including many African American ones, opposed that kind of separatism.[90] Moreover, because the student militants had little experience with academic procedures and expected immediate action, they often viewed the faculties' drawn-out deliberations about establishing black studies programs as a manifestation of their underlying racism. As a result, implementing these programs often resulted in what one scholar called "the creation of academic chaos, misunderstanding, and mutual ill will."[91]

In such a situation, it was obvious that some of the early black studies programs would be thoroughly politicized. They were, after all, artifacts of the larger black power movement. As the head of San Francisco State University's program explained, "A black-studies program which is not revolutionary and nationalistic is, accordingly, quite profoundly irrelevant." Staffing these programs created further problems, for the newness of the field meant that scholars with the appropriate academic credentials were in short supply, and many who had those credentials were reluctant to take positions where, as Yale's John Blassingame put it, they might be forced to "kowtow to the black students."[92] In some cases as well, the organizers of these programs cared more about their instructors' political qualifications than their academic ones. Cornell's initial offerings, for example, included a course called Black Ideology, taught by a former SNCC field secretary with only two years of college.[93]

Because of the contested genesis of these black studies programs, faculty members on many campuses evinced considerable skepticism about their academic quality—and with some justification. The curriculum proposals that the SUNY Albany Black Students' Alliance put forward in 1969, for example, included the following:

> Mastery of ONE of the following disciplines:
> A) Basic reading knowledge of either Swahili, Yoruba, Arabic, Spanish, Portuguese, or Chinese.
> B) Sufficient mastery of either Akido, Karate, Gung Fu, Judo, Riflery, or Stick Fighting.[94]

Admittedly, such a course of study was unrepresentative of the more academically oriented black studies programs that were also being developed at the time. Even so, many of these programs did differ from the rest of the curriculum in their emphasis on community service and their interdisciplinary nature. Their lack of an organizational home in an already established department, along with the not always justified perceptions of the intellectual weakness of their offerings, did not help these embattled and often poorly funded programs gain legitimacy on their campuses.[95] Even their supporters feared that they might inadvertently ghettoize their students and, in the name of empowerment, provide them with an inferior education.[96] Nonetheless, such was the pressure from militant students and the guilt and fear of liberal faculties and administrators that even institutions where there had been no unrest rushed to offer some kind of a black studies program. By the early 1970s there may have been more than five hundred of them. Ten years later, half were gone, done in by budget cuts and low enrollments as well as by the overall political shift to the right and an inability to translate the black nationalist agenda into acceptable scholarship.[97]

The programs that remained became respectable. As one scholar put it, black studies had been transformed from "a field pursuing a radical educational and political agenda into an almost conventional area of inquiry," one that had been "forced to jettison or at least reframe [its] liberatory mission."[98] That so many programs survived, even in an attenuated form, testifies to the tenacity of their practitioners and the quality of their teaching and research. From the first, the men and women who studied the African American experience had to face considerable opposition from colleagues who questioned the intellectual validity of their work. As the philosopher Judith Thompson notes, innovative scholarship invariably challenges more conventional faculty members. Threatened by the prospect of being bypassed, older scholars often demand that the new field prove its "academic respectability."[99] That black studies was also burdened by its association with a radical political movement simply increased the difficulties it faced in gaining acceptance. Even so, many brilliant academics, both black and white, were drawn to the field. Using new sources and asking new questions, many of these people, including Eugene Genovese, produced pathbreaking work that reinvigorated whole areas of inquiry. And as this scholarship seeped into the academic mainstream, it completely transformed the way succeeding generations of Americans, both on and off the campus, thought about race.

Expanding the Curriculum: Women's Studies

Different problems plagued the equally politicized field of women's studies. Although the feminist scholars who introduced women's studies to the academy faced considerable hostility during the first decade of their discipline's existence, they had no trouble attracting students or producing innovative research. Many of the field's pioneers were already credentialed and academically employed, albeit in other areas and in the peripheral positions to which women were then relegated.[100] As a result, instead of organizing demonstrations or taking over buildings, they mounted low-cost stealth infiltrations into the curriculum by offering courses on women as an overload or as a collective enterprise. The courses were oversubscribed and the field took off at once. Within a year of its introduction, for example, the women's studies program at SUNY Buffalo had 1,400 students; by the mid-1970s, anywhere from 10 to 33 percent of the women at schools where women's studies courses were offered were taking them. Administrators, faced with declining enrollments in the liberal arts throughout the 1970s, swallowed hard and coughed up the resources for the field's expansion. As a result, from a handful of courses and a single program in 1969, women's studies grew to 270 programs and 15,000 courses at 1,500 schools in 1976 and to 350 programs five years later. By 2000, there were more than 600 programs, some even offering advanced degrees.[101]

What women's studies did have in common with African American studies, however, was its connection to a major social movement. The field grew directly out of second-wave feminism; it was, one scholar noted, "the educational arm of the women's liberation movement."[102] As such, it had a strong political agenda, one that was readily embraced by its early practitioners, former New Left activists who viewed their teaching and research as part of the broader feminist struggle against the patriarchal oppression of women. "From the beginning," historian Marilyn Boxer explained, "the goal of women's studies was not merely to study women's position in the world but to change it." There was thus a "continuing commitment . . . to advocacy—that is, to political action in the interest of women."[103] As a result, the early scholars in the field were as devoted to obtaining day care centers or access to abortions as they were to uncovering overlooked female writers or countering male-centered notions of universal human traits in the anthropological literature.[104]

At some schools, the women who organized these programs concealed their activist agenda, stressing, as the University of Arizona's Myra Dinnerstein noted,

> the merits of feminist scholarship which we believed in—rather than our political aims to change the university and inspire a feminist consciousness in our students. What administrators didn't realize, of course, was that it was almost impossible to take a women's studies class, as scholarly as it might be, without developing a feminist consciousness, or at least a new way of thinking about women's issues.[105]

At other institutions, the women were more open about their intentions. "This education will not be an academic exercise," the mission statement of the SUNY Buffalo women's studies program proclaimed, "it will be an ongoing process to change the ways in which women think and behave. It must be part of the struggle to build a new and more complete society."[106]

Such an agenda was hardly designed to appeal to the traditional male academics who prided themselves on their objectivity in the pursuit of knowledge.[107] Nor did the subject's interdisciplinary nature help, since its practitioners could enlist no preexisting department or discipline in their defense.[108] Even left-wing scholars were unsympathetic. A colleague involved in organizing the Socialist Scholars Conferences that grew out of the teach-in movement of the mid-1960s recalled that Eugene Genovese simply giggled when a proposed panel on women's issues was put on the table. Male NUC members charged that feminism was "trivial, exclusively personal, or divisive to left activism."[109] Ridicule was common, as was the assumption that women's studies was just a passing fad.[110] The strength of the opposition they encountered surprised the early feminist scholars. One recalled the "radically disillusioning" impact of the hostility that greeted a proposed women's studies program. She and her colleagues had assumed that "reasoning and evidence" would guide the university's decision-making; instead,

> we came up against levels of prejudice, anger, perhaps fear, that overrode commitments to rational process. Whatever might be the case in other areas, when it came to . . . admitting women to full intellectual and professional equality in the university, the deepest springs of irrationality came to the surface.[111]

Other feminist scholars had similar experiences. Misogyny was common. An eminent historian, noticing that his department had admitted more female graduate students in 1969 than previously, commented that he hoped it "will not affect the University of Chicago's high standards." At other schools, male administrators and colleagues rejected proposals for women's studies courses and programs out of hand, often without reading any of the documentation the women had painstakingly prepared.[112]

The prejudices that caused male academics and administrators to make it hard for women's studies courses and programs to win acceptance within the academy afflicted individual scholars as well. Tenure denials were common, as senior professors overlooked substantial publications and other forms of scholarly productivity by claiming that the field had little intellectual value.[113] "I suddenly realized with dismay," one scholar recalled of her harassment by a dean and department chair,

> that my association with *women's* studies meant, in the minds of these administrators, that I was intellectually, academically, and professionally suspect. It didn't matter that I had attended elite schools, had a distinguished academic record, had outstanding letters of reference, and that I had published with a major university press.[114]

At many institutions, structural forms of gender discrimination prevailed. Nepotism rules, in particular, made it impossible for women to teach at the same schools as their husbands, a career breaker in areas where there were few other institutions of higher learning nearby.[115]

Despite the obstacles, the field's pioneers persevered, buoyed by the support of the feminist community that had stimulated their original interest in learning and teaching about women's lives. Especially in its early days, women's studies developed as a collective enterprise. By the late 1960s, feminists in New Orleans, Seattle, Chicago, and New York City were offering courses on women in the alternative institutions sponsored by such groups as the New University Conference. Graduate students, undergraduates, part-time teachers, assistant professors, administrators, faculty wives, and community activists met in living rooms, kitchens, and unused offices to plan the early courses, gathering reading materials from the pamphlets and position papers the women's liberation movement was then producing.[116] Unlike the people who taught African American studies, these women had no preexisting body of scholarship to rely upon; they had to invent everything. As Sheila Tobias, whose 1970 collection of syllabi helped to shape the field, put it, "There was no structure, no 'story line,' not yet any agreed-upon topics in women's studies. We had to sculpt a new field for ourselves and, eventually, for our students."[117]

Like the men and women who taught black studies, the early feminist scholars faced structural as well as intellectual obstacles. Should they seek to create a separate department, with its own course of studies, degrees, and tenure lines, or should they remain an interdisciplinary program that shared its offerings and personnel with already existing departments? Each model had its advantages and disadvantages. Departments ensured independence but risked ghettoization and isolation, while programs could develop mainstream alliances but depended on other units to hire their instructors and cross-list their courses. Because the bureaucratic politics of the situation varied so much from one institution to another, no single configuration prevailed. Even after women's studies gained respectability in the mid-1980s, its structural diversity remained, revealing its multiple identities as, in the words of one of its practitioners, "*both* a discipline and an interdisciplinary field."[118]

From the start, what a group of SUNY Buffalo academics called "the essential duality of feminist scholarship"—its simultaneous roots "in the disciplinary structures of contemporary intellectual inquiry and in a social movement"—shaped the teaching and research of people in the field.[119] In every discipline, those scholars' work, Marilyn Boxer noted, "questions conventional knowledge, dissolves boundaries, and facilitates the quest to integrate one's intellectual, professional, and personal experiences."[120] It was, in other words, *relevant* scholarship, designed both to help women understand their subordinate position in society and to encourage them to change it. Much of the academic feminists' early work resulted in uncovering the masculinist biases of their own disciplines, which were, in the words of the SUNY Buffalo scholars,

> an intellectual mirror of the sexism in society; as subjects for scholarly research women were given little attention or ignored altogether and, where they were studied, they were often portrayed in a distorted or stereotyped manner. Moreover, it was discovered, this intellectual reflection of social prejudice was far from inconsequential. It provided continuing

> ideological support for conditions and policies oppressive to women: certain stereotypes and misapprehensions could even be used to justify women's marginal status in the academic world itself.[121]

From the start, feminist scholars were acutely aware that their marginal position required them to prove themselves intellectually. In 1975, when she founded the pioneering journal *Signs*, the literary scholar Catharine Stimpson was determined "to beat the academics at their own game." And so she and her colleagues did. Within a decade, the flood of first-rate scholarship by and about women that ensued not only brought legitimacy to the field of women's studies but, more important, forced a rethinking of almost every other field as well. No longer could scholars make assumptions about the objectivity of their work; even before poststructuralism made it fashionable, feminists were questioning the concept of the "natural." In fact, scholarship by and about women had become so sophisticated that, as Marilyn Boxer pointed out, "curricula that lack women's studies content can no longer meet the test of scholarly currency." [122]

Not only had feminist scholarship, in Florence Howe's words, "shifted the paradigms and changed the content of most disciplines," it had also adapted itself to a multicultural perspective before most of the rest of the academy. Initially, the women's liberation movement and its academic offshoot, though radical in many respects, came out of a white, middle-class milieu. But it soon came to include the perspectives of working-class women and women of color.[123] By the mid-1980s, nearly two-thirds of all women's studies programs offered at least one course on minority women; many programs actually required their courses to contain material on women of color.[124]

At the same time as they were struggling to bring a feminist perspective to the traditional disciplines, the founders of women's studies were also experimenting with pedagogy. In fact, outside of schools of education, probably no other group of academics paid as much attention to teaching. Viewing the traditional college classroom as a mechanism for reproducing social inequality, the early feminist scholars not only questioned the nature of professorial authority, but also strove to create a community that would empower themselves and their students.[125] They arranged the chairs in circles, encouraged student-led discussions, and even carried out joint political actions. Some militant teachers even barred men from their classes and offered courses in auto mechanics.[126] Of course, not every feminist scholar was comfortable with such drastic measures. After all, as one who retained a more traditional approach explained, simply "seeing women able to assume authority would help students break out of gender hierarchies."[127] It was also common, at least in the early days of women's studies, for both traditionalists and innovators to ground some of their teaching in the personal experience of their students. As the field developed, however, and more useable scholarship came into being, this form of what came to be known as "personalized teaching" fell into disuse. Ultimately, most women's studies professors eschewed experimental pedagogy and maintained traditional academic standards. No longer would they, if they ever did, award grades on the basis of the strength of someone's feminist commitment, organize their students to demand day care on campus, or refuse to say something negative about another woman's work in a book review.[128] As with black studies, academic respectability had been achieved at the expense of activism.

Unionization

As the New University Conference entered its final throes, some of its members had already turned their attention to a new development on campus: the formation of faculty unions. Overshadowed during the mid-1960s by the campus drama of black power demonstrations and antiwar protests, faculty members at a few colleges and universities had begun to take some tentative steps toward collective bargaining. Encouraged by the relaxation of the ban on public employee unions in New York state, professors in the CUNY and SUNY systems began to organize with the help of Albert Shanker's American Federation of Teachers.[129] Shanker, though a gifted organizer, was no radical, and the NUC's activists were quite ambivalent about linking themselves to a labor movement that they considered racist and pro-war.[130] Still, as the Rutgers activist Wells Keddie noted, forming unions would help left-wing faculty members

> establish ourselves in a position of earned trust and respect in the eyes of those we are trying to reach, so that our analyses of the existing order can be of real help to the working class in its battles. To do this requires, as a major first step that we recognize our own true identities as educational workers.[131]

Other academics turned to unionization to restore or reinvigorate faculty governance, as well as to protect their academic freedom—not to mention their jobs and salaries. By the fall of 1971, 50,000, or about 6 percent, of the nation's 836,000 college and university teachers were in collective bargaining units at some 180 schools.[132] Less than two years later, there were unions at 304 institutions, representing about 10 percent of the nation's faculty, mainly at public colleges and universities.[133]

Many academics did not welcome this development. Half of the sixty thousand respondents in a 1973 Carnegie Foundation survey opposed collective bargaining. This was especially the case with senior professors at top-tier universities. They viewed it as divisive and in some way as a threat to their status. Unions, they seemed to feel, were for the academy's losers.[134] The AAUP was torn apart by the issue. By the early 1970s, a few of its chapters had opted for collective bargaining and had been certified by the National Labor Relations Board. The organization's leadership agonized over the issue for several years before ultimately deciding to support unionization on the grounds that it was inevitable and that the AAUP could provide a better template for a faculty union than a more traditional labor organization could. Many of the association's old-line members were not so sure; they feared unionization would bring in people from outside the academic profession, while "it would violate our principles, our policies, and our basic philosophy."[135]

As we shall see, when we examine the activities of faculty unions more closely in the following chapters, that debate continues today within the AAUP and elsewhere—as do similar controversies over the other issues that first surfaced during the 1960s and early 1970s. Those years have bequeathed a complex legacy to American higher education, opening it up to previously excluded groups and individuals as well as to new ideas about power and learning. These changes were not always well received, both within the academic community and outside of it. But as we examine how the backlash against the 1960s evolved, it is important to remember that much of it was stimulated by broader political issues. The barrage of conservative criticism that has been pummeling American higher education over the past few decades often (though not always) reflects an underlying discomfort with the major social changes that occurred during the 1960s and early 1970s, not just quibbles about the content of the curriculum or the quality of someone's research and teaching. In a sense, therefore, the university has become a surrogate for everything that its critics dislike about American society. The academy's dual role as the sole remaining haven for serious dissent as well as the main vehicle for social mobility in the United States ensures that those critics get a broader hearing than they might otherwise deserve.

Chapter 4

"A LONG-RANGE AND DIFFICULT PROJECT": THE BACKLASH AGAINST THE 1960S

Everyone on the campus was tense as eighty-some students from the Afro-American Society marched out of Cornell's Willard Straight Hall student center on Sunday afternoon, April 20, 1969. They had taken over the building at 6:00 A.M. the previous day to oppose both the disciplining of some of their members for an earlier demonstration and a cross burning in front of a black women's dormitory, as well as to emphasize their concern about what they perceived as the university's dilatoriness in establishing an African American studies program. In order to clear the building and avoid a violent confrontation between its occupiers and a group of white athletes and fraternity boys who had tried to storm it, Cornell's administrators gave in to most of the blacks' demands. But as the occupiers left the student center some of them were carrying guns. By the next day, pictures of the armed black students—bandoliers over their leather jackets, their clenched fists in a black power salute—were on front pages everywhere.

The crisis, however, was only beginning, for the local authorities had mobilized, bringing in hundreds of sheriff's deputies from the rural towns and villages of upstate New York, rednecks who, one observer noted, "were loading their shotguns with double-0 buck and saying, 'Tonight we're going to get us some niggers and them Jew commies.' "[1] Terrified by the prospect of bloodshed, Cornell's administration banned guns on campus, while trying to keep outsiders from entering the university. The next few days were a maelstrom of meetings, speeches, demonstrations, counterdemonstrations, manifestoes, and press releases. Student radicals—both black and white—talked of revolution and retaliation against "racist" professors and administrators. The faculty was in turmoil; first it decided to discipline the African American students and then, under student and administration pressure, rescinded its initial vote.

That vacillation and the administration's apparent capitulation to the students' demands horrified a group of academic traditionalists in Cornell's government and history departments.[2] A few, several of whom were already planning to leave Ithaca, resigned on the spot; others left soon after. The classicist Donald Kagan was "absolutely so miserable," he recalled, "that I just couldn't bear being there. And so I packed my family into the car and we just drove off to New York to get the hell away from it." Political scientist Allan Bloom was so distraught that he had a near breakdown, actually disappearing for a few days before resurfacing to deliver an ultimatum, refusing to return to class until all guns were removed from the campus.[3] Actually, even before the Willard Straight takeover, Kagan, Bloom, and their allies had become increasingly alienated by what they saw as the university administration's abandonment of traditional standards of academic excellence as well as President James Perkins's failure of nerve in the face of student protests. In the years that followed, many of these people—Kagan, Bloom, Walter Berns, Thomas Sowell, Alan Keyes, and Donald Downs, to name the most prominent—were to figure in the so-called culture wars that came to dominate public discussions of the academic world during the 1980s and 1990s. It is unclear to what extent, as Kagan later claimed, the Cornell crisis pushed him and his colleagues to the right, but it is certainly the case that they looked back on it—and on the 1960s as a whole—as, in Bloom's words, "an unmitigated disaster" for American higher education.[4]

Bloom and his colleagues were hardly alone in their dyspeptic attitude toward the changes that the 1960s brought to America's colleges and universities. From the start, there was strong opposition both on and off the campus to the student radicals and to the academics and administrators who tolerated and/or supported them. As I show in the rest of this chapter, that opposition was to feed a backlash against the so-called liberal academy that came to dominate the public perception of American higher education by the end of the twentieth century and beyond and was to erode the public's support for traditional academic freedom as well as for the academic profession as a whole. Naturally, none of this happened in a vacuum; the attack on the academy was part of a broader conservative campaign that sought to roll back the social, political, and cultural changes of that more liberal era. By the 1980s the entire political spectrum had shifted so noticeably to the right that the regular academic work of the nation's faculties came to be seen as radical, elitist, and somehow alien to most ordinary citizens, even as those citizens also recognized how essential a college degree had become for their own and their children's economic futures.

From the start, the general public had little sympathy for what was happening on the nation's campuses during the 1960s and early 1970s. The media fed that aversion. Even when it was not overtly hostile, it contributed to the antipathy toward the academy by focusing on the most sensational aspects of the student unrest. Violence, rioting, and Viet Cong flags were, one TV reporter explained, "what sells. You always go after the extremes." [5] Coverage of the Berkeley Free Speech Movement, for example, picked up on the Red-baiting that California's president Clark Kerr engaged in, and often emphasized that the movement was under radical control.[6] Admittedly, most of the main newspapers in the San Francisco Bay area were notoriously conservative, but even the more moderate *New York Times* evinced little sympathy for the student movement and the faculty's tolerance of its demands. Although it had originally given extensive coverage to the early teach-ins, its pages were by no means supportive. After all, as the nation's paper of record and a bastion of the Establishment, the *Times* tended to defer to the powers that be and, at least until late in the decade, it followed the Johnson administration's lead. Columnist James Reston, for example, bemoaned the one-sided nature of some teach-ins, asserting that "these nocturnal marathons have not been debates at all but anti-Administration demonstrations disguised as 'teaching' and in many cases backed by propaganda of the most vicious nature." [7] By the end of 1967, with campus unrest escalating, the *Times* was condemning "disruptive student action" and castigating faculty members for "irresponsibility" and "for forgetting the fact that to ignore the twin concepts of the sanctity of dissent and government by law, on and off campus, is a threat to academic freedom itself." [8]

The paper's treatment of the Willard Straight Hall takeover, for example, was clearly influenced by Bloom and the other faculty conservatives. Homer Bigart, who was covering the crisis in Ithaca, hung out with the Cornell administration's critics in the government and history departments and quoted them at length about school's "abject surrender" to "an atmosphere of coercion." [9] The *Times*'s editorial page echoed that perspective. In editorials entitled "Reform by Bully" and "Campus Totalitarians," the paper excoriated the "spineless response on the part of administrations and faculties to intolerable challenges by radical students" and claimed that "these outrages against academic freedom" would impose the kind of "orthodoxies of political revolutions [that] has been the mark of Fascist, Nazi and Stalinist totalitarianism." [10]

For the *Chicago Tribune*, the professoriate's sins went beyond capitulation to the students' political demands to encompass acquiescence in their immoral lifestyle. "Drug addiction among youth," the *Tribune* thundered,

> is so widespread that we are treated to the spectacle at great universities of faculty-student committees solemnly decreeing that this is no longer a matter for correction . . .
>
> At countless universities, the doors of dormitories are open to mixed company, with no supervision. . . . Dress is immodest. Pornography floods the news stands and book stores. "Free speech" movements on campuses address themselves to four-letter words. . . . We are knee-deep in hippies, marijuana, LSD, and other hallucinogens. We do not need any of these: we are self-doped to the point where our standards are lost.[11]

All the evidence we have shows that ordinary citizens were just as hostile to the campus unrest. Ninety-eight percent of the 186,000 messages that poured in to California's educational authorities in response to the Free Speech Movement, for example, opposed the student activists. In November 1968, the state's voters overwhelmingly rejected a large bond issue for the California state colleges.[12] And by the spring of 1969, the Gallup Poll was reporting that 82 percent of its respondents wanted to expel campus militants, while 84 percent supported withdrawing their federal student loans. Three years later, according to the same poll, "campus unrest" still registered as the single most important issue confronting the nation.[13]

It is thus no surprise that right-wing politicians picked up on the same themes. Though McCarthyism had subsided within the political mainstream, it hadn't completely disappeared. We have already seen how the demand for the removal of Rutgers professor Eugene Genovese figured prominently—though unsuccessfully—in the 1965 New Jersey gubernatorial race. At the same time, the U.S. Senate's Internal Security Subcommittee trotted out its old witch-hunting apparatus to report on "substantial Communist infiltration" in the teach-in movement. The subcommittee's staff zeroed in on the University of Colorado and listed the supposed subversives who coordinated its teach-in, while its vice chair, Connecticut senator Thomas Dodd, insisted that "control of the anti-Vietnam movement has clearly passed from the hands of the moderate elements who may have controlled it, at one time, into the hands of Communists and extremist elements who are openly sympathetic to the Vietcong and openly hostile to the United States." It was unclear what damage, if any, the subcommittee's error-ridden report actually inflicted on Colorado's academics; nonetheless, if nothing else, it suggested that, just as in the 1950s, colleges and universities could again become tempting targets for conservative politicians.[14]

But it was Ronald Reagan, in his 1966 campaign for governor of California, who transformed the attack on the academic community into a winning political formula. From the start, Reagan ran against Berkeley. At a major rally at San Francisco's Cow Palace in May, Reagan inveighed against "the University of California at Berkeley, where a small minority of beatniks, radicals, and filthy-speech advocates have brought such shame to a great university." Alluding to "happenings which cannot be mentioned," the movie-star-turned-politician then noted that all "this has been allowed to go on in the name of academic freedom. What in heaven's name does academic freedom have to do with rioting, with anarchy, with attempts to destroy the primary purpose of the university, which is to educate our young people?"[15] Given the strength of the backlash against the Watts riot of the previous summer, Reagan probably would have won the election without attacking the university. Nonetheless, his tirades against student unrest consistently drew applause, and he explained that he took a strong position on the issue primarily because he felt the voters demanded it.[16]

Moreover, throughout his governorship, he continued to indulge his supporters by attacking the university and the "criminal anarchists and latter-day fascists" it sheltered. While his condemnation of higher education did little to stem the unrest (and, in fact, probably intensified it), he did cut back on funding for the state's colleges and universities and was able to impose previously unheard-of tuition charges on the grounds that they would "weed out the non-serious student and promote respect for school property."[17] Faculty members drew fire as well; by December 1968, Reagan was threatening to implement "a concerted plan to get rid of those professors, who have made it apparent that they are far more interested in closing the school than they are in fulfilling their contract to teach."[18] He also bemoaned the one-sidedness of "certain departments" where, he claimed, "if a man is not far enough left, he doesn't get hired." Social scientists were particularly guilty in this respect; they were "shirking responsibility and short changing the students and subjecting them to indoctrination and not education."[19]

Nor was Reagan unique. Especially as the turmoil spread throughout the nation's campuses, other politicians recognized the political payoff involved in attacking radical students and professors. We have already seen Richard Nixon's early effort to bolster the campaign against Eugene Genovese in New Jersey. Two years later he published an article in *Reader's Digest* reprising his criticism of the academy and its supposed elitism and complaining that "our teachers, preachers, and politicians have gone too far in advocating the idea that each individual should determine what laws are good and what laws are bad, and that he then should obey the law he likes and disobey the law he dislikes."[20] The same idea was being espoused at the same time by George Wallace, albeit in earthier language. Insisting that he was merely speaking for the "workin' folk fed up with bureaucrats in Washington, pointy-headed intellectuals, *swaydo* intellectual morons tellin' 'em how to live their lives," the former Alabama governor promised to "institute action . . . including treason charges" against the likes of Genovese, "that left-winger in New Jersey who says he *longs* for—that's what he said, he *longs* for a Vietcong victory."[21]

The most formidable voice, or at least the most frequently cited one, was that of Vice President Spiro Agnew, the designated heavy in the Nixon administration. In his own and his speechwriter Pat Buchanan's overblown prose, he articulated the conservatives' case against the academy, the home of what he called the "effete corps of impudent snobs who characterize themselves as intellectuals." He also echoed Wallace's populist allegation that liberal academics (and, often, just plain liberals) were "elitists" who "would have us believe that they alone know what is good for America."[22] Like Reagan, the vice president considered the social sciences particularly culpable, since they were "subjects which can accommodate any opinion and about which the most reckless conjecture cannot be discredited."[23] Affirmative action was just as bad. Reiterating the complaints of conservative professors about how poorly prepared minority group students threatened the educational quality of their institutions, Agnew claimed to be concerned about the damage that the demands of college might inflict upon those in "the lower half of the intelligence scale . . . I do not feel that our traditional four-year institutions should lower their sights or their standards for the sole purpose of opening their doors wider."[24] Reprising another common theme, Agnew explained that if academic freedom was suffering, it was an inside job, brought about by the "sordid surrenders and conspicuous cave-ins to intimidation and force" of so many faculty members and administrators.[25] After enumerating the many travesties occurring on the nation's campuses, the vice president summed up his case against the academy by noting "that record hardly warrants a roaring vote of confidence in the academic community that presided over the disaster."[26]

As the student movement spread, politicians matched their words with action. State legislators, who, after all, had considerable control over the nation's public colleges and universities, introduced dozens of bills cracking down on students and threatening to withhold funds from institutions and their faculties. There were more than seventy such measures in California and twenty in Wisconsin, including one that called for the dismissal of professors who assisted student strikers. In February 1969, to take another example, the New York State Senate voted 38–15 to ban student aid to anyone convicted of crimes "committed on the premises of any college." A similar measure went through Congress, though it was somewhat watered down by the education lobby, which managed to ensure that it would come into play only at the request of an institution's administration. A few months later, New York's legislators reacted to the events at Cornell by passing a law banning guns on college campuses.[27]

It is, of course, an oversimplification to view the negative response to what happened on American campuses during the 1960s as if it originated entirely outside the academic community. Such was certainly not the case. Cornell was hardly the only institution whose faculty members deplored the students' behavior and criticized those colleagues and administrators who accommodated themselves to it. As early as 1964, their apprehensions about the Free Speech Movement induced a few Berkeley professors to abandon the university. "I know personally of five or six faculty members who are leaving," one of them wrote to the *New York Times*,

> not because of lack of sympathy with 'free speech' or 'political action,' but because, as one put it, who wants to teach at the University of Saigon? The net result, I fear, will be a sharp decline in public support for what was the finest state university in America; a rift within the faculty and the departure of some of its best members; and the persistence of suspicion and animosity in a world where suspicion and animosity have no place.[28]

Predictably, the neoconservative Sidney Hook, who had done so much fifteen years before to disseminate the notion that Communists were unfit to teach, lost little time in deploring the "lawlessness" of the Berkeley students. But what he found "really disgusting" was the behavior of the university's faculty. In a January 1965 article in the *New York Times Magazine*, Hook denounced "the failure of the faculty to condemn the action. Indeed, by failing to couple their call for an amnesty for the students with a sharp rebuke for their actions, the faculty seemed to condone indirectly the students' behavior."[29] The passage of time only sharpened Hook's critique of what he came to call "a turning point in the history of American higher education." Bemoaning the "sad, sad role of the faculty at the University of California," in a piece entitled "Second Thoughts on Berkeley," Hook reiterated the standard complaint that "this *approval* of student lawlessness on the part of the faculty" not only "constitutes the most shocking aspect of the role of the faculty in the Berkeley episode" and "can only serve to encourage further lawlessness," but it also "runs the risk of provoking representatives of the public . . . into actions directed against the abuses."[30]

Such a portrayal, though polemically useful and, in some respects, partially correct, nonetheless distorted the faculty's position. To begin with, the academic profession was hardly of one mind with regard to the student unrest. In summarizing the results of two foundation-sponsored surveys of faculty opinion in 1969 and 1972, Everett Carll Ladd Jr. and Seymour Martin Lipset describe a seriously divided professoriate that they characterized as "ambivalent" about the student movement's political and educational demands. What surprised them, however, was that even those faculty liberals who sympathized with the students' position on national issues often deplored those students' actions. Thus, for example, while 63 percent of Ladd and Lipset's respondents agreed with the goals of the 1968 student activists at Columbia, only 5 percent supported their takeover of the campus. Moreover, when it came to matters of university governance, faculty members from every point on the political spectrum opposed significant student participation in academic affairs.[31] Though willing to give power to the students on matters such as dress codes or dormitory regulations, they would not cede control over such key professional responsibilities as curriculum and personnel decisions. At most, they would let a few token students sit on committees.[32]

The AAUP reflected the splits within the academic profession. Though the delegates to the association's annual meeting in May 1969 managed to adopt a resolution on the Vietnam conflict that "welcomes any efforts to bring the war to an end" and were even able to pass one warning "that the present tragic season in our intellectual life must not be made the occasion for premature or punitive intervention by public officials or law enforcement officers," they could not reach a consensus on what to do about student demands for a say over educational policy.[33] By the following year, the organization was embroiled in a debate about whether, given the contentious nature of the contemporary situation, it should take *any* stand on political issues. Generational divisions surfaced as younger and more radical academics insisted that universities were already so enmeshed in the state that not to take an overt position (presumably one in opposition to current U.S. policies) was in effect to support the status quo.[34] More conservative voices, however, argued that, in the words of a long-time AAUP leader, "the intrusion of political or moral questions into academic deliberations" not only "weakens the capacity of faculties to cooperate in accomplishing their educational task" but also risks the loss of external support.[35]

A similar debate about the advisability of taking political positions was raging throughout the academic community—within disciplinary organizations and on campuses all across the country. On the whole, faculty members tended to take sides in accordance with their own political proclivities. The well-known conservative Russell Kirk believed that academics should steer clear of political controversy. "If the scholar deserts his realm of scholarly competence for the agora, he is liable to attain neither wisdom nor the public good."[36] Insisting that political advocacy would undermine the rationale for academic freedom and thus expose the academy to external attacks, Sidney Hook also argued that abandoning neutrality would split the university wide open. "How long," he wondered, "could a faculty survive in which one faction regards the other as guilty of complicity in murder, and the other faction regards the first as traitors and apologists for political genocide, and both require *the* university to choose between them."[37] His qualms were not without substance. Berkeley's history department, to take one example, voted to condemn the Nixon administration's invasion of Cambodia in 1970, but did so over what one scholar called the "hysterical" opposition of some of its most illustrious members.[38]

It was clear, however, that with regard to the turmoil on their own campuses most faculty members, whatever their personal views on the issues of the day, supported whatever tactic seemed most likely to allay the unrest—the supposedly spineless behavior that their more conservative colleagues deplored.[39] After all, as the decline in faculty productivity during the University of California's most tumultuous years revealed, the turbulence was hardly good for research and scholarship.[40] Significantly, one phenomenon that Ladd and Lipset noted—though they admitted they had little hard evidence for it—was that the moderate and liberal professors who accounted for the majority of faculty members at schools like Berkeley, Harvard, and Columbia did not maintain a consistent stance on their school's troubles but shifted their positions in accordance with the developing crises. Thus when administrators authorized a violent police action, faculty members sided with the students; when the students' demands became more radical and began to target professors, the faculty dug in its heels and supported the conservatives' calls for resistance.[41]

The Campaign Against the Liberal Campus

To what extent the disorders of the 1960s can be considered violations of academic freedom remains an open question. It is something of a surprise to find that few scholars or public intellectuals addressed the issue once the crisis passed. Certainly there were moments when militant students and their allies interfered with faculty members' teaching and research. Strikes and building takeovers, not to mention something like the burning of a Columbia historian's research notes during the occupation of his office in the spring of 1968, prevented professors from carrying out their normal academic functions.[42] But it is not necessarily the case that these actions—some of which were clearly criminal—constituted violations of academic freedom in the traditional sense of the term. They disrupted the universities, to be sure, but they were not ordinarily directed against faculty members, nor did they target the collective privileges of the professoriate. In fact, some student radicals actually believed that faculties took advantage of the turmoil to gain more power and autonomy.[43] In any event, however we assess the impact of that turmoil, it is clear that *something* changed on campus. And, as we shall see, the controversies surrounding those changes, occurring at exactly the same time as an economic crisis was transforming the structure of American higher education, ultimately eroded the faculty's professional status and independence.

For many academics, mainly conservatives, the students' demands and the faculty's capitulation to them struck at the heart of the university's mission. In particular, they were upset about the way in which the radicals' insistence on relevance undermined the faculty's core educational responsibilities by diminishing its control of the curriculum. Moreover, the attempt to pacify campus militants by opening institutions of higher learning to more minority group students and designing special programs for them would, these conservatives feared, politicize the university. Not only would such measures abandon the cherished neutrality of the academic profession, but they would also create what Donald Downs called "a new conception of the university as an instrument of social progress and social justice," thus negating its time-honored role as "simply . . . an instrument for the Socratic pursuit of truth."[44]

What was at stake here was a confrontation between two different approaches to higher education: one the traditional ivory tower conception of the academy as an institution devoted to the pursuit of truth, the other a more activist vision of the university as an institution embedded in and contributing to the society around it. Historically, of course, as the AAUP's 1915 Declaration of Principles on Academic Freedom and Academic Tenure acknowledged, American colleges and universities have combined both missions—and more.[45] Clark Kerr's much reviled depiction of the "multiversity" as a "confused" and "inconsistent" but effective institution of higher learning remains as apt today as when he proffered it in 1963.[46] But, given the controversies over the changes that took place later in that decade, defining the nature of the university turned into a highly charged partisan struggle that rages to this day.

A connected and equally contentious matter was the assertion that the academy had lowered its standards by acceding to demands for educational and social reforms. Affirmative action was the main culprit here. But even before any major changes had been implemented, there were voices on campus anticipating the plaints of Spiro Agnew that the quality of the American university was under assault. These Cassandras were not just talking about the influx of new groups of presumably less well-qualified students or the creation of new and less rigorous courses of study. The faculty, too, was losing its distinction. The expanding system of higher education had attracted a new breed of college teachers, "a kind of *Lumpenprofessoriat*" who, in the words of one critic, pandered to students and treated radical political activity as "a respectable substitute both for classroom performance and for scholarly productivity."[47] Not only did such people flock to graduate school to avoid the draft but, another critic explained, they "combine little real interest with small ability to fulfill the old-fashioned research ideals. And when they try, their best simply is not good enough to warrant publication."[48] Unionization was also seen as a threat to academic quality. As some faculty members embraced collective bargaining in the late 1960s, others warned that it would undermine standards by substituting such bureaucratic criteria as seniority for the meritocratic process of peer review.[49]

Though a few of the academy's internal critics insisted that the responsibility for the supposed decline of the university "lies partly with faculty members who abandon teaching in favor of plush research jobs," most blamed their unruly students and compliant colleagues.[50] There was more than a whiff of elitism to their disapproval, for they rarely looked beyond the Harvards and Berkeleys of their self-enclosed universe. As a result, they displayed a stunning inability to recognize that even in the 1960s the real world of academe encompassed nearly three thousand institutions and hundreds of thousands of instructors far removed from the competitive precincts of the major research universities and top liberal arts colleges. Nor did such critics acknowledge that most college students in America were far more likely to be studying accounting and elementary education than physics or philosophy. At the same time, while ignoring the nonelite schools and their nonelite students, these individuals bemoaned the passing of what they considered the university's golden age, a time when intellectually serious undergraduates eschewed politics and lounged appreciatively at the feet of their professors to soak up the truths purveyed by Plato, Shakespeare, and the other greats.[51] That these prelapsarian students were, like their instructors, privileged white males seems not to have registered as any kind of a problem. Nor did the Eurocentrism and narrowness of the curriculum bother those who automatically assumed that Charlemagne was more important than the Qianlong emperor.

Nonetheless, despite their elitist provenance, these complaints about the decline of the university had remarkable staying power. They did, it is true, change over time. The *Lumpenprofessoriat* of the sixties became the tenured radicals of the late eighties and early nineties. The lamentations about the lowering of standards were now embellished with tales about the jettisoning of Western civilization and its literary canon. Similarly, the rampaging radicals of the late sixties and early seventies had morphed into the politically correct thought police who patrolled the campus for unwary souls cracking ethnic jokes or commenting about someone's personal appearance. Highly exaggerated though it was, by the early 1990s this demonized portrayal of American universities and their faculties had become entrenched in the popular mind. The pervasiveness of such negative scenarios, however, reflects something other than the salience of their analyses. They became prevalent, at least in part, as the result of a highly self-conscious and well-financed campaign to destroy the influence of the academic left, a campaign that has had serious consequences for all of American higher education.

Such a statement does, I know, smack of a conspiratorial mind-set. But the evidence for such a campaign is too overwhelming to ignore. Let us begin by looking at the business community. Complacently prospering until the mid-1960s, it suddenly faced an economic slowdown and decline in profits as well as an increase in government regulation. Forced into a defensive position by what they saw as a hostile public climate, a few corporate leaders began to formulate a long-term strategy for regaining power: they would make America's political culture more business-friendly. Though much of this program consisted of intensive lobbying and public relations efforts by groups such as the recently established Business Roundtable, it also contained a significant educational component. As these businessmen saw it, academia—its social scientists, in particular—stood in the way of the ideological reorientation they sought. The nation's colleges and universities were, in the words of Hewlett-Packard's David Packard, "havens for radicals who want to destroy the free enterprise system" and "are to a large degree, responsible for the anti-business bias of many of our young people today." If the corporate sector was to reverse that situation and counter what it considered the academy's malign influence, it somehow would have to create an alternative and more conservative source of expertise.[52]

An influential memorandum that the future Supreme Court justice Lewis Powell sent to the chair of the U.S. Chamber of Commerce's Education Committee in August 1971 laid out the strategy for doing so. To begin with, the business community would have to "be far more aggressive than in the past" and engage "in careful long-range planning and implementation . . . over an indefinite period of years, in the scale of financing available only through joint effort, and in the political power available only through united action and national organizations." It would have to mount a sophisticated public relations campaign to insert conservative ideas into the nation's public discourse. It would also have to monitor textbooks, campus lectures, and television newscasts, as well as establish its own network of speakers and scholars. "Perhaps the most fundamental problem," Powell explained,

> is the imbalance of many faculties. Correcting this is indeed a long-range and difficult project. Yet it should be undertaken as a part of an overall program. This would mean the urging of the need for faculty balance upon university administrators and boards of trustees.[53]

Conservative business leaders, thus, had a double mission: they would have to create their own intellectual infrastructure while at the same time they would also have to destroy the credibility of the already existing academic one.

Powell was hardly alone in his diagnosis, and within a few years, the strategy that he had outlined began to produce results. Nixon's former secretary of the treasury, William Simon, was a key figure here, both in convincing the business community that it needed to underwrite an ideological offensive and in helping to develop the institutional structure to carry it out. As the head of the John M. Olin Foundation in the late 1970s, he was also in a position to use his organization, as a recent admirer put it, "not as a charitable foundation, but as a source of venture capital for the vast right-wing conspiracy."[54] With the help of the neoconservative Irving Kristol, who considered himself "a liaison to some degree between intellectuals and the business community," Simon began to direct corporate money to conservative intellectuals, student interns, alternative campus newspapers, and right-wing faculty groups.[55] Nor was Olin the only funder involved; the Lynde and Harry Bradley, Sarah Scaife, Coors, and Smith Richardson foundations also poured money into this project.

They were particularly generous to the conservative think tanks that housed right-wing intellectuals and former public servants. By the late 1980s, the Hoover Institution, Heritage Foundation, and American Enterprise Institute, to name the most prominent, were receiving millions of dollars to arrange conferences and produce policy documents for federal officials, politicians, and the media. Thus, for example, by 1991, less than twenty years after its founding, Heritage had 145 staff members, 22 fellows, 50 adjunct scholars, and a budget of $19.3 million. It produced two hundred publications a year and mounted a major marketing operation to distribute the position papers and op-eds its people had written.[56]

The conservative funders reached onto the nation's campuses as well, where they established special programs and endowed professorships to gain an academic imprimatur for the ideas they championed. The Olin Foundation set up several such centers, among them the Social Philosophy and Policy Center at Bowling Green State University, the Olin Center for Policy at the University of California, Los Angeles (UCLA), and the University of Chicago's John M. Olin Center for Inquiry into the Theory and Practice of Democracy. Individual scholars received similar largesse. Conservative political scientists Samuel Huntington and Harvey Mansfield got substantial grants, while Allan Bloom, the co-director of the Chicago center, raked in more than $3 million from Olin between 1986 and 1989.[57] Significantly, the conservative foundations and corporations spread their bounty to second- and third-tier institutions as well as to the big leagues. Among the nearly one hundred beneficiaries of Free Enterprise chairs were faculty members at schools such as Middle Tennessee State University, Washington and Jefferson College, and Troy State University as well as at the universities of Texas and Virginia.[58]

Naturally, the holders of these chairs, as well as the denizens of the right-wing think tanks and policy centers, advocated free market ideas. The Law and Economics programs established by Olin at such prestigious institutions as Chicago, Harvard, Stanford, Yale, and the University of Virginia were particularly influential in this respect; not only did they produce pathbreaking scholarship, but they ensured its dissemination by paying students to enroll in their courses and organizing training sessions for judges. At the same time, in the field of foreign relations, programs such as Georgetown's Center for Strategic and International Studies (CSIS) pushed a hard-line cold-warrior approach to international affairs. Though marketed as scholarship, not all of the material that emerged from these programs met academic standards. Some seemed to be simple cheerleading for the conservatives' economic and foreign policy agendas. In 1986, for example, Timothy Healey, Georgetown University's president, was so worried about the overly partisan nature of the CSIS's work that he convened a committee of outside experts to assess it. After receiving the panel's conclusion that the center was turning out one-sided propaganda, Healey severed his school's relationship with it.[59]

But most of the ventures established deeper roots, and it did not take long for the conservative philanthropists to develop a sizable network of institutions and endowed chairs that, in Simon's words, "provided a nesting place . . . for brilliant scholars whose research and teaching would otherwise be rejected by academic chic."[60] As a result, by the mid-1980s, these individuals and their sponsors were furnishing the media and the nation's political elites with an alternative source of expertise that looked, at least superficially, like scholarship.

They also were beginning to marginalize mainstream academic work by directly attacking the nation's colleges and universities. That attack took place on several fronts. There were, for example, the more than fifty alternative student newspapers subsidized by the Institute for Educational Affairs that Kristol and Simon had founded, While many of these publications soon folded, others remained, not only offering strident and frequently tasteless right-wing critiques of their home institutions but also serving as incubators for future conservative journalists. Perhaps the most successful alumnus of this venture was Dinesh D'Souza, the founder of the *Dartmouth Review* and author of the 1991 best-seller *Illiberal Education*, which he produced as an American Enterprise Institute fellow with the help of $120,000 from Olin. Similar outlays subsidized both the writing and the publicity for such other book-length critiques of the academic world as Roger Kimball's *Tenured Radicals* and, of course, Allan Bloom's *Closing of the American Mind*.[61]*

Another contribution of the right-wing foundations to the campaign against the academic left was the establishment of the National Association of Scholars (NAS) in 1987. Heavily supported by Olin et alia, the organization claimed to represent those faculty members who felt themselves alienated by what Herbert London, one of the group's early leaders, called the "ideological orthodoxy [that] has insinuated itself into the Academy." The NAS would, its founders agreed, stand fast against the influence of "structuralism, semiotics, deconstruction, [and] social history, to cite a few examples," by upholding "what is admirable about Western civilization" and "those principles on which our profession and our institutions depend."[62] By opposing feminism,

---

* Sometimes, it must be admitted, the right-wing foundations did support real scholarship if it fit into their ideological agenda. Thus, for example, Olin, Bradley, and Smith Richardson all contributed to the publication of John Haynes and Harvey Klehr's Yale University Press volumes of documents from the Soviet archives and, presumably, to the employment of an outside public relations firm to publicize the work.

multiculturalism, Marxism, and all the other intellectual remnants of the 1960s, the NAS sought to position itself as the main institutional champion of traditional academic scholarship. It was equally hostile to affirmative action and to the measures taken on many campuses to create a more hospitable atmosphere for minority-group students and faculty members.[63] Viewing itself as an activist, rather than merely intellectual, organization, the NAS issued position papers and indulged in lobbying, while seeking to project an image of itself as speaking for the supposedly suppressed right-wingers within the professoriate. It also mimicked its radical adversaries by forming conservative caucuses inside disciplinary organizations like the American Historical Association and the MLA.[64] Within four years, the association had 1,700 members in twenty-five affiliates. Today it boasts 5,300 members, but, claiming to fear that its adherents might suffer retaliation from the intolerant liberals who run the nation's colleges and universities, it keeps its membership secret.[65]

There are as well a number of other organizations that, while not specifically concerned with higher education, have had a significant impact on it. The Center for Individual Rights, for example, a public interest law firm that litigates against alleged governmental excesses, has been instrumental in opposing affirmative action in admissions as well as in taking up cases against speech codes and other campus measures that it claims constrict the rights of students and teachers. A more recent and more academically oriented outfit, the Foundation for Individual Rights in Education (FIRE), deals with similar issues. Though one of its main founders, Alan Kors, is also a stalwart of the NAS, FIRE's libertarian stance complicates an assessment of its impact on higher education, since some of its actions do, in fact, support free speech and academic freedom against unjust administrations, while others seem more narrowly ideological or at least blind to the more serious problems of the day. And then there's the American Council of Trustees and Alumni (ACTA), established in 1995 by Lynne Cheney and Senator Joseph Lieberman with the mission of encouraging donors, trustees, and policy makers to brush off the faculty and take a more active role in pressing for such academic "reforms" as the restoration of the traditional curriculum.

What is so striking about the conservatives' two-pronged campaign against the academy is how self-conscious it was. In a 1989 speech at the Heritage Foundation, a former Reagan official openly acknowledged that he and his colleagues were seriously engaged in "a counteroffensive on that last Leftist redoubt, the college campus."[66] As we shall see, that counteroffensive paid off handsomely in the late 1980s when Bloom and D'Souza's books and similar articles in the mainstream press touched off the so-called PC (political correctness) controversy that generated considerable popular distaste for the academy. At the same time, thanks in part to the sophisticated production and dissemination of the work of the conservative think tanks and professors, the nation's intellectual discourse shifted noticeably to the right. The ideas that the conservative philanthropists were supporting about the harm of governmental intervention in the economy, the disadvantages of direct aid to welfare recipients, and such other tenets of the academic right gained traction within the political mainstream. This is not to say that such ideas were created by the business community. "The rise of neoconservatism and the revival of market-oriented economics would have occurred in any event," Berkeley political scientist David Vogel explained.

> Rather, the role played by business and by conservative foundations was that of a catalyst: they accelerated the rate at which neoconservative and market-oriented studies were produced and gave them far more visibility and influence than they might otherwise have received.[67]

Moreover, and this is crucial, in a circular process that further amplified the impact of this campaign, conservative intellectuals were proclaiming that most of the scholarship being produced on campus was worthless, while, in the words of Alan Kors, "what's coming out of certain think tanks and certain foundations and certain institutes is very exciting and much more central to the real debates about the problems of American society."[68]

Political Correctness and the Culture Wars

The culture wars over political correctness, or PC, that began in the late 1980s brought into the mainstream the critiques of the academic community that had been simmering for years within the "counterintelligentsia" that William Simon and his allies had so self-consciously been nurturing.[69] Most of those critiques harked back to the sixties, when, according to the conservatives' indictment, radicals infiltrated the nation's colleges and universities and inflicted serious intellectual, political, and social harm. Much of the damage came from what the culture warriors considered the misguided attempt to open the university to previously excluded women and minorities, a project that not only lowered educational standards but also deformed the curriculum, substituting trendy multiculturalism and feminism for the traditional Western canon. Further injury occurred when schools catered to their new recruits by imposing politically correct restrictions on racist and sexist speech and behavior, restrictions that seriously violated the individual rights and academic freedom of students and faculty members alike. A final indictment was that some of the disciplines, especially in the humanities, had been so perverted by radicals, feminists, and deconstructionists that their practitioners no longer engaged in the scholarly pursuit of truth.

Not all these charges were off the wall. As we shall see, some of the measures that university administrations took to create a more welcoming atmosphere for women and racial minorities did infringe on people's rights. And some of the humanities scholarship of that period was perhaps unnecessarily opaque. Taken as a whole, however, the scenario that emerged during the PC controversy presented a skewed and demonized—and ultimately damaging—portrayal of American higher education.

The Reagan administration offered a nurturing environment for the development of that scenario. It also gave its proponents real clout. There was William Bennett, for example, who, first from his position as head of the National Endowment for the Humanities (NEH) between 1981 and 1985 and then as secretary of education, used his bully pulpit to articulate the standard narrative about the decline of America's institutions of higher learning. In a 1984 report, Bennett bemoaned the destructive impact of the "failure of nerve and faith on the part of many college faculties and administrators," which led them to abandon the teaching of Western civilization and allowed faculty members to treat the humanities "as if they were the handmaiden of ideology" or else as if they "have no inherent meaning because all meaning is subjective and relative to one's own perspective."[70] His successor at the NEH, Lynne Cheney, took up the same themes, focusing in particular on the academy's failure to imbue students with a sufficiently patriotic vision of the nation's history. But it was the unexpected success of Allan Bloom's indictment of higher education in 1987 that gave the conservatives' charges a mass audience.[71]

An impassioned jeremiad against the academic reforms of the 1960s, *The Closing of the American Mind* recycled most of the main arguments against the supposedly liberal academy. Much of Bloom's passion, it is clear, stems from the desperation he felt during the 1969 crisis at Cornell. While he indicts rock music and divorce for the insipid nature of his current students, his real target is the flabby liberalism of academic administrators and their failure to mount a coherent defense of their university's sacred mission. "The imperative to promote equality, stamp out racism, sexism and elitism (the peculiar crimes of our democratic society), as well as war," Bloom wrote,

> is overriding for a man who can define no other interest worthy of defending. The fact that in Germany the politics were of the Right and in the United States of the Left should not mislead us. In both places the universities gave way under the pressure of mass movements and did so in large measure because they thought those movements possessed a moral truth superior to any the university could provide.[72]

Nostalgia for the "true intellectual longing" of his undergraduates in the 1950s and early 1960s pervades the book.[73] Having been educated at a major Ivy League university during those years—when women were barred from the intellectual camaraderie Bloom romanticizes—I found his description all too familiar. It took many years, and contact with a liberatory gay and lesbian movement, to get over my fury at the homosocial exclusivity of a certain kind of precious and erudite male bonding. Bloom's racism is as blatant as his misogyny. He devotes considerable attention to what he considers the damaging effects of opening selective institutions to minority students who are intellectually inferior—and "everybody knows it."[74] Not that he cares much for anyone outside of a "small band of prestigious institutions" and that "group of rare individuals," philosophers mainly, who "engage in rational inquiry in the small number of disciplines that treat the first principles of all things."[75] It is, in short, a depressing and arrogant piece of work.

So why, given its elitist and cranky tenor, did *The Closing of the American Mind* gain so much influence? I am not alone in wondering whether most of the people who bought the book ever read it.[76] But, thanks to its embrace by the mainstream media, they knew what it said. It appealed to conservatives, of course, and since it recapitulated the main themes of the right's well-subsidized "counteroffensive," it also resonated with ordinary citizens among whom repetition had turned those themes into common knowledge. Moreover, as the campaign against political correctness continued (Bloom's bestsellerdom having attracted others into the field), few influential voices were raised in the academy's defense.[77] The issues involved in the PC debate seemed confusing, while the political climate had shifted so far to the right that *liberal* had become a dirty word. And unlike the 1960s, when Bobby Kennedy praised the New Jersey authorities for defending Eugene Genovese, no major figure outside higher education was willing to stand up for academic freedom.[78] On the contrary, by 1991 the attack on the academy had become so widely accepted that even the president endorsed it. Claiming that PC "replaces old prejudices with new ones," George H.W. Bush told the University of Michigan's graduating class that "what began as a crusade for civility has soured into a cause of conflict and even censorship."[79]

Paradoxically, the conservatives themselves claimed the mantle of victimization, complaining that their academic freedom was under attack from the tenured radicals who controlled the nation's institutions of higher learning. In his 1991 best-seller, *Illiberal Education: The Politics of Race and Sex on Campus*, Dinesh D'Souza offers a compendium of incidents in which the PC thought police subjected undergraduate syllabi and unwary professors to rigid political tests. Some of the incidents D'Souza and his allies describe, such as the supposed victimization by black students of the Harvard historian Stephen Thernstrom, are spurious, but some are not.[80] Though often exaggerated and endlessly recycled throughout the anti-PC literature, there were enough real incidents of persecution by overzealous campus administrators to give the conservative campaign credibility.

Before we look at some of those incidents, however, it helps to put them into perspective and to recognize that until the 1960s, American higher education, like most of American society, was essentially segregated. Reversing that situation and overcoming centuries of institutional racism proved more challenging than the well-meaning individuals who ran the nation's colleges and universities had anticipated. The occupation of Willard Straight Hall in 1969 and the similar takeovers and strikes at schools from Brandeis to San Francisco State indicate how difficult it was to integrate black students into the previously white institutions of higher learning. Over time, many schools did develop institutional structures and educational programs to facilitate that integration, but the process was by no means easy.[81]

From the start, however, conservatives opposed these measures. In particular, they fought attempts to expand access to selective institutions by claiming that those attempts led to divisiveness, reverse discrimination, and lowered standards. Their campaign against what they considered the academy's preferential treatment of minorities spread from the media to the courts and the voters. Though the Supreme Court, in the 1978 *Bakke* case about racial and ethnic quotas at the University of California–Davis medical school, while overturning an institution's use of explicit racial quotas, did allow race to play some role in its admissions process, the opponents of affirmative action pressed on and, with funding from Olin and the other right-wing foundations, began to whittle away at the measures taken to increase minority enrollments. In 1996, for example, California's voters supported Proposition 209, banning the use of racial categories in university admissions. In the same year, the Olin-supported Center for Individual Rights, which was suing a number of institutions, won a major victory in Texas and essentially forced the university there to drop its explicit racial preferences.[82]

Carried out in the name of fairness, merit, and individual rights, the conservatives' attack on affirmative action certainly contributed at least indirectly to legitimizing the exhibitions of more blatantly racist behavior that occurred on campuses during the late 1980s. A fraternity at the University of Wisconsin held a "slave auction," while one at George Mason University affronted both women and African Americans with its "ugly woman" contest featuring students decked out in blackface. Racist graffiti appeared in dorms and racist remarks were directed against black students at schools ranging from Stanford to Michigan. For the men and women who were subjected to them, these insults hurt. Described by one of the main proponents of academic speech codes as "a slap in the face," a racial epithet

> functions as a preemptive strike. The racial invective is experienced as a blow, not a proffered idea, and once the blow is struck, it is unlikely dialogue will follow. Racial insults are undeserving of first amendment protection because the perpetrator's intention is not to discover truth or initiate a dialogue but to injure the victim.[83]

At the same time, previously ignored instances of date rape and sexual harassment also emerged from under the rug. Such racist and sexist (as well as homophobic) language and behavior was clearly painful and demeaning to many of the women, gay, lesbian, and minority students and faculty members on campus and did, as many commentators noted, create an atmosphere that made it hard for them to study or teach. Thus, whatever one thinks of the way in which an institution handled such incidents, there is no question but that they were unacceptable.[84]

Unfortunately, however, the sensitivity training, speech codes, and other measures that many colleges and universities adopted to deal with such expressions of bigotry failed on several counts. To begin with, they violated people's First Amendment rights and were thus thrown out by the courts, especially after a 1992 Supreme Court decision ruled that all restrictions on freedom of expression had to be "content neutral" and could not just ban offensive or racist speech.[85] In addition, the imposition of sanctions on that speech enabled the offenders to pass themselves off as victims.

The situation is muddled, however, because we still need to acknowledge that, even though it may be protected by the Constitution, racist and sexist language should not be tolerated or treated as a "mere difference of individually held opinion," to use Patricia Williams's words. Uncomfortable as it may be for everyone, Williams's advocacy of openly confronting—though not punishing—the exponents of racism and sexism seems the best policy. This is certainly the case within the classroom, where a certain level of discomfort is to be expected. If we ignore the bigotry, Williams warns us, if

> my white or male colleagues pursue the same path (student insult, embarrassed pause, the teacher keeps on teaching as though nothing has happened), we have collectively created that peculiar institutional silence that is known as a moral vacuum.[86]

But Williams was asking for a kind of everyday heroism that few academics, let alone administrators, were able to supply. It turned out to be much easier to adopt a bureaucratic response to racist behavior that would demonstrate to the aggrieved groups and individuals that the institution was taking action on their behalf. And by 1990, nearly two-thirds of the nation's colleges and universities had adopted policies against bigotry or harassment.[87]

Unfortunately, however, the implementation of those policies turned out to be problematic, especially with regard to the faculty. Take the case of Michael Levin, for example. A tenured philosopher at the racially diverse City College of New York, Levin had published three pieces (a letter to the *New York Times*, a book review in an Australian journal, and a letter in the American Philosophical Association's *Proceedings*) that expressed negative views about the intellectual ability of African Americans. Although no students had ever complained of unfair treatment by Levin on racial grounds, the administration—over the philosophy department's objections—decided to create alternative "shadow" sections of his introductory course in the spring of 1990 for those students who wanted to switch out of his class. The school's president then set up an ad hoc committee "to review the question of when speech both in and outside the classroom may go beyond the protection of academic freedom or become conduct unbecoming a member of the faculty, or some other form of misconduct." (There was considerable irony here, since the CUNY system had fired dozens of allegedly Communist teachers for just such "conduct unbecoming" in the 1940s and 1950s.) Though the committee recommended no action against him, Levin sued nonetheless. The administration's actions had, he claimed, violated his academic freedom as well as his First Amendment rights. Both the district and appellate courts agreed with Levin; they found that the shadow sections had a "chilling effect" and ordered CCNY to discontinue them.[88]

Levin's case was unusual in that he was being punished for his off-campus remarks. Most of the professors who came under attack for politically incorrect behavior had erred in the classroom. They had run afoul of their schools' speech codes and antiharassment policies. Disastrous in almost every way, not only did these regulations violate people's free expression, but they also allowed the NAS and other conservatives to clothe their critique of the liberal academy as a defense of academic freedom and the First Amendment—which in part it was. To begin with, the speech codes were often vague. Not only did they proscribe remarks and/or actions that the perpetrators sincerely believed were innocuous, but their imprecision invited judicial disapproval. Michigan's regulations were the first to be thrown out. Its prohibitions on "any behavior, verbal or physical, that stigmatizes or victimizes an individual on the basis of race, ethnicity, religion, sex, sexual orientation, creed, national origin, ancestry, age, marital status, handicap, or Vietnam-era veteran status" were, Judge Avern Cohn declared in 1989, "constitutionally overbroad." They did not even exempt the classroom and were, in fact, used to charge a graduate student with sexual harassment for questioning the biological nature of homosexuality.[89] Nor did the more narrowly designed code drawn up by the University of Wisconsin survive in the courts. Its prohibition of "racist or discriminatory comments, epithets or other expressive behavior directed at an individual" when such behavior "demean[s] the race, sex, religion, color, creed, disability, sexual orientation, national origin, ancestry or age of the individual or individuals" or "creates an intimidating, hostile, or demeaning environment for education" was, a district court judge explained, "unduly vague." Moreover, he continued, "by establishing content-based restrictions on speech, the rule limits *the diversity of ideas* among students and thereby prevents the 'robust exchange of ideas' which intellectually diverse campuses provide."[90]

First Amendment issues aside, when universities created lists of the language or actions that could be considered offensive and thus vulnerable to sanctions they exposed themselves to ridicule. In their 1998 book decrying the academic speech codes, Alan Kors and Harvey Silverglate supply a stunning compendium of inanities. Students at the University of Maryland had to avoid "idle chatter of a sexual nature" or "comments about a person's clothing, body, and/or sexual activities," while those at the University of Connecticut were warned against "inappropriately directed laughter." The University of West Virginia told its students, "DO NOT tolerate 'jokes' which are potentially injurious to gays, lesbians, and bisexuals." And at Syracuse, "sexually suggestive staring, leering, sounds, or gestures," not to mention "offensive remarks . . . or jokes," could get someone in trouble. At Sarah Lawrence, a student was actually punished for laughing when another undergraduate called someone a "faggot."[91]

While the intent behind these efforts to avoid offense to vulnerable groups and individuals may have been laudable, in practice such regulations proved counterproductive. To begin with, they rarely brought enlightenment to the alleged offenders, who, even if they only had to undergo sensitivity training, understandably felt victimized and resentful. As Henry Louis Gates Jr. pointed out, they can "turn a garden-variety bigot into a First Amendment martyr."[92] All too often, the codes were enforced with little regard for due process. Secret proceedings, anonymous accusations, and a lack of legal counsel were only a few of the irregularities that occurred when people faced charges of improper behavior.[93] In many cases the administrators who handled these proceedings were affirmative action officials or diversity educators who were hardly impartial and seemed strangely insensitive to infringements of individual rights and free expression. Kors and Silverglate also charge that the hate speech sanctions were selectively applied, with conservative students and faculty members singled out for punishment.[94] Whether that implies a biased system of enforcement or just that right-wingers were more prone to be offensive than leftists is, of course, unclear. In any event, there is no question but that serious injustices did occur in the name of eliminating racism and, in particular, sexual harassment.

The case of Donald Silva illustrates those injustices. In particular, it shows how a ham-handed attempt to implement policies forbidding what the Supreme Court called a "hostile environment" in the workplace could backfire when applied to the classroom.[95] A tenured professor at the University of New Hampshire, Silva had been teaching technical writing for nearly thirty years when he was charged with sexual harassment early in 1992. His offense was that he had tried, in his words, "to catch the attention of my class" by using a sexual comparison to explain how to focus an essay.

> You seek a target. You zero in on your subject. You move from side to side. You close in on the subject. You bracket the subject and center on it. Focus connects experience and language. You and the subject become one.

Two days later, he offered the same class an example of a working definition by paraphrasing Little Egypt's description of her job: "Belly dancing is like jello on a plate with a vibrator under the plate."[96] Several female students immediately complained that they felt "disgusted" and "degraded" by his remarks. Within a week, the administration had set up "shadow" sections so that the offended students could switch out of Silva's classes. A month later, the school gave him a letter of reprimand stating that his "behavior is in violation of University policy prohibiting sexual harassment . . . and will not be tolerated." Silva was then formally charged and suspended without pay for the following semester. The official hearings and appeals lasted until May 1993, when a final ruling not only extended his unpaid suspension for at least a year but also required him to seek counseling at his own expense.

Silva sued, claiming that the university had violated both his First Amendment right of free speech and his Fourteenth Amendment one of due process. He won the case and was reinstated with nearly a quarter of a million dollars in back pay and legal expenses.[97] While Silva's classroom remarks may have been outrageous, the district court explained in its September 1994 decision, " 'outrageousness' in the area of political and social discourse has an inherent subjectiveness about it which would allow a jury to impose liability on the basis of the jurors' tastes or views, or perhaps on the basis of their dislike of a particular expression." Furthermore, the court concluded, the University of New Hampshire's sexual harassment policy "employs an impermissibly subjective standard that fails to take into account the nation's interest in academic freedom." Significantly, in their discussion of the university's policies, the New Hampshire jurists cited numerous articles from the mainstream press about the then-ongoing PC controversy.[98]

The University of New Hampshire was not the only school that reached into the classroom to enforce its policy against sexual harassment. In 1992, San Bernardino Valley College launched similar charges against a remedial English instructor on the grounds that his assignment of papers with sexual themes had created "a hostile learning environment." Warned that further violations might lead to dismissal, the instructor was ordered to attend a seminar on sexual harassment and to send copies of his syllabi with an explanation of his teaching policy to his department chair. Like Silva, he sued and won—again on the grounds that the school's sexual harassment policy was unconstitutionally vague.[99] There were incidents as well at, among other schools, the University of Nebraska, Mesabi Community College, Chicago Theological Seminary, and Dallas Baptist University. Not all such cases reached the courts or even the AAUP. Sometimes the threat of litigation was enough to force the institution to give in, especially when it became clear that the plaintiffs would probably win. At other times (and we may never know how widespread this was) the individual involved reached a private arrangement with the institution.[100]

The speech codes presented a dilemma for the AAUP. Unlike the NAS and its allies, it welcomed the academy's commitment to diversifying the campus; at the same time, however, it could not accept any content-based limitations on free expression. Accordingly, it often defended teachers accused of offensive speech and submitted amicus briefs in their cases, including that of Michael Levin.[101] In its 1994 statement "On Freedom of Expression and Campus Speech Codes," it acknowledged how damaging "hostility or intolerance to persons who differ from the majority (especially if seemingly condoned by the institution)" can be and how "verbal assaults and use of hateful language" can hurt "new members of the community" and "create an atmosphere inimical to learning." Even so, the AAUP's official pronouncement continued,

> rules that ban or punish speech based upon its content cannot be justified. An institution of higher learning fails to fulfill its mission if it asserts the power to proscribe ideas—and racial or ethnic slurs, sexist epithets, or homophobic insults almost always express ideas, however repugnant. Indeed, by proscribing any ideas, a university sets an example that profoundly disserves its academic mission.

The statement also urged administrators and faculty members to condemn hate speech as strongly as possible—without, of course, banning it—and to adopt measures that would punish physical intimidation, the defacing of property, and other forms of unacceptable behavior.[102] But, adopted as the PC controversy was winding down, the AAUP's thoughtful formulation had little impact on the public's increasingly negative perception of the academic world.

The Canon Wars

An equally deleterious image of academe emerged from the campaign against the post-1960s curricular changes. As the conservatives saw it, student and faculty radicals had so politicized the curriculum in the name of relevance and multiculturalism that the traditional course of study within the humanities was on the verge of extinction. No longer was Western civilization and what William Bennett (paraphrasing Matthew Arnold) called "the best that has been thought and written about the human condition" the required core of an undergraduate education. Instead, students were offered, in Bennett's words, "a mere smorgasbord or an expression of appeasement politics."[103] To a certain extent, Bennett et alia were responding to a genuine problem.

Students were no longer taking courses in the humanities. (Students were, as Katha Pollitt pointed out, no longer even *reading*—which may explain why the conflict over the few books they did have to read was so intense.)[104] From 20 percent of all undergraduate degrees in 1966, the humanities had fallen to 12 percent by 1993—with huge declines in fields such as English, history, philosophy, and foreign languages. But it was the growing vocationalism of higher education, not the takeover of the curriculum by tenured radicals, that was at fault. Moreover, the flight from the traditional humanities occurred at the second- and third-tier public institutions that educated the overwhelming bulk of American undergraduates, not at the elite schools where the decline-of-the-curriculum debate churned.[105]

This is not to say that higher education's failure to give students at least some exposure to the traditional humanities is a good thing; it is not. And many who deplore the situation do so from the left as well as the right. The radical sociologist Stanley Aronowitz, for example, thinks that "virtually all postsecondary students should encounter the crucial elements of the canon of Western thought." Not only do those works contain "much of value," but they also provide the knowledge that is needed for a thoughtful critique of the society that created them. Where Aronowitz disagrees with the conservatives is in his insistence that such an education be given to *all* undergraduates—the single mothers, working-class adults, and the ethnic and racial minority group members who attend community colleges and third-tier public institutions—not just, as someone like Allan Bloom would have it, to the inhabitants of the Ivy League and other selective colleges and universities.[106] For mainstream liberals, like the historian Arthur Schlesinger Jr., the traditional curriculum provided the intellectual glue for a shared "national identity that absorbs and transcends the diverse ethnicities that come to our shore" and through which "a highly differentiated society holds itself together."[107]

Actually, for all the sound and fury of the older canon's defenders, there was little evidence that the professors who opened their syllabi to previously ignored writers had dropped Plato or Shakespeare from their reading lists. They recognized the liberatory elements of the Western tradition; they just wanted to view it from a critical rather than a celebratory perspective. Thus, according to that bête noire of many culture warriors, Edward Said,

> it is probably correct to say that it does not finally matter *who* wrote what, but rather *how* a work is written and *how* it is read. The idea that because Plato and Aristotle are male and the products of a slave society they should be disqualified from receiving contemporary attention is as limited an

> idea as suggesting that *only* their work, because it was addressed to and about elites, should be read today.[108]

Like Said, the academics who embraced the expansion of the canon simply wanted to incorporate voices that had long been marginalized by higher education's emphasis on the Eurocentric visions of—yes—dead white men. They saw themselves as adding to the curriculum, not diminishing it. In fact, as feminist scholars noted, on those campuses where most students majored in vocational subjects, women's studies courses often offered the only exposure to the humanities or social sciences that many undergraduates received. And, of course, canon revision was hardly an innovation. After all, until the middle of the twentieth century, *Moby-Dick* had usually been treated as an adventure story for boys.[109]

Nor was there evidence to support the conservatives' oft-quoted aperçu that Alice Walker's *The Color Purple* was being taught more often than Shakespeare. A survey of reading lists at one major university revealed only one course that assigned the Walker novel, while twenty courses offered a total of a hundred Shakespeare plays.[110] In other words, the campaign against the expanded canon sometimes embroidered the facts. Take the treatment of the 1987 curricular revisions at Stanford, when the faculty renamed the core course in Western culture Culture, Ideas, and Values (CIV) and pared down the list of required books from fifteen to eight. Under this reform, students could choose from eight different CIV courses, seven of which adhered to the traditional canon. The eighth, Europe and the Americas, treated Western culture as simply one among several cultures. Because the original set of readings had long been seen as too constricting for the course's teachers, as well as too onerous for the students, the Stanford faculty embraced these changes—which were not especially earthshaking. But the culture warriors seized upon them as a betrayal of everything civilization stood for.[111] Dinesh D'Souza devoted an entire chapter to the new course and its subversive readings; William Bennett labeled it "an unfortunate capitulation to a campaign of pressure politics and intimidation"; the columnist George Will called it "political indoctrination supplanting education."[112] Such comments seriously distorted the nature of the new curriculum. That every undergraduate, no matter what CIV course he or she selected, would still have to read Shakespeare, Aristotle, Augustine, Freud, and the Bible was, it seems, irrelevant. The conservatives were bent on treating the Stanford reforms as an example of a major university and its wishy-washy faculty surrendering to their campus's radicals by jettisoning the West's cultural treasures and replacing them with inferior but politically correct texts.

A similar but more disheartening story deals with the aborted revision of the University of Texas's freshman composition course in the fall of 1990. Again, pedagogical problems spurred the changes, for the course was taught by poorly trained graduate assistants who had trouble finding paper topics that interested their students. To rectify this problem, the English Department decided to create a unified syllabus dealing with racial issues that would not only relieve the TAs of having to design their own courses but also generate assignments that freshmen actually wanted to write about. The English professors who created Writing About Difference: Race and Gender, as they called the new course, hoped that dealing with controversial topics would encourage their students to develop critical skills and learn "not to agree or disagree with an opinion, but to locate an unquestioned assumption and explore (argue) its possible ramifications."[113]

Unfortunately, many of the course's supporters, as well as its critics, mistakenly thought that it had been designed to counter racism, a misapprehension encouraged by the choice of an overtly one-sided textbook (as if white supremacists wrote for the academic market). Though the text was dropped, the course's critics, with faculty conservatives and the National Association of Scholars in the lead, attacked it as an example of "the current mania for converting every academic subject into a politicized study of race, class, and gender." The *Houston Chronicle* claimed that the course was "elitist cant masquerading as tolerance" and had been pushed by "latter-day versions of the Hitler Youth or Mao Tse-Tung's Red Guards." In the face of that kind of pressure, the Texas administration caved in and, despite the unhappiness of the English department, scuttled the new course before it was ever taught.[114] The thought police had triumphed—though not quite in the way that the conservatives had fantasized.

That the Texas controversy erupted over a syllabus dealing with racial issues was hardly a coincidence. Not only did the opponents of the new curricula worry about what was being dropped, but they were equally, if not more, upset about what was being taught. They zeroed in on two different, though sometimes overlapping, scholarly trends: one, which took hold in the literature departments of major research universities, applied the critical approach to knowledge and power that was derived from such theories as deconstruction, while the other had a more overtly political cast and emphasized what one conservative academic called "the sacred if dogmatic trinity of

Race, Class, and Gender."[115] That these approaches had become increasingly accepted within the mainstream academic community only infuriated the traditionalists, who considered this scholarship a key ingredient in the left's broader assault on American society. Of course, as many observers noted, such intellectual triumphs bore little relation to real struggles in the real world. "It sometimes seems," Henry Louis Gates Jr. remarked, "that blacks are doing better in the college curriculum than they are in the streets or even on the campuses."[116]

Ironically, many academic leftists also looked askance at the theoretical turn within the American university. The highly abstract and consciously esoteric language that characterized much of the new scholarship—especially in literary studies—struck them as a renunciation of serious political engagement. They believed that the theorists' inability to communicate their, admittedly sometimes radical, ideas to people outside their field doomed them and their ideas to marginality within the broader culture.[117] Even though many conservatives also noted how "out of touch with the mainstream of American life and society" such scholarship was, they nonetheless believed it posed a serious threat to American higher education. This was because by insisting on the social construction of reality and denying the existence of objective and universal truths, the poststructuralists and their allies were subverting the very basis of traditional learning. They wanted, in the words of the Olin Foundation's William Simon, "to place ideology over the pursuit of truth."[118] And as Lynne Cheney, then head of the National Endowment for the Humanities, put it, "Higher education should be about . . . trying to tell what is true." Professors who believed that "there is no truth to tell" were indoctrinating, not educating, their students.[119]

Even worse, according to the culture warriors, the subjective nature of the new scholarship and its abandonment of rationality not only undermined the nation's traditional values and beliefs but threatened its political cohesion as well. "An openness that denies the special claim of reason," Allan Bloom explained, "bursts the mainspring keeping the mechanism of this regime in motion."[120] Cheney made the same point about "the view that reality is nothing more than different perspectives advanced by different people in order to promote their interests" when she noted:

> Some who have observed the increasing influence of this idea see it as a threat to democracy. How can a self-governing people survive if they reject even the possibility of objective standards against which competing interpretations and claims can be measured?[121]

Even more ominously, the deconstructionists' relativistic view of the world carried within it the seeds of Orwell's *1984* or worse. "There is," the critic Paul Berman noted with regard to that postmodern worldview,

> the idea that we are living under a terrible oppression based on lies about liberal humanism, and that with proper analysis the hidden vast structure of domination can be revealed. There is the temptation to flirt with irrationalist and racial theories whose normal home is on the extreme right.

Berman was not alone in citing as proof of the protofascist tendencies of such scholarship the pro-Nazi articles that the Yale literary theorist Paul de Man wrote for a Belgian newspaper during World War II.[122]

An equally if not more serious threat to the United States came, so the culture warriors claimed, from the insertion of race, class, and gender into the academic mainstream. To a large extent, the conservatives believed that feminism and multiculturalism were the vehicles through which the university was being corrupted by the irrationality and relativism of the poststructuralists as well as by the identity politics and Marxism of the academic left.[123] According to Dinesh D'Souza,

> Because the old notion of neutral standards corresponded with a white male faculty regime at American universities, minority and feminist scholars have grown increasingly attached to the *au courant* scholarship, which promises to dismantle and subvert these old authoritative structures. They view it as a mechanism to change the structure and content of what is taught in the classroom. . . . Not coincidentally, the new scholarship also offers a comprehensive critique of those institutions and procedures of liberal society—democracy, free markets, due process—that seem to hinder social progress.[124]

In other words, the combination of postmodern methods and antiracist and antisexist content transformed contemporary scholarship into a weapon aimed not only at traditional academic practices but also at the nation's most cherished values.

It was as easy for conservative critics to find examples of exaggerated Afrocentrism or near-pornographic feminist scholarship in the course catalogues of major universities and annual meeting programs of the MLA as it was to find absurdities in campus speech codes.[125] The opponents of this new learning also operated under the assumption that it not only politicized the academic community but also undermined its quality. In addition, for someone like Arthur Schlesinger Jr., the multiculturalist emphasis on ethnic identity evoked the fear that it might actually "sanction and deepen racial tensions."[126] Schlesinger, to his credit, did recognize the value of studying black and women's history. So, too, at least on the surface, did many conservatives who often mouthed the standard litany about the advantages of adding a few non-Western, female, or minority voices to the curriculum, though they otherwise saw little of value in the new scholarship. Rarely, it seems, did they try to understand (or even read) the works they were panning. There was an arrogance here and a willingness to engage in stereotyping that contradicted their stated concern with high evidentiary standards.

Thus, for example, because the traditionalists were still wedded to the notion that only great works deserved academic attention, they dismissed cultural studies, with its critical perspective on popular culture (and much else besides), as an exercise in pandering to the anti-intellectualism of contemporary undergraduates.[127] Other fields, especially those that dealt with women or previously oppressed minorities, were derided as studies in victimhood taught by unqualified "people with certain kinds of social resentments."[128] This was the case, for example, with African American studies, which the conservatives often dismissed as an intellectually vacuous discipline whose main function was to make poorly prepared black students feel good about themselves by blaming all their problems on whites. Admittedly, some African American academics with their own separatist agendas did push dubious Afrocentrist theories and denigrate white Western culture; but their influence was much more limited than one might guess from reading D'Souza and others who simply ignored how the pathbreaking work in black history, for example, enriched the rest of the discipline.[129] Women's studies received somewhat more respect, but it was still viewed by many conservatives as an impermissibly politicized field, dominated by a "combination of revolutionary rhetoric, passion, and hatred." Roger Kimball, for example, regarded radical feminism "as the single biggest challenge to the canon as traditionally conceived." Traditionalists of both sexes agreed. Not only were "professional feminists" what one female conservative called "a prime carrier of leftism," but their "standpoint unabashedly advocates the dismissal of value neutrality in the pursuit of knowledge."[130]

Politicized and without any redeeming intellectual value, the emphasis on diversity also victimized students—or so the culture warriors believed. Thus, for example, the insertion of race, class, and gender into the curriculum led, they claimed, to the quashing and isolation of white male students who refused to admit that American society invariably oppresses women and minorities. Though such instances of classroom repression were rarely documented, stories about them circulated widely and were later to give rise to lists of supposedly dogmatic radicals compiled by David Horowitz and his allies.[131] Worse yet, as one NAS stalwart noted, standards had degenerated so seriously under pressure from the academic left that professors routinely indulged in "such flagrant abuses of academic freedom as irrelevant political harangues, known falsehoods presented as fact, and biased grading," while their "students graduate 'knowing' little more than that Western civilization is racist, sexist, and 'homophobic.' "[132]

Such travesties were, the conservatives claimed, particularly prevalent in the field of history. The dirty word here was *revisionism*. Actually, revisionism is what historians do; each generation looks at different issues, finds different sources, or offers a different interpretation than those of its elders. No doubt the crises of the 1960s sped up the process as historians responded to the Vietnam War, the civil rights and women's movements, and the neo-Marxist scholarship that was emerging in Great Britain and the European continent. As a result, by the 1970s work that had been marginalized only a few years before became mainstream as, in Jonathan Wiener's words, "established historians observed—and experienced—the social and political upheavals that swept American society and politics."[133] Social history, African American history, women's history, cultural history—new fields and new approaches overshadowed such traditional areas as political, intellectual, and diplomatic history.

The culture warriors, however, complained that this new historical scholarship had been "written from the counter-cultural perspective by oppression-minded people who trashed the dean's office in the 1960s (or wish they had)."[134] When, for example, an NEH-sponsored group of historians and high school teachers developed a set of national standards for the teaching of history in 1994, its report encountered the wrath of Lynne Cheney, talk radio host Rush Limbaugh, and others. By departing from the traditional view of the American past and attempting to provide a more inclusive portrayal of that past, the group was, Cheney explained, "pursuing the revisionist agenda."[135] Its choice of subject matter, though informed by the latest scholarship, was unacceptably infected with political correctness. "What is a more important part of our Nation's history for our children to study," one critic asked,

> George Washington or Bart Simpson? Is it more important that they learn about Roseanne Arnold or how America defeated communism as

> the leader of the free world? . . . According to this document . . . the answers are not what Americans would expect. With this set of standards, our students will not be expected to know George Washington from the man in the Moon. According to this set of standards, American democracy rests on the same moral footing as the Soviet Union's totalitarian dictatorship.[136]

Portraying such ideas as unpatriotic or worse, the opponents of the standards were able to persuade Congress to repudiate them.

A similar outcry occurred in the summer of 1994 with regard to the Smithsonian Institution's plans for exhibiting the *Enola Gay* on the fiftieth anniversary of its dropping the first atomic bomb. A panel of distinguished scholars had provided a serious proposal that thoughtfully explored the main historical issues associated with Hiroshima. Unfortunately, even to raise the question of whether it had been necessary to drop the bomb was to encounter the wrath of the patriotic right. A congressional resolution called it "revisionist and offensive," and the mainstream media attacked the proposed exhibit. "What I don't understand," the TV newsman David Brinkley commented, "is why a very strong element in the academic community seems to hate its own country and never passes up a chance to be critical of it."[137] What makes Brinkley's comment so disturbing is the fact that his own son, Alan, was a highly respected historian who presumably would have conveyed a more nuanced view of the profession to his father.

That such an important voice of the establishment (and there were others) could buy into the conservatives' stereotyping of the American academy indicates as well as anything else how successful the anti-PC campaign of the culture warriors had become. By the mid-1990s, these journalists, academics, and political figures had been circulating charges against mainstream academic scholarship for more than a decade. And by the mid-1990s, most other Americans had accepted as authentic the portrayal of a system of higher education subverted by unpatriotic, politically correct, and radical faculty members. This negative view of the university was devastating. It undermined support for public higher education just at a moment when that system was undergoing structural changes that would raise questions about its affordability. At the same time, this damaging stereotype deprived the academic profession of its previously respected voice within American political discourse, thus clearing the way for further attacks on academic freedom in the aftermath of 9/11.

Chapter 5

"PATTERNS OF MISCONDUCT": WARD CHURCHILL AND ACADEMIC FREEDOM AFTER 9/11

How many of the three hundred people who gathered around the Dalton Trumbo Fountain in front of the University of Colorado's student center on March 3, 2005, to hear Ward Churchill speak understood the irony of the location?[1] A successful screenwriter and Colorado alumnus, Trumbo had been one of the so-called Hollywood Ten, who were imprisoned and blacklisted for defying the House Un-American Activities Committee in 1947. Churchill, like Trumbo an outspoken radical, had just become the target of a nationwide campaign to eject him from his position as a tenured professor of American Indian studies on the Colorado faculty. In a hasty essay, written to explain why the perpetrators of the attack on the World Trade Center would have been so hostile to the United States, he had characterized the 9/11 victims as "little Eichmanns." That unfortunate phrase, unremarked at the time, emerged with a vengeance three years later in conjunction with a planned speech he was to give at Hamilton College in upstate New York. Catapulted into notoriety by right-wing bloggers and talk-show hosts, Churchill then came under attack by Colorado politicians who forced the university to investigate and then dismiss its controversial faculty member.

Since Churchill's outrageous comment and presumably sloppy scholarship were to provide ammunition for his critics, his case is not as clear-cut a violation of free expression as Trumbo's conviction for contempt and subsequent blacklisting or as the dismissals of such squeaky wheels as Ralph Gundlach and Chandler Davis. But in the late 1940s, when Trumbo was fighting for his First Amendment rights, most contemporaries refused to support him. He was a Communist, and everybody knew the Constitution did not protect Communists. So, one wonders, will the good folk of Colorado have second thoughts once the current furor subsides? Admittedly, it may be too soon to answer that question, but a closer look at what happened to Churchill may help us understand how the contraction of civil liberties that characterized the so-called war on terrorism affected the already beleaguered academy. That Churchill was one of Colorado's squeakiest wheels and specialized in the kind of multicultural studies so reviled by conservatives should come as no surprise.

Before we examine the Churchill case in detail, we must recognize that the academic community was hardly in a strong position to ward off a renewed assault from the right in the aftermath of 9/11. Nearly thirty years of ideological warfare, as well as the structural and economic changes that we will be examining later on, had put the nation's universities on the defensive. Thus, while the crackdown on civil liberties that accompanied the war on terror was not as directly devastating to the academic community as that of the early Cold War, it may well be as damaging in other ways. True, we have not seen anything like the widespread purges of political undesirables that afflicted the nation's faculties in the late 1940s and 1950s. On the other hand, McCarthyism occurred during the golden age of academe, when American colleges and universities were expanding and the professoriate was held in high esteem. The situation today is very different, with institutions competing for resources in an often hostile political climate that cuts little slack for universities or their faculties. While many of the problems that confront the academic community today are the result of deeper structural changes within the world of higher education, the heightened concern for national security that accompanied the Bush administration's war on terror has worsened those problems and created new ones. Thus, while Ward Churchill might have lost his job in any event, his long-standing notoriety on top of the University of Colorado's financial and political vulnerability was to prove lethal.

It was the Emerald Society of Rockland County, New York, that touched off Churchill's troubles when its members protested Hamilton's appointment of Susan Rosenberg to teach a one-month course on memoir writing in the fall of 2004. Hired by the college's Kirkland Project for the Study of Gender, Society, and Culture, Rosenberg, a 1960s radical and member of the Weather Underground, had been connected to the fatal Brinks robbery of 1981. Arrested in 1984 as she was delivering an automatic weapon and 740 pounds of explosives to a storage facility in New Jersey, she was serving a fifty-eight-year sentence when she was pardoned by President Clinton in 2001, apparently because of her exemplary record in prison. Until her Hamilton appointment unleashed a storm of protest, she had been teaching quietly as an adjunct at the John Jay College of the City University of New York. Shaken by the unfavorable publicity, Rosenberg and her Hamilton sponsors backed down and cancelled the course. When the by-then controversial Kirkland Project announced its speakers for the coming semester, a political science professor noted that Churchill was on the roster. When he discovered the "little Eichmanns" essay on the Web, he forwarded it to the administration, urging them to cancel Churchill's appearance. He also alerted the editor of Hamilton's student newspaper, who published an article about Churchill's 9/11 piece on January 21, 2005. Five days later, the *Syracuse Post-Standard* ran the story, which got picked up by a conservative weblog. Such is the power of the Internet that within hours, hundreds of readers were contacting the Colorado press and politicians. Then on January 28, Bill O'Reilly jumped into the fray, claiming that Churchill should be arrested for sedition and calling on his viewers to demand that Hamilton cancel Churchill's appearance.[2]

Deluged by thousands of e-mails, Hamilton's administration initially stood firm. It had, it is true, forced the Kirkland Project's director to transform Churchill's planned address on prisons and Native American rights into a forum on his controversial article. But, as the school's president, Joan Hinde Stewart, explained on January 30, free speech was at issue; were Hamilton to call off the talk, "we would be abandoning a principle on which this College and indeed this republic are founded."[3] For a president who had only just begun her tenure at a campus already polarized by her predecessor's plagiarism, Stewart's attempt to protect free expression was commendable, though temporary. Two days later, citing her responsibility for the "safety and security of our students, faculty, staff and the community in which we live" in the face of "credible threats of violence," she cancelled the talk.[4]

Other cancellations followed, as many schools, including Churchill's own, panicked at the prospect of hosting such a notorious speaker. A few institutions—Berkeley, the University of Wisconsin–Whitewater, and the University of Hawaii–Manoa—did give the controversial scholar a platform. As was the case at Hamilton, Colorado's administrators initially cited safety concerns in their decision to cancel the lecture, but when a group of students sought an injunction against them, they reversed themselves and, on February 8, let the scheduled event take place.[5] Addressing a standing-room audience, the embattled professor lashed out at his critics and mounted an impassioned defense of his activism and scholarship.

By then, it was no longer a matter of being allowed to speak; Churchill's job was on the line. After several decades of conservative attacks on the academy, the liberal consensus that had allowed New Jersey's governor to protect Eugene Genovese in 1965 had dissipated. Colorado's Republican governor,

Bill Owens, wanted Churchill out. While claiming that "no one wants to infringe on Mr. Churchill's right to express himself," Owens insisted that "we are not compelled to accept his pro-terrorist views at state taxpayer subsidy nor under the banner of the University of Colorado. Ward Churchill besmirches the University and the excellent teaching, writing and research of its facility [*sic*]."[6] The legislature had unanimously voted for a resolution demanding that the controversial professor be fired, and two local talk-show hosts took an ad in the Boulder paper calling for his dismissal. In response, the university's Board of Regents held an emergency meeting on February 3 at which the interim chancellor, Philip DiStefano, announced that he was about to launch a preliminary investigation of Churchill's writings and activities in order to ascertain whether there were sufficient grounds for taking action against him.[7] A day later, the university's president, Elizabeth Hoffman, addressed the Boulder faculty. Already damaged by a football recruiting scandal, Hoffman invoked the McCarthy era as she cited the threat to academic freedom that Churchill's case might pose.[8] Within three days, she was gone, forced out by Owens and the regents because, as she later explained, she had refused to obey the governor's demand that she "fire Churchill tomorrow."[9]

Controversy was nothing new for Ward Churchill. A prolific public intellectual, Churchill had a thirty-seven-page CV (now fifty pages) that listed two dozen books and hundreds of articles. Many, like his "little Eichmanns" essay, are highly polemical attacks on the past and present policies of the federal government, published by small presses and obscure journals far outside the academic mainstream. A longtime activist in American Indian affairs, Churchill's confrontational style and radical politics had earned him enemies on both the right and the left, as well as on the Boulder campus. The fact that he claimed to be speaking as a Native American particularly outraged former allies within the faction-ridden American Indian Movement who questioned his authenticity, calling him a "wannabee" and trying to destroy his reputation as a Native American spokesman and scholar.[10] Whatever his background (and I am in no position to judge that issue), it is clear that Churchill's energy, intelligence, and literary skill made him one of the Indian cause's main public voices. Given his take-no-prisoners rhetoric, his message—that whites have committed a form of genocide by undermining Native American culture—was bound to alienate many both within and outside the academic world. But, as one of his supporters noted, "while at times tendentious and almost always pushing the envelope, if not tearing it to pieces," Churchill "has helped to shape the discourse of the modern Indian rights movement."[11]

His academic career was unorthodox, though not quite as aberrant as his critics suggested. He began teaching courses in Indian studies in the University of Colorado system in the 1980s while also working as an administrator in the university's American Indian Education Opportunity Program. By 1991, when he received his first regular faculty appointment as an associate professor with tenure, he had already gained a national reputation. According to Evelyn Hu-DeHart, the then head of Colorado's Center for Studies of Ethnicity and Race in America, even though Churchill could have been hired directly as a "special opportunity" candidate, the center mounted a national search before offering him a position. Since he may also have been under consideration for a full professorship at another university, Colorado's administration, which wanted to increase the "cultural diversity on campus," felt some pressure to make the appointment. His lack of a PhD was a problem, but, as the vice chancellor for academic services explained in an e-mail to the dean of arts and sciences, "it would be a shame to lose him because of a standard which may be irrelevant in this case."[12] Other scholars like Arthur Schlesinger and Colorado's own Kenneth Boulding had achieved academic success without doctorates, and Churchill was hardly the first faculty member to parlay an outside offer into a tenured position.

Over the years, Churchill continued his career as a controversial public intellectual and faculty member, winning teaching awards and compiling a publications record that, Hu-DeHart noted, "most faculty would die for." In 1994, his enemies within the American Indian Movement alerted the Colorado administration to what they claimed was the spurious nature of his identity as a Native American. But the authorities determined that the statute of limitations had expired with regard to the job application on which he had claimed that ethnicity, and they dismissed the complaint.[13] Anyhow, as Hu-DeHart explained, "He was not hired based on his genealogy. He was hired because of his expertise." Three years later, Churchill was promoted to full professor. In 2002, he became chair of the Ethnic Studies Department when Hu-DeHart left for Brown; the following year, he got a massive raise as "part of a retention offer," which the dean explained was designed "to recognize your outstanding contribution to scholarship and teaching in the area of Native American studies. Retaining you as a valued member of our faculty is a high priority for both the department and the college."[14] Though Churchill had neither muted his rhetoric nor abandoned his activism (he had, in fact, been arrested in the fall of 2004 for trying to disrupt Denver's Columbus Day parade), it was clear that the university would not have questioned his scholarship had the "little Eichmanns" furor not erupted.

Churchill's problems, though certainly exacerbated by his outrageous language and confrontational demeanor, were not solely of his making. He had become a convenient target for the already wide-ranging attack on American higher education. Had Churchill been a professor of marketing or electrical engineering, the campaign against him might have been less virulent (though, as we shall see, being a computer scientist did not protect the University of South Florida's Sami al-Arian). But he was the chair of Colorado's ethnic studies department, an academic haven for left-wing and minority group activists. Formed in 1994 by combining the departments of African-American and Chicano studies, ethnic studies, like women's studies, queer studies, and similar departments at other schools, had emerged from the struggles over diversity in the 1960s and 1970s. Its political agenda as well as its interdisciplinary and often unorthodox faculty members and academic programs put the department on the defensive as it fought for resources and respect within the university.[15] It was, as two of its supporters noted in a letter to the Colorado administration, "a collective attempt on the part of anti-racist activists of all stripes to transform an exclusionary and essentially racist, as well as sexist and homophobic, educational system."[16]

Such a mission was not guaranteed to win much support among the conservative citizens and politicians of Colorado. And, as the hate mail that poured into the ethnic studies office during the height of the frenzy over Churchill revealed, the department's opponents did not hide their views. "Fire his sorry ass!" was one of the milder messages that the department forwarded to the administration and regents in its request for assistance in coping with the more than one thousand e-mails it was receiving each day. Churchill was far from the only target; the entire department came under fire. One message, for example, urged that "the proper response to . . . Chief Ward Churchill is to shut down the ethnic studies department entirely," while another called the department "a collection of f*cking faggots and victocrats. No wonder 'ethnic' studies is a universal joke." And still another gloated, "I'm glad the Indians were wiped out."[17]

The failure of either the administration or the regents to respond to the department's appeal for help is suggestive. More genteel—and more powerful—voices than those of the e-mails' authors were ganging up on ethnic studies. Some were allied with the educational conservatives who had been struggling for years against what they saw as a drive by the likes of Ward Churchill and his academic allies to dismantle traditional standards. Governor Owens, for example, was a key combatant in those culture wars, as was regent Tom Lucero, who had helped Owens sponsor a retreat for his fellow regents put on by the American Council of Trustees and Alumni, the lead organization in the crusade against multiculturalism and the academic left. Hank Brown, the former Colorado senator who took over the presidency of the university after Hoffman resigned, had been an early ACTA supporter and was an entrenched member of the GOP's conservative establishment. One does not have to be a conspiracy theorist to recognize that the Churchill case gave Colorado's partisans of traditional higher education a perfect opportunity to take on the unpopular department, and they rushed to do so. At its March 24 meeting the regents decided to examine both the women's studies and ethnic studies departments, requesting them to provide syllabi, course evaluations, and information about their majors and minors.[18]

Outside of Colorado as well, Churchill's notoriety encouraged many right-wing commentators to resume the offensive against the educational legacy of the 1960s that had been such an important component of the culture wars of the late 1980s and early 1990s. "How Many Ward Churchills?" a 2006 ACTA publication asked, its authors tallying up the courses that "too often look more like lessons in political advocacy and sensitivity training than objective and balanced presentations of scholarly research."[19] Among the dozens of courses at forty-seven of the nation's top colleges and universities that ACTA cited as examples of "academe's increasingly unapologetic ideological tilt" were those in traditional humanities and social science departments as well as in interdisciplinary programs. Courses with the words *race*, *gender*, *sex*, *whiteness*, and *ethnicity* in their titles made it to ACTA's list, as did "The Post-Colonial Novel," "International Human Rights Law," "Introduction to Women's Studies in the Humanities," and "Environmental Justice Movements in the United States."[20]

ACTA was hardly unique in treating Churchill as a symptom of what was wrong with the academic profession. Picking up on themes that had surfaced during the earlier PC debates, academia's critics not only questioned the intellectual credibility of such new fields as ethnic studies but also viewed them as, in the words of the right-wing commentator Phyllis Schlafly, "university-financed 'movements' of the Left." Besides indoctrinating their students, Schlafly claimed, leftists controlled their universities "because of the lock that the radicals have on the hiring of new professors, the granting of tenure, and selections of publications by academic journals and the university press."[21] David Horowitz's online magazine, FrontPage, featured a similar critique of ethnic studies. Calling the Colorado department a "cult," FrontPage's authors explained,

> CU has evidently downplayed academics in order to present a collection of pampered, job-protected scholars platforms to express their political views . . . [I]n presenting such a one-sided perspective about the manifold opportunities America gives to peoples of all races and ethnicities . . . the college is shirking its educational responsibilities in favor of treacherous partisan indoctrination.[22]

It is significant that, both in Colorado and elsewhere, much of the rhetoric unleashed against Churchill and the academic left he supposedly represented focused on the issue of tenure. Especially at a time when, as Schlafly perspicaciously noted, there was an "exorbitant rise in tuition," the economic security tenured professors enjoyed was bound to stir envy and resentment among less privileged individuals and thus gain allies for those who had other complaints against the academic profession.[23] The issue was particularly acute in Colorado because of Churchill's unconventional background and the seemingly unorthodox manner in which he had gained his permanent appointment. From the start, both regents and legislators complained about Churchill's tenure. As regent Patricia Hayes explained, they wanted to find out "how that happened, . . . have assurances that it is not happening now . . . and see if we need to make changes to add more scrutiny."[24] After learning that all the people responsible for Churchill's appointment were no longer at CU, Hayes noted, "There is no one we could actually string up for this at this point." Instead, at its March 24 meeting, the board agreed to collaborate with the faculty in establishing an advisory group of regents, professors, and student and community representatives, chaired by a "distinguished individual from outside academia," to review the whole tenure process. There was a sense of urgency about the review, since it was widely believed that if the university did not act, the state legislature might do so instead.[25] Even so, it took two years before the panel, which was headed by a retired air force general and had hired the PricewaterhouseCoopers consulting firm, came up with some rather minor reforms. But at least it had prevented the legislature from imposing more drastic measures.[26]

At the same time, the university had begun to grapple with the issue of what to do about Churchill. Although the interim chancellor, DiStefano, had outraged many faculty members by acting unilaterally and not following the university's preexisting procedures, his announcement that he would mount a preliminary investigation managed to—as it was no doubt intended to—head off more damaging probes by outside politicians and regents.[27] While acknowledging that he found Churchill's remarks "offensive," "appalling," and "repugnant," DiStefano emphasized that it was important for the university to grant its notorious professor all the protections due process provides. Along with the deans of the law school and the arts and sciences, he was planning to comb through Churchill's speeches and writings to see whether he had so "overstepped his bounds as a faculty member" that the university could begin proceedings against him. "Two primary questions will be examined in this review," DiStefano explained. "(1) Does Professor Churchill's conduct, including his speech, provide any grounds for dismissal for cause . . . ? And (2) if so, is this conduct or speech protected by the First Amendment against University action?"[28]

It took a few weeks for DiStefano and his two-dean committee to study Churchill's record. In the report that they rendered to the regents on March 24, 2005, they explained that, after consultations with administrators, attorneys, and other academics at Colorado and elsewhere, they had concluded that Churchill's "little Eichmanns" remark, "though repugnant in many respects," was protected by the First Amendment. Years of Supreme Court decisions had made it clear that public institutions like the University of Colorado could not punish their employees for statements about matters of public concern as long as those statements did not keep the employees from fulfilling their responsibilities on the job. Since Churchill had resigned his position as chair of ethnic studies at the beginning of the controversy but had continued to teach his classes, there were no grounds for a complaint on that account.[29]

His research, however, was more problematic. Although DiStefano admitted that the university had begun to question Churchill's scholarship as a result of the storm over the "little Eichmanns" article, because "adherence to minimum standards of professional integrity is a contractual requirement," he believed that it was legitimate to investigate that scholarship no matter how its flaws had been discovered. Since the partisan nature of Churchill's work had been attracting opposition for years and his enemies within the American Indian Movement had earlier complained to the administration about his ethnicity, DiStefano may have been, in the words of the faculty investigating committee, "disingenuous" here. It is more likely that the university knew that there was criticism of Churchill's scholarship but chose to ignore it because of his prominence as a public intellectual.[30] Nonetheless, after obtaining information from Churchill's critics within the field of American Indian studies, DiStefano and the deans concluded that there was enough evidence of "research misconduct"—namely, "plagiarism, misuse of others' work, falsification and fabrication of authority"—to refer the case to the university's Standing Committee on Research Misconduct for a full-scale investigation. DiStefano also wanted the committee to reassess the allegations that Churchill had fraudulently claimed to be an Indian, since such a misrepresentation might also be an instance of research misconduct.[31] All told, the administration formulated nine separate charges for the faculty to investigate.

The political nature of the preliminary report was obvious. The administration was under so much pressure from Colorado's politicians and regents that, although it might have bought off Churchill with an early retirement package, it felt compelled to investigate.[32] No doubt it hoped that treating its notorious professor as an academic transgressor rather than a political one would ensure that the inquest would remain in faculty hands—even if the expected outcome would be the same. Moreover, by conducting that investigation in accordance with the university's elaborate procedures for the dismissal of a tenured professor, the Colorado administration might be able to deflect criticism from civil libertarians and the AAUP. It was, above all, a question of damage control—although, as the McCarthy-era cases of people like Ralph Gundlach and Chandler Davis reveal, whether such a process actually protected Churchill's rights or preserved academic freedom, as DiStefano claimed to believe, is by no means clear.[33]

The Standing Committee on Research Misconduct was in no hurry. A subcommittee spent four months studying the allegations against Churchill's scholarship before recommending, in early September 2005, that two be dropped, including the one about his allegedly fraudulent claim to be an Indian. The other seven, it decided, should be examined in detail by a five-person special investigating committee.[34] There were problems staffing that investigation. Although Churchill did not know this at the time, the law school professor who became its chair had expressed hostility to him in an e-mail, calling him an "unpleasant (to say the least) individual" whose defense "reminds me unhappily of the rallying around O.J. Simpson and Bill Clinton and now Michael Jackson and other charismatic male celebrity wrongdoers."[35] At the same time, conflict-of-interest regulations were so stringently applied that they disqualified people who, like the Colorado professor who had signed a general statement in support of academic freedom, could be suspected of sympathy with Churchill. Similarly, the two outside scholars in American Indian studies who had originally agreed to serve on the investigating committee resigned after they were attacked in the local press. As one explained, "the level of discourse on this issue in the Denver area has become nearly hysterical" and the atmosphere so "toxic" that the group would be unable to do its work.[36]

It took nearly a year for the panel to sort out its membership, examine the evidence, hold hearings, and write up its 124-page report, which it formally submitted on May 9, 2006. While the bulk of the report was an exhaustive analysis of the seven allegations against Churchill's scholarship, it began with the disclaimer that the committee had not considered his "little Eichmanns" essay and other political writings, since it was clear they were under the protection of the First and Fourteenth Amendments. The committee also admitted that it had qualms about the context of the inquiry and noted that it was "troubled by the origins of, and skeptical concerning the motives for, the current investigation." Nonetheless, the report continued, "serious claims of academic misconduct have been lodged and they require full investigation."[37] The committee modeled its inquiry on the rigorous examination by a group of eminent historians of the work of the Emory professor Michael Bellesiles, who had also been charged with research misconduct a few years before. As the Bellesiles investigators did, the Colorado committee decided to ignore the political issues swirling around their inquiry and focus single-mindedly on Churchill's scholarship.[38] The committee then compared its work to a situation in which a police officer gives someone a ticket for speeding instead of a warning because he was offended by the motorist's bumper sticker. Whatever the police officer's motives, the driver had violated the speed limit. So, too, with Churchill. Just as speeding was speeding, fraudulent scholarship was fraudulent scholarship—or so the committee claimed.[39]

There were two sets of allegations: four charged Churchill with falsifying evidence or misrepresenting the facts about specific events or pieces of legislation, and three charged him with plagiarism. Whether or not these transgressions should have cost him his job, it is clear that in several instances Churchill went beyond the available evidence and was less than scrupulous about documenting his sources. As even some of his defenders admit, he seems to have stretched the truth in order to make a polemical point. The committee was not, however, going to let him get away with that. As Eric Cheyfitz, a Cornell specialist in American Indian literature, noted, "these guys were really nitpicking," focusing on a few of Churchill's more problematic assertions and doggedly tracking down their references and sources. Thus, for example, the committee criticized Churchill for citing books without supplying specific page numbers—a practice common among scholars (the present author among them) who want to alert their readers to the most useful works about the subject under discussion without necessarily documenting a particular fact. In many places, the report reads like a prosecutor's brief, in which every dubious citation or omission is pounced upon as reinforcing the case against the controversial professor, while alternative interpretations get overlooked. "What's happened here," Cheyfitz explained with regard to committee's treatment of the disputed passages, "is that what should be an academic debate they turned into an indictment."[40]

More specifically, the report analyzed Churchill's allegations, in several of his publications, that two federal statutes, the General Allotment Act of 1887, or Dawes Act as it is called, and the 1990 Indian Arts and Crafts Act, reinforced what he considered to be a racist definition of Native American identity. Both of these examples had been brought to the university's attention by John LaVelle, a law professor at the University of New Mexico and longtime critic of Churchill's work, who claimed, correctly, that neither statute contained the explicitly racist wording about "blood quantum" that Churchill said they did. Churchill had cited the two laws to support his argument that they were part of a broader campaign that pressured the Indians to abandon some traditional forms of tribal membership and adopt the federal government's essentially racist "eugenic code" with its assumptions about the biological basis for Native American identity. This was an issue that had roiled the American Indian community for years—and one in which LaVelle was hardly a disinterested bystander. Significantly, the committee conceded that while LaVelle's indictment was technically correct, Churchill's interpretation of the broader implications of the government's standards for identity was historically "accurate or, at least, reasonable." Still, it noted, the Colorado professor had "deliberately embellished" that otherwise valid account.[41]

The committee also looked at two passages, again appearing in several of Churchill's works, in which he discussed what he considered to be the genocidal transmission of smallpox to the Indians, first by Captain John Smith in New England in 1614 and then in a lethal epidemic that began at Fort Clark, North Dakota, in 1837. Again, Churchill cited these episodes as part of his larger argument that the demographic mayhem that accompanied the expansion of the European whites in North America was as deserving of the label "genocide" as anything the Nazis perpetrated against the Jews. In assessing this scholarship, the committee relied on a narrowly literal reading of Churchill's statement that there was "circumstantial evidence" of the John Smith episode in which, for example, it noted that the source he cited as supporting his statement that Smith had visited the Wampanoags in Connecticut did not use the word "Wampanoag" though, in fact, that source had mentioned a tribe of the Wampanoags, the Pokanoket.[42] The most exhaustive section of the report was its forty-four pages devoted to the Fort Clark epidemic that showed there were no documentary sources to back up Churchill's statement that the U.S. Army had deliberately provided smallpox-infected blankets to the Mandans and their neighbors. Churchill had countered the charge that he had fabricated this story by claiming that he had relied on the Indians' oral traditions. The committee admitted that such an attribution was plausible but noted that since he hadn't cited those traditions in any of his publications about the epidemic, he was actually guilty of "considerable disrespect for the native oral tradition by employing it as a defense against research misconduct while failing to use or acknowledge it in his published scholarship" and, in any event, he had "created myths under the banner of academic scholarship."[43]

The committee paid less attention to the charges of plagiarism, actually dropping one of them because Churchill admitted that he had, in fact, written one of the essays he was accused of plagiarizing. While not plagiarism, the committee explained, such ghostwriting was nonetheless "research misconduct" because it constituted a "failure to comply with established standards regarding author names on publications" and because Churchill's citations of that and other work he published under someone else's name were designed to make it appear as if it came from another scholar instead of himself.[44] The other two cases involved (1) the appropriation in several publications of the text of a pamphlet about water rights written by Dam the Dams, a Canadian environmental group, and (2) the unauthorized inclusion of an article credited to the Institute of Natural Progress, but actually written by Fay G. Cohen, in a volume edited by M. Annette Jaimes, Churchill's former wife. While Churchill did give Dam the Dams credit in the first reworking of its material, he did not later on, though he did cite the pamphlet in his footnotes and claimed that the editors of *Z Magazine* dropped the group's name from one version of the piece without his consent. Moreover, it is quite likely that the group, which apparently wanted him to draw attention to the water rights issue, did not mind having their information disseminated under his name; in any event, as the piece evolved, more and more of it was obviously written by Churchill. That was not the case with the Cohen article; it was definitely plagiarized, though whether the offense had been committed by Churchill or by someone else was less than clear. Cohen had originally published the essay in a volume edited by Churchill; it was slated to reappear in the Jaimes volume as well, but for some reason Cohen decided to withdraw it. While denying that he was involved in plagiarizing the article, Churchill admitted that he had a hand in editing the Jaimes volume and he was one of the two main principals in the Institute for Natural Progress. The committee found that assertion "implausible," though one of Churchill's supporters noted that the essay, while obviously plagiarized, is much too "crude and unintelligent" to have been produced by Churchill.[45]

In its overall assessment of Churchill's scholarship, the committee insisted that it was the broader "patterns of misconduct," in particular the "pattern of failure to understand the difference between scholarship and polemic, or at least of behaving as though that difference does not matter," that convinced its members to charge him with "research misconduct."[46] It viewed Churchill's "shoddy and irresponsible work" as particularly serious because it was damaging to his associates, as well as to "the reputation of ethnic studies as a field and to the University of Colorado as an institution."[47] Contributing to the committee's negative assessment was Churchill's attitude: he was "unwilling to acknowledge any serious wrongdoing" and insisted that "he has been singled out for unfair scrutiny by those who oppose his political views."[48] The committee, however, was not unanimous in its recommendation of sanctions: two members thought he should be suspended without pay for two years, two others thought a five-year suspension appropriate, and one supported dismissal.[49]

Although it was to take more than another year before the university finally managed to dismiss Churchill, the investigating committee's report seems to have legitimized that process in the minds of most academics. It was exhaustive, it gave Churchill ample opportunity to defend himself, and, above all, it was conducted entirely by faculty members.

A month after the investigating committee's report was submitted, the full Standing Committee on Research Misconduct delivered its verdict. It agreed with the investigating committee that Churchill's violations were not trivial, but rather

> extreme examples of research misconduct, particularly in this area of study. Providing misleading or incorrect citations, bending accounts to fit one's desired interpretation, or simply making up information all strike at the foundation of scholarly historical work. Scholars rely upon the accuracy of each other's work to create a cumulative and incremental basis for extending our understanding of events. When that foundation turns out to be based on intentionally fallacious and misleading information, the usefulness of subsequent information is called into question and the work of many scholars may be compromised.[50]

Like the investigating committee, the standing committee was concerned about the "erosion of public trust" that Churchill's "deliberate" misconduct had contributed to and upset "that Professor Churchill is unable, or at least unwilling, to acknowledge legitimate critique. If he is unwilling to acknowledge the critiques, we are pessimistic that he is likely to change his behavior."[51] Again, like the investigating committee, the standing committee did not reach a consensus about sanctions, though this time, "six of the voting members of the committee recommended dismissal, two recommended suspension without pay for a five-year term, and one recommended suspension without pay for a two-year term."[52]

On June 26, 2006, the interim chancellor made the expected announcement that "after conducting the due diligence I felt was necessary," he had "issued to Professor Churchill a notice of intent to dismiss him from his faculty position at the University of Colorado, Boulder."[53] Churchill appealed and, in accordance with the university's regulations, took his case to the Faculty Senate Committee on Privilege and Tenure, which appointed yet another committee to consider the matter. That panel studied the transcript of the earlier investigation, reexamined the evidence, heard witnesses, and delivered its own seventy-seven-page report on April 11, 2007. Churchill had asked the committee to dismiss the charges against him on two procedural grounds: that the whole investigation was illegitimate because it was a "selective enforcement" precipitated by his constitutionally protected political writing about 9/11, and that the investigating committee's behavior had violated his right to due process in several instances. While rejecting Churchill's charges, the appeals panel did recognize that "but for his exercise of his First Amendment rights, Professor Churchill would not have been subjected to the Research Misconduct and Enforcement Process or have received the Notice of Intent to Dismiss presently at issue."[54] Even so, it could not find enough evidence to prove that the university's motivations were "inappropriate."[55] It also noted several irregularities in the investigation such as the committee's inability to provide Churchill with a clear explanation of the standards it was applying to his work and its failure to alert him to the committee chair's hostile e-mail.[56] Ultimately, however, the tenure committee decided that the evidence for the lack of due process was simply too "ambiguous" for it to comply with Churchill's appeal.[57]

With regard to the more substantive issues involved, the appeals committee was somewhat less ambivalent. Even so, it did not support all the findings of the original investigators. It did not, for example, consider Churchill's lack of precision with regard to the 1887 General Allotment Act to be something that "falls below minimum standards of professional integrity. Indeed," it added, "academic debate seems a more appropriate method for deciding the question than disciplinary proceedings."[58] The panel also threw out the charges relating to John Smith's involvement with a seventeenth-century smallpox epidemic because of the ambiguity of the evidence that Churchill had, after all, only claimed was "circumstantial." Nonetheless, it did agree with most of the previous investigators' conclusions, finding that Churchill had indeed fabricated some evidence, plagiarized or at least been "involved" with plagiarizing two papers, and misused sources, especially when he sought to pass off "as an independent authority a paper really written by himself."[59]

As their predecessors had been, the members of the appeals committee split over the issue of sanctions and in their conclusions listed the arguments both pro and con dismissing someone who, they all agreed, had "demonstrated conduct which falls below minimum standards of professional integrity." Convinced that academic freedom and the good of the university would be protected by showing that Colorado "will not tolerate unethical conduct," two panelists recommended dismissal. Three opposed it and suggested that he be reduced in rank and suspended for a year without pay. They were concerned about proportionality, believing that Churchill was guilty of "misbehavior, but not the worst possible misbehavior."[60] They also noted the conflicts within the fledgling field of American Indian studies and worried about the impact that dismissing such a prominent champion of one faction might have on that field as well as on the academic community as a whole. With that clearly ambivalent recommendation, the faculty's role in the Ward Churchill case came to an end. It would be up to the president and Board of Regents to make the final decision.

That decision was never in doubt. Hank Brown, who already had the Churchill case on his plate at the time he became the University of Colorado's president, evinced no hesitations about recommending dismissal; he even restored the two counts against Churchill that the appeals panel had deleted. "The university," he told the regents in a letter dated May 29, 2007, "cannot disregard allegations of serious research misconduct simply because the allegations were made against a professor whose comments have attracted a high degree of public attention." His concern about maintaining "the integrity of the scholarly enterprise" inclined him toward the most extreme punishment, since he believed that Churchill's "severe" and "deliberate . . . misconduct seriously impacts the university's academic reputation and the reputations of its faculty."[61] Not surprisingly, the regents concurred. By an 8–1 margin at their July 24 meeting, they decided that "the good of the university required dismissal because Professor Churchill engaged in repeated and deliberate conduct that fell below the minimum standards of professional integrity."[62]

Just as academic officials during the McCarthy era had done, both the regents and the president appropriated the language of scholarly integrity, faculty governance, and academic freedom. They emphasized that they were not punishing Churchill because of his "little Eichmanns" statement. "Like every citizen of the United States," the regents explained, "he has the right to make controversial political statements." It was his academic misconduct that was at issue. And here, both the president and the governing board stressed that their decisions were, in the regents' words, "guided by the findings of three faculty committees, made up of more than 20 tenured faculty members from CU and other universities, which unanimously determined that Professor Churchill had engaged in acts of research misconduct, including fabrication, falsification and plagiarism." The president reiterated that observation: "Three separate panels of more than 20 tenured faculty, from the University of Colorado and other universities, unanimously found" Churchill intellectually dishonest.[63] Not only did Churchill's dismissal have a faculty imprimatur but, according to the regents, it was also consonant with the academic freedom they were "committed . . . to promote and respect."[64] Hank Brown made a similar point, noting in one of the many op-eds he produced at the time his belief that "academic freedom—the ability to challenge conventional views or put forth unpopular ideas—is fundamental to any university. But it does not excuse academic fraud and intentional fabrication."[65]

Churchill's fate provoked little outrage either on the Boulder campus or anywhere else in academe. Although both the local Colorado chapter of the AAUP and the ACLU's Colorado affiliate protested the firing, few Boulder professors became involved. Churchill's abrasive personality had not endeared him to his colleagues; as one of them, who did feel that Churchill should not have been dismissed, told me, "There just isn't a lot of energy out there for us to mount the barricades for a guy that everybody hates."[66] A handful of radicals supported him, at Boulder and elsewhere, but on the whole, most faculty members who had given any thought to the matter did not see it as a serious violation of academic freedom. Once the quasi-judicial faculty committees took over and operated in accordance with the traditional procedures for dealing with professorial misconduct, it was hard to accuse Colorado of abusing Churchill's rights. And, in any event, he had violated scholarly norms.

Since there seemed to be no solution within the academy, Churchill decided to seek reinstatement through the courts. At the time of his suit in June 2006, only one of the six experts on academic law that a Denver journalist canvassed thought Churchill might succeed on First Amendment grounds. The others, all highly respected and knowledgeable legal scholars, explained that because the judiciary had recently been deferring to university administrators when academic freedom has been at stake, Churchill would probably lose the case.[67] Ordinary citizens, however, took a different position. On April 2, 2009, a Denver jury unanimously decided that Churchill's firing had been an illegitimate violation of his First Amendment rights, since it had been precipitated by his "little Eichmanns" statement. Although five of the six jurors also wanted to award a generous financial settlement, they ultimately compromised on $1, rationalizing their action on the grounds, as one juror later explained, that Churchill's attorney "kept saying this wasn't about money, and in the end, we took his word for it."[68] Three months later, however, Judge Larry Naves vacated that verdict, ruling that Colorado's regents were immune from litigation. He also claimed, in a statement that followed the rulings that deferred to university administrations in the *Urofsky* and *Hong* cases, that "reinstating Professor Churchill would entangle the judiciary excessively in matters that are more appropriate for academic professionals."[69]

Because an appeal is in the works, the case will probably drag on for years. One thing, however, is clear: Churchill would not have been fired had Colorado's politicians not called for his scalp. He had not faced a legitimate inquiry into his scholarly misconduct. Despite all the trappings of academic due process, politics drove the investigation. All the committees involved recognized that fact but pursued the inquiry anyhow. Because the case is currently under litigation and none of the panel members can speak about it, it is impossible to know what motivated them. It is possible—and here I can only speculate—that at least some were impelled to carry out the investigation by a combination of concern for the university and a sense of responsibility for the maintenance of professional standards. Perhaps if they had adopted a broader perspective, they might have taken a different position. In any event, one can certainly question the severity of the sanction. Churchill did not have to be fired. Plagiarists and charlatans remain on other faculties. In 1991 an eminent scholar at the University of Chicago published a graduate student's paper under his own name. His punishment: no graduate teaching for five years.[70] After historian Joseph Ellis was exposed for having lied to his classes about serving in Vietnam, Mount Holyoke College put him on unpaid leave for a year, revoked his chair, and barred him from teaching about the Vietnam War.[71]

Whatever their rationale, the actions of Colorado's faculty committees may have deleterious consequences. Only by construing academic freedom in the very narrowest of procedural terms can we conclude it was not violated. The case was tainted from the start: because of outside political pressures, a major American university's squeakiest wheel, an unpopular and outspoken professor, who may have been guilty of scholarly misconduct, was fired. Admittedly, there was no way that his colleagues could have saved Churchill's job; Hank Brown and the trustees would have fired him no matter what the faculty panels recommended. Still, had the committees refused to punish Churchill on the grounds that the investigation was illegitimate, they could have offered a stronger defense of free speech and academic freedom.*

Academic Freedom After 9/11

Ward Churchill was unquestionably the most notorious academic casualty of the crackdown on civil liberties after 9/11. But he was not alone. Other professors also lost their jobs, many because they had some kind of connection to the Middle East or were recalcitrant or contentious individuals—the squeaky wheels who figure so disproportionately in the history of academic freedom. Besides these dismissals, the war on terror also inspired renewed attempts to ban controversial speakers as well as increased efforts by politicians and other outsiders to regulate what should be taught and who should teach it. In addition, the academic community found itself facing a variety of heightened security measures that seriously interfered with its ability to recruit students and carry out research.

The first such dismissal, and, in many respects the most predictable, was that of the computer scientist Sami al-Arian at the University of South Florida (USF). Al-Arian was a Palestinian nationalist whose outspokenness and questionable associations not only got him fired but also led to a five-year incarceration, a botched federal prosecution, and a pending deportation from the United States. At no point in its dealings with al-Arian, who had been at the Tampa institution for sixteen years, did the USF administration formulate charges of academic misconduct or take him before a faculty committee. Citing supposed security concerns, it suspended him and barred him from the campus after an appearance on *The O'Reilly Factor* led to a media blitz in the fall of 2001. And it dismissed him out of hand when the federal government arrested him at the beginning of 2003.[72]

---

* How faculty committees can avoid collaborating with politically inspired investigations of errant colleagues is a particularly vexed issue—and one that requires further consideration. As someone who has recently been appointed to a special AAUP subcommittee to look into just that problem, I am currently trying to figure out exactly what kind of policy would allow faculties to protect academic freedom in situations such as the one that arose at Colorado.

The denial of tenure to the DePaul University political scientist Norman Finkelstein in June 2007 was another high-profile case. Much reviled in certain Zionist circles for his aggressive attacks on the defenders of the Israeli occupation of Palestine, Finkelstein was nonetheless a good teacher and a competent, though highly polemical, scholar. His department had voted him tenure by a 9–3 margin, as did a college-wide faculty panel in a 5–0 vote. But outsiders intervened, especially the Harvard Law School professor Alan Dershowitz, who sent large packets of material to everyone involved. Thus, when the decision reached the administration, the dean weighed in against Finkelstein. Admitting that there were no problems with his teaching or the content of his scholarship, Dean Charles Suchar claimed to "find the personal attacks in many of Dr. Finkelstein's published books to border on character assassination," which, he declared, is "inconsistent with DePaul's Vincentian values, most particularly our institutional commitment to respect the dignity of the individual and to respect the rights of others to hold and express different intellectual positions."[73]

DePaul's president, the Reverend Dennis Holtschneider, echoed the same concerns about civility when he rejected Finkelstein's tenure bid after the administration-dominated University Board on Promotion and Tenure voted 4–3 against the controversial scholar. Noting his "ad hominem attacks" on other scholars, Holtschneider explained that Finkelstein's failure to fulfill his academic "obligations to 'respect and defend the free inquiry of associates,' 'show due respect for the opinions of others,' and 'strive to be objective in . . . [his] professional judgement of colleagues'" disqualified him from the faculty.[74] Again, as in the case of Ward Churchill, the university sought to present its rejection of Finkelstein as a professional rather than political matter, and actually claimed that denying tenure to such a contentious scholar showed that "academic freedom is alive and well at DePaul."[75]

As many critics of the decision noted, not only did DePaul's administration overrule the favorable verdicts of the two faculty groups that had the most responsibility for tenure decisions, but it also couched its opposition to Finkelstein in the language of collegiality, a highly suspect category that, as the AAUP explains, sometimes conceals illegitimate personal or political agendas.[76] Of course, one can argue that Finkelstein was asking for trouble by intervening in the highly fraught debate over Israel and Palestine in such a belligerent manner. But someone's style, however unfortunate, should not be grounds for expulsion from academe if the person's teaching and scholarship hold up. Moreover, since Finkelstein's sojourn at DePaul was apparently without incident, he might well have received tenure had not the current war on terror heightened the emotional intensity of and attention devoted to anything that dealt with the Middle East.

Other post-9/11 dismissals have received less attention, mainly because most have affected contingent faculty members who, like CUNY's Susan Rosenberg, fired from John Jay College after her troubles at Hamilton College, lack the procedural protections of tenured and tenure-track faculty members. Thus, for example, the CUNY administration forced Mohammed Yousry from his position as an adjunct lecturer at York College in April 2002 after he was indicted in connection with the case of attorney Lynne Stewart, for whom he had served as a translator, and a Chicago municipal college fired a part-time lecturer in computer programming when it learned he had been convicted in Israel of supporting Hamas.[77] There have also been a few dismissals of opponents of the Iraq war, such as that of the first-year English instructor at Forsyth Technical College in North Carolina who talked about the war in a class.[78] Academics who question the destruction of the World Trade Center have also come under attack. These are the so-called 9/11 deniers, conspiracy theorists who claim that the whole business was staged by the Bush administration so that it could invoke a national emergency to implement its right-wing agenda. Although the universities of Wisconsin and New Hampshire did protect their controversial faculty members, Brigham Young University forced a physics professor into early retirement.[79]

On the whole, however, given the emotional intensity of the war on terror, as an AAUP special committee examining academic freedom in 2003 admitted, "incidents involving outspoken faculty members have been fewer than one might have expected in the aftermath of so momentous an event as September 11. Moreover, with few exceptions . . . the responses by college and university administrations to the events that have occurred have been reassuringly temperate."[80] This relative paucity of politically inspired dismissals suggests that academe may well have learned at least some lessons from the purges of the McCarthy era.

Even so, academic freedom has been violated in less striking ways. Loyalty oaths have reappeared. In 2006, for example, the Ohio legislature passed a law requiring all new state employees, including teachers at its public colleges and universities, to sign a disclaimer that they do not belong to or support any organization identified as terrorist by the U.S. State Department.[81] Meanwhile, older oaths that had been ignored for years were suddenly resuscitated. In the midst of its investigation of Ward Churchill, the University of Colorado discovered that he had not signed the required loyalty oath. Nor had many other faculty members. That oath, instituted in 1921 when the Ku Klux Klan ran the state government (and coincidentally tried to eliminate all Catholics and Jews from the faculty), was revived in 1951 at the height of the McCarthy era and used to fire a handful of nonconformists. In the late of 1960s, while similar oaths were being invalidated by the Supreme Court, Colorado managed to revise its wording enough to pass judicial scrutiny. As a result, all faculty members were required to swear or affirm "that I will uphold the constitution of the United States and the constitution of the state of Colorado, and I will faithfully perform the duties of the position upon which I am about to enter." Perhaps because it was so harmless, the oath soon fell into desuetude, and few administrators even knew of its existence. Still, it was on the books; and fearful that the state's attorney general might crack down on the Boulder authorities if they did not implement it, the administration ordered all faculty members who had not yet taken signed the oath to do so.[82] A similar oath requiring California teachers to swear to "defend the Constitution of the United States and the Constitution of the State of California against all enemies, foreign and domestic" was also enforced, leading to the dismissal and threatened dismissal of two pacifist instructors.[83]

Speaker bans have also reappeared. As we have seen, during the height of the early Cold War, universities routinely prevented Communists and other political undesirables from speaking on campus. More recently, religious fundamentalists have tried to ban what they considered offensive speakers, performers, and artworks. The events of 9/11 added political censorship to that already present threat of suppression. Not only was Ward Churchill barred from Hamilton College and elsewhere, but such controversial individuals as the filmmaker Michael Moore were also denied academic platforms. Most of the post-9/11 cancellations involved people who wrote about or came from the Middle East, especially if, like Norman Finkelstein, they criticized Israeli policies. Thus, for example, St. Thomas University in Minnesota tried to call off a speech by the South African Nobel laureate Bishop Desmond Tutu, only to reverse the ban after a massive outcry.[84] Columbia University faced a similar outcry in 2006 when it cancelled a talk by the Iranian president Mahmoud Ahmadinejad on the grounds that it would create too many "logistical" problems and would not "reflect the academic values that are the hallmark" of a Columbia event. The following year the university relented and invited Ahmadinejad to campus, only to have its president, Lee Bollinger, directly attack the Iranian leader before letting him speak.[85] As the attempt to cancel Bishop Tutu's appearance reveals, the current speaker bans are reaching highly respected individuals as well as marginal ones. Criticize America's ties to Israel and, as such mainstream scholars as Chicago's John Mearsheimer and Harvard's Steven Walt have discovered, speaking engagements get rescinded.[86] Sometimes, as in the 1950s, the censorship comes in the form of demands that controversial speakers be "balanced" by someone with an opposing view. Thus, when former president Jimmy Carter was scheduled to speak about Palestine at Brandeis in the beginning of 2007, university authorities—unsuccessfully, it must be noted—tried to force him to share the platform.[87]

In the most recent outbreak of cancellations, the content of the presentations by William Ayers, a former acquaintance of Barack Obama, was not even at issue. Once a notorious sixties radical, Ayers had long since eschewed the violence of his Weather Underground career and established himself as a respected professor of education at the University of Illinois–Chicago. During the 2008 presidential campaign, however, when the Republicans attacked Obama for his connection to Ayers, several institutions rescinded the latter's speaking engagements. Citing security concerns and, in one case, its desire not to upset the family of a Boston police officer whose 1970 murder a local radio host had incorrectly linked to Ayers, the University of Nebraska–Lincoln, Boston College, and Georgia Southern University cancelled his appearances. Not every school caved in. Millersville State University in central Pennsylvania defied the demands of several state legislators to call off Ayers's lecture, though it did make arrangements with the local emergency response unit to patrol the campus.[88] For universities to clamp down on controversial speakers indicates not only a serious lack of confidence in the ability of their students to handle conflicting ideas and a less than solid commitment to the intellectual freedom they claim to espouse but also an inability or unwillingness to resist outside pressures.

What makes the post-9/11 situation so worrisome is that the organized pressure groups that have sought to silence speakers have also tried to interfere with the core teaching and research functions of the nation's colleges and universities. They have not yet succeeded. The threat is unprecedented nonetheless; even during the height of McCarthyism, the witch hunt never reached directly into the classroom. Fortunately, however, the academic community seems to be drawing a line here. Although it has not always protected controversial faculty members from outside pressures, it has displayed more backbone when it comes to curricular matters. Even though the school faced a lawsuit and considerable pressure from state legislators, administrators at the University of North Carolina refused to drop the book about the Koran that had been assigned as summer reading for its incoming freshmen in 2002.

The university held the line again the following year when a similar campaign was launched against that summer's freshman reading, Barbara Ehrenreich's *Nickel and Dimed.*[89]

A particularly problematic campaign has been the attempt of the conservative activist David Horowitz to impose his so-called Academic Bill of Rights on the nation's institutions of higher learning. Although it seems to have fizzled out, at its peak in 2005 and 2006, about twenty state legislatures were considering the measure, and some of its language, albeit much watered down, almost made its way into the reauthorization of the federal Higher Education Act. Designed to promote "intellectual diversity," it called for universities to ensure that faculty, syllabi, and course offerings were balanced and that instructors presented all points of view on a subject, a requirement that critics feared might force evolutionary biologists to teach intelligent design or historians the virtues of slavery. In its rhetorical support for academic freedom, the Academic Bill of Rights cleverly played upon the liberal value of tolerance as well as the postmodern insistence on the relative nature of truth. It also operated on the assumption that most colleges and universities were dominated by tenured radicals who spew polemics in class and mistreat their conservative students. But what neither Horowitz nor his allies seemed, or seemed to want, to understand is that even if America's faculty members are more to the left than their fellow citizens (and they probably are), they do not indoctrinate their students. And, with only a very few exceptions, they never did. As we have seen, none of the professors fired for political reasons during the McCarthy era was ever accused of abusing the classroom. Nor were Ward Churchill and Norman Finkelstein. Even so, the myth of the doctrinaire instructors persists. It got some exposure in Pennsylvania where the legislature formed a special committee to investigate Horowitz's charges, only to discover no—that's right, no—examples of classroom bias. In fact, Horowitz actually had to admit that he lacked evidence for his tales of left-wing abuse. "It seems to me we may be overblowing this problem," one of the legislative committee members commented. "I don't have streams of people coming to me."[90]

Undaunted by his failures in Pennsylvania and elsewhere, Horowitz went on to publish a book in which he listed "the 101 most dangerous academics in America."[91] As one might expect, most of those miscreants were people in fields like ethnic and women's studies or else were scholars who studied Islam and the Middle East. Here Horowitz's efforts blend in with those of right-wing Zionists like Daniel Pipes, whose Campus Watch Web site purports to monitor the supposedly biased academics in Middle East studies, or the Boston-based David Project, which circulated a videotape in the fall of

2004 documenting the allegedly abusive behavior of members of Columbia's Department of Middle East and Asian Languages and Cultures. In the immediate aftermath of 9/11, ACTA put out (and then retracted) a similar list of professors whose hate-America rhetoric, the organization claimed, put them completely at odds with the rest of the country. There is, as both Joe McCarthy and the editors of *U.S. News & World Report* well knew, nothing that gets as much attention from the media and the public as a list. Nonetheless, I doubt that Horowitz, Pipes, and the others expected the men and women they named to lose their jobs; most, after all, are tenured and many are eminent. Rather, the function of these folks' campaigns is to delegitimize the work of mainstream scholars, especially those in Middle East studies who do not support the Israeli hard line.

They have had some success. In the beginning of 2003, for example, former senator Rick Santorum introduced legislation to cut off federal funding to universities that allowed their faculty members, students, and student organizations to openly criticize Israel. While Santorum's initiative quietly faded from view, a more serious congressional attempt to regulate Middle Eastern studies got under way. At a June hearing, a Hoover Institution scholar convinced a subcommittee of the House Education and Workforce Committee that the late Palestinian literary critic Edward Said had cast such a spell over the field that just about every center of Middle Eastern studies subscribed to "post-colonial theory" and displayed an "extremist bias against American foreign policy." Worse yet, not only were these centers engaging in the trendy theorizing that marked so much of the nation's academic discourse, but they were also discouraging their students from entering the nation's public service. Accordingly, the committee and then the full House signed on to a measure that would create an outside advisory board to supervise the federal funding of area studies centers under Title VI of the Education Act. Though H.R. 3077, as the measure was called, never got to the Senate, its unanimous adoption by the House reveals how readily the nation's political elites have accepted a right-wing Zionist scenario about Middle Eastern studies.[92]

The Federal Government and Academic Freedom

That the academy's conservative critics may have more traction within the public sector than the private one shows something about the nature of the current threat to academic freedom. Much of it comes from the federal government. During the McCarthy era, the universities handled much of the repression, firing and blacklisting alleged Communists whom the FBI and congressional investigators had identified. There are few such cases today. Instead, individual academics and, in some cases, whole fields are hampered by official constraints imposed in the name of national security. While not necessarily politically motivated or violating academic freedom in the traditional sense of term, these measures, such as the heightened secrecy and visa restrictions that were imposed in the aftermath of 9/11, nonetheless interfere with people's research. Whether intentionally or not, they have the effect of limiting what professors can study, teach, and publish. Moreover, by hyping the dangers of terrorism and implementing an unnecessarily repressive internal security program to deal with them, the Bush administration created a political atmosphere that offered support to extremists like Horowitz and Pipes.

The case of University of Buffalo professor Steven Kurtz exemplifies these problems. A conceptual artist who uses biological specimens to protest against such things as genetically modified food, Kurtz ran into trouble when his wife died of a heart attack in May 2004. The local law enforcement officials who responded to his 911 call spotted the petri dishes and laboratory equipment at the house and notified the FBI. The feds showed up in full bioterrorism regalia, impounded Kurtz's artworks, and, after discovering that the materials he was working with were harmless, indicted him for mail fraud along with Robert Ferrell, the University of Pittsburgh biologist who had supplied the bacteria the Buffalo artist was using. Since the culprits' main crime was that they planned to use microorganisms intended for research for artistic purposes, the government's actions seem arbitrary in the extreme. Ferrell, who was suffering from cancer, was so devastated physically and emotionally by the case that he took a guilty plea. Kurtz, however, faced a four-year ordeal before the trial judge finally threw out the charges against him. There may have been political reasons for the government's refusal to drop the case. The Critical Art Ensemble, to which Kurtz belongs, is a collective enterprise that explores what it calls "the intersections of art, technology, radical politics, and critical theory" by using the paraphernalia of the laboratory to produce performance pieces and installations that challenge the mystification of science and question the corporate and military control of biotechnology.[93] Were Kurtz an apolitical landscape painter, it is hard to imagine that he would have been so relentlessly prosecuted, though it is also possible that the Justice Department simply could not admit it had goofed.

Bizarre as the experiences of Steven Kurtz may be, they are, alas, not unique. As the case of the Texas Tech professor Thomas Butler reveals, the government's panicky response to 9/11 not only damaged people's lives and careers but also was counterproductive with regard to national security, not to mention destructive to scientific research. Unlike Kurtz, Butler was a Republican, not a radical. A medical researcher, he had dedicated his career to eradicating infectious killer diseases like cholera and bubonic plague. Butler got into trouble when he discovered that some vials containing plague germs were missing from his laboratory in January 2003. When he couldn't find them, he notified his superiors, who then contacted the authorities. The prospect that potential terrorists might have gotten their hands on Butler's bacteria threw the Federal Bureau of Investigation into high alert. Even though there was no way the materials could be turned into a weapon, the FBI was taking no chances. Having failed to find the source of the previous year's anthrax attacks, its credibility was at stake and it was under enormous pressure to solve the plague case. After hours of interrogation, a sleep-starved Butler caved in to a polygraph-wielding agent and confessed that he must have inadvertently destroyed the vials. "I told him destruction was not something that I remembered," Butler later explained, "but he told me it must have happened. And he convinced me, because I wanted to believe him."[94]

His confession was only the beginning of Butler's ordeal, however. In the aftermath of 9/11 the government had imposed stringent restrictions on the handling of the dangerous bacteria known as "select agents." Butler had been doing fieldwork in Africa at the time and was unaware that his usual methods of transporting plague germs were no longer legal. Plus he was already embroiled in a nasty battle with the Texas Tech administration over the funding of his grants. Perhaps as a way of warning other scientists to be more careful about working with such materials, the government decided to prosecute him. Accordingly, the Justice Department threw the book at him, indicting him on sixty-nine counts of mishandling dangerous substances and defrauding his university with a maximum sentence of 469 years in prison and $17 million in fines. Though the jury acquitted him of the charges with regard to the plague vials, it convicted him on the financial ones. Not only did he have to repay Texas Tech more than $250,000, but he served two years in prison and lost both his job and his medical license.[95] His fellow scientists were outraged. Butler's work with cholera victims in Bangladesh had led to a breakthrough that had saved literally millions of children's lives. Here was an important scientist who had done nothing wrong being punished because, as the Bush administration's top bioterrorism advisor noted, "they wanted to make an example of him," even though "it has only succeeded in making the country less safe by losing the services of a good scientist."[96]

In other ways as well, Washington's heavy-handed treatment of the nation's scientists has been astonishingly counterproductive, reminding those with long memories of the harassment inflicted on the physicist J. Robert Oppenheimer and his colleagues in the 1950s. The regulations governing the use of "select agents," for example, became so burdensome that some investigators simply stopped working with them. Even before 9/11 the government had been monitoring dangerous pathogens; the panic-inspired Patriot Act expanded that regulation to dozens of rather commonplace agents. It also increased the paperwork required for using them and barred certain types of people from working on them, including nationals from unfriendly countries like Iran, Syria, and North Korea, as well as American citizens who had been convicted of a crime, used illegal drugs, or had been dishonorably discharged from the military. Complying with these regulations and ones that were later imposed by other federal agencies threatened to become so onerous that, an MIT committee noted, "at some point, MIT may rightfully decide that on-campus research in areas governed by these regulations is no longer in its interest or in line with its principles." Nor was this speculation; scientists elsewhere have given up work in the field.[97] Moreover, the regulatory burden has spread from obviously sensitive subjects into fields like urban design, community development, and landscape architecture.[98]

The government's heightened secrecy created additional obstacles to research. One of the Bush administration's earliest responses to 9/11 was to increase the classification of documents. Reversing Clinton's policy of encouraging openness, the Bush regime drastically curtailed access to information about its activities by, for example, allowing such federal agencies as the Agriculture and Health and Human Services Departments to classify documents. So much material has been unnecessarily withheld that one federal official estimated that at least 50 percent of it "really should not be classified." Unclassified documents also became harder to obtain. In October 2001, the attorney general released a memo decreeing that Freedom of Information Act requests should be denied whenever possible. Similarly, the government sought to expand the vague category of "sensitive but unclassified" information that could also be withheld from the public. Many agencies complied at once, yanking previously available documents from public Web sites. As a result, many researchers found themselves unable to obtain basic data from the government about public health or environmental hazards on the grounds that such information could be of use to terrorists.[99] The Obama administration has pledged to roll back its predecessor's secrecy, but it is always easier to close files than to open them.

Scientists were also forced to withhold information. For years the Defense Department and other national security agencies had been trying to keep people in fields like cryptography and optical engineering from publishing the unclassified results of their research. The scientific community resisted more or less successfully, obtaining a directive from President Reagan in 1985 ordering that "the products of fundamental research remain unrestricted." The war on terror changed the rules. The heightened pressures for secrecy were particularly intense in the field of biotechnology. Facing what they felt was a genuine threat of federal censorship, many journals voluntarily collaborated with Washington's demand that they keep potentially sensitive information from their pages. In February 2003, the editors of more than twenty major publications in the life sciences issued a statement that expressed their concern about "the potential abuse of published information" and recommended the creation of special procedures for vetting "papers that raise such security concerns." Similarly, the National Academy of Sciences suggested that universities monitor research in those areas that might have applications to bioterrorism.[100] Such restrictions, whether they stem from federal regulations or self-censorship, directly contravene the openness that makes scientific communication, and thus scientific progress, possible.

The government's repressive treatment of foreign students and scholars has created additional problems for the academy. Not only have tightened security procedures made it more difficult for these people to gain entry into the United States, but once they are here, federal regulations discriminate against some of them on the basis of their country of origin. Imposing what are known as "deemed" export controls, the authorities have barred students and scientists from nearly two dozen countries from undertaking certain kinds of research, handling certain kinds of materials, or working with certain kinds of technology. While the need to prevent potential terrorists from gaining access to dangerous pathogens is obvious, these restrictions are overly broad and out-of-date, and they extend to technologies and materials that are readily available in other countries.[101] In any event, such screening can best be done on an individual basis rather than by imposing a blanket prohibition that bars even opponents of those hostile regimes from working in a sensitive laboratory or, as happened recently, that keeps the president of Johns Hopkins University from overseeing one of his own institution's labs because he is a Canadian citizen.[102]

Other types of regulations are similarly onerous. A truly remarkable Treasury Department ruling tried to prevent American journals from editing submissions from people who lived in the allegedly "terrorist" nations of Cuba, Iran, Syria, Sudan, and North Korea on the grounds that such editorial assistance would constitute trading with the enemy. And there are now provisions in place requiring grant makers to ensure that none of their funds go to anyone on a long list of alleged supporters of terrorism.[103]

The war on terror has also allowed the State Department to reintroduce the ideological exclusions that had been common during the McCarthy era. Of course, since the government refuses to explain why it barred these people, we actually don't know why it kept out a Greek economist, a Bolivian historian with a Georgetown PhD, a European Islamicist with a named chair at the University of Notre Dame, the deputy vice chancellor of the University of Johannesburg, and sixty-five Cuban academics invited to attend the annual meeting of the Latin American Studies Association in 2004. But since most were left-wingers or critics of American foreign policy, it is likely that their politics were at issue.[104] Those bans may now be easing. Although the Obama administration initially sought to maintain its predecessor's exclusions, in January 2010 it finally relented on the high-profile cases of the Islamicist Tariq Ramadan and the South African Adam Habib.

Even more damaging to the academic enterprise than the politically motivated exclusions of individual scholars has been the overall tightening of the visa process for all overseas applicants. Unexplained rejections and delays became common, and foreign scholars and students who visited their homelands between semesters risked being barred when they tried to return to the United States. Although the situation has eased somewhat over the past few years, the new visa regulations and delays kept many students out of the United States while deterring unknown numbers of others from applying. The problems are worse for students and scientists from some twenty-five largely Muslim nations. In many cases, people from these supposedly "sensitive" nations have had to undergo full security clearances before their visas are approved. Moreover, once here, foreign students and scholars have to comply with the federal government's onerous reporting requirements, as do the schools where they matriculated or worked.[105] Because of the academic community's dependence on foreign students (especially in the sciences), all of these immigration restrictions can lead to serious problems. Since foreign nationals obtain nearly a third of the graduate degrees in science and engineering, making it hard for them to study in the United States threatens the very future of American science. Moreover, Washington's thoughtless and insensitive treatment of international scholars and students can only be counterproductive. Not only does it alienate the nations and individuals whose support and goodwill are vital in an increasingly globalizing world, but it also prevents the academic community from engaging in that unconstrained exchange of ideas upon which the life of the mind depends.

Even so, the obstacles to free inquiry caused by the post-9/11 political repression, as well as by the imposition of heightened security restrictions on academic research and scholarly communication, may pale into insignificance in the face of the present financial crisis. As we shall see, the ideological warfare that has troubled the academy over the past forty years might not have inflicted so much damage after 9/11 had the academic community not at the same time been experiencing massive structural changes. It is the combination of the traditional violations of academic freedom with the almost revolutionary transformation of the way in which the nation's colleges and universities operate that is currently endangering American higher education.

Chapter 6

"TOUGH CHOICES": THE CHANGING STRUCTURE OF HIGHER EDUCATION

Even if 9/11 had not created new threats to the autonomy and academic freedom of America's college and university teachers, it was clear that by the end of the twentieth century structural changes were challenging the faculty's traditional role within American higher education. Beginning in the late 1960s and 1970s, while most professors attended to their classes and careers, the institutions that housed them were evolving into ever more bureaucratized organizations with an increasingly market-oriented set of priorities that reinforced the university's long-standing hierarchical structures while weakening its traditional intellectual and educational commitments. In the process, moreover, professors were losing much of their power to determine the educational policies of their institutions and to protect their own academic freedom and that of their colleagues.

These changes did not just happen. As we well know, the academic community has never been immune to the broader political, cultural, and economic forces that have transformed American society. In recent years, those forces, in particular the economic upheavals of the past thirty years along with the neoliberal assault on the welfare state, swept across the nation's campuses, not only threatening their financial security but also imposing new, and not necessarily academic, values. In this chapter and the next, I am going to look at how the changes those forces created affected—and continue to affect—higher education.

I take the faculty's perspective here. Students, administrators, alumni, parents, taxpayers, and other campus professionals and workers all have an interest in the fate of America's colleges and universities. But professors still are, in today's ghastly parlance, academia's key "stakeholders," the only men and women whose entire working lives, as well as their professional identities, have been devoted to higher education. Yet they are becoming increasingly marginalized within its precincts. Whether or not the institutions that have traditionally employed these people are now ready to dispense with them, it is clear that the changes tending toward such an outcome have taken place without much, or any, faculty input. That may or may not be a tragedy, but it is certainly not a laughing matter.

Let us not romanticize the academic past. No golden age ever existed, nor have the nation's institutions of higher learning ever been isolated from change. In fact, despite the academy's longevity (and academics love to dwell upon the fact that almost every Western institution that has existed since the Middle Ages has been a university), change has been a constant—certainly within the United States.[1] The academy's mission has never been static. From the small religiously oriented training schools for clergymen and educated professionals of the eighteenth and early nineteenth centuries, America's institutions of higher learning have evolved into the multiversities Clark Kerr described in 1963: institutions that not only engaged in cutting-edge research in dozens of fields but also offered training and liberal education to undergraduate and graduate students and provided expertise to the state and the rest of society.[2] That evolution continues. "Higher education today," former Stanford president Donald Kennedy noted a generation later,

> is challenged to fulfill a new and staggering burden. Always expected to make young people more skilled, mature, cultured, and more thoughtful, it is now seen as the motive power for regional economic improvement and even for international competitiveness. It is looked to for research underlying everything from better health care to military preparedness. And we are disappointed if it does not provide us with cultural inspiration and, on weekends, athletic entertainment.[3]

Kennedy ignored, perhaps because of Stanford's privileged student body, what is arguably the most important social function of American higher education: its value as a sorting mechanism. A BA or similar degree has become the main engine for economic mobility within the United States, required for entry into and retention within the middle class.[4] For that reason, access to higher education has become an increasingly fraught issue, one that provides critics from every point in the political spectrum with an indirect way to address or avoid the nation's main social problems.

In response to the demand for that all-important educational credential, the academy has grown enormously. But, again, that growth is nothing new; throughout the twentieth century, a national consensus in support of higher education led to ever increasing numbers of institutions, students, and professors. Even during the Great Depression, America's colleges and universities grew in size, with faculties expanding by more than a third.[5] That growth continued after World War II, with the GI Bill doubling prewar enrollments to reach an unprecedented two million students in 1947.[6] Even after the veterans graduated, the boom in higher education continued. Enrollments grew 78 percent during the 1940s, 31 percent during the 1950s, and an astonishing 120 percent during the 1960s before slacking off to 45 percent in the 1970s and 17 percent in the 1980s, when it was believed that a college education brought few economic returns.[7] To take but one example, UCLA, which served 10,000 students before the war, doubled in size by the end of 1950s, while its faculty expanded from 220 members to over 900. Today it has more than 38,000 students and over 4,000 faculty members.[8] The number of institutions grew as well, and continued to grow even after the boom years of the 1960s came to an end. In 1974 there were just over 3,000 institutions of higher learning; by 2006 there were 4,314.[9] There were also more than 1.3 million faculty members, as well as nearly 18 million students.[10]

The schools these students attend very enormously. After all, the most idiosyncratic and, some observers claim, admirable characteristic of the American postsecondary educational system is its enormous variety. Ranging from proprietary vocational schools to the flagship state and elite private research universities, American higher education offers a much broader array of academic options than any other system. These options, however, are far from equitably distributed. Like the rest of American society, U.S. institutions of higher learning are highly stratified and, despite a stated commitment to open admissions, by no means universally accessible. At the top, elite schools normally take in the ambitious and well-educated sons and daughters of the upper middle classes and turn out well-paid professionals and business leaders, while at the bottom, community colleges and for-profit vocational schools train working-class men and women for positions as medical assistants and air-conditioning technicians.[11] The ostensibly meritocratic ethos of the system legitimates its stratification, thus, at least in part, deflecting criticism of the underlying inequality of American society.

At the same time, both between and within these institutions, a ferocious struggle for prestige takes place. What money is to Wall Street and most other sectors of the American economy, status is to the academy. Such has been the case ever since the late nineteenth century, when the modern university emerged and prestige came to substitute for more pecuniary rewards. Today, as higher education has moved deeper into the penumbra of the market, financial remuneration has also come to reinforce the formal and informal rankings that constitute the academy's stratified reward system.[12] At the top are football coaches with seven-figure salaries and university presidents with high six-figure ones. Professional academics at somewhat less rarified levels, from full professors with named chairs and independent research centers down to part-time instructors and graduate student teaching assistants, operate within a carefully calibrated set of hierarchies and privileges. That stratification extends to disciplines as well. People who work in fields that are more closely tied into the market usually reap higher salaries and better working conditions. A professor in computer or health sciences can sometimes make 30 percent more than someone at the same rank in foreign languages or education.[13]

But, whatever the discipline, research is the coin of the realm. Though teaching is the main activity of most faculty members and many perform community service as well, status and money accrue to those professors whose research gains major funding and attention. These are the stars, the men and women with national and international reputations who command high salaries and fancy perquisites because of the supposed prestige they confer upon their institutions. That reward system inevitably lures academics away from the classroom and into laboratories and libraries. Widely deplored but rarely rectified, this obsession with research has, its critics claim, seriously detracted from the quality of undergraduate education. Over the years, these charges have only intensified in response to the spectacle of big-name academics offering one or two graduate seminars a year, while teaching assistants and part-timers handle the introductory courses that most students take. In many respects, this depiction of arrogant professors ignoring their instructional responsibilities oversimplifies the situation, but it contains enough validity to provide ammunition to the academy's enemies and to politicians concerned about the students of their states.[14] Even so, as Sheila Slaughter and Larry Leslie observe, "if faculty were offered more resources to teach more students, it is not clear that they would compete for these moneys with the same zeal with which they compete for external research dollars."[15]

Naturally, Slaughter and Leslie's thought experiment will never take place, for the institutions that employ these striving academics are themselves engaged in a similar struggle for status. Top-tier universities raid each other's faculties for professional stars to boost their ratings; second-tier schools establish and expand graduate programs to acquire the capacity for research and the cachet that it confers. Again, there's nothing new here. The competition for institutional prestige has been under way for years. Stanford, for example, began to push itself into the academic stratosphere in the 1950s by consciously cultivating what its ambitious provost Frederick Terman called "steeples of excellence." Not only did the university's leaders scramble to capture research money from industry and the federal government, but they also refused tenure to many people the departments had wanted to retain.[16] There is a contradiction here, for the institutional pursuit of prestige could and often did conflict with the autonomy of the faculty whose members were themselves also struggling for recognition.

Much of that struggle, on the institutional level at least, has become ever more enmeshed in what Slaughter and Leslie identify as "marketlike" activities, attempts on the part of the nation's colleges and universities to sell themselves and their services to whatever customers they can find. In the process, these institutions make structural changes that, whether intentional or not, diminish, if not eliminate, the power of the faculty and its ability to protect its traditional independence and academic freedom. The proliferation of interdisciplinary research centers, for example, permits administrators to appoint people to their faculties without having to go through already established departments.[17] Similarly, schools that create distance education programs often bypass regular academic channels when they hire part-time or temporary personnel to develop and staff those programs. Few of the administrators who implemented these measures were consciously trying to downgrade the professoriate; they simply believed that what they were doing was necessary for their institution's well-being, especially after the prosperity of the early 1960s began to recede.

Economic Crisis and Academic Realignments

"The American university," Colin Campbell, the president of Wesleyan University, announced in 1979, has "passed from its Golden Age to its Age of Survival."[18] We now know that Campbell had greatly exaggerated the academy's peril, but at the time he offered that assessment, the situation seemed so dire that the nation's educational leaders had few hesitations about proposing drastic action. The financial upheavals of the 1970s had eaten away at higher education's traditional sources of support, and many observers were speculating that anywhere from 10 to 30 percent of the nation's colleges and universities would go under. Those same observers were also—but again incorrectly—predicting that enrollments would fall once the last baby boomers had graduated.[19]

Many factors fed this crisis. Inflation shrank endowments; states reduced their appropriations; federal funding slowed and no longer went directly to institutions. It's a long list, reflecting, above all, the serious economic turmoil that was then convulsing the rest of the nation. It also reflected the political backlash against the campus unrest of the 1960s and early 1970s as well as against the movement to open the academy to more women and people of color. Ronald Reagan's attack on the University of California was only the most notorious of the measures that took a heavy financial toll on public higher education as state legislators began to cut back on their previously unstinting support. But the times were bad for all kinds of educational institutions, not just the public ones. By the late 1960s, Harvard, Stanford, Princeton, and many other top schools were operating at a deficit, and by the 1970s, up to one-quarter of the nation's colleges and universities were drawing on their endowments to pay operating expenses. Brown University had actually gone through one-third of its endowment.[20]

The academy panicked. Some institutions responded to this crisis with massive job cuts. In 1973 Southern Illinois University fired 104 faculty members, 24 of whom had tenure, while one of the branch campuses of the University of Wisconsin lopped off 88 tenured people. The City University of New York imposed a tenure quota in 1973, which it implemented a year later by seeking to deny tenure to 200 teachers without an explanation.[21] When, in 1980–81, the regents cut $11.6 million from the budget of the University of Michigan, the school took 600 people off its payroll.[22] Yale simply refused to fill 75 vacant faculty positions.[23] These may have been extreme cases, but the sense of crisis that provoked them permeated most American campuses.

Except in a few instances, revenues hadn't actually declined. But what had changed, especially for the research universities that established the prototypes for the rest of the academy, was that by 1968 the expansion of the boom years had slowed down, leading to what one historian called "a persistent, incremental scaling back of the commitments made during the post-Sputnik era." Research funding became harder to find as foundations and the federal government modified their operations and no longer gave money directly to colleges and universities.[24] Two changes in particular had a major impact on higher education. One was the decline in the percentage of state funding in the budgets of the nation's public colleges and universities, and the other was the shift of federal aid to higher education from institutions to individuals. Both of those changes, as well as the increasing competition for research money, encouraged academic administrators to look more intensively for other sources of income.

While state support still represents the largest percentage of most public institutions' budgets, that percentage has been shrinking for years. It began to decline in the 1960s and 1970s and is still going on. Until the current crash, the actual amounts of money going to the nation's public colleges and universities did not usually drop off, but the percentage of their budgets covered by their state governments dwindled inexorably.[25] According to one authority, that funding declined by 25 percent between 1980 and 2000. Taken as a whole, state support for public institutions of higher learning fell from 45 percent of those institutions' budgets in 1981 to 36 percent in 2000. And it continued to plummet. In 2004, for example, nearly half the states were allocating less money to their institutions of higher learning than they had the year before, some with cuts of over 5 percent.[26] Just to give a few examples: The University of California system received 37 percent of its income from the state in 1990 but only 23 percent in 2004, while the figures for Penn State showed a decline from 21 percent in 1990 to 13 percent in 2002.[27] The University of Virginia, which gets only 8 percent of its income from the commonwealth, has already privatized its law and business schools and is thinking of leaving the state system altogether.[28] The president of the University of Michigan—where state funding had declined from 70 percent in 1960 to 36 percent in 2000—put the situation succinctly: "We used to be state-*supported*, then state-*assisted*, and now we are state-*located*."[29] The current financial meltdown promises even more drastic reductions.

Actually, despite their criticisms of some academic practices, most state legislators had not abandoned their support of higher education; they were simply caught in a fiscal bind. The taxpayers' revolts of the 1970s—California's Proposition 13, in particular—made it politically impossible for them to raise taxes even if they wanted to. At the same time, they faced other and equally pressing financial demands, especially for the rising costs of medical care and incarceration. Moreover, while there was no other way to cover those expenses, many of which were mandated by law, colleges and universities did have another source of revenue: they could raise their tuitions.[30]

The transformation of the federal government's policy toward higher education further encouraged the academy to seek more income from its students. Although Washington had been spending money on the nation's campuses for years, it usually directed its largesse to specific research projects in agriculture, medicine, and the physical sciences. It was not until 1965 that Lyndon Johnson's Great Society program directly subsidized institutions of higher learning. That funding, however, did not last very long. The Nixon administration, while still willing to support higher education, decided to replace direct grants to colleges and universities with financial assistance to individual students. Not only was such a program in keeping with the egalitarian goal of increasing access for previously underserved populations, but it also accorded with the administration's ideological proclivities. As a 1971 internal Health, Education, and Welfare Department document explained, direct aid to students would allow "a freer play of market forces" that would "give individuals the general power of choice in the education marketplace." In addition, such a measure would let the government funnel assistance to private colleges and universities, many of them religious ones, without encountering political or constitutional roadblocks.[31]

Actually, by the time Washington made the switch to student aid in 1972, many schools were already reassessing their tuition policies and pondering ways to increase their enrollments. Thus, for example, because they feared losing potential male applicants, Princeton and Yale decided to go coed in 1968. They also began to raise their tuitions. By 1989 the cost of attending Yale had doubled in real terms.[32] Yale, of course, had other sources of income and was hardly threatened with extinction, but for smaller schools and for the many state institutions whose public funding had begun to decline, the federal government's subsidies to their students proved a lifesaver. This was especially the case by the late 1970s when Washington expanded its support for higher education from outright grants to lower-income students to the extension of loans to any student who applied.[33] By the 1980s, loans—and in the 1990s tax credits—had largely replaced grants in the overall mix of federal financing, tipping the government's aid program away from its original focus on expanding access to the by then more politically popular one of subsidizing middle-class students who would have gone to college anyhow. As a result, by 2002, loans, which had accounted for 20 percent of all student aid in 1975–76, had risen to 69 percent of that aid. While those loans enabled many students and their families to afford the growing cost of higher education, by 2007 the $13,275 debt they bestowed upon the average graduate cast shadows over many students' educational and career choices.[34]

Before we look at the institutional changes that the academy's increasing reliance on tuition income fostered, we cannot overlook its deleterious impact on the provision of access to postsecondary education and to the social mobility it affords. Even with the federal government backstopping financial aid and many schools offering deep discounts, the enormous rise in the cost of college has priced many otherwise qualified individuals out of higher education altogether. This lack of affordability seriously blights the prospects for the men and women at the lower end of the economic spectrum. Where earlier generations of New Yorkers could once go to CCNY for free, it now costs them nearly $5,000. Similar hikes have occurred throughout the academy. In 1980–81, the average price of a year of higher education was $3,101; in 2007–8 it was $16,245. Even at bargain-rate community colleges tuition had risen from $2,230 to $7,645 over the same period of time, while the average rate at four-year private schools was nearly $30,000, with high-end institutions charging in the neighborhood of $50,000.[35]

By the 1980s, as tuitions funded ever larger percentages of their budgets, academic administrators became concerned about attracting paying customers and began to focus on boosting—or at least maintaining—their enrollments. They began, in other words, to market themselves. Admissions now became a competitive project in which colleges and universities struggled to distinguish themselves from each other, establish special niches, and gain some kind of comparative advantage. Such behavior was hardly alien to a set of institutions that had been competing for status since long before the financial crunch of the 1970s. Still, the attention and resources that went into what came to be known as "enrollment management" were considerable. According to one recent study, for example, the average four-year private college spent $2,000 to recruit a newly enrolled student, while public institutions spent $500. And this competition was to reshape much of American higher education.[36]

Look, for example, at how financial aid got manipulated. Originally designed to subsidize the neediest students on campus and later used to recruit minority group members, enrollment managers then turned it into an instrument to attract talented undergraduates regardless of need. Bringing gifted students onto the campus would, many administrators believed, raise an entering class's average SAT scores and thus improve the institution's standing in the all-important *U.S. News & World Report* rankings. Accordingly, schools used all kinds of devices to appeal to such students—merit scholarships, honors colleges, and even, at Vanderbilt University, the creation of a Hillel house in order to lure the Jews who, it was believed, would elevate the overall cultural and intellectual level of the institution. Elsewhere, institutions actually raised their tuitions as a marketing tool on the assumption that their higher cost would indicate their higher quality.[37]

As schools scrambled to increase enrollments, they became caught up in what a recent study calls an "amenities arms race" that devoted considerable resources to improving the lives of undergraduates outside of class.[38] They provided state-of-the-art computers, elaborate fitness centers, and gourmet dining facilities. They also expanded student services and introduced big-time athletic programs. They did not, however, increase their support for the academic side of the institution—except, of course, for the recruitment of faculty stars. Students now had to be catered to, and if they did not actually gain the power that they had presumably struggled for in the 1960s, their needs and demands did carry weight in certain areas. They could not, for example, receive poor grades. Grade inflation, the bête noire of so many conservative pundits, owes more to the need to placate—and thus retain—tuition-paying undergraduates than it does to their increasing intellectual prowess or the wishy-washy behavior of left-wing ideologues.[39] Especially at institutions where student evaluations of their teachers went into those teachers' personnel files, maintaining high standards could cost people their jobs. As a result, although 39 percent of all students received a C or lower between 1966 and 1970, that figure had dropped to 9 percent in 1987–91. At the high end, only 6 percent of all grades were B+ and above in the earlier period, by the 1990s they had reached 33 percent.[40]

More important, however, as institutions sought to provide programs and courses that would bring in more tuition revenue, the transformation of students into consumers changed the curriculum. Except at the very top tier of elite colleges and universities, whose degrees traditionally ensured access to the upper levels of American society and which therefore did not have to provide their graduates with any specifically job-related skills, vocational education edged out the traditional liberal arts. At community colleges, such had always been the case. But elsewhere, particularly as the cost of college rose, students and their parents began to demand that education lead directly to employment.[41] Especially at second- and third-tier state schools and at the small private colleges that came to award most of their degrees in professional fields, liberal arts majors declined precipitously—from 47 percent in 1968 to 26 percent in 1986. The humanities took the heaviest hit, from 20.7 percent of the total majors in 1966 to 12.7 percent in 1993, and though the social sciences held up, the natural sciences did not.[42] Not surprisingly, the outside economy dictated what students wanted to study. Thus, in the 1980s, with neoliberalism riding high, business programs attracted the most undergraduates. Computer science was also a draw. Recently there has been more interest in the health professions, and it is likely that the previously scorned but presumably secure field of education will also pick up again, especially as the undergraduate student body becomes increasingly female.[43]

This shift in student interest had widespread ramifications for the overall structure of the university. Strangely enough, though, it did not lead to massive cuts in traditional departments. Some less popular programs were eliminated, but most colleges and universities hustled to meet student demands by adding more vocationally oriented courses and staffing them with contingent faculty members. These instructors, mainly part-time and non-tenure-track teachers, had a much more tenuous relationship with their students and with the institution that employed them than did traditional academics. They could be let go at any moment—a serious problem for the individuals involved, but a very attractive feature for the institutions that were scrambling to adjust their curricular offerings to the fluctuations of the economy. Intellectually as well, vocationalism brought significant shifts, as many disciplines reoriented themselves to meet student demand. Thus, for example, sociology departments beefed up their offerings in criminology, while philosophers began to teach courses on business ethics.[44]

This redirection of the academy could, however, create new problems, for at the same time as so many colleges and universities are repositioning themselves to provide more job training, they are also coming into competition with the for-profit sector of higher education. Because federal student aid can be applied to any kind of postsecondary program, private proprietary institutions, which tailor all their offerings to the job market, are also expanding.[45] As of the spring of 2009, for example, enrollment at the University of Phoenix, the largest such venture, grew by more than 20 percent over the previous year, to more than 400,000 students. Neoliberals within the federal government welcomed these operations with open arms (and loans and tax credits), forcing traditional educators who wanted to protect their turf to seek the assistance of accrediting bodies and state legislatures. How this competition eventually plays out may well be determined by the effectiveness of each sector's state and Washington lobbyists. What is not in question, however, is the fact that the increasing vocationalization of the academy now determines what so many American students do and do not learn.

Research and the Corporatization of the University

Its growing participation in the market is also reshaping the university's other major activity: research. Unlike teaching, not every academic participates in active scholarship or scientific investigation; most, in fact, do not. But because of the contemporary drive for both personal and institutional advancement, faculty members at almost every level feel themselves under increasing pressure to produce original research—even as it has become ever more difficult to obtain the resources that such investigations require. Moreover, because both public and private donors, as well as university administrators, target their funds to certain kinds of projects, scholars and scientists, who have become increasingly sensitized to the whims of those donors, all too often skew their research to what they think such funders want. These problems are particularly acute for natural scientists, whose work often requires major infusions of cash. While scholars in the humanities and social sciences have had similar trouble winning outside grants, their research is less expensive and is usually supported by their institutions in the form of sabbaticals and course releases.

It is important to note that scientists are not facing an overall decline in funding. Their problems result from changes in the way that funding gets awarded and from the increased competition for it. Nor has the source of that funding changed. Even as universities intensify their courtship of industrial donors, the federal government still supports most of the nation's on-campus research. In 2007, according to the National Science Foundation (NSF), Washington supplied more than $30 billion out of a total of $49 billion spent on academic research, with the institutions themselves contributing another $9.6 billion.[46]

The government has been bankrolling university scientists ever since World War II. Before that time, the academy, along with the Rockefeller and other foundations, had funded its own research, but the war brought both big science and the government onto the campus. The University of California ran the Manhattan Project that produced the atomic bomb, MIT managed the Radiation Lab project that developed radar, and schools like Johns Hopkins and Michigan operated smaller programs that turned out proximity fuses and other weapons. Even before the war ended, it was clear that the government would continue to support scientific research, though the form that support would take was a matter of contention. Most leading scientists wanted a "best science" system based on peer review. Such an approach, however, encountered political opposition because of its ostensible elitism and so did not get implemented until the Soviet Union launched its Sputnik satellite in 1957.[47] Then, panicked by the prospect of falling even further behind in the space race, Washington ramped up its support for basic science and poured money into graduate training, buildings, and individual projects.

Actually, the government, through the use of military contracts, had already been funding large amounts of academic research. Though some of that support went directly to weapons development at institutions like MIT, the rest was funneled to individual scientists mainly through the Office of Naval Research, which was, until the National Science Foundation was up and running, the chief patron of pure science. In fact, by the late 1950s, the Defense Department and the Atomic Energy Commission together were responsible for 76 percent of all the federal spending on academic research.[48] But even before the Vietnam War rendered it unpopular, that military connection was not without its drawbacks. Some universities, Harvard among them, refused to let classified research take place on their campuses, while others welcomed it, and still others, such as MIT, established separate, off-site research centers to handle such work. For the most part, however, few administrators or scientists had qualms about accepting military money for their research. Some, at least during the early years of the Cold War, actually viewed it as a source of prestige. "The feeling was that if the memos and reports you wrote weren't stamped 'secret,' they just weren't important," one scientist recalled, "they didn't involve 'real' science or engineering."[49]

Within a few years, however, ambivalence developed within the academy as it became clear that relying so heavily on military funding was, at least in part, distorting scientific priorities. Ethical matters aside (and they did not surface in any significant way until the mid-1960s), skewing an institution's resources toward fields that could be subsidized by defense industries and the Pentagon left other areas, including the humanities and the less militarily relevant sciences, underfunded. This was certainly the case at Stanford in the 1950s, where Provost Frederick Terman consciously hired faculty members in fields like electrical engineering and then steered their work into areas that he knew would produce research contracts from the Defense Department and its industrial partners. Since these people were as eager as Terman to obtain that funding, they did not hesitate to tailor their research projects to the military's specifications. A related, and still unresolved, problem that this collaboration spawned involved the distinction between basic and applied research and whether academic scientists should participate in the latter. Terman, as later proponents of similar efforts in biotechnology were to do, explained that "an organizational split along lines of applied work vs. basic work, or classified work vs. unclassified work . . . is not always realistic." In addition, he noted (again, as later academic entrepreneurs would as well) that for outside critics to prevent faculty members from undertaking research they wanted to do was to compromise academic freedom.[50]

Perhaps because almost everybody—scientists, academic administrators, government funders, and the public—was still under the sway of Los Alamos and the Manhattan Project, much of the federal money went to "big science," major enterprises that spent heavily on equipment and enlisted large numbers of graduate students and technicians. Individual researchers lost out as their more modest, though not necessarily less worthy, projects elicited less excitement, both on campus and in Washington.[51] That preference for big science also reinforced the hierarchical nature of the academic system, since few smaller institutions could compete with the large research universities that got most of the grants. In 2000, for example, 80 percent of the federal grants went to some one hundred schools, while in 2006, twenty schools received 35 percent of the billions of dollars Washington spent on research in science and engineering.[52]

At least in the beginning, peer review was crucial to the allocation of the federal government's research support. Even the military, when it was not contracting for specific weapons systems, operated on the assumption that only fellow scientists could assess the quality of someone's research proposal. As a result, throughout the 1950s and 1960s, the nation's most distinguished practitioners routinely screened grant applications for agencies like the National Institutes of Health (NIH) and the National Science Foundation. They also funded most of them, or at least most of the legitimate ones. By the late 1960s, however, as the government's support for research expanded, it had to recruit from a larger and less eminent pool of assessors, leading some observers to perceive a decline in standards.[53] At the same time, other—and not necessarily scientific—criteria began to determine what and what kind of research the government would fund.

In many areas, merit would no longer decide where Washington's dollars went. Politics intruded, both as a reflection of the underlying suspicion with which the public viewed supposedly head-in-the-clouds professors and a response to the Vietnam-era turmoil on the nation's campuses. Even Lyndon Johnson, during whose administration the funding for basic research reached its apogee, wanted to see practical results. "What," he asked his science advisors, "can I do for grandma?"[54] Actually, his administration had already been doing quite a lot, if not for Grandma, at least for her state's politicians, as it began to press for a wider geographical distribution of its research funding. Several undertakings, including a NASA-sponsored graduate fellowship program and the Defense Department's THEMIS project, explicitly sought to build the infrastructure for research at second-tier universities. Though partially designed to avoid the antiwar demonstrations that had targeted their schools' collaboration with the military at such prominent institutions as Wisconsin and Columbia, the grantors also recognized the political value of dispersing money and prestige more widely than would have been the case if they had maintained their programs' "best science" approach.[55]

Congress got into the act as well. Not only did its members begin the process of allocating research dollars to those special undertakings that later became known as earmarks, but they also exhibited a decided preference for big projects that would channel dollars and publicity into their home districts. At the same time, some congressional leaders were becoming skeptical about the value of basic research as a whole. In 1974, for example, Senator William Proxmire inaugurated the Golden Fleece awards, which highlighted what he considered the government's most frivolous and wasteful scientific grants.* A few years before, the so-called Mansfield Amendment barred the Defense Department from subsidizing any research that was not related to weapons development, thus depriving the academic community of an important, though controversial and already dwindling, source of support.[56] Medical research, on the other hand, had always been popular. Nobody, after all, wanted to lose the war on cancer, and even in the early years of the Cold War, it was not hard for biologists and medical school scientists to get grants from the National Institutes of Health, then under the Public Health Service's aegis. Over time, the NIH was to become an ever more important patron of the scientific establishment.

Although the government largesse did not dry up, by the 1980s it had become increasingly harder to obtain. There was simply more competition, much of it caused by the institutional scramble for prestige that ensued as second- and third-tier institutions developed graduate programs and pushed their faculty members to produce more fundable research. Moreover, that research became increasingly more expensive. The easy problems had been solved; the harder ones often required major capital investments in laboratories, equipment, and personnel. As a result, by the mid-1990s, costs were growing at the rate of 6 to 7 percent a year.[57] In addition, because of the political pressures for geographical distribution and big science, the NSF, which was now academia's main funder, was tailoring its grants to what it thought Congress wanted, rather than to what the scientific community felt should be studied. Not only did such developments threaten to eviscerate peer review, but they also led scientists to become risk-averse—to avoid difficult projects that might not pay off immediately and to concentrate on safe ones that could be more easily funded.[58] Complicating everything was the enormous amount of time and paperwork that developing a grant proposal required.[59]

Increasingly, scientists and universities began to explore other sources of funding for their research. The most obvious such resource was the private sector. Again, there was nothing unprecedented here. MIT had been particularly adept at developing connections with corporations during the early

---

*A neurobiologist friend actually won a Proxmire award for her federally funded work on leech penises—a subject that, neurobiologically at least, was not as silly as it sounded.

twentieth century, while professors elsewhere in fields like chemistry and engineering had long worked closely with private companies.[60] Traditionally those relationships had taken the form of outside consulting or individual grants. What changed, beginning in the 1980s, was the scale of those relationships and their impact on the way in which academic science was being pursued. This despite the fact that as of 2007 industry was supplying less than 6 percent of the academic community's nearly $50 billion research budget.[61]

The universities' drive to cultivate corporate sugar daddies accelerated in the 1980s for a variety of reasons. To begin with, the academy could hardly isolate itself from the growing influence of the neoliberal reverence for the private sector. Accordingly, as they responded to the economic crunch of the late 1960s and 1970s, many institutions sought to reorganize their operations in a more businesslike manner that borrowed managerial practices from the corporate world. For obvious reasons, such a transformation increased the universities' willingness to collaborate more closely with the corporations they were copying. At the same time, Washington was also prodding the academy to develop closer ties with the private sector.[62] More important, however, the commercialization of academic research seemed to promise previously undreamed-of riches, especially once universities figured out how to capitalize on the products of their scientists' research.

Here again, the federal government rode to the rescue, this time in the form of the 1980 Bayh-Dole Amendment. Originally designed to help small businesses compete successfully with the Japanese, this measure allowed institutions to patent the discoveries that their federally funded faculty members had made. Before then it was rare for a university to profit directly from the research done on its campus. But by the late 1970s, after two West Coast biologists cashed in on their discovery of a gene-splicing technique and earned $300 million for Stanford and the University of California–San Francisco, many schools started to pay attention to the commercial opportunities their faculties presented. At the same time, the corporate world also realized that it could profit from federally subsidized academic research, especially in the burgeoning field of biotechnology. Bayh-Dole simply eased the process. So, too, did the Supreme Court, which in a 1980 decision allowed researchers to take out patents on biological organisms. Suddenly, it became possible to generate big money from commercially licensing the products of academic laboratories—or so it seemed. In 1979 the nation's colleges and universities were awarded 264 patents; in 2001 they received 3200.[63]

Of course, it wasn't only institutions that profited from these discoveries; individual professors found them lucrative as well. Following the example of the University of California gene splicer who co-founded the Genentech Corporation and made $82 million when it went public, other scientists and engineers also sought to capitalize on their research by establishing start-up companies. Even if they didn't form their own businesses, they could still negotiate generous arrangements with the private sector to exploit their discoveries. There was a serendipitous quality to these developments, for it turned out that the most cutting-edge work in the field of molecular biology also happened to have commercial applications, and by the 1980s some 45 percent of all academic research within the field of biotechnology was funded by corporations. There were similar developments in smaller fields like optical and materials science as well. For the scientists involved, the money they received from their entrepreneurial activities, though obviously welcome and a source of prestige, was mainly viewed as a way to fund their research without having to wade through the red tape of an NSF or NIH grant application. In addition, these entrepreneurs claimed, their corporate ventures were speeding up the process by which their academic research could be transformed into socially beneficial products.[64]

There was a downside, to be sure. Some corporate practices, in particular the requirement that researchers keep their findings secret in order to protect their sponsors' commercial interests, clashed directly with the scientific community's traditional culture of openness and publication. A 1994 study found that more than 80 percent of the industry-funded academics it surveyed admitted that they withheld their results for months at a time, nearly half of them for more than three months—and this in a highly competitive field where rapid advances demanded immediate publication. Such secrecy damaged both science and scientists. Even when publication occurred, for example, some authors were not allowed to release the data on which their results were based, making it impossible for other scientists to confirm the accuracy of those results.[65] In other cases, professors were prevented from sharing their work with their own students. For younger scientists whose academic careers depended on publishing their research, the obstacles imposed by their funders' demand for confidentiality made it hard for graduate students to find jobs and for junior faculty members to gain tenure and promotion.[66]

In other ways as well, business values clashed with academic ones, often to the detriment of the overall scientific enterprise. To begin with, the privatization of academic research blurred the distinction between an invention and a discovery, turning the fruits of scientific investigation into a commodity that could be bought and sold. As a result, once a discovery was patented, it was transferred from the intellectual commons to the marketplace. Traditional collegiality disappeared.[67] No longer could scientists freely share their virus strains or experimental techniques with each other, since the corporations and universities that now owned such pieces of intellectual property expected to profit from them. Not only did this practice of treating gene sequences and other such scientific discoveries as "confidential property" conflict with the traditional communitarian values of the scientific world, but it sometimes made it too difficult or expensive for people to pursue certain types of research. Biologists had the most trouble, especially when the materials they were studying were in the hands of corporations or universities that could deny licenses to people whose work they did not like. When, for example, an Ohio State researcher published her findings that genetically altered sunflowers produced so many seeds that they were becoming "superweeds," the companies involved refused her further access to the plants or their seeds. In another case, a group of investigators at the University of Pennsylvania simply dropped their study of breast cancer genes rather than risk a suit for patent infringement. As one critic noted, "It's as if somebody just discovered English and allowed the alphabet to be patented."[68]

Within the academy, the commodification of scientific discoveries intensified the drift away from curiosity-driven investigations. It also marginalized research in lines of inquiry and whole fields that could not be commercialized or that imposed costs on the private sector. The once thriving specialty of labor studies, for example, has almost entirely disappeared, while that of occupational health is also threatened. Similarly, although plant biology attracts support from agribusiness, environmental studies does not, a shift in funding that doomed Berkeley's Department of Plant Pathology. As a result, few agricultural scientists look at biocontrol mechanisms or crop rotation. After all, as the former president of the Weed Science Society explained, "if you don't have any research other than what's coming from the ag chemical companies, you're going to be doing research on agricultural chemicals. That's the hard cold fact."[69]

The bottom line established another "hard cold fact" for those scientists who rely on corporate support for their research: they had to turn a profit. Businesses operate under a very different set of constraints and assumptions than academic institutions. Not only do they need to make money, but they are also more willing to tolerate risk and less willing to take a long-term perspective. They see universities as "sheltered environments" whose inhabitants "could not," one observer noted, "work on partial information, . . . were not fluid enough," and would not even fill out time sheets.[70] Academics, on the other hand, felt that companies had little patience for "research in a systematic manner" and were relentless in their pursuit of immediate results. If someone's research did not pan out or deliver a marketable product quickly enough, the sponsor could drop the project. As one chemist explained, "With private support, one day you think you're on easy street, the next day they pull their funding and you're stuck." Thus, for example, some of the scientists Slaughter and Leslie studied were stranded when the company that was backing their work went bankrupt. And, as we shall see, a similar fate befell the controversial collaboration between the University of California and the Novartis corporation when, after five years and no patentable results, the company changed hands, lost interest in plant biology, and dropped the venture.[71]

As the relationships between the private sector and academe intensified, many universities took on some of the characteristics of their new partners. Some schools even began to impose the same demand for secrecy as corporations—and for the same reasons. "If you think you have something that is commercially relevant," a young biologist explained,

> you are required to file a disclosure to the university before you publish it. So they are essentially sort of censoring what's being published . . . [T]he university is in business too . . . [A]nything that you think is commercially relevant has to be filed first and then they have up to six months to decide the fate of what you are working on . . . and that includes presentations at meetings. So, I don't know. The lines between industry and universities are sort of merging.[72]

Profits were now as important as publications. As a result, postdocs and junior faculty members in fields that were penetrated by the market felt they had to show proficiency in both the commercial and the scientific realms. The rules for academic success had changed, creating a double whammy for those scientists who had to delay publication and whose research was insufficiently profitable.[73]

Sometimes—as when some institutions charged such outrageous fees for access to their faculty's research that they shocked even members of the business community—the academy's desire to make money turned out to be counterproductive. Hewlett-Packard, one of its executives explained, "has found that it simply can't afford to make a product if universities demand such steep royalties on all the pieces of technology it needs to build that product. It's increasingly looking to universities overseas that don't impose such costly licensing agreements."[74] Moreover, the impression that the nation's institutions of higher learning cared more for money than for the broader social good did little for their public relations.[75]

Even more damaging to the reputation of American higher education were the revelations that the corporate ties of academic scientists were deforming their research. When eighteen-year-old Jesse Gelsinger died during a gene therapy experiment at the University of Pennsylvania in 1999, it turned out that the doctors conducting that experiment had not only misinformed their subjects about the project's risks but had also concealed their own financial interest in the company whose product was being tested.[76] Similar scandals occurred elsewhere at institutions as reputable as Brown, Harvard, and the universities of Washington and California. In October 2008, for example, the NIH cancelled a major grant to Emory University because its chief investigator had not disclosed the nearly $2 million he had received from a major drug company.[77]

In many fields, conflicts of interest were almost unavoidable. Faculty entrepreneurs were, after all, conducting research for their own spin-off firms or for other companies in which they held equity. Medical school professors were particularly vulnerable here, since pharmaceutical companies sponsored almost all the clinical trials that tested their drugs. When the *New England Journal of Medicine* decided that it would bar authors with "any financial interest in a company (or its competitor) that makes a product discussed in the article," it had to add the word *significant* in 2002 because its editors had found only one submission over the previous two years that could comply with their journal's stringent requirement. Similarly, in a survey of the Food and Drug Administration's scientific advisory committees in the fall of 2000, *USA Today* discovered that half the panelists had conflicts of interest.[78] A more recent study found that nearly two-thirds of the chairs of departments of medical schools and teaching hospitals had some kind of financial or other ties to industry.[79]

Although such sleazy practices as lending one's name to a company-written article did exist, most scientists with corporate ties did not intentionally distort their research or falsify their results.[80] Nonetheless, as Marcia Angell, the *New England Journal of Medicine*'s former editor, noted, "papers submitted by authors with financial conflicts of interest were far more likely to be biased in both design and interpretation."[81] In clinical trials, for example, company-sponsored investigators sometimes offered higher dosages of their patron's drugs than those of rival firms, or else they measured those drugs against placebos rather than against older medications in common use.[82] As the case of Jesse Gelsinger illustrates, such practices could lead to tragedy, especially when researchers treated unfavorable results as "confidential commercial information."[83] Thus, for example, although eight academics knew that information about the life-threatening side effects of Pfizer's arthritis medication Celebrex had been withheld from an article praising the product, none of them mentioned that fact. They all had ties to the company. So, too, did the medical experts who pooh-poohed the news that the diabetes drug Rezulin damaged the liver.[84]

At the same time, researchers who did uncover that kind of unfavorable information sometimes encountered pressure to conceal their findings. In 1994, when Betty Dong at the University of California–San Francisco found that the drug she had been studying was no better than the cheaper ones, the pharmaceutical company involved threatened to sue her if she published her results. Since the university refused to cover her legal expenses, Dong withheld publication until the *Wall Street Journal* broke the story two years later. By that time, the delay in disseminating her results had cost consumers (and presumably their insurers) hundreds of millions of dollars.[85] The University of Toronto's Nancy Olivieri also encountered drug company opposition to her work. Because she was finding serious problems during the clinical trial of a treatment for a rare children's blood disease, Olivieri felt obligated to warn her patients and publish the results of her investigation. In response, Apotex, the company that was funding her research, claimed that she had violated the confidentiality clause in its contract with Toronto. The university, which had been angling for a multimillion-dollar gift from Apotex, then removed Olivieri from the project and would have fired her had there not been a huge international outcry.[86]

Ironically, while whistle-blowers such as Nancy Olivieri risked sanctions for speaking out, the institutions that employed them rarely tried to regulate or even learn about the corporate affiliations of their faculty members. In many cases, knowledge about these people's conflicts of interest emerged only when a disaster occurred, a drug had to be recalled, or an investigative journalist poked around. Not only did researchers often conceal their financial connections to pharmaceutical and other companies, but outside attempts to monitor those connections were nonexistent or weak.[87] No institution—neither the academy, the professional journals and associations, nor the federal government—seriously policed the field. Even where regulations specifically banned conflicts of interest, as they did for advisors to the Food and Drug Administration, loopholes existed. People could get waivers if they were deemed essential to a panel—and about half of them did so.[88] By the 1990s, federal guidelines for academic research did exist, but they were voluntary and most universities left it up to their faculty members to determine whether or not they were in compliance. Some schools did, it is true, try to prevent the most flagrant abuses; Harvard, for example, did not allow its professors to do research for a company if they owned more than $20,000 of its stock or received more than $10,000 in consulting fees or spent more than one day a week in its employ. Significantly, however, by the year 2000, it was thinking about easing up on these restrictions and only refrained from doing so because of the outcry after the death of Jesse Gelsinger.[89]

Academic administrators had adopted these "don't ask, don't tell" policies in large part because they feared that if they cracked down on conflicts of interest, the high-powered researchers on their faculties might just pack up their laboratories and move to another school. Journals had similar concerns about losing their contributors.[90] And federal officials claimed that they did not want to infringe upon the academy's autonomy by imposing yet more restrictions on their grants. Such restrictions, the NIH explained, "would effectively, if not legally, transfer the locus of responsibility for managing 'conflicts' from the grantee institution to the federal government."[91] It should be noted as well that few of the organizations involved—from federal agencies to professional associations and universities—had the resources for stringently enforcing any regulations.[92] Recently, however, as revelations about conflicts of interest continued to pile up and politicians at both the state and federal levels began to express concern (and even pass legislation), academic bodies as well as government agencies have started to talk about greater transparency and tighter controls. Not surprisingly, some corporate-sponsored scientists are fighting back, claiming that increased regulation will interfere with academic freedom and push biomedical research down the slippery slope to "totalitarianism."[93]

It is significant, however, that until very recently, institutional (as distinguished from individual) conflicts of interest received little attention. Yet, as we have already seen, many universities were as immersed in profit-making activities as the most entrepreneurial professors on their campuses. Often, in fact, they encouraged those faculty members to develop businesses and even in many cases supplied them with seed money in return for equity. Not only would such a venture contribute to those institutions' bottom lines, but it would also enable them to respond to the growing political demands for them to serve as catalysts or, in the then-current phrase, "incubators" for economic development. Here, the model was the massive archipelago of high-tech corporations that had developed around Stanford in northern California's

Silicon Valley and Route 128's semicircle of MIT-spawned companies outside of Boston, as well as North Carolina's Research Triangle corporate park near Duke and Chapel Hill. It was widely—though incorrectly—believed that by supplying the requisite intellectual capital, universities could somehow stimulate the growth of entire sectors of American industry. Accordingly, many schools set aside parts of their campuses for research parks and, often in collaboration with state and local officials, devoted considerable resources, and even more rhetoric, to the pursuit of economic development.[94]

Few of these ventures proved as successful as their proponents hoped. Some schools, in fact, lost money. Boston University, for example, squandered 20 percent of its endowment on a start-up named Seragen.[95] Elsewhere it turned out that replicating Silicon Valley required a stronger academic infrastructure as well as more assistance from the military-industrial complex and a more sophisticated financial network than was available, for example, to the chancellor of the University of Wisconsin–Eau Claire, who wanted to "build economic growth and entrepreneurship in the Chippewa Valley." Nonetheless, the academy did win some big corporate partnerships. Most of these, it must be noted, involved major research centers and universities, not the eager second- and third-tier institutions that were looking to jump-start economic development in places like northwestern Wisconsin.[96] A few fields—mainly in the biological sciences and engineering—received the bulk of that largesse. Pharmaceutical and related companies were the main donors, especially to the multiyear packages like the $85 million that the dermatology department of Massachusetts General Hospital, a Harvard Medical School teaching hospital, received in 1989 from the Japanese cosmetics firm Shiseido or the $300 million sixteen-year grant from the Sandoz pharmaceutical company that went to the Scripps Research Institute in 1997.[97]

The most well-known of these arrangements, no doubt because it encountered the most opposition, was the agreement that was forged between the Novartis biotechnology company and the University of California–Berkeley's Department of Plant and Molecular Biology in 1998. What was unusual about the Novartis deal was that instead of establishing a separate research center, as so many large corporate donors did, the company funded an entire department. In return for $25 million over five years and access to the firm's special technology, Novartis got first crack at the same percentage of the department's research as it supported, whether that research had been produced with Novartis money or that of agencies like NSF and NIH. While the overwhelming majority of the department's professors supported the arrangement, other Berkeley faculty members and graduate students were outraged. They questioned, in the words of one of them, "the rightness, appropriateness, the morality of a private company sponsoring research at a university using facilities paid for with tax money for the company's eventual profit." These critics also evinced concern about the deleterious impact on faculty governance of the secrecy with which the Novartis contract had been negotiated as well as the way in which the company's preferences might skew the department's research. Eighteen months later, a California State Senate investigating committee under Tom Hayden also questioned the venture.[98]

In order to quell the controversy, the administration and faculty reached an agreement to have an outside group study the arrangement and its implementation. A cluster of Michigan State University educational researchers received the assignment; their report, released in 2004, assessed the project as pretty much a wash. It had, in the report's words, "resulted in modest benefit and very little harm to the PMB department." The company had awarded a total of $14,240,000 in grants to members of the department but had not commercialized any of their research. Moreover, even before the grant expired, Novartis had lost interest in agricultural research and transferred the project to a spin-off company. In short, as far as the Michigan State observers were concerned, the arrangement was neither as deleterious as its critics feared nor as productive as its sponsors hoped. Nonetheless, it did have a broader impact on the academic community, for the controversy that it spawned brought to the surface the underlying tensions engendered by the growing corporatization of the university—even if it didn't prevent the Berkeley administration from making a similar ten-year $500 million deal with the BP corporation in 2007 to do research on biofuels in collaboration with two other institutions.[99]

Administrative Expansion and Accountability

The university administrator who announced the Berkeley-BP agreement was Carol Mimura, the Assistant Vice Chancellor for Intellectual Property and Industry Research Alliances.[100] Mimura, who had been managing Berkeley's corporate research arrangements since the early 1990s, is one of three Assistant Vice Chancellors (including one for Research Administration and Compliance and another for Research Enterprise Services) as well as an Associate Vice Chancellor who report to Berkeley's Vice Chancellor for Research. These people are only a few of the thousands of administrators added to the payrolls of the nation's colleges and universities over the past few decades to deal with their increasingly complex operations. In the field of technology, for example, once the Bayh-Dole amendment cleared the way for capitalizing on the research of faculty members, Berkeley, like many other universities, recognized the need for managerial expertise to handle the commercial arrangements involved and hired accordingly.

That development and similar ones in other areas of American higher education have contributed to the enormous expansion of academic administrations over the past few decades. Not only have administrative costs become the fastest-growing component of most college and university budgets but, according to the Education Department's National Center for Education Statistics, as of the fall of 2006, the percentage of full-time professional employees in administrative positions in U.S. institutions of higher learning was higher than the percentage of such employees in faculty positions: 51.4 percent to 48.6 percent.[101]

This proliferation of academic bureaucrats owes much to the developments we've already examined. As colleges and universities competed for higher enrollments, lobbied for state and federal aid, and looked to the corporate sector for research grants, they hired more staff members to handle the load. The federal government, because it forced schools to generate huge amounts of paperwork, was largely responsible for this expansion. Institutions had to comply with regulations about everything from access for disabled individuals and the treatment of laboratory animals to labor laws and equal employment practices. At the same time, the financial accounting requirements for federal research money became increasingly onerous, with demands for meticulous reporting of income and expenses, as well as for detailed budgets in every grant application. Institutional review boards that monitor the use of human subjects in faculty research added another—and in fields like anthropology, genuinely detrimental—layer of regulation. So burdensome have federal requirements become that whenever former secretary of education Lamar Alexander delivers a speech on higher education, he brings along a five-foot-high stack of boxes that, he claims, contain all the government's rules affecting the nation's colleges and universities.[102]

But federal regulations account for only part of the administrative bloat. Think as well of all the nonacademic operations that take place on the nation's campuses. Bookstores, dining halls, athletic teams, publishing houses—all require considerable managerial capacity. Then there's all the effort involved in acquiring, developing, and supervising the institution's physical plant and dealing with the local regulations and vendors involved. And, of course, security (not to mention parking) issues require most schools to have their own police forces.[103]

Much of this work devolved upon the academy's burgeoning legal departments. Besides the routine business of higher education, the amount of litigation facing American colleges and universities has also mushroomed. Not only were the nation's institutions of higher learning drawn into cases dealing with policy matters like affirmative action and graduate student unions, but they also faced individual lawsuits about tenure denials, student expulsions, and sexual harassment. Moreover, commercial relationships required corporate-savvy lawyers to draw up contracts for patents, licenses, and other forms of intellectual property. In fact, many schools generated so much business that their legal counsels' offices resembled small law firms, whose lawyers handled, as the official statement from my own institution puts it, "a broad array of specialties, including corporate; finance; contracts; trusts and estates; real estate; tax; labor and employment; commercial litigation; intellectual property, patents, trademarks, and technology agreements and licensing."[104]

As we have already seen, many of those operations spawned their own set of administrators. Thus, for example, although the first individuals who, like Carol Mimura, handled the process of what came to be called "technology transfer" tended to work out of their school's legal offices, they soon became independent.[105] By the early 1980s, these administrators had already formed their own professional organization, the Association of University Technology Managers (AUTM), a vibrant outfit of more than 3,500 specialists that encourages networking and holds annual conferences. At its 2003 meeting at Disney World, AUTM members interested in the best ways to commercialize the work of their institutions' scientists and engineers could attend panels on such topics as "Dirty Little Tricks in Licensing," "Make $10 Million with No Money Down," and "Getting Value out of Mice."[106]

Nor are technology transfer officials unique. Academic administrators in every field have established their own professional organizations, each with its own career tracks, status hierarchies, and specialized forms of knowledge. Thus, for example, the people who worked in admissions offices could join the American Association of Collegiate Registrars and Admissions Officers, while financial officials had the National Association of College and University Business Officers and lawyers the National Association of College and University Attorneys. There's also the International Association of Campus Law Enforcement Administrators, the National Association of Student Financial Aid Administrators, the National Association of Collegiate Directors of Athletics, and the National Association of College and University Food Services. While these and similar organizations help their increasingly professionalized members keep up with new developments and make contacts with others in their field, they also undermine those people's local loyalties—a problem that had long bothered academic reformers concerned about faculty members identifying more with their disciplines than their schools. Such concerns were not far-fetched. These organizations of college and university administrators sometimes took positions that conflicted with the well-being of their institutions, as, for example, when the college bookstore managers' association endorsed a tax policy that would have hurt higher education.[107]

Whether academic administrations expanded because they had gained more power or whether they gained more power because they had increased in size, it is clear that they have taken on ever greater responsibilities for running their institutions. Again, much of this is the result of the fiscal crisis of the 1970s. As colleges and universities struggled to keep afloat, they looked to the business sector for financial solutions, often bringing in managers from private companies to handle their affairs. But, as we have seen, the corporate world operates within a very different culture than the academy; it prizes risk taking, decisiveness, hierarchy, and, of course, the bottom line. For managers with that worldview, therefore, the academic community's traditional shared governance was simply too slow, too inefficient, and too wedded to the status quo. "Institutions that choose to ignore the realities of the emerging marketplace either because of complacency or simply because of glacial pace of their governance," Michigan's former president warned, "are at considerable risk."[108] Change was essential, though what it entailed and why it was necessary was often left unsaid.

In any event, as these new—and often highly paid—administrators surveyed the institutions they had been brought in to save, they concluded that they would need much more authority to carry out their jobs. "In the 1980s," a University of Minnesota vice president explained, "universities must either make tough choices or stagnate. And there is no way to make tough choices except centrally."[109] "Flexibility" became their mantra, presumably because they felt it was impossible to make those "tough choices" without it. Moreover, because they were unused to academic norms, many seemed unaware that it might be possible to combine that flexibility with the university's decentralized and democratic form of decision making.

These administrators were caught in a bind, especially when they confronted fiscal exigencies that seemed to require major surgery. Some behaved in an autocratic manner, risking an AAUP sanction by blowing off their faculties. Other, and usually more effective, leaders recognized that they needed professorial support for their reforms but chafed at their faculties' refusal to take strong actions or to adopt a broader perspective. Noting that "sunset is an hour that almost never arrives," the former Stanford president Donald Kennedy complained about his faculty's collective defense of each other's turf. Faced with a call for considerable belt-tightening, they opted for across-the-board cuts instead of mounting a triage operation and eliminating the university's weakest units. Another former president, George Washington University's Stephen Trachtenberg, had a similar grievance: the entrenched leaders of his school's Faculty Assembly were so "completely risk averse" that they even refused to discuss, let alone act on, revisions to the academic calendar. Many administrators found the faculty's failure to take responsibility for solving the university's problems, while blaming the administration for those problems, particularly frustrating. "Faculty think we administrators have more power than we actually do and have more money than we actually do," one educational leader explained. "Faculty do not understand or are aware of the great power they have. Faculty hold the key to change and institutional transformations but most are not aware of that."[110]

Departments were a major stumbling block; their members' vested interests in their own disciplines and subfields made them, many academic administrators believed, the most serious structural and intellectual obstacles to meaningful change. They had, one critic explained, a "tendency to ossify," cloning themselves instead of reaching out beyond the traditional boundaries of their disciplines to recruit the men and women doing cutting-edge work. Certainly there have been instances in which the self-protective behavior of insecure, narrow, and hidebound academics has, in fact, perpetrated mediocrity and irrelevance. How to handle that behavior without infringing on faculty rights has long been a serious challenge to their institutions—and to their colleagues. Some administrators skirted the problem by creating interdisciplinary programs and research centers outside of departmental controls.[111] Such units can attract exciting new scholarship and science as well as reward particularly entrepreneurial and innovative faculty members, but they can also—and sometimes at the same time—demoralize the rest of the faculty and undermine traditional forms of academic governance.[112] Moreover, because such ventures can infringe upon the professoriate's traditional control over curriculum, hiring, promotion, and tenure, these programs and centers can threaten the quality of the institution's educational mission, especially when they reflect corporate rather than academic values.

But we may be overstating such conflicts; a 2001 survey of some nine hundred institutions of higher learning indicates that most faculty members and, surprisingly, administrators felt that shared governance worked fairly well on their campuses.[113] Whether such a positive assessment can be maintained when major cutbacks occur remains an open question. And in any event, generalizations about administrative behavior and its impact on faculties may not be too helpful here. Clearly, some particularly entrepreneurial professors may have been empowered by their administration's more corporate approach, while those in less marketable specialties have undoubtedly felt marginalized. The key, of course, is to ensure that the faculty's collective voice gets listened to. Even so, there is no guarantee that the famous herd of cats so many administrators identify as their faculties will speak with a single voice. Divisions *within* the professoriate may very well be more of a threat to its traditional position within academe than the corporatelike ventures of its business-oriented administrations.

Still, those enterprises can create serious problems when administrators put them into place without consulting their faculties. A particularly egregious example of such a managerial presumption was the course on "Guerrilla Marketing" that was foisted on the Department of Film and Media Studies at CUNY's Hunter College in the spring of 2007. Developed by the administration with a $10,000 grant from the Coach handbag company, the course was designed to further the luxury leather goods industry's campaign against low-cost knockoffs by creating a Web site that would purportedly show the traumas of purchasing such counterfeit goods. Not only was the instructor, an untenured assistant professor of computer design with no expertise in the area, forced to teach the course, but he was given no control over its content. "Only a single point of view," a faculty committee later complained, "a distinctly non-scholarly perspective that came from outside of the academy and hence not subject to the usual rigor of peer-review and other academic standards of higher education, was presented during the course." But in return for flouting the faculty's control of the curriculum as well as violating both the students' and the instructor's academic freedom, the college received a million-dollar donation from Coach's CEO.[114]

Few of the ostensibly educational undertakings that emerged from the offices of academic administrators were quite as crass as the Hunter course. Most such projects tended to follow the fads of the day, implemented in order to cash in on a supposedly eager market for them. They were far from uniformly successful and sometimes exploited the men and women who staffed them. In the late 1990s, these enterprises usually involved the Internet or some other form of supposedly profit-making, money-saving, customer-attracting distance education. In 1999, for example, Columbia created Fathom, a highly touted consortium of fourteen prestigious institutions, among them the universities of Chicago and Michigan, the London School of Economics, the New

York Public Library, the American Film Institute, the British Museum, and the Woods Hole Oceanographic Institute, that was going to offer a wide variety of online courses and seminars. Three years later, after investing nearly $15 million in the project and reaping all of $700,000 in return, Columbia shut it down. Similar ventures at Temple and New York University proved equally unrewarding.[115] In 2009, faculty displeasure with the poor quality of the offerings sank the University of Illinois's online Global University. His colleagues, the chair of the faculty senate pointed out, were reluctant to participate in what seemed to be a moneymaking venture designed by the administration.

> Teaching is not a delivery system, and I think most faculty were just not interested in giving up their course content to be "delivered" by adjuncts with whom they might have little to no contact. . . . you can't divorce the syllabus from the delivery.

Had the faculty been involved with the program from the start, creating a more academically oriented model, the venture's critics suggested, the outcome might have been different.[116]

At the moment, the academy is surfing the wave of globalization, as dozens of American colleges and universities set up satellite campuses everywhere from Singapore to Madrid. As of the fall of 2009, there were seventy-eight such campuses.[117] The Persian Gulf is a particular draw for institutions interested in, as one commentator put it, "franchising their brands." Already Carnegie Mellon, Cornell, Georgetown, Northwestern, and Texas A&M, among others, have set up shop in Qatar, while dozens of other schools have gone prospecting in China, "the Klondike of higher education," in the words of one astute observer.[118] NYU, for example, has programs in London, Paris, Buenos Aires, Madrid, Berlin, Prague, Florence, Shanghai, Accra, and Tel Aviv, as well as several dozen summer ones in Russia, Cuba, Greece, and elsewhere; it is also building a completely new campus in Abu Dhabi. Already a quarter of the school's undergraduates spend some time abroad, freeing up expensive New York City dorm and classroom spaces, while living in what Andrew Ross calls an "edu-tourist bubble" with other American students.[119]

Not all these ventures pan out. George Mason's campus in Ras al Khaymah, near Dubai, closed after three years, a victim of unrealistic expectations, inadequate funding, and not enough students. And the recent tanking of Dubai's financial structure threatens the programs established by Michigan State and the Rochester Institute of Technology.[120] Ostensibly established to offer the same education as that which takes place on their home campuses, all these schools are still figuring out how to staff their classes. Local teachers are inexpensive but may not attract paying customers; bringing out their own faculty members can be pricey. NYU plans to lure its professors to Abu Dhabi by offering them one and a half times their regular salary. And, of course, academic freedom issues may arise if the hardly democratic local rulers who are subsidizing these projects intervene to ensure that nothing subversive occurs in class.

External pressures for accountability are posing additional problems for higher education, especially when administrators respond to those pressures without sufficient consultation with their faculties. These pressures have been accumulating recently in response to concerns about the soaring cost of higher education and its alleged inadequacies. After tuitions rose 35 percent at private schools and 51 percent at public ones between 1995 and 2005, politicians, journalists, parents, students, and ordinary citizens began to ask how effectively the nation's colleges and universities are spending the taxpayers' dollars.[121] At the same time, confronted with data that participation levels are falling behind those in other industrialized countries while graduation rates are also lagging, these folks also want to know whether the academy is actually fulfilling its educational mission. The culture wars have muddled the situation. Well-publicized surveys that show how few college graduates, for example, can identify the founding fathers allow ACTA and the other culture warriors to promote the academy's failings. By attacking so much of what goes on in academia, they have given additional grounds for questioning what higher education is doing.

There have been some congressional investigations into college costs, but little action.[122] State legislatures have been busier, responding to this situation by taking steps that, while seemingly correcting abuses, do not look at the diversion of funding and attention away from undergraduate teaching that constitutes the main problem of higher education. Instead, they investigate and, in some cases, even specify how much time professors must spend in their classrooms. In other cases, they demand action to ensure the English-language competency of teaching assistants. Most of the time they call on colleges and universities to evaluate their own progress, though without much in the way of specificity.[123] Recently, the most serious pressure for accountability came not from the states but from the federal government in the form of the Commission on the Future of Higher Education, set up in 2005 by Secretary of Education Margaret Spellings. Ironically, given the group's corporate makeup and pro-business ideology, it recommended a federally mandated program of largely quantitative outcome assessments designed, the commission's businessman chair explained, to "hold postsecondary institutions accountable for their performance."[124] Though Congress refused to support that initiative, the idea of imposing some kind of standardized evaluation procedures on higher education remains popular with politicians and officials, including many in the Obama administration.[125]

The academic establishment is giving in. Instead of mounting a campaign to explain what really ails higher education and how the states' dwindling support for their public colleges and universities has contributed to their perceived defects, much of the academy's official leadership is scrambling to show that it can evaluate itself. Just as administrators purged their faculties of suspected Communists in the 1950s in order to keep outsiders from doing it, they are now struggling to implement accountability procedures before trustees and politicians devise ones for them. Some have been hyping the so-called College Learning Assessment that was developed by the Rand Corporation.[126] At the institutional level, individual schools are implementing various other "learning-outcome assessments" to measure how much their students learn, though it is by no means clear what those instruments actually show or, more important, how they can be used to improve instruction.[127]

As it now stands, the process of assessing student progress all too often turns into additional paperwork that is submitted to accreditation agencies and then gets filed away. Here, for example, is the testimony of a CUNY professor who views his administration's current demands for accountability as a way

> to torture the faculty. The need for measures of assessment, accountability, reporting of activities, periodic departmental reviews with self-study and outside visitors, etc. really takes up a lot of time and . . . creates (in me at least) greater resentment of the obligation and drains energy. My department is just beginning a periodic review. So I have just reread the last departmental self-study and outside committee report from about five years ago. The self-study was all bullshit; I am embarrassed for my colleagues who were able to write it. We have been told we have to outdo it this year (phrased in terms of telling the administration all the good things about us that they ignore). The outside report contained a number of suggestions, some reasonable and some off the wall, but as far as I remember none of them were discussed nor was any attempt made to implement them when we returned in the fall (it was done at the very end of the spring semester).[128]

Given the amount of busywork it creates, it is no wonder that what the sociologist Gaye Tuchman calls "the accountability regime" engenders considerable opposition within the academy, from both the right and the left.[129] Though it might be useful to find out what undergraduates actually learn, poorly designed measures based on unrealistic assumptions threaten all of higher education. According to Diane Auer Jones, a former official in the Bush administration's Education Department and an outspoken critic of the Spellings Commission's exclusive focus "on a narrow band of outcomes," relying so heavily on something such as graduation rates could prove counterproductive. After all, as has long been known, students drop out of college because they can't afford it, not because they are receiving a poor education. Moreover, Auer notes, there is the serious danger that the assessment process can turn into a series of cookie-cutter examinations in the No Child Left Behind mode that "reduces colleges to the least common denominator." Not only would such a standardized process disregard the enormous variety of types of institutions, but it would encourage the further dumbing down of the curriculum in order to teach to the test. As the executive director of the National Association of Scholars points out, such measures rely upon a "severely impoverished view of what higher education should be." There is, he pointed out, no way that the liberal arts can be quantified.[130]

It is unclear whether the current economic crisis will ease the demands for outcomes assessment or intensify them. The Obama administration is sending contradictory signals. It is, to its credit, at least talking about redirecting more money to needy students, if not to higher education as a whole. On the other hand, the prospect of harder times in academe may well result in an even greater call for accountability, thus exacerbating many of the problems that are already undermining the faculty's professional autonomy and academic freedom. At the moment, however, while most of the public's attention has been drawn to the plight of the nation's undergraduates who face rising tuitions and restricted enrollments, the situation of their teachers is already dire, as the next chapter will reveal.

Chapter 7

"UNDER OUR NOSES": RESTRUCTURING THE ACADEMIC PROFESSION

In 1990, Ernest Boyer, president of the Carnegie Foundation for the Advancement of Education, published *Scholarship Reconsidered*, a highly touted jeremiad about the state of higher education. Decrying the academy's overemphasis on a narrowly delimited and hierarchical type of research, Boyer called for a reconceptualization of scholarly work that would restore undergraduate teaching and service activities to their central position within the academic profession. He developed an elaborate four-part definition of scholarship that not only included traditional research—what he called "the scholarship of discovery"—but also viewed "integration," "application," and "teaching" as equally valuable forms of scholarship.[1] A pathbreaking textbook or piece of policy analysis, a stimulating classroom discussion—all should earn as much credit for tenure and promotion as a scholarly monograph or peer-reviewed article. It was an ingenious model, one that was widely admired as a way of maintaining intellectual standards while eliminating the proliferation of often trivial research and publication that the then current academic reward system encouraged.

It was, of course, ignored.

Instead of heeding Boyer's call for more attention to undergraduate education and community service, the nation's colleges and universities focused ever more heavily on research. They upped their requirements for tenure, even as many senior professors confessed that they could never have met their own demands for what the Modern Language Association called "publication productivity."[2] As we have already seen, much of that pressure came from the competition for resources that transformed American higher education at the end of the twentieth century. In that struggle, almost every institution of higher learning sought to raise its perceived status. A faculty that won grants, developed graduate programs, and published extensively would, it was believed, add to the school's prestige and thus make it a hotter commodity in the academic marketplace. Prolific authors like Ward Churchill could often write their own tickets. Second- and third-tier state universities were particularly culpable here, as they pursued productive scholars and offered ever more doctoral degrees. But even liberal arts colleges tried to play the game, diverting attention and resources away from undergraduate education while pressuring faculty members to compete for grants and to publish, publish, publish.[3] Teaching, the traditional responsibility of the academic community, received little attention and offered few rewards. And, as we shall see, it devolved increasingly onto a cadre of subfaculty contingent instructors who taught most undergraduate classes and who had essentially no academic freedom.

In order to understand how this drive for ever more research affected the nation's faculties, their students, and the institutions that housed them, this chapter will look at the ways in which the broader structural changes that accompanied the corporatization of higher education transformed the academic profession. No longer isolated from the pressures of the bottom line, most college and university teachers found themselves working within an increasingly competitive operation that sometimes bore little resemblance to the traditional academic system that had existed for most of the twentieth century. Professional academics lost control over the conditions of their employment in ways that not only deformed their teaching, research, and participation in faculty governance but also diminished their ability to preserve their intellectual autonomy. The rules had changed, as had the contours of most academics' jobs. And not always for the better.

Professors were complicit here; in fact, many actually welcomed the new emphasis on research. They were, after all, as deeply invested in the quest for status as anyone else on campus, though they may also have been responding to the growing demand for grants and publications that came from their institutions' high commands. Until the mid-1980s, when colleges and universities began to put priority on scholarship in tenure and promotion decisions, surveys of faculty members showed that they preferred teaching to research. But as their employers' expectations changed, so, too, did these people's proclivities. Moreover, by the 1980s, the job market was making it easy for the academy to emphasize research. With the rapid expansion of higher education at an end and a growing surplus of unemployed PhDs, lower-ranked institutions discovered that they could hire faculty members with the kind of qualifications that previously only the Ivy League and Big Ten universities had been able to command. Trained at the nation's top graduate schools, these young academics expected to replicate their mentors' careers by pursuing an active research agenda. Their employers accommodated them, often using scarce resources to provide them with state-of-the-art laboratories and minimal teaching loads while hiring low-cost adjuncts and teaching fellows to take over their classrooms.[4]

And, of course, their paychecks and those of their colleagues reflected that research orientation. Productive scholars and scientists simply earned more. In 1988–89, for example, the average salary for professors who produced less than one publication every five years was $35,500, while those with two or more publications a year got $51,901. Although, as we have seen, a faculty member's remuneration varies significantly in accordance with that person's field, this discrepancy in favor of active researchers held steady no matter what the discipline. The only activity that offered similar rewards for full-time college teachers was—no surprise—participation in administration. Even more troubling, there seems to have been a negative correlation between the amount of time a professor spent in the classroom and his or her salary.[5]

Ironically, as institutions scrambled for the prestige conferred by their faculties' research, the individual members of those faculties were experiencing what one authority has called a "conflict of commitment."[6] They were coming to identify themselves and their professional careers with their disciplines, not with the colleges and universities where they taught. "The market for professors," Louis Menand noted with regard to the humanities, "is a national market run by the disciplines, not a local market run by provosts or trustees." This ebbing of local loyalties had been going on for decades, as academic professionals became increasingly immersed in the hierarchical reward structures of their own scholarly communities. By the mid-1990s, this process had become so widespread that in one study, 77 percent of the professors surveyed said that their discipline was important to them, while only 40 percent said their campus was.[7] Such priorities did not augur well for a healthy level of participation in such relatively unremunerative chores as advising students or serving on committees, let alone teaching undergraduates.

Nor, unfortunately, did this professorial disengagement appeal to the ordinary citizens and politicians who neither shared the academy's regard for research nor cared what college teachers did outside of class.[8] "The public," Harvard president Derek Bok explained,

> has finally come to believe quite strongly that our institutions—particularly our leading universities—are not making the education of students a top priority . . . With the passage of time, the public is

> beginning to catch on to our shortcomings. They may not have it quite right—they are often wrong about the facts—but they are often right about our priorities and they do not like what they see.[9]

Misunderstandings were rife, since it was hard to make outsiders understand, for example, that a professor's twelve-hour teaching load comprised only a fraction of his or her academic work. In this regard, the urban legends about college teachers mowing their lawns on a weekday afternoon were damaging in the extreme, especially when so many students had firsthand experience of unavailable senior professors and overcrowded classes staffed by adjuncts. While there had probably never been a golden age of undergraduate education, certainly not on the massive scale of the late twentieth century, the academic profession's seeming disregard for its students created considerable resentment—and not just among the hoi polloi. Within the academy as well, critics on both the left and the right found the downgrading of teaching unconscionable. And, as we have already seen, not a few state legislatures responded to this situation by imposing minimum course loads and other requirements on faculty in their public institutions of higher learning.[10]

Nonetheless, although it alienated the public and clashed with the traditional missions of most institutions of higher education, this pattern of downgrading undergraduate teaching and community service came to dominate the academic world. Top-tier universities provided the template by rewarding their leading professors with tiny teaching loads—usually a few graduate seminars with an occasional large lecture course thrown in. Some of these luminaries had even managed to buy out their undergraduate teaching and were rarely on campus. Admittedly, not every big-time academic avoided the classroom, but many did and it was increasingly common for prominent universities to staff their introductory courses with contingent faculty. As early as 1974, the Yale historian George Pierson acknowledged that one-third of his school's undergraduate instruction was being handled by adjuncts, graduate students, and visiting faculty members. More recently, another authority estimated that part-timers and graduate students taught 25 percent of the top-tier institutions' undergraduate courses—especially at the freshman and sophomore level. And at the University of Chicago, with its famously rigorous liberal arts core curriculum that was the pride of its eminent faculty, two-thirds of that core's humanities and social science courses were in the hands of teaching assistants and non-tenure-track instructors.[11]

Its impact on elite undergraduates all to one side, the dissemination of this research model from prestigious schools to less well-endowed institutions created serious problems. To begin with, setting up laboratories and lowering teaching loads to attract faculty stars drained resources away from those institutions' basic educational functions. In addition, some of those schools lacked the capacity to handle major research projects, thus contributing to the proliferation of mediocre science and scholarship while diverting support from more worthwhile undertakings. To make matters worse, many of these ambitious projects were funded by earmarks, obtained through the efforts of paid lobbyists and politicians eager to bring resources to their home districts. "Academic pork," in Jennifer Washburn's felicitous phrase, these noncompetitive awards not only created public resentment but also undermined the system of peer review.[12]

Actually, despite the earmarking, the bulk of the nation's research money still went to the same handful of major universities it always had, prompting more than a few observers to question the drive for institutional advancement at second- and third-tier schools.[13] In a February 2009 letter to the Republican senator and former secretary of education Lamar Alexander, Robert Berdahl, the president of the American Association of Universities and a former Berkeley chancellor, asked, "How many research universities does the United States realistically require in order to maintain its agenda of innovation and advanced training?" While Berdahl did not call for any specific cutbacks, he did imply that at a time of straitened financing it might be a good idea to reconsider whether lower-tier institutions should set up graduate programs or try to do big-time research. Though the suggestion that such schools should limit their ambitions may well reflect the elitism endemic among the nation's most high-powered academics, no one can deny that a lot of irrelevant and overly narrow scholarship does get churned out in the quest for academic status.[14]

After all, when an institution is looking to raise its profile, it will press its members to produce whatever adds to its ranking. Quantity in such a situation almost always trumps quality, which is, of course, much harder to measure.[15] It is easy enough for department chairs, deans, and promotion committees to count the number of somebody's grants and publications. Whether those achievements add significantly to the store of human knowledge is another matter. All too often the growing emphasis on productivity not only encourages sloppy (or even fraudulent) work but also, as we have seen, deters investigators from pursuing quirky or ambitious undertakings or ones that take too long to pay off. Since experiments fail as often as they succeed, it is not surprising that more and more scientists focus on safe projects that can be easily funded, even if they do not produce groundbreaking results.[16] They also publish more quickly, often rushing into print prematurely, especially if they sense a competitor is on their tail. And they churn out "salami publications," lots of small papers that all come from a single project.[17] In the humanities, where books rather than articles are the currency of choice, the reverse is true. As the MLA noted in a 2006 report, the tenure crunch encourages young faculty members to produce monographs that the report calls "articles on steroids," transforming what could be fine scholarly essays into full-length books that may reach a few hundred readers, if that.[18]

The pressure to publish more has not, however, led to a reduction in the professoriate's other duties. As a result, many full-time faculty members are encountering a serious speed-up. Even as the academic reward system mandates greater attention to research, the professoriate's instructional and administrative workloads are also increasing. The growing public concern about accountability and student outcomes, for example, has encouraged many institutions to schedule more meetings, require more paperwork, and impose more evaluations. Moreover, as the percentage of tenured and tenure-track faculty members shrinks, those who remain find that they must handle ever more administrative duties, especially in the hiring and supervision of the growing numbers of part-time and other contingent instructors who now account for more than two-thirds of the nation's teaching staff. For conscientious faculty citizens, participation in institutional governance can be quite onerous, as the following plaint reveals:

> I spend 30 to 40 hours a month in service roles in assignments and meetings for university curriculum councils, a college diversity committee, a subcommittee that reviews course proposals and media plans for a general education program, faculty council meetings, undergraduate faculty meetings and now strategic plan meetings and accreditation meetings.[19]

Mentoring PhD candidates and junior faculty members is also time-consuming. A colleague at a research center with me several years ago spent the entire first month of his residency writing letters of recommendation for his graduate students. Nationally ranked scholars have the additional burden of service to their discipline in the form of reviewing manuscripts, fellowship applications, and other institutions' candidates for tenure and promotion. Technology, as we shall see, has also added to the professoriate's burdens. Finally, teaching loads have risen—not necessarily for all faculty members, but they have rarely declined. At one-third of the departments that Sheila Slaughter and Gary Rhoades studied in the late 1990s, administrative demands for "instructional productivity"—in other words, larger numbers of students—brought bigger classes and more of them.[20]

It is no wonder, then, that academics at every level are feeling stressed. "Formerly our role was to produce top quality research and graduate education, and to do a reasonable job of teaching," the chair of a science department explained to Slaughter and Rhoades.

> Now [the dean's] told us to return [*sic*] undergraduates at a certain rate, to be diverse, to use technology in teaching, to be innovative, to do outreach in the community, and to keep doing the research and graduate education. All with no new resources.[21]

Similar complaints abound, and it's not as if the nation's academics had been loafing. By the early 1970s faculty members were putting in some fifty hours a week, with professors at the University of California working sixty. In 1988–89, according to another survey, the average college professor was spending fifty-five hours a week on the job.[22] Junior people were particularly burdened. Stanford's former president described one beginning assistant professor who worked seventy to seventy-five hours a week, putting in anywhere from seven to eleven hours preparing each lecture.[23] Similarly, the three hundred faculty members whom William Tierney and Estela Bensimon interviewed in 1992 were unanimous in reporting that they worked most of the time. "I don't know if I am a distance runner, biker and swimmer," one respondent grumbled.

> I feel like I'm asked to do everything at once and all the time. At work I had one job, one task, and maybe one on the drawing boards. Here, you have one project going, one in planning, one or two you're writing grants for, and the constant submission/revision of articles. Then there are the students. My graduate students line up outside the door, the undergraduates want their exams back, and somebody's always in crisis. And then there's the service side where you're asked to sit on committees. Who can do all this? Whoever thinks faculty life is the leisurely pursuit of knowledge should follow me around for a while.[24]

Tenure in an Era of Higher Expectations

The situation is particularly stressful for the men and women on the tenure ladder—especially since, thanks to what one authority calls the "academic rachet," they face much heavier demands for scholarly productivity than their predecessors.[25] Whatever the field, the expectations have been increased. By the mid-1990s, a top-tier university like Stanford was requiring its scientists to have 50 percent more funding than they had received in the early 1980s. Junior faculty at Emory University's Medical School, to take another example, must now get two grants in order to receive tenure. Moreover, at least at the more prestigious schools, tenure became harder to get. At Stanford, where half of the junior people in science and engineering won permanent appointments in the 1960s, by the 1990s that figure had dropped to between one-third and one-fourth. And all of this at a time when grants had become so competitive that even major scientists did not always get funded.[26]

A similar situation prevails in the humanities and social sciences. An MLA task force created in 2004 to study the rising requirements for tenure discovered that

> over 62% of all departments report that publication has increased in importance in tenure decisions over the last ten years. The percentage of departments ranking scholarship of primary importance (over teaching) has more than doubled since the last comparable survey . . . in 1968: from 35.4% to 75.7%.[27]

Moreover, that scholarship had to be substantial. The "tenure monograph" was obligatory, of course, but in addition to that "gold standard," nearly a third of all the departments surveyed reported that they expected candidates to exhibit "progress toward the completion of a second book."[28]

Unfortunately, the ramping up of publication requirements coincided with cutbacks inside the world of academic publishing that made it harder for junior faculty members to find outlets for the monographs upon which their academic careers depended. The financial crunch that afflicted their home institutions hit university presses hard. Not only did the schools that supported them reduce their subsidies, but they also expected those presses to pay more attention to their bottom lines. As a result, esoteric scholarship in fields like medieval studies or literature in languages other than English lost out to more profitable ventures like cookbooks and the serious trade books that mainstream commercial houses no longer wanted to publish. University presses were, it is true, still producing large numbers of titles (more than ten thousand in 2005), but some also began to prune their lists. Cambridge University Press stopped publishing in the field of French studies, Northwestern cancelled all translations, and Stanford curtailed its publications in the humanities. To make matters worse, prices for scholarly works rose—from an average of $29 for a hardcover volume in the humanities in 1986 to $51 in 2004 (an increase of 77 percent).[29]

At the same time, college and university libraries, which have long been the main market for most academic books, were also cutting back. No longer did they place automatic orders for everything that a major university press put out, and instead of purchasing 600–1,000 copies of the initial print run for a work of scholarship, they were now buying 250. Their budgets had shrunk or, if they had not, a much larger percentage of those budgets was being absorbed by the astronomical increases in the cost of scientific and technical periodicals, subscriptions to which ran into thousands of dollars a year—$2,845 for an average chemistry journal and $2,538 for a physics one. In 1980, the University of California library system spent 65 percent of its acquisitions budget for books and 35 percent for journals. By 2000, only 20 percent was going to books, with 80 percent to periodicals.[30] To a certain extent, that problem was the result of what the University of Chicago sociologist Andrew Abbott called " 'the crisis of abundance'—too many scholars, too much scholarly output." Journals proliferated in part because all that research required an outlet, but also because hosting such a publication was considered a mark of institutional prestige.[31]

Libraries were also spending considerable sums on technology, as was the rest of academe. Here, too, junior faculty members in pursuit of tenure were receiving mixed signals. Instructional technology was initially viewed by many academic leaders as the panacea for their financial problems. To a certain extent, the academy's romance with the computer stemmed from its growing corporatization. "Colleges and universities," the former president of the University of Michigan insisted,

> must learn an important lesson from the business community: investment in robust information technology represents the stakes for survival in the age of knowledge. If you are not willing to invest in this technology, then you may as well accept being confined to a backwater in the knowledge economy, if you survive at all.[32]

Once they figured out how to deliver courses over the Internet, many administrators believed, the efficiency of their operations would soar, their personnel expenditures would fall, and they would be able to tout their institutions as leading the way into the twenty-first century. The former president of MIT actually claimed that the new technologies would somehow make higher education less impersonal.[33]

Such, at least, was the rhetoric, though the reality was somewhat different. Computers and the software and technicians to run them were expensive and prone to obsolescence. (According to one recent study, revamping a major university system's information management operation could run anywhere from $50 million to $100 million.)[34] Nor, with some exceptions, did students flock to online classes.[35] Staffing raised serious questions. Who would design these courses and who would teach them? Would those tasks be assigned to regular faculty members or would they be farmed out to contingent labor? What about compensation? Would the men and women involved in creating these courses get extra pay or would their efforts in the area be considered part of their normal workload? And how would quality be maintained? Moreover, if administrators asserted control over the content of this technology, they would be chipping away at the faculty's instructional responsibilities—with all the implications for shared governance and academic freedom that such an undertaking implied. Finally, there was the perplexing matter of intellectual property: who would own the pedagogical materials that were created? Though universities could technically claim to possess the fruits of their faculties' labor, they had rarely done so, following the traditional practice of letting professors reap what profits they could from their monographs and textbooks. But an online course that could be licensed and sold to other users might have the same commercial potential as a new drug or computer code. Moreover, since more institutional resources went into the creation of such a course than into the writing of a monograph, the university could legitimately claim to own it, especially if the men and women who produced such materials were doing it at the school's behest under the terms of a "work for hire" contract.[36]

Nonetheless, despite these problems, computers did have their uses in the classroom, even if they did not fulfill the utopian fantasies of their early proponents. At the same time, however, many of the junior faculty members who were incorporating the new media into their teaching found it hard to figure out exactly how that work—and it was work—would help them get tenure. After all, the older professors who were evaluating these people often had little experience with technology and were thus unable to assess its scholarly value. As one tenure candidate explained, the faculty members on his committee viewed his creation of a set of online teaching materials as "not being a research project—it counts sort of like service, but it's also sort of a hobby." In other words, even as their institutions were exhorting them to use the new technologies in their classes, junior faculty members were also being advised by their mentors to avoid such "risky" ventures and "stick to traditional academic activities like publishing journal articles."[37]

Not only was technology hard to evaluate, but so, too, was teaching. And since teaching was what constituted the bulk of most nontenured people's work, the haziness about its assessment constituted the most confusing element in a young academic's career. Good teaching may, in fact, be such an elusive practice that it can never be precisely measured. Classroom visits aside, the most common instruments for evaluating someone's pedagogy leave much to be desired. Student questionnaires, for example, though useful for showing how well professors communicate and how fairly they grade, cannot assess a course's intellectual quality or whether it is up-to-date. Moreover, there is no clear correlation between high ratings and student learning.[38] Teaching portfolios and similar types of evidence impose substantial burdens on their creators as well as on the faculty members and administrators who must assess them. Furthermore, the haphazard attention to pedagogy during the socialization process by which most younger academics acclimate to their institutions rarely offers much help. According to Tierney and Bensimon, the frustrating lesson that gets imparted "is that teaching is not that important; if it were, there would be more discussions about what constitutes good teaching."[39]

No doubt much of that frustration has to do with the academy's essentially hypocritical insistence on the importance of teaching in the face of its overwhelming preoccupation with research. As the following online response to a *Chronicle of Higher Education* article about the increase in assessment reveals, even if it was possible to identify the elements of good teaching, its subordination to research can only produce cynicism about its value.

> I'm a faculty member at a "teaching institution," where teaching is officially stated to be the most important factor in faculty review. In fact, as everybody knows, research is the only criterion that matters. Why spend a lot of time implementing the results of assessments—that is, worrying about teaching—when that time could go into research?[40]

Yet teaching does matter. Student evaluations do count, especially since every candidate for tenure is expected to be above average, unless, as one unfortunate young professor learned, her exceptionally high teaching scores showed that she was spending too much time on it.[41] Damned if one does, damned if one doesn't. No wonder junior faculty members feel so much stress.

Ironically, however, even though the criteria for tenure keep rising, the rate at which it gets awarded remains the same. It is surprisingly high—except, of course, at places such as Harvard or Berkeley, where untenured people rarely expect to stay on. Sometimes, it is true, an ambitious institution will seek to boost its standing by raising the bar on its junior faculty members. This is what happened recently at Baylor, where the administration decided to transform the school into a major research university and unilaterally imposed higher standards for tenure. The denial rate shot up from about 10 percent to 40 percent.[42] At most colleges and universities, however, more than 90 percent of the applicants for tenure receive it, a percentage that has held steady for years. This seems to be the case no matter what the discipline or type of institution. At the Penn State university system, to take one example, an internal survey reported "that the approval percentage at the university level has almost always been over 90 percent," while a similar study done in 2003 by the American Historical Association revealed a 94 percent success rate for historians at all institutions, with a 92.3 percent rate at doctoral and research universities.[43]

Reassuring as such figures are, they tell only part of the story, for as the MLA discovered, at least 20 percent of the individuals who were hired to tenure track positions left them before coming up for review.[44] Did they anticipate denial, or did they find the process so "dehumanizing," as one of Tierney and Bensimon's respondents characterized it, that they simply dropped out? For many women, their own biology created additional obstacles. The time period during which they were striving for tenure usually coincided with their prime childbearing years. Even at schools that boasted family-friendly policies, raising children while meeting the intense pressures for productivity "during the 'make or break,' assistant-professor years," the head of Berkeley law school's Center for Economics and Family Security explained, "frightens some top scholars away from a tenure-track job and defeats others who attempt it."[45]

But what was most disheartening about the MLA's survey was its discovery that even with the high rate of success that tenure-track faculty members encountered, those successful candidates comprised only about 35 percent of the men and women who received PhDs in the fields the organization represented. Studies from other disciplines revealed similar statistics: "fewer than 40% of the PhD recipients who make up the pool of applicants for tenure-track positions obtain such positions and go through the tenure process at the institutions where they are initially hired." Traditional academic jobs had disappeared.[46]

The Casualization of Academic Labor

It had been a gradual process, this hemorrhaging of tenure-track positions. It started in the late 1960s, when the academy began to confront the prospect that the seemingly unlimited growth of the previous decade was coming to an end. Actually, some of the practices that were to undermine the academic profession had begun even earlier. The enormous expansion of American higher education in the years after World War II had been accompanied by an even greater expansion of graduate training. Spurred by fears that there would not be enough faculty members to handle the anticipated flood of baby-boom undergraduates, American universities, which had granted fewer than ten thousand PhDs in 1960, awarded three times that many in 1970, while the number of institutions offering the doctorate grew from 180 to 250.[47] Federal and foundation subsidies (not to mention the military draft during the Vietnam War) fed this process, enticing into academe many young men and women who otherwise might have opted for different careers.*

Despite some concern that the expansion of doctoral programs might get out of control, many universities admitted increasing numbers of graduate students; they could, they discovered, use them to handle their overflowing classrooms. Thus, in part to provide their PhD and MA candidates with financial aid as well as teaching experience, their departments put them to work. As a result, by the early 1960s, 40 percent of the lower-level courses at Berkeley and Michigan were being taught by graduate instructors. Soon such teaching fellowships became a staple of university life as teaching assistants took over more and more introductory courses, especially in the humanities and social sciences. At the same time, academic scientists came to rely ever more heavily on doctoral candidates to carry out their research.[48]

But within a few years the jobs that these graduate students expected to fill began to disappear. The demographics were discouraging. The baby boom

* Such was the case with this author, who had planned to become a high school teacher and only decided to go for a PhD when I was nominated for and received a Woodrow Wilson Fellowship.

that had packed so many classrooms with eighteen-to-twenty-four-year-olds was coming to an end, and although enrollments were still expected to rise during the 1970s, few academic leaders counted on them doing so at a rate that could absorb the growing horde of newly minted PhDs. Nor could those job candidates take over the positions of the college teachers who retired, for there were relatively few such individuals. The massive expansion of the nation's faculties during the boom years had created a youthful cohort of tenured people who would not stop working for decades. But even when senior professors did leave, their institutions did not replace them. Plunged into uncertainty by the fiscal crisis of the late 1960s, many schools cut back on hiring tenure-track faculty members.[49] Administrators did not want to lock themselves into long-term commitments to particular fields of study at a time when course enrollments were fluctuating and students were turning away from the traditional liberal arts. As a result, instead of having department chairs lined up seeking interviews with job candidates at the professional association meetings, as had been the case during the late 1950s and early 1960s, aspiring academics suddenly found themselves in a Darwinian struggle for employment.[50]

The awareness that there were not enough jobs to go around surfaced for the first time at the MLA's 1968–69 annual meeting, where shell-shocked candidates wandered the halls in despair. People with prestigious degrees suffered along with the products of lower-tier schools. In 1973, for example, of the fifty-five graduate students and new PhDs from the Berkeley English department looking for jobs, only twenty-four found them. And the situation only got worse. While 68 percent of all new PhDs found tenure-track jobs in 1970, only 51 percent did so in 1980, although enrollments had actually risen 41 percent. To take another example, when the Berkeley sociology department advertised two openings in the late 1970s, more than 300 people applied.[51]

Despite these troubling statistics and the tens of thousands of dollars of debt that PhD recipients amassed, graduate school enrollments held up.* Few institutions wanted to forgo the prestige that a doctoral program conferred or abandon their reliance on low-cost teaching fellows.[52] Moreover, there was reputed to be a light at the end of the tunnel. According to an important 1989 study of the academic job market by William G. Bowen, the former president of Princeton, the tenured professors who had been hired during

* By 2004, some 60 percent of all PhDs had taken out an average of nearly $50,000 in loans (Paul D. Thacker, "PhD's in Debt," *Inside Higher Education*, December 8, 2006).

the 1960s and early 1970s were aging and would soon need to be replaced. By the 1990s, PhDs would again be in demand; by 1997, Bowen predicted, "there will be only seven candidates for every ten positions" in the humanities and social sciences. But Bowen had not reckoned with the growing tendency to replace full-time tenure-track positions with contingent ones; he had, in fact, explicitly eliminated adjuncts from his study. As of the mid-1990s, America's colleges and universities were filling only one-third of the tenure lines vacated by retiring professors. Between 1994–95 and 1999–2000, to take an even more striking example, while student enrollments grew by 35,000 in the California State University system, only one full-time tenure-track faculty member was appointed. All the system's other teaching assignments went to part-timers or people on temporary contracts.[53]

Those positions were the wave of the future. Ostensibly created as stop-gap measures designed to give an institution the flexibility it claimed to need during a time of flux, these off-the-ladder appointments came to account for ever higher percentages of the academic workforce. Even at the start of this transformation, it was clear that, as a department chair explained in 1973, "the word 'flexibility' has come to have one meaning: the ability to reduce my staff or my funds." It was, Judith M. Gappa and David W. Leslie pointed out in a widely cited 1993 study of part-time academics, "a frequently used euphemism for saving money."[54] For all the rhetoric about needing to stay on top of current trends, everybody knew that the low wages and lack of security that characterized these contingent faculty positions constituted their main attraction—at least for the colleges and universities that hired such people.

Part-time instructors were not a new phenomenon. Some institutions had been relying on adjuncts for years. Community colleges, for example, had long been staffing their classes with moonlighting high school teachers or professionals in fields like real estate, accounting, and engineering who taught vocationally oriented courses in their areas of expertise and who would have been too expensive to hire on a full-time basis. And, as we have already seen, graduate students performed a similar function at research universities. The fiscal crunch of the 1970s encouraged other types of institutions to recruit more adjuncts; as a result, by the end of the decade part-timers had climbed from 24 to 33.9 percent of the professoriate.[55] But even as the crisis ebbed, the push to hire ever more contingent instructors continued. As the table below shows, by 2007 nearly 70 percent of all faculty positions were either part-time or off the tenure track.[56]

	1975	1989	1995	2007
Tenured	36.5	33.1	30.6	21.3
Tenure-track	20.3	13.7	11.8	9.9
Full-time non-tenure-track	13.0	16.9	16.7	18.5
Part-time	30.2	36.4	40.9	50.3

Distressing as these figures are, they are in accord with the broader trend toward a more contingent labor force throughout American society. Think of Wal-Mart, think of McDonald's, and think of all the downsized autoworkers whose jobs once offered them entrée into a middle-class style of life now working as waiters and telemarketers. Actually, academics have it even worse. Only about one-fifth of the nation's labor force is part-time. As one adjunct activist noted,

> The casualization of the faculty workforce . . . represents one of the few recent instances in the United States economy (another is taxi driving) where an entire occupation has been converted from permanent career status to temporary, often part-time status in the space of a single generation of workers.[57]

Budgetary concerns drove this transformation. By the 1970s, as state legislatures started to pull back and no longer automatically increased their appropriations for higher education, many institutions found themselves in a precarious situation. Though their enrollments continued to grow, they could not be certain of sufficient funding in time to mount a search for new full-time faculty members. Instead, they resorted to the last-minute hiring of adjuncts and other temporary instructors to staff their classes. Those contingent faculty members were "the buffer," one department chair explained. "They take care of the budget surges and shortages."[58] However, since this pattern repeated itself year after year and many, if not most, part-timers and non-tenure-track instructors were rehired to teach the same courses every semester, it was obvious that relying on contingent labor had become something more than a short-term solution.

Much of this transformation was, it must be noted, inadvertent. In a recent study of contingent faculty at ten major research universities, John Cross and Edie Goldenberg, the dean and associate dean of the University of Michigan's College of Literature, Science, and the Arts, admitted that

> we never anticipated the significant increase over time in employment of part-time and full-time non-tenure-track instructors in our own college. Our office was entrusted with academic appointment policy, and yet we observed substantial growth in a type of appointment that we never consciously decided to make. The expanding role of non-tenure-track instructors was taking place under our noses but without our being fully aware of it. We were also surprised to learn about some of the employment circumstances of lecturers in our college that were established without our participation.

Michigan was not unique; the same process was occurring everywhere in academe. Short-term solutions, such as an English department's decision to give its own PhDs who failed in that year's job market postdoctoral teaching positions, morphed into the creation of "a cadre of semipermanent NTT [non-tenure-track] English instructors holding PhDs from their own institution."[59] Some folks tried to rationalize the situation, claiming that relying on adjuncts was the best way to ensure access "to a greater segment of society. Without part-time faculty, we would still be an elite organization. If you want mass education and modern access, the use of part-time faculty is the model for how to do it."[60] However, since the use of non-tenure-track instructors had spread to elite as well as nonelite, institutions, it was clear that, with the possible exception of small liberal arts colleges outside of metropolitan areas, all the nation's faculties were being restructured.

Still, while financial considerations certainly fueled this phenomenon, there were legitimate educational reasons for the employment of at least some kinds of adjuncts. High school teachers, for example, were in demand to staff the remedial classes that many institutions, community colleges in particular, increasingly had to offer. It was also customary for many of those schools to hire outside practitioners to teach courses in business, engineering, and other vocational fields. Most of these people held full-time jobs elsewhere and taught either for their own personal satisfaction or else as a community service or professional obligation—as some Silicon Valley engineers did—to ensure that their companies would benefit from a pool of well-trained future workers. They did not need the money and, in any event, probably would not have taken a full-time academic position that normally paid so much less than what they were already earning in their off-campus jobs.[61] Similarly, more well-endowed institutions sometimes enriched their curricula by luring major writers, artists, and former politicians onto their campuses with lucrative part-time teaching deals or visiting professorships.

But what has become increasingly more common (and, as we shall see, more problematic) is the employment of fully qualified academic professionals to teach standard liberal arts courses on a part-time or temporary basis. Some departments use more of these contingent instructors than others, especially for the required introductory general education courses in foreign languages, math, and freshman composition that few regular faculty members want to teach. At one school that Gappa and Leslie studied, adjuncts were responsible for 75 percent of the introductory math courses and 25 percent of the higher-level ones. To take an even more extreme case, as of 1999 only 7 percent of all freshman writing classes were being taught by tenured and tenure-track professors. And, according to the NYU Italian department's Web site, no regular faculty members were handling any of its language classes. English composition and the modern languages may well be the worst offenders, no doubt because of the oversupply of unemployed PhDs in their fields. But the fine arts are another area where part-timers do much of the teaching (some 40 percent nationwide)—again because educational institutions can take advantage of the large pool of artists and musicians who cannot earn a living from their creative work.[62]

In point of fact, however, the casualization of academic labor is affecting almost every field of study. Even scientists, who usually had been able to find jobs outside the academy, are feeling the pinch. In physics, the *Chronicle of Higher Education* reported in 2007, nearly 70 percent of newly minted PhDs took temporary postdoctoral positions, whereas only 43 percent did so in 2000. The situation does not look much better for people in a hot area like biomedicine, where the number of tenured and tenure-track positions has not increased in the past two decades even as the number of doctorates granted has nearly doubled.[63] Another indication of how pervasive contingent employment has become is the fact that the average age at which people receive doctorates is thirty-three, while that at which successful candidates land their first tenure-track job is thirty-nine.[64]

Perhaps this situation would not be so distressing if the holders of these contingent faculty appointments did not want regular academic employment. But, except for retirees, outside experts with other jobs, and the handful of freelancers who welcomed the flexibility of part-time teaching, large numbers of the men and women who worked on a contingent basis did so because they had to. It was the only way they could remain within the academy. Moreover, despite the odds, many continued to hope for a tenure-track appointment. In a 1980 survey, 60 percent of the adjuncts in the California State University system indicated that they would like a regular academic position.[65] They were, after all, highly educated, middle-class professionals who had always done well in school and who had not anticipated the serious decline in status that confronted them once they received their degrees. "We've been the ones to get the fellowships and the scholarships and the TAs [teaching assistantships]," one unsuccessful job candidate explained in the mid-1980s, "Without recognizing it, when we hear that the job market is bad, we remember that some people get jobs and we think, 'Well, I will, too.' "[66] But, of course, they don't. One critic actually claims that the acquisition of a PhD signals the end, not the beginning, of someone's academic career, since that person is no longer eligible for the teaching fellowships that supported her through graduate school. And it is often the case that working on a part-time or temporary basis usually ensures that someone will never find a traditional faculty job, since such people are assumed to be losers—"damaged goods," one adjunct activist calls them. Moreover, the longer these academics stay off the tenure track, the harder it is for them to do research and the easier it is to assume that they are no longer as au courant with their fields as someone fresh out of graduate school.[67]

Perhaps the most striking characteristic of academia's contingent labor force is its gender composition. In 1988, 58 percent of all adjuncts were men, while 42 percent were women, though the ratio for full-timers was 73 percent to 27. As of the late 1990s, women constituted 67 percent of the part-timers in the humanities and only 33 percent of the full-time faculty, while the reverse was true for men. Some of this discrepancy can be attributed to the fields that women gravitate toward—literature and the fine arts in particular. But it is also hard to deny that some discrimination—even if not overt—also plays a role. Sidelined in many instances by a lack of geographical mobility and the still widespread assumption that they do not want regular academic positions because of their family responsibilities, many part-time and non-tenure-track female teachers are particularly dissatisfied with their situation. According to a 1981 study of twenty-two Ohio institutions, these women viewed their positions as "an unhappy substitute for regular full-time employment." They felt hobbled by what one explained were assumptions "that we should think ourselves lucky to get the work [at ridiculous wages in view of our educations]—after all, if we weren't teaching part-time, we would just be housewives anyway." That assumption—"the marriage plot," one scholar calls it—condemns many highly qualified academics to part-time employment.[68]

Of course, not every adjunct or off-the-ladder instructor resents his or her situation. Most, after all, love their work and gain enormous satisfaction from their teaching. In addition, because of the diversity of the American system of higher education, the circumstances under which these men and women labor vary widely, though low pay and a lack of security are common. But such statements are mainly educated guesses, for we know surprisingly little about these teachers. We don't even know how many there are. In fact, unless there is a union, record keeping with regard to contingent faculty members is so inadequate that well-informed observers concede they lack reliable figures and could be undercounting the ranks of part-time and temporary college and university teachers by as much as several hundred thousand.[69] As a result, information about contingent faculty members and what they do often relies heavily on anecdotal evidence—the result, perhaps, of that cohort's overrepresentation among writing instructors, whose field encourages the publication of personal narratives.[70] Understandably, these accounts tend to highlight the dissatisfactions of the underemployed and underpaid, rather than the experiences of happier campers.

My own experiences off the ladder, though far from wretched, were not atypical. I taught on a contingent basis for nearly fifteen years after I got my PhD in the mid-1970s. For much of that time I did not look for a tenure-track job because I was in the process of raising children and switching fields. Instead, I worked as a full-time off-the-ladder instructor at two Ivy League universities—with benefits, an almost adequate salary, a low teaching load, a nice office, and even, at one school, the prospect of promotion into a permanent, albeit irregular, position, plus a letterhead that was prestigious enough to help me secure a tenure-track job. I also taught a few graduate and undergraduate courses as an adjunct in New York City, sometimes for real money, sometimes for pocket change. Admittedly, those part-time jobs provided no benefits, but since I was on my husband's health plan, that was not a problem. Even so, despite my relatively cushy situation, at no point could I have supported my family on what I made. Like most contingent faculty members, I was one of "those persons who," as Marc Bousquet points out, "are in a financial position to accept compensation below the living wage."[71]

For contingent faculty members without other sources of income or gainfully employed partners, in particular for adjuncts who must cobble together several gigs in order to get by, the situation is grim. Part-time teaching positions pay very badly, sometimes as low as $1,200 for a three-credit course. The average, as of the 2006–7 academic year, is $2,758 a course, which, given the amount of preparation required, comes out to not much more than $10 an hour, not counting the time spent commuting. Altogether, part-timers earn an average of $12,100 a year from their teaching. Nearly a third of them work at more than one school, while 73 percent have some kind of outside employment. Some rely on food stamps. Ironically, the compensation is sometimes higher on rural campuses, where the cost of living is low, than in the more expensive urban areas with their larger pools of underemployed academics. Adjuncts at the City University of New York, for example, make an average of $10,000 a year from their teaching. One Tennessee part-timer taught ten courses during the academic year 2007–8 and earned $15,210. "Literally, I could quit my job," she explained, "and get a job at the local Wal-Mart full time and make more money and have benefits." At the high end, Keith Hoeller, the organizer of the Washington Part-Time Faculty Association, teaches between eight and ten courses a year in the Seattle area for about $35,000 before taxes.[72] Nor, unless they are unionized, do part-timers ordinarily receive merit or cost-of-living raises, benefits, or unemployment compensation. Moreover, few institutions make a financial distinction with regard to credentials; a PhD with prolific publications will receive the same flat rate as a beginning MA student. The pay is so bad, in fact, that many people who began adjuncting to support themselves during graduate school could not finish their degrees.[73]

Such conditions give rise to the notorious "freeway flyers," the men and women who teach at several different institutions over the course of a semester. The stress these people can experience is, to put it mildly, considerable. "One year I taught at five colleges simultaneously," explained a man who was still hoping that one of those schools would give him a full-time job.

> Thursdays I started at the university for an 8 A.M. class. Then I went [across town] for a 9:45 A.M. class, which went to 11 A.M., then to [a nearby institution] for mid afternoon. [Finally, I returned] to the university for an evening extension class. I finished teaching at 9 P.M. I think I taught well. I never sacrificed the classroom. The colleges lost the out-of-class interaction. It really compromised my personal life. But it would be too embarrassing to be unprepared for class.[74]

Another adjunct, a self-described "artist who does academic piecework to survive," recounts similar experiences when she taught at as many as four different colleges in one semester. Not only was there a time-consuming (and uncompensated) commute, but she also had to juggle each school's different academic calendar and paperwork requirements.[75] Another former part-timer recalls the inconvenience of having to adjust his lectures for the different lengths of the class periods at the three schools where he was teaching.[76] For one Los Angeles instructor, the commute was the killer.

> During the fall term I was driving to three places. One is one and a half hours to the north, a little more than sixty miles from here. The second is just twenty miles from here and the third is seventy-five miles from here. Sometimes I could go from one to the other, but, in general, I was driving at least forty and frequently eighty miles a day. . . . I've hardly met any of my colleagues because I drive to a place, park, and run up to teach and then get back in the car and drive to some place else and run up to teach. I can't publish because half of my time is spent driving from one place to the other.[77]

Compounding their difficulties were the other disadvantages part-timers faced: the lack of offices, telephones, mailboxes, coat hooks, supplies, or access to photocopying and computers. One-third of the adjuncts in the CUNY system, for example, had no office; two-thirds had no computer.[78] Horror stories abound, but the bottom line here is that the poor working conditions of part-time faculty members make it hard for them to teach as effectively as they could. For the men and women who handle freshman composition courses, in particular, the lack of a private office militates against their ability to offer the one-on-one instruction their writing students need.

Nor do part-timers and temporary instructors find it easy to do the research that might land them a better job. Some, in fact, do not even have library privileges. Moreover, unlike their tenure-track colleagues, contingent faculty members rarely get opportunities for professional development, although they often have the same training and commitment to scholarship. To begin with, especially if they must commute to several different institutions, their teaching loads are too heavy to allow them to do any research. "You teach part-time here at the expense of research," one adjunct complained as he bemoaned the opportunities he had to forgo.

> I don't have time for research or even to prepare properly for class. I know I've devoted too much energy to teaching and should have done more research. I deeply regret this choice, but [I] had no alternative at my age and with my family commitments. I needed to provide a stable income.[79]

Rarely do contingent faculty members get sabbaticals or travel money to give papers at scholarly conferences and do the networking that allows them to keep up in their fields. The instability of their employment is a further impediment. "I can't begin any research that will extend beyond a year or two," one contingent instructor explained, "because I don't know where I will be to finish it up. Everything gets foreshortened into these six month segments and you don't plan on anything more than six months ahead of time."[80]

An even more serious problem—and one that surfaces in every survey of contingent faculty members—is the insecurity of their employment. Part-timers are usually hired a semester at a time and are often called in at the last minute after a cursory local search that relied on personal contacts rather than formal peer-review procedures.[81] According to one source, fewer than half of these people get as much as six weeks notice of their teaching assignment, a practice that not only generates anxiety but also makes it hard for part-timers to plan courses properly and order books. "For seventeen years," one community college instructor commented, "I have worked never knowing whether I had a job or not until the day or so before the classes started. I wish there were a better way to arrange things."[82] Whether administrators consciously create that insecurity in order to procure a more expendable and docile workforce, as some critics of the practice believe, or whether it stems from inadvertence and poor planning on the part of the harried and often inexperienced department chairs who hire most of their schools' part-timers, these last-minute appointments are, for the most part, completely unnecessary. Especially in those departments that use large numbers of contingent faculty members in courses such as freshman composition and elementary calculus, adjuncts and off-the-ladder instructors are almost always rehired on a regular basis. Nearly half the part-timers Gappa and Leslie surveyed had taught more than four years; some had spent more than twenty years in the same position.[83]

Despite the casual and, for many, demeaning process through which these teachers are appointed and reappointed, unless they turn out to be a disaster (a not uncommon phenomenon, given how perfunctorily they were hired), they can count on fairly automatic renewals as long as their course enrollments hold up.[84] Rarely do their departments evaluate their performance. After all, what already overworked chairs or professors have the time to assess the teaching of perhaps dozens of adjuncts and short-term instructors? As a result, inertia ensures that many of these contingent academics keep their jobs indefinitely. Union contracts and state laws against capricious dismissals of long-term employees protect some of them; others remain simply because it would be too much of a hassle to dispose of them. "For all intents and purposes," a high-level administrator at a research university explained, "general faculty (those without tenure) are tenured. It's hard to let them go. If you have been reappointed twice, you have the expectation of continuing employment." Moreover, their institutions depend upon them. "We've never tried to get rid of general faculty members. To get rid of them, we'd have to eliminate the entire program."[85]

Nonetheless, de facto tenure is not real tenure. And the insecurity that plagues off-the-ladder appointees, the fact that their institutions will make no formal long-term commitments to them, can be demoralizing in the extreme. It makes "the work . . . very alienating because we are all disposable, like Kleenex," one adjunct explained. "We are basically in the same position as migrant workers," another noted. "There is a lot of wasted energy and unnecessary expense in trying to stay alive with part-time teaching."[86] And a not inconsiderable psychic cost.

Contingent faculty members get no respect. Almost everything about their appointments and their working conditions shrieks second class. And, as members of a profession where status is at the heart of the system, their lack of it turns out to be one of the most debilitating characteristics of their marginalized careers. They are, as the title of Gappa and Leslie's book so tellingly puts it, "the invisible faculty." Their institutions do not even bother to count them. "When departments hire NTT [non-tenure-track] people, they can throw any title at them they want," one administrator explained, "I don't include them in my tables." Nor, in many cases, do their supposed colleagues on the tenure track acknowledge their presence. "Who are these people?" a senior professor at Yale was said to have asked when informed that a third of his school's undergraduate instruction was in their hands.[87] As one longtime adjunct noted, his regular faculty colleagues treated him "like the ghost that goes between people, they see you, they are cordial, but you don't really count."[88] Such perceptions were common. "I don't even think they know who I am," another part-timer complained. "I'm just someone filling a hole, and they don't know about my experiences; they don't know about my ideas. . . . [T]hey don't care who I am; they just want someone in there teaching classes."[89] In many cases, either because they work at several campuses or else teach in the evening or at other unpopular hours, part-timers never even encounter other faculty members.[90]

What these contingent instructors resent above all is the often overtly expressed opinion that because they are not on the academic ladder, they are therefore inferior. Adjuncts, as the vice president of a large community college told a group of them, "should realize that you are not considered faculty, or even people. You are units of flexibility."[91] The accounts of contingent life abound with stories of the indignities suffered at the hands of regular faculty members. One adjunct, for example, was at an English conference where her comments

> as a member of a group amicably discussing student writing . . . were cordially received. In the course of the conversation, however, my part-time status was revealed. In effect, the group moved away from me, and, for the rest of the conference, they not only ignored me but would not even establish eye contact.[92]

An adjunct who taught composition at Ohio State recalls a similar "feeling of having no meaningful affiliation with the department as a whole but only with the other lecturers . . . [W]hen we weren't ignored, we were treated with condescension."[93]

Not surprisingly, part-timers and temporary instructors rarely, if ever, participate in faculty governance. Administrations, like that at Rensselaer Polytechnic Institute, which abolished its faculty senate because it included adjuncts, are often loath to give them a voice.[94] Nor are many tenured and tenure-track professors eager to entrust their off-the-ladder colleagues with administrative responsibilities; they do not want to let these people vote on the grounds that their connection to the institution is too tenuous. Especially in departments with large numbers of contingent employees, traditional faculty members fear being outvoted by people who, one senior professor emphasized, "aren't held accountable the way we are."[95] Equally unfortunate is the fact that in many cases, adjuncts and off-the-ladder appointees have little autonomy in their classrooms. Unlike regular faculty members, they can rarely choose what to teach. Almost invariably they are assigned sections of their department's introductory courses—over and over and over again, at the worst hours in the worst classrooms. Nor can they teach the way they want to. In order to maintain standards, many departments impose uniform syllabi and textbooks on the courses they assign to adjuncts. While such a system can be helpful to beginners, many experienced teachers find those requirements demeaning, a symbolic statement that they cannot be trusted to do the right thing in their classrooms.[96]

These contingent faculty members are further plagued by what the adjunct organizer Joe Berry calls their "double-consciousness." As far as their students are concerned, these men and women are professors who, to maintain their professional identity and authority within the classroom, must behave as such. Thus, despite being seriously exploited on the job, they cannot "treat our students the way we are treated by our employers. If we did, little learning would take place and many students would exit the classroom." Worse yet, they must grapple with the "great contrast between the public perception of their status and the reality of their existence. The brittleness resulting from this state can cause contingent faculty to fear revelation of their true status to students for fear of losing respect and the ability to teach effectively."[97]

The Impact of Casualization on Student Learning and Academic Freedom

Given all the obstacles that contingent academics have to overcome, it seems obvious that their insecure situation and poor working conditions must have a negative impact on their students. That may well be so. But given how difficult it has been, despite its trendiness, to assess the educational progress of America's undergraduates, it must be admitted that we actually know very little about how effectively most adjuncts teach. At best, according to Cross and Goldenberg, the quality of these people's work is "an open question."[98] There does not seem to be any evidence that contingent instructors are any less competent in the classroom than their full-time, tenure-track peers.[99] Nonetheless, their lack of continuity may create educational problems. Some recent research, for example, reveals lower student retention rates for part-timers than for other teachers. After all, "adjuncts are often trying to patch together a living, running back and forth between three different campuses," the author of one such study explained. "If they don't have office hours and can't often be found on campus, their students are likely to become frustrated or disengaged with the course material."[100] In addition, some part-timers have admitted that their commutes and heavy teaching loads force them to cut corners. Thus, for example, they spend less time on class preparation and assign fewer essay exams. Moreover (and this is a common observation), because they realize that they must not offend their students if they want to be rehired, many adjuncts and short-term lecturers feel compelled to dumb down their courses and give high grades.[101]

Maureen Watson, however, was not one of them. She was an off-the-ladder instructor who was not afraid to fail the weak students in her math classes at Nicholls State University in Thibodaux, Louisiana. Perhaps she should have been, for on May 18, 2007, Watson was notified by her department head that she was being dismissed right away. The administration, which had been pressing the faculty to stop flunking so many students, gave Watson a number of flimsy excuses for its action, but it was clear that it was retaliating against her for refusing to compromise her academic standards. Though Watson had been teaching full-time at Nicholls for twelve years, she was not on the tenure track and was thus vulnerable to the capricious behavior of the school's administrators. In its report on the case, an AAUP investigating committee charged that firing Watson because of "her determination to grade according to her best professional assessment of the merits of student performance" not only violated her academic freedom but, in fact, "warranted not dismissal but commendation."[102]

It is clear that the Nicholls State administration's demand for easier grading—itself an incursion against the classroom autonomy (and thus the academic freedom) of its faculty—was designed to maintain enrollments in response to the cutthroat competition for warm bodies so characteristic of the twenty-first-century academy. Other schools elsewhere engaged in similar maneuvers to retain weak students—athletes in particular. Nor was the Nicholls administration's dismissal of Watson an unprecedented exercise in the arbitrary use of managerial authority over part-time and non-tenure-track instructors. Many other institutions treated their contingent faculty members in a similarly capricious way. Because those teachers have few rights to their jobs, they can be hired and fired at will, providing the "flexibility" that makes them so attractive to so many academic administrators. Except when protected by a state law, a union contract, or a strong campus faculty culture, adjuncts and temporary instructors can be dismissed for almost any reason (or no reason) without any advance notice or the ability to appeal. As the AAUP's general secretary, Gary Rhoades, points out, "in layoff actions, part-time faculty are accorded virtually no due-process rights." Completely at the mercy of their employers, they do not, in other words, have academic freedom.[103]

In fact, when we look at some of the more egregious violations of academic freedom that have occurred over the past few years, almost all of them involve contingent faculty members, most of whom were canned because they said something controversial in class. There's Douglas Giles, an adjunct instructor at Roosevelt University in Chicago, terminated and told by his chair in September 2005 that he would never be hired there again because he had allowed a discussion of Israel, Zionism, and Palestine in his world religions class.[104] There's Nicholas Winset, also an adjunct, teaching a course on financial accounting at Emmanuel College, ordered by his administration to discuss the recent Virginia Tech killings in his class and then fired the following day without a hearing because of student complaints about that class. Winset had apparently called the killer an "asshole" while giving his opinion that the murders did not constitute a national crisis for students but had been hyped by the media because so many of the victims were young white women.[105] There's Jeffrey Nielsen, a practicing Mormon, who had been teaching philosophy part-time for five years at Brigham Young University, let go by his department in June 2006 a few days after he published an op-ed piece in support of same-sex marriage.[106] There's Teresa Knudsen, who put in seventeen years as a contingent instructor at Spokane Community College, also dropped after writing an opinion article in a local paper—this one about the poor treatment of adjuncts. And finally, there's Steve Bitterman, a part-time history teacher at Southwestern Community College in Red Oak, Iowa, who explained to his Western civ class that one could view the Adam and Eve story as a myth. After some students and their parents complained, Southwestern's vice president called and, according to Bitterman, "told me I was supposed to teach history, not religion, and that my services would no longer be needed."[107] These people are not unique. There are similar cases elsewhere, though, since most such dismissals never reach the media or the AAUP, we will probably never know how many part-timers and short-term lecturers were fired because of what they said or wrote.

It is, of course, no surprise that contingent faculty members are so much more vulnerable than their tenured and tenure-track peers. "When push comes to shove," Knudsen told the *Chronicle of Higher Education*, "we do not have academic freedom. We can be fired for what we say or what we teach."[108] Tenured and tenure-track professors rarely suffer such blatant violations of academic freedom. As we have seen, they have usually lost their jobs either because they were squeaky wheels who antagonized their administrations or else, as happened with Ward Churchill, because outside political forces demanded that they go. Even at the height of the McCarthy era, no faculty members were punished for what they did in the classroom or wrote outside of it. Yet because they lack the professional privileges and due process protections of their tenure-track colleagues and because their schools have become so worried about maintaining their enrollments, part-timers and short-term instructors are seriously at risk for losing their jobs for the most trivial of reasons—as well as for organizing unions, grading too stiffly, or assigning too much work.[109] They are employed at will and can be dismissed on a whim. Their inability to invoke due process only reinforces their inferior status.

It also constrains them from expressing themselves freely in class. When student complaints can lead to unemployment, a vulnerable instructor will think twice before saying something that might upset a Christian fundamentalist or religious Zionist. Not only do many contingent faculty members hesitate to voice provocative opinions or deal with controversial subjects, but some have also admitted that the precarious nature of their employment has made them less willing to be innovative in their teaching. Composition teachers are especially at risk here: employing critical pedagogy and thus encouraging their students to question their own situations can open up their classrooms in intellectually productive ways, but it can also backfire. There is considerable irony here, for the rhetoric of "liberation" pervades the field of composition studies, even as so many of its practitioners quite self-consciously curtail their own freedom.[110] Of course, part-timers and short-term instructors are hardly the only academics to censor themselves in class. Especially during times of political or social stress, it can be tempting to hold back a bit in order to keep from having one's class turn ugly. Still, the unique vulnerabilities of contingent faculty members understandably encourage them to keep their classrooms bland. And since those individuals now teach over two-thirds of all classes in America's colleges and universities, we need to ask some very serious questions about the status of intellectual freedom in the United States.

What Is to Be Done? Collective Action and Other Solutions

For the past twenty years, especially after the adjuncts began to organize themselves into unions in the late 1990s, a consensus has been developing among those scholars who pay attention to such matters that the growth of the contingent faculty has seriously undermined the status of the entire academic profession and eroded the quality of American higher education. That concern surfaced as early as the late 1970s, when the AAUP with a grant from the Ford Foundation commissioned a survey of the adjunct labor force. Other studies followed. By the end of the 1980s, faculty unions, as well as the MLA and other professional organizations, were issuing reports—all bemoaning the casualization of academic labor and all making suggestions about what the nation's colleges and universities should do about it.[111] In its 1984 report on the situation, for example, the National Institute of Education's Study Group on the Conditions of Excellence in Higher Education recommended that "academic administrators should consolidate as many part-time teaching lines into as many full-time positions as possible."[112]

Similar proposals came from accrediting bodies, which began to include language about adjuncts in their policy statements. In its 1991 handbook, for example, the Southern Association of Colleges and Schools not only insisted that "the number of part-time faculty must be properly controlled" but also recommended that they get better working conditions. The Middle States Association evinced the same concern, emphasizing the importance of retaining a strong core of full-time tenured faculty, while the American Assembly of Collegiate Schools of Business actually specified that part-timers should handle no more than 40 percent of the instruction at any institution. Prodded in some cases by unions and adjunct organizations, some state legislatures also got into the act, setting limits on the use of part-timers and granting them such benefits as prorated health insurance and sick leave. Florida, for example, ruled that no more than 40 percent of any community college's faculty salaries should go to adjuncts.[113] California's legislature passed a similar—but, alas, unfunded—resolution in 2001 mandating that 75 percent of the teaching positions in the California State University system be filled by tenure-line faculty members.[114]

From the start, the most common proposals were those that would convert part-time positions into full-time ones. These suggestions were hardly pathbreaking. Many schools had already implemented such reforms, developing new cadres of teaching-intensive faculty members whose ranks are now the fastest growing sector of the academic workforce. "Lecturers," "faculty specialists," "instructors," "university teachers," "preceptors," "faculty fellows," "clinical professors"—these positions come with different titles, but all offer more security, pay, and benefits than part-time work. For many administrators and faculty members, such appointments seem to provide an effective and humane solution to the metastasizing growth of their schools' adjunct labor force. Beginning in 1999, for example, Georgia State decided to create nearly a hundred new full-time faculty slots to be filled primarily by the part-timers on its payroll. By reducing the school's reliance on adjuncts, these new positions would, it was anticipated, provide a more stable and committed faculty. Even so, despite their better benefits, salaries, and prospect of promotions, these renewable lectureships—like similar positions at schools ranging from the University of Nevada–Reno to Syracuse—still pay less than traditional faculty positions, have higher teaching loads, and do not provide for tenure. Nor do they eliminate the second-class status that a contingent appointment confers.[115]

As a result, there is considerable ambivalence about these measures. In 2006, the head of the University of Denver's composition program, which had just created a number of such positions, admitted that he might be collaborating in helping to chip away at the tenure track. Could his program, he wondered, become "a composition Vichy regime"?[116] After all, as Marc Bousquet points out, "what a large sector of composition labor . . . 'really wants' is not to be *treated as* colleagues but instead to *be* colleagues."[117] These instructors wanted regular tenure-track jobs, not tenure-light jobs that still preserved the two-tiered division (and divisiveness) of America's faculties. The AAUP, in a recent report, makes a similar demand. While applauding the conversion of part-time appointments to full-time ones, it calls for those holding such appointments to be given the opportunity for tenure within their present jobs subject to the same kind of evaluation and peer review that their research-oriented colleagues receive. Anything less than full faculty status will, the association believes, continue to undermine the professional infrastructure of academe.[118]

At the moment, given the current economic crisis, it is hard to tell whether the growing attention to the plight of contingent faculty members will hasten the process, in Joe Berry's words, of converting "what has always been *good work* into *good jobs*."[119] At least one recent report seems to indicate that, for all the rhetoric, there has been little progress in turning part-time and temporary positions into tenured and tenure-track ones.[120] A more realistic approach to the problem, however, may be to obtain so many improvements in the economic status, security, and working conditions of contingent academics that it will "ultimately," Berry believes, "break down the barriers between part-timers and full-timers" and eliminate the two-tiered structure of the nation's faculties. Such a gradualist scenario may be the best we can hope for. After all, when his union was negotiating for a raise at Chicago's Columbia College, Berry recalled, the administrators, "did say that if we pay $3000 a course, the board of trustees might not want to hire so many part-time teachers and might make more full-time teachers, as if that was some sort of threat to us."[121]

For Berry, as for many other activists and observers, it was clear that collective bargaining has become the most effective (though not the only) way for contingent faculty members to improve their situation. Not only does it win some real concessions from employers, but it also prods other institutions to follow suit in the hopes of avoiding unionization.[122] Those have been hard-earned victories, for part-time academics are notoriously difficult to organize. To begin with, they are not easy to find. Without offices, e-mail, or telephones, simply making contact with these people is a major challenge, all the more so if they teach at several campuses.[123] The psychological barriers are even more daunting, for the vulnerability of contingent faculty members makes them skittish about joining a union, especially when administrators pick off their leading organizers. They know they are being exploited, but many are too relieved to have landed an academic position to risk losing it. "Without job security," one activist explained, "adjuncts are afraid to do almost anything—both on campus and also in their union."[124] In addition, many still cling to the individualistic worldview inculcated by their graduate training that they will somehow end up okay as a result of their own merit and hard work. There was, they felt, something déclassé about collective action. Working-class men and women belonged to unions, not academic professionals like themselves, who were, they believed, only temporarily in a tough position.[125]

Nonetheless, once they finally became convinced of the advantages of collective action, adjuncts and off-the-ladder instructors were willing to join the labor movement, either within their own separate organizations or else as part of a larger faculty union. For many of them, collective bargaining brought pay raises, benefits, and even such professional perks as money for travel to conferences. In the late 1990s, for example, after a major struggle, the part-timers at the University of Massachusetts–Boston managed to negotiate a prorated half-time status with full medical, dental, and pension benefits as well as a floor of $4,000 per course.[126] A few years later, composition teachers and other adjuncts without terminal degrees obtained a minimum compensation of $4,785 per section at some schools in the Pennsylvania higher education system.[127] Some unions were able to win additional full-time and even tenure-track jobs for their members.[128] Pay raises were easier to obtain than job security. Though some institutions did provide longer-term contracts and procedural protections for their contingent faculty members, others refused to surrender any portion of their managerial control. Administrators who are forced to bargain with their part-timers, an experienced organizer noted, are "willing to make substantial concessions on pay, less on health benefits, but hold very tightly to all issues regarding power, flexibility, or the job security of contingent faculty."[129] This is what happened in 2008, for example, when the CUNY faculty union renegotiated its contract. It represented both part-time and full-time teachers, and although it got raises and professional development funding for the former, it could not persuade the intransigent administration to grant the adjuncts any greater job security. In response, some disgruntled part-timers then tried to scuttle the whole contract.[130]

As the CUNY struggle shows, the demands of contingent academics can become a divisive issue within the unions that represent both tenure-track and off-the-ladder appointees—just as the process of unionization itself had been so disruptive within the academy as a whole. All too often, efforts to enlist faculty members in the defense of other college and university teachers flounder in the face of the stratification of the academic profession. Differences in real and perceived status exacerbate the situation. Leaders in UMass Boston's full-time faculty union, for example, initially refused to let adjuncts join their unit on the grounds that their presence would undermine the prestige of the research-oriented professors on the tenure track.[131] Opponents of collective bargaining elsewhere, fearing that personnel decisions would be made with regard to seniority rather than scholarly merit, evinced a similar distaste for the egalitarianism that unionization brought. "My degree," a CUNY faculty member complained,

> is a hard-won Ph.D. in Economics, ten years at Princeton including bachelor's, master's, and doctorate degrees. My publication record is good, and I teach a full load. And under the union contract a community college teacher with a "cheap" master's, one year beyond his bachelor's, from any two-bit teacher's college, will get approximately the same pay and benefits. In my opinion the outcome of the union contract is disgustingly unprofessional, even anti-professional.[132]

There are other divisions as well. Several studies, including an influential one by Everett Carll Ladd Jr. and Seymour Martin Lipset in the early 1970s, at a time when many academics were just beginning to join the labor movement, found a "relative lack of support for unionization among professors of high attainment." Collective bargaining, Ladd and Lipset explained, was for faculty who were "in the least professional components of higher education," teachers at community colleges and lower-level public institutions—second-raters, in other words, who lacked the individual bargaining power of their more productive colleagues. Elite professors, on the other hand, not only viewed unions as undercutting academic standards but also believed (and still believe) that they had enough personal clout to protect themselves and their colleagues from incursions against their autonomy and power.[133]

Those individuals voted with their feet when the AAUP endorsed collective bargaining for its members in 1972. It had taken several years of agonizing debate within the organization for its leaders to drop their aversion to what its general secretary lamented in 1965 was the "gravitation from our professional role as 'officers' of our separate institutions to mere 'employees' thereof."[134] As the momentum for engaging in collective bargaining continued, traditionalists within the organization feared that it could be seen as "an organ of class warfare" that would undermine the AAUP's ability to preserve academic freedom.[135] "Our objection is one of basic principle," two of the organization's leading members wrote.

> The notion of collective bargaining, supported by most of us in the industrial context, is wholly inappropriate in the academic situation. A university is not a corporation in which the interest of labor and management

> are opposed, a zero-sum arrangement in which one group gains only at the expense of the other. On the contrary, trustees, regents, and board members have nothing to gain by depressing our salaries. They have no personal financial interest in the matter and they win prestige only as they provide stipends high enough to attract the most capable scholars and scientists among us to their institutions.
>
> We could not possibly support union tactics in negotiation because they denigrate and ultimately deny our professional status. We do not consider ourselves employees. Whatever the legal definition may be, there is a genuine sense in which we can assert that we *are* the university.[136]

In particular, these people feared the rigidities of industrial-style unionism, raising concerns about heavies from Detroit forcing one-size-fits-all formulas on highly individualistic faculty members. They also opposed the inclusion of nonprofessorial types in a bargaining unit. "To lump them [non-faculty members] together with faculties and at the same time to remove some of those who can properly claim those rights," the organization's first vice president, Robert K. Webb, wrote,

> will leave faculties mere adventitious interest groups, without clear definition and lacking either historical or present purpose. In some respects, of course, faculties are interest groups—they are concerned about their remuneration and conditions as compared with other groups inside and outside the academic profession. But they are also defenders of the central ideals of the academic community, and it is those ideals that collective bargaining—in this country at any rate—may render precarious.[137]

But the desire of so many academics to organize in the face of fiscal retrenchment and the infusion of corporate practices into their institutions, as well as the fear that if it did not act the American Federation of Teachers (AFT) and the National Education Association (NEA) might put it out of business, pushed the AAUP into union organizing. Within a year, however, the association's membership fell from 97,106 to 87,649, with many of the dropouts explaining that they did so out of hostility to collective bargaining. By 1975, 22 percent of the AAUP's members at the top thirty research universities had quit—and that decline continues to this day.[138]

Meanwhile, however, faculties were organizing. Not, it is true, at flagship state universities or the Ivy Leagues, but at dozens of campuses across the country from the California State University system to less prestigious private schools like Rider University outside Trenton, New Jersey. By the mid-1970s, more than two hundred institutions of higher education housed collective bargaining units. The Supreme Court dealt some of these units a death blow in 1980 when it ruled in the case of the independent Yeshiva University Faculty Association that professors at private institutions were "substantially and pervasively operating the enterprise," to quote the words of Lewis Powell, who wrote the majority decision. Since they controlled the appointment and promotion of their colleagues, developed the curriculum, and evaluated their students, Yeshiva's faculty members were managers and thus could not engage in collective bargaining. Powell's ruling ignored the realities of academic life in the 1970s, when business-oriented administrators were responding to the perceived financial crisis by adopting a corporate style of decision making that shunted faculties aside. The *Yeshiva* decision also created an artificial distinction between public and private institutions that bore no relationship to the working conditions of professional academics in either sector.[139] Once they had the Supreme Court's imprimatur, Yeshiva's authorities raised their managers' teaching loads from three courses a semester to four. Though other private institutions took advantage of *Yeshiva* to decertify their faculty unions, organizing at public schools continued apace. As of January 2006, there were collective bargaining units at more than twelve hundred campuses, representing nearly 320,000 faculty members.[140]

These unions—and there are about ten different ones, though the AAUP, AFT, and NEA represent the bulk of the organized faculty—are all becoming concerned about the casualization of the academic profession. Whether they have enough clout at this point to reverse the process remains unclear. Unfortunately, the increasing stratification of the professoriate and the elite's withdrawal from the AAUP (which is, after all, the only organization that represents faculty members qua faculty members) have made it harder for the academic profession to stem the erosion of tenure-track jobs. There is no powerful faculty voice in today's debates about the status of higher education, an absence that stems, at least in part, from the disappearance of a shared community within the academic profession. Although today we can easily fault the eminent academics who founded the AAUP for their racism, sexism, and elitism, not to mention their feckless behavior during World War I, they nonetheless shared a sense of collective responsibility for the entire professoriate as well as an underlying commitment to promoting what they called "the common good." They also recognized the seamlessness of the academic enterprise and the need for faculty members, well-established ones in particular, to put up a collective front in its defense. No longer.

There is little solidarity in academe. Distinctions of status eat away at whatever exists of a community of scholars. Although, as Gary Rhoades points out, "the key fault line in the academic profession" is between part-timers and others, there is considerable hostility on every side.[141] Resentment of the privileged position of senior professors, for example, runs so deep that some 40 percent of the junior faculty members in a recent poll approved of the statement that the "abolition of tenure would, on the whole, improve the quality of higher education."[142] Upset about the racheting up of the requirements for tenure and promotion and/or their lack of access to them, the folks at the bottom of the ladder grumble about the deadwood in their departments who barely teach and rarely publish yet pull down substantial salaries. Particularly galling to members of the academic proletariat is the insensitivity to their situation evinced by so many self-identified liberals and even radicals within the higher reaches of the academic establishment. All too often these well-paid and well-connected senior professors act as if they have no more in common with the freeway flyers who shuttle from one community college to another than Daniel Boulud and Jean-Georges Vongerichten have with the high school dropouts who flip burgers at Wendy's. Yet the parallel is false, for the academic profession is not the restaurant business. Teaching and scholarship, at whatever level, are more than just a job.

Other fissures have opened up in the wake of attempts to organize graduate students at some of the nation's leading universities. Although schools like Berkeley, Wisconsin, and Michigan have had TA unions since the 1960s and 1970s and by now most major public research universities host such organizations, no academic administration has actually welcomed them. Most, in fact, are hostile in the extreme. Insisting that teaching assistants are apprentices, not employees, whose work is part of their training for future faculty jobs, universities—NYU being the most notorious—have hired union-busting law firms and mounted major public relations campaigns to deny their graduate students the right to organize. Even schools that have been dealing with organized TAs for years still dig in their heels when contracts come up for renewal—a posture that brings strike threats and increased ill will. Money may not be the issue. According to Michigan's Graduate Employees Organization, it cost the university almost as much in the salaries of its negotiating team as the union had been demanding in benefits. Similarly, most institutions, when confronted by organizing campaigns and the threat of organizing campaigns, respond by increasing the benefits and pay of their graduate students. The issue is clearly a matter of principle and control. As universities become increasingly assimilated into the corporate world, their top administrators take on the values of that world, especially the antilabor ideology that so many of the businesspeople who dominate their boards of trustees adhere to.[143]

That a university president, whose 16.5 percent raise in 2003 added $122,000 to his take-home pay while the salaries of his faculty were frozen, might consider himself on the side of capital against labor is hardly a surprise.[144] That so many of those faculty members supported his position requires more explanation. In this particular case, when NYU's frustrated graduate students called a strike in response to the administration's refusal to negotiate a second contract after a National Labor Relations Board decision against the teaching assistants at Brown, many professors did not side with the students. Though they may have sympathized with the TAs and may even have been upset about the administration's failure to consult the faculty about the situation, less than half the professors in the Faculty of Arts and Sciences supported the strike, and even fewer did so in NYU's other divisions. Professors at Yale and Columbia, where there had also been graduate student job actions, were even less sympathetic to their TAs.[145] Faculty members in Yale's French department actually warned their students that participating in the strike "could legitimately be taken into account in faculty evaluations of a student's aptitude for an eventual academic career." Walking out on their classes was, many professors believed, something that conscientious academics simply did not do.[146]

Such a lack of solidarity bodes ill for the future of the academic profession at a time when so many of its members are already working under stressful and insecure conditions. The current fiscal crisis can only worsen matters. In order to surmount what promises to be a genuinely catastrophic situation for all sectors of American higher education, the faculty needs to overcome its internal divisions. Only then can it confront the increasingly corporatized administrators who seem to have lost sight of their schools' educational mission in their quest for institutional aggrandizement. Some educational leaders, to their credit, do recognize the need for solidarity. "The university administration," the former president of Stanford warned his colleagues,

> needs to be a more active advocate for its own faculty and for a public understanding of its role. If presidents and Boards of Regents, trustees,

> deans, and administrators would express pride in, and understanding of them, the work of teaching and scholarship, faculty morale, and faculty responsibility would benefit greatly.[147]

Not until the men and women who lead the nation's colleges and universities jettison their business orientation and come to recognize how much their institutions depend on having a stable and independent faculty will the American academy recover its soul.

Epilogue

"EVERYTHING IS ON THE TABLE": THE ACADEMY'S RESPONSE TO THE GREAT RECESSION

At a recent scholarly meeting, I ran into a former close friend turned university administrator and (not so) innocently asked how things were going. "We're fine," he replied, "we didn't fire anybody," explaining that because his school had already pared its faculty (and earned an AAUP censure) before he arrived, his administration did not have to take advantage of the recession to implement the changes it wanted to make. Other institutions, he implied, would be using the financial meltdown to justify the reforms they had long wanted to impose. His honesty was refreshing, even if the message he delivered was unsettling.

The recession—or Great Recession, as it is beginning to be called—landed on an academic community that was already on the defensive. For years, the nation's colleges and universities had been trying to meet public demands to keep tuitions low, improve graduation rates, stimulate economic growth, develop lucrative research, and field winning teams by refashioning themselves in a corporate mode and adopting business practices to improve their bottom lines. When the economic tsunami washed over them in 2008, almost every institution of higher learning, from the Ivy League to the community colleges, feared that it was in trouble. States cut back their funding, while endowments plummeted. Though each school handled the loss of income in its own way, their early responses indicate that the current crisis will only intensify many of the deleterious trends we have already examined and further diminish the role of the faculty. Administrations usually acted unilaterally, sometimes by implementing long-sought strategic plans without consulting their faculties. Most strove, it is true, to avoid laying off tenured and tenure-track faculty members and instead resorted to hiring freezes, tuition increases, pay cuts, and reductions in everything from pension contributions to trash collection.

The University of Florida even talked about taking the phones out of its professors' offices.[1]

For the nation's college and university teachers, both tenure-track and contingent, the situation could hardly be more stressful. If the economic picture does not improve, their jobs might be on the line, and in any event, they are facing lower salaries, larger classes, smaller pensions, and fewer resources for their research. Given the precariousness of their economic situations, few professors outside of the AAUP worried about the fate of academic freedom. Yet the crunch demands even greater vigilance on the part of the professoriate if it is to retain its ability to protect itself, its students, and the quality of American higher education. Even if there had been no financial meltdown, critics of the status quo like Juan Hong would still be facing restrictions on their professional activities in the wake of the *Garcetti* decision. Now they and their colleagues must also cope with administrative efforts to use the crisis to further whittle away at shared governance and preempt the faculty's traditional responsibility for curricular and personnel matters.

As we have seen, public institutions have been dealing with dwindling state appropriations for years. In some states, the financial panic simply turned a bad situation into a disaster, although it is possible that in many cases administrators may be exaggerating the potential shortfall. Nonetheless, in states like California and Florida, where the housing bubble wreaked enormous damage on an already dysfunctional tax structure, the cutbacks were particularly brutal. The legislature slashed its appropriations for California's once vaunted institutions of higher learning by 20 percent. Hawaii, Tennessee, and Washington suffered similar cuts. But just about every state reduced its budget for higher education, if not by as much as California, by nearly 10 percent in some cases. The SUNY system in New York, for example, faced a 6.6 percent decrease.[2]

Yet the situation for many public institutions is hardly so dire. Although state legislatures did reduce their appropriations, they had been increasing them for the previous few years. Moreover, as many observers noted, these cuts were buffered by the federal stimulus that went to the states in 2009. And in any event, as the percentage of state funding has declined over the years, institutions have found ways to cover their reduced state appropriations with other revenues. Were states still funding 60 to 70 percent of their universities' budgets, a 10 percent cut would be disastrous. But when one is looking at 10 percent of the 30 percent that many states supply, the cuts seem less drastic. The figures for the University of Illinois system, for example, reveal that although the state's appropriations subsidize a smaller percentage of the system's budget, its income from tuition and fees, pumped up by higher enrollments as well as tuition increases, has more than compensated for that decline.[3]

Private schools are also worried. Tuition-driven institutions fear that they might lose customers to lower-cost public schools. Endowments took major hits, especially at those of the nation's wealthiest colleges and universities, which had relied on their investments to fund big chunks of their operating expenses. Harvard, whose financial managers had plunged into the riskiest of derivatives and hedge funds, saw the value of its endowment drop 29.8 percent by 2009. Accustomed to spending big on everything from trophy architecture to financial aid, the university's administrators predicted drastic reductions. "There are going to be a hell of a lot of layoffs," one explained. "Courses will be cut. Class sizes will get bigger." Nor was Harvard alone. Yale lost 28.6 percent of its endowment, Johns Hopkins 20 percent, and Vassar 18 percent. Like Harvard, Vassar's investments had covered one-third of its budget, and like Harvard, it began to pare its staff and make other economies.[4]

Not all the news was bad, at least in certain quarters. For many of the administrators, politicians, and pundits who had long been trying to restructure American higher education, the financial meltdown brimmed with promise. As one of them told the National Association of College and University Attorneys, the crisis offered "a unique opportunity to get costs under control, and to make the kind of changes [in employment policies] you can only dream about in flush times." Others urged their hearers to "seize the day," to expand facilities while cutting back on unwanted programs and departments. At last, they explained, academic institutions would be able "to use a systemic approach to *change*." What that change implied was clear: "We've got to improve productivity."[5] Though much of the impetus for those changes originated in the offices of corporate-minded administrators, some came from politicians and other outsiders who had long been critical of the academy's supposed flaws. In allocating its budget cuts, for example, the Indiana Commission for Higher Education decided to impose the steepest reductions on those institutions with the highest costs per student and the lowest graduation rates. Tennessee enacted similar reforms, its legislature almost unanimously passing a bill that would also tie the budgets of individual schools to their graduation rates.[6]

Nonetheless, there seemed to be a consensus among the academy's leaders that although, as the chancellor of the State University of New York put it, "everything is on the table," at least initially they would try to preserve the jobs of their core full-time faculty members. They were, however, planning drastic reductions in the ranks of other university employees. The numbers were big: 600–800 at the University of Washington, 600 at Michigan State, 1,200 at the University of Minnesota, 175 at the University of Maryland, 230 at Miami-Dade Community College, and 2,000 at the University of California. Temple University decided to reorganize its administrative staff by firing every single worker and then selectively rehiring only those people it wanted to keep. Most institutions avoided such extreme measures; they would, they announced, retain their tenured and tenure-track faculty members and reduce their payrolls through attrition, retirement incentives, and the nonrenewal of temporary employees and adjuncts.[7]

Unfortunately, not every school was so protective of its tenured professors. The most egregious dismissals occurred in early February 2009 at Clark Atlanta University, where, citing something it called an "enrollment emergency," the administration peremptorily fired nearly sixty full-time professors, twenty of whom had tenure. Formed in 1988 by the merger of two historically black institutions, Clark College and Atlanta University, the school's faculty and administrators had been at odds for years, and it was clear to the AAUP investigating committee that looked into the case that the president had manufactured the so-called emergency in order to purge the faculty of people he did not want. The AAUP had developed procedures for schools to follow during a "financial exigency" when the institution's survival seemed to require shedding some faculty members. Clark Atlanta ignored them all, summarily dismissing one-quarter of its teaching staff with only a month's worth of severance pay and no opportunity to defend themselves. The remaining faculty members, assigned unpaid overloads of two to three of their former colleagues' classes, were understandably demoralized, especially since the school's enrollment had barely declined and the administration had made no effort to pursue alternative ways to save money. Nor had it consulted with the faculty.[8]

No other institution has made quite such drastic across-the-board cuts; a more common expedient was for trustees and administrators to divest their institutions of programs and departments that did not attract enough students or seemed extraneous in one way or another. That some of the units slated for what one college president called "right-sizing" were central to the traditional liberal arts curriculum seemed irrelevant. Thus, for example, when the University of Louisiana's Board of Regents trimmed the "low completer" majors at its Lafayette campus, it targeted the school's philosophy department; so, too, did Pennsylvania's higher education authorities at

East Stroudsburg University. The University of Southern Mississippi actually eliminated its economics department, while Michigan State contemplated the demise of geology, among other fields, and a Kansas institution lopped off five majors including political science. Elsewhere, foreign languages, whose enrollments had been dwindling for years, were being gutted or replaced by online instruction. Nor was it much of a surprise to find that some schools were planning to cut programs in such politically controversial fields as Africana and women's studies.[9] Whether administrators are also using the crisis to rid themselves of their critics and similarly undesirable faculty members is not entirely clear. We might expect that to be the case, but there is little hard evidence at the moment.[10]

Nor do we know how many adjunct and non-tenure-track positions are being sacrificed in order to meet budget shortfalls. Since, as we have seen, even obtaining an accurate count of the nation's contingent faculty members is a daunting task, we may never know how many of them are losing their jobs to the current crunch. After all, unless they are protected by a union contract, most adjuncts are "at will" employees who can be let go with few if any formalities. Their dismissals rarely, if ever, receive the attention even of the specialized education press. There is some anecdotal evidence. At one of the New York City municipal colleges, a colleague reports that one-third of his department's adjuncts are gone, while some of the campuses in the California State University system have not rehired up to 25 percent of their long-term lecturers.[11]

What makes the situation even worse is that the full-time tenure-track positions so many contingent faculty members hoped to fill are also disappearing. Even before the full extent of the catastrophe became known, some schools had begun to eliminate new hires. In November 2008, for example, Brown imposed a freeze on all staff positions and announced that faculty searches would be "carefully reviewed." At my own institution, where a reluctant administration had finally agreed to a much-needed addition to our department in 2008, the provost pulled the plug before we could review the applications. The American Historical Association found that similar cancellations occurred in 15 percent of the other history searches that had been advertised at that time. By the following year, the job freeze had spread throughout the entire academic community. According to a September 2009 survey by the *Chronicle of Higher Education*, 40 percent of the 166 institutions responding said that they had stopped hiring new faculty members.[12]

The competition for the few jobs that remain is astronomical. "At least a couple of my friends," a dispirited graduate student in English told the

Chronicle in December 2009, "have applied to upwards of 100 positions in a single year and have landed two, maybe three interviews." The MLA, which had been tracking the market for several years, predicted that job openings in English were expected to fall 35 percent in 2009–2010, which on top of a decline the previous year came to a total of 51 percent over the past two hiring seasons. For scholars in literatures other than English, the figures were even worse, 39 and 55 percent. People in other disciplines face an equally gloomy prospect. During the 2008–9 academic year, there were ninety-four applicants for each job in American history and eighty for each one in European history, and the situation is only worsening. When we reopened our search for an American historian in the fall of 2009, we received more than 175 applications. Even in fields that normally face a more buoyant market, the news was bad. Academic employment for economists fell 19 percent, while jobs outside the academy suffered a 24 percent decline. Adding to the crunch in every discipline was the reluctance of senior professors to retire as they watched their pension accounts decline.[13]

Many of these people also saw their paychecks shrink or at least remain static. In August 2009, the Minnesota state university system froze its professors' salaries. A concurrent survey of private colleges and universities showed that two-thirds of the participating campuses had imposed similar freezes. There were pay cuts as well; Greensboro College reduced its faculty's salaries by 20 percent. At public institutions, these reductions, often designated "furloughs," proliferated, though whether the authorities designed them as PR measures to show trustees and legislators that they could tighten their belts or whether they were responses to a genuine shortfall is unclear. Stalled contract negotiations led the administration at the University of Hawaii to impose a 6.7 percent cut on its faculty members; Arizona State offered its employees the option of taking either a furlough or a pay cut. Colleges and universities elsewhere mandated furloughs of varying lengths. California's were among the earliest and most extensive. But almost every major state university from Maryland to Wisconsin was imposing unpaid vacations on its employees. Sometimes, as at Georgia, these furloughs constituted across-the-board pay cuts; more often, it seems, they were applied on a graduated scale. This was the case, for example, in California, where the furloughs were adjusted according to people's salaries, with faculty members taking cuts that ranged from 4 to 10 percent. A similar system at Iowa State imposed a four-day furlough on low-paid employees, while top administrators surrendered ten days of pay. In some cases, especially at schools like Rutgers, where there were collective bargaining units on campus, faculty members agreed to such givebacks in return for administrative guarantees against layoffs.[14]

But faculty members were hardly the only victims of the academic community's financial woes. As institutions stopped hiring, shed adjuncts, and laid off staff members, students suffered as well. Even as they sought out higher education to improve their own job prospects, overcrowded and cancelled classes prevented many of them from taking the courses they needed to meet graduation requirements. These cutbacks fell disproportionately on students from lower socioeconomic groups at community colleges and local state universities. The City College of San Francisco, just to take a particularly egregious example, cancelled eight hundred classes for the 2009–2010 academic year, including human biology, elementary French, and financial accounting. At the nation's largest community college, Miami-Dade, faculty and staff reductions shut thirty thousand students out of courses they needed to take. But even top-tier schools cut back their academic programs. UCLA, for example, reduced its offerings in English as a second language by scheduling most of its ESL sections in the summer, when it could charge more for them—and when the mainly immigrant students who needed those classes had to get paying jobs.[15]

California's system was particularly stressed. Where it had once led the rest of the nation in the provision of mass higher education, the state's drastic budget cuts forced it to the unimaginable expedient of turning away students. The California State Universities planned to reduce their enrollments in 2009–2010 by forty thousand undergraduates. Not only did the system simply stop admitting undergraduates in the spring of 2009, but individual campuses tightened up their requirements and flunked marginal students to keep their enrollments down. These cutbacks fell particularly heavily on the working-class and minority-group men and women who were trying to transfer from community colleges to the four-year state university system.[16]

Adding to the obstacles these people faced in California and elsewhere were the higher fees they had to pay. The University of California system imposed a two-year tuition increase of 32 percent. The University of Washington raised its sticker price 28 percent for the same period of time, while Iowa's state universities imposed a $100 surcharge on every student. The Oregon authorities not only raised tuitions 8.5 percent at its three most popular campuses but also reduced the funds available for financial assistance. Even when an institution did not cut back on its student aid budget—and most schools claimed that their scholarship money was sacrosanct—the growing tendency to award it on the basis of merit rather than need served as another barrier to broader access. At the same time, many public colleges and universities actively recruited foreign students and undergraduates from out of state who could be charged a higher rate, again reducing the number of slots for more local (and poorer) applicants. Private institutions, which did not raise their tuitions as sharply, sought higher enrollments mainly by lowering their standards for admission.[17]

None of this occurred without opposition. Dozens of students disrupted meetings or sat in at Berkeley, UCLA, Santa Cruz, and San Francisco State. The California protests garnered the most headlines, but there were demonstrations and even building takeovers in New York, Maryland, and Pennsylvania. Angered by the educational cutbacks and tuition hikes, students were, as one Santa Cruz activist explained, tired of having the state's budget "constantly being balanced on our backs." The high salaries and raises that top administrators—and football coaches—received have only added to the outrage. And students are not the only protesters. Their parents are also up in arms. In fact, even such ordinarily staid individuals as University of California department chairs have been jolted to consider forms of direct action in the face of 8 percent salary cuts, while normally hard-to-organize adjuncts and even postdocs at schools as varied as Cooper Union, Rutgers, and Montana State are seriously talking union.[18]

It would be heartening to think that these activities signal the advent of a major movement on the nation's campuses that would unite students, teachers, and members of the general public in a broad drive to push back against the corporatization of the university. It is possible that the feckless and high-handed behavior of so many administrations in the face of the Great Recession will energize the nation's faculties to reassert their own responsibility for the welfare of their own institutions. Certainly there are signs that the academic community is ripe for collective action. At schools like Rutgers and the University of Akron, where unions have been on top of the situation, faculties have been better able to resist the cutbacks than elsewhere. Major organizing drives are under way at some of the nation's larger universities, and it may well be that the economic crisis will dissolve much of the opposition to collective bargaining within the rest of the professoriate.[19]

Even so, there are so many divisions within the academic community at every level that there is no guarantee the crisis will unify rather than further polarize America's campuses.[20] We have seen how poorly the American professoriate has treated its own squeaky wheels, and we have noted its apparent acquiescence in its own casualization. Still, there is a growing awareness that something is very wrong with American higher education and that both its quality and availability are at risk. Obviously, priorities need to be changed. That California's governor has proposed a constitutional amendment requiring more spending on higher education than on prisons indicates a recognition on the part of a not always sympathetic politician that his state's institutions of higher learning are in trouble.

More than money is at stake here. One can envision a dystopic set of institutions, dominated by vocationalism and the bottom line, where the drive for productivity transforms most faculty members into temporary workers with little job security or control over the content of their courses, while scientists and engineers churn out patentable results in industrialized laboratories that service their corporate sponsors. Such a constricted model of the academic community not only would stunt the careers and futures of students and teachers but also would undermine the very idea of the university as a place for intellectual growth and meaningful scholarship. Academic freedom is in danger here, as is the future of the well-informed citizenry that our democratic system requires. An academy transformed into a site for job training and corporate research will be increasingly hard-pressed to retain its function as the last remaining haven for reasoned dissent and the home of serious ideas that do not lend themselves to sound bites.

Perhaps I paint too grim a picture. Perhaps the current crisis will finally rouse the nation's faculties to put aside their internal divisions and take advantage of their hitherto latent power to restore the intellectual vitality of American higher education and renew its democratic mission. It can be done, though whether it can be done without also undertaking the even more formidable project of reshaping the nation's corporate-dominated value structure and depoliticized public discourse is an open question. But we have few alternatives. Without an aware and energized academic community that can fight for all its members, higher education as a bastion of freedom and opportunity will, like the polar bears' glacial habitat, slowly melt away.

NOTES

Introduction: "Official Duties": Juan Hong and the Crisis of the University

1. Juan Hong, "Opening Brief," Ninth Circuit Court of Appeals, n.d., in possession of the author.

2. *Garcetti v. Ceballos*, 544 U.S. 410, 126 S. Ct. 1951 (2006).

3. Amici curiae brief of the Thomas Jefferson Center for the Protection of Free Expression and the American Association of University Professors in *Hong v. Grant*, Ninth Circuit Court of Appeals, March 17, 2008 http://www.aaup.org/NR/rdonlyres/E0C569DB-DE60-4D19-8208-C5C8EC584132/0/HongAmicusBriefFILED031708.pdf (accessed February 5, 2010).

Chapter 1: "So Fragile and So Indispensable": What Is Academic Freedom and Why Should We Care About It?

1. DePaul University Statement on the Tenure and Promotion Decision Concerning Professor Norman Finkelstein, June 8, 2007, http://www.normanfinkelstein.com/article.php?pg=11&ar=1070 (accessed February 3, 2008).

2. Statement from University of Colorado Board of Regents, https://www.cusys.edu/regents/communique/churchill-reg-stmt.html (accessed January 11, 2008); Statement from University of Colorado President Hank Brown, https://www.cusys.edu/regents/communique/churchill-brown-stmt.html (accessed January 11, 2008).

3. Statement by Albion W. Small and Nathaniel Butler in *Shaping the American Educational State*, ed. Clarence J. Karier (New York: The Free Press, 1975), 41.

4. Matthew W. Finkin and Robert C. Post, *For the Common Good: Principles of American Academic Freedom* (New Haven, CT: Yale University Press, 2009), 6.

5. David M. Rabban makes the same point about the confusion attending the term in his important article, "A Functional Analysis of 'Individual' and 'Institutional' Academic Freedom Under the First Amendment," *Law and Contemporary Problems* 53, no. 3 (Summer 1990): 255.

6. For a particularly lucid explanation of the varied nature of academic freedom, see Joan W. Scott, "Academic Freedom as an Ethical Practice," in *The Future of Academic Freedom*, ed. Louis Menand (Chicago: University of Chicago Press, 1996), 163–80.

7. This material on the German academic profession comes from Richard Hofstadter and Walter P. Metzger, *The Development of Academic Freedom in the United States* (New York: Columbia University Press, 1955), 383–89.

8. Hofstadter and Metzger, *Development of Academic Freedom*, 393.

9. There is a fairly extensive scholarly literature on the growth of middle-class professionalism and the universities. The seminal work is Robert H. Wiebe, *The Search for Order, 1877–1920* (New York: Hill and Wang, 1967). See also Burton J. Bledstein, *The Culture of Professionalism: The Middle Class and the Development of Higher Education in America* (New York: W. W. Norton, 1976); Mary O. Furner, *Advocacy and Objectivity: A Crisis in the Professionalization of American Social Science, 1865–1905* (Lexington: University Press of Kentucky, 1975); and Lawrence P. Veysey, *The Emergence of the American University* (Chicago: University of Chicago Press, 1970).

10. "1915 Declaration of Principles on Academic Freedom and Academic Tenure," in American Association of University Professors, *Policy Documents and Reports*, 9th ed., (Washington, DC: American Association of University Professors, 2001), 295.

11. For a recent assessment of the relationship between academic freedom and intellectual quality under authoritarian regimes, see John Connelly and Michael Gruttner, eds., *Universities Under Dictatorship* (University Park: Pennsylvania State University Press, 2005).

12. Claude Bowman, *The College Professor in America* (1939, New York: Arno Press, 1977), 20–74; Richard Shryock, "The Academic Profession in the United States," *AAUP Bulletin* 38, no. 1 (Spring 1952): 51–55; Theodore Caplow and Reece J. McGee, *The Academic Marketplace* (New York: Basic Books, 1958), 122–35; Robert H. Knapp, "Changing Functions of the College Professor," in *The American College*, ed. Nevitt Sanford (New York: John Wiley and Sons, 1962), 298–303; Anthon Ostroff, "Economic Pressure and the Professor," in *The American College*, ed. Sanford, 447–58.

13. "1915 Declaration of Principles," 298–99.

14. "1940 Statement of Principles on Academic Freedom and Tenure," in AAUP, *Policy Documents and Reports*, 3–10.

15. American Historical Association, "Statement on Standards of Professional Conduct," 2005, http://www.historians.org/pubs/Free/ProfessionalStandards.cfm?pv=y (accessed November 20, 2007).

16. American Physical Society, "Guidelines for Professional Conduct," 2001, http://www.aps.org/policy/statements/02_2.cfm (accessed November 20, 2007).

17. American Sociological Society, "Code of Ethics," 1997, http://www.asanet.org/cs/root/leftnav/ethics/code_of_ethics_introduction (accessed November 20, 2007).

18. Modern Language Association, "Statement of Professional Ethics," 2004, http://www.mla.org/repview_profethics#one (accessed November 20, 2007).

19. Scott, "Academic Freedom as an Ethical Practice," 168.

20. For a good discussion of the ways in which fields incorporate or resist new knowledge, see Judith Jarvis Thompson, "Ideology and Faculty Selection," *Law and Contemporary Problems* 53, no. 3 (Summer 1990): 155–76. For a more recent discussion of the process of peer review, see Michele Lamont, *How Professors Think: Inside the Curious World of Academic Judgment* (Cambridge, MA: Harvard University Press, 2009).

21. For some examples of such early cases, see Walter P. Metzger, ed., *Professors on Guard: The First AAUP Investigations* (New York: Arno Press, 1977).

22. Rabban, "A Functional Analysis," 236; J. Peter Byrne, "Academic Freedom: A 'Special Concern of the First Amendment,' " *Yale Law Journal* 99 (November 1989): 256.

23. *Sweezy v. New Hampshire*, 354 U.S. 234 (1957).

24. *Keyishian v. Board of Regents*, 385 U.S. 589 (1967).

25. Rabban, "A Functional Analysis," 231, 268; Byrne, "Academic Freedom," 299–300.

26. Byrne, "Academic Freedom," 254.

27. *University of California Regents v. Bakke*, 438 U.S. 265 (1978), 312–13.

28. Amy Gutmann, *Democratic Education* (Princeton, NJ: Princeton University Press, 1987), 179.

29. Byrne, "Academic Freedom," 261.

30. Ibid., 307.

31. Ibid., 323–36.

32. Rabban, "A Functional Analysis," 258–62.

33. *University of Pennsylvania v. EEOC*, 493 U.S. 182 (1990).

34. Rabban, "A Functional Analysis," 263–65.

35. William A. Kaplin and Barbara A. Lee, *The Law of Higher Education: A Comprehensive Guide to Legal Implications of Administrative Decision Making*, 3rd ed. (San Francisco: Jossey-Bass, 1995), 299–300, 306–7.

36. *Bishop v. Aronov*, 926 F.2d 1066 (11th Cir. 1991), cited in Kaplin and Lee, *Law of Higher Education*, 310.

37. *Urofsky v. Gilmore*, 216 F.3d 401, 410, 415 (4th Cir. 2000), cert. denied, 531 U.S. 1070 (2001).

38. Brief of amici curiae, Thomas Jefferson Center for the Protection of Free Expression and the American Association of University Professors, on Writ of Certiorari to the U.S. Court of Appeals for the Ninth Circuit, in the case of *Garcetti v. Ceballos*, July 21, 2006, http://www.aaup.org/NR/rdonlyres/FA297466-D642-4040-987D-BAF46DDA0CA0/0/GarcettiSupremeCourtFinal.pdf (accessed February 5, 2010); *Garcetti v. Ceballos*, 547 U.S. 410 (2006).

39. Nat Hentoff, "Academic Freedom: The Indivisibility of Due Process," in *Academic Freedom on Trial: 100 Years of Sifting and Winnowing at the University of Wisoconsin–Madison*, ed. W. Lee Hansen (Madison: Office of University Publications, University of Wisconsin–Madison, 1998), 219.

40. For an overview of the impact of McCarthyism on the universities, see Ellen Schrecker, *No Ivory Tower: McCarthyism and the Universities* (New York: Oxford University Press, 1986).

41. My favorite epithet identifies me as "the Lucille Ball of anti-anti-communism," Glenn Garvin, "Fools for Communism," Reason Online, April 2004, http://www.reason.com/news/show/29095.html (accessed December 2, 2007). See also John Earl Haynes and Harvey Klehr, *In Denial: Historians, Communism and Espionage* (San Francisco: Encounter Books, 2003).

42. Fritz Machlup, "In Defense of Academic Tenure," in *The Case for Tenure*, ed. Matthew W. Finkin (Ithaca, NY: Cornell University Press, 1996), 22.

43. James C. Hearn, "Faculty Salary Structures in Research Universities: Implications for Productivity," in *Faculty Productivity: Facts, Fictions, and Issues*, ed. William G. Tierney (New York: Falmer Press, 1999), 124.

44. "1915 Declaration of Principles," 294.

45. "1940 Statement of Principles," 3.

46. Hearn, "Faculty Salary Structures," 134.

47. Much of this argument comes from the brilliant essay by Michael S. McPherson and Gordon C. Winston, "The Economics of Academic Tenure: A Relational Perspective," in *Case for Tenure*, ed. Finkin, 99–123.

48. Daniel T. Layzell, "Higher Education's Changing Environment: Faculty Productivity and the Reward Structure," in *Faculty Productivity*, ed. Tierney, 15–16.

49. Richard P. Chait and Andrew T. Ford, *Beyond Traditional Tenure* (San Francisco: Jossey-Bass, 1982), 52.

50. William G. Tierney and Estela Mara Bensimon, *Promotion and Tenure: Community and Socialization in Academe* (Albany: State University of New York Press, 1996), 43–74.

51. Modern Language Association, "Report of the Task Force on Evaluating Scholarship for Tenure and Promotion," December 2006, http://www.mla.org/pdf/taskforcereport0608.pdf (accessed July 1, 2009).

52. Chait and Ford, *Beyond Traditional Tenure*, 42.

53. William Van Alstyne, "Tenure: A Summary, Explanation, and 'Defense,'" in *Case for Tenure*, ed. Finkin, 4.

54. Gary Rhoades, *Managed Professionals: Unionized Faculty and Restructuring Academic Labor* (Albany: State University of New York Press, 1998), 83–129.

55. Van Alstyne, "Tenure," 87.

56. Ibid., 5.

57. Chait and Ford, *Beyond Traditional Tenure*, 219.

58. Ibid., 6–7.

59. Kaplin and Lee, *Law of Higher Education*, 282; Chait and Ford, *Beyond Traditional Tenure*, 236.

60. Chait and Ford, *Beyond Traditional Tenure*, 71–75.

61. Ibid., 42–43, 59.

62. "On the Relationship of Faculty Governance to Academic Freedom," in AAUP, *Policy Documents and Reports*, 224.

63. Ibid., 226.

64. Donald Kennedy, *Academic Duty* (Cambridge, MA: Harvard University Press, 1997), 141–46; Robert O'Neil, *Academic Freedom in the Wired World: Political Extremism, Corporate Power, and the University* (Cambridge, MA: Harvard University Press, 2008), 117.

65. Christopher Jencks and David Riesman, *The Academic Revolution*, rev. ed. (1968; Chicago: University of Chicago Press, 1977), 17–18, 130.

66. Gabriel E. Kaplan, "How Academic Ships Actually Navigate," in *Governing Academia*, ed. Ronald G. Ehrenberg (Ithaca, NY: Cornell University Press, 2004), 175.

67. O'Neil, *Academic Freedom*, 117; Kennedy, *Academic Duty*, 144–45.
68. Arthur T. Hadley, quoted in Bowman, *College Professor in America*, 105.

Chapter 2: Academic Freedom Under Attack: Subversives, Squeaky Wheels, and "Special Obligations"

1. For a more extensive discussion of the development of academic freedom through the McCarthy period, including the University of Washington case, see Ellen Schrecker, *No Ivory Tower: McCarthyism and the Universities* (New York: Oxford University Press, 1986). Although that book is over twenty years old, I do not see any need to revise it, and much of the following material is drawn from that earlier work. I am not, therefore, providing the original references for that information.

On the University of Washington, see Vern Countryman, *Un-American Activities in the State of Washington: The Work of the Canwell Committee* (Ithaca, NY: Cornell University Press, 1951); and Jane Sanders, *Cold War on the Campus: Academic Freedom at the University of Washington, 1946–1964* (Seattle: University of Washington Press, 1979).

2. Ralph Gundlach, interview with Paul Tillett, June 20, 1962, in Paul Tillett papers, Seeley Mudd Library, Princeton University.

3. James A. Thompson '47, in Nancy Wick, "Seeing Red," *Columns: The University of Washington Alumni Magazine*, December 1997, http://www.washington.edu/alumni/columns/dec97/red1.html (accessed October 11, 2007).

4. Countryman, *Un-American Activities*, 228–29.

5. Ibid., 222, 228, 231.

6. Sanders, *Cold War on the Campus*, 39–43.

7. Countryman, *Un-American Activities*, 256; Peter Charles Schaehrer, "McCarthyism and Academic Freedom—Three Case Studies," PhD diss., Columbia University Teachers College, 1974, 95.

8. Countryman, *Un-American Activities*, 267–69.

9. Gundlach, Tillett interview; Sanders, *Cold War on the Campus*, 95.

10. Lawrence Veysey, *The Emergence of the American University* (Chicago: University of Chicago Press, 1965), 394–95, 418–28; Carol Gruber, *Mars and Minerva: World War I and the Uses of the Higher Learning in America* (Baton Rouge: Louisiana State University Press, 1975), 176, 193–95.

11. For a fuller discussion of the Davis and Moore cases, see Schrecker, *No Ivory Tower*, 219–40.

12. *Schwimmer v. U.S.*, 279 U.S. 644, 655–56.

13. *Trotman v. Bd. of Trustees of Lincoln Univ.*, 635 F. 2d 216, 226 (3rd Cir. 1980), cited in *Hong v. Grant*, AAUP brief, in possession of the author.

14. Benjamin G. Rader, " 'That Little Pill': Richard T. Ely and the Emerging Parameters of Professional Propriety," in *Academic Freedom on Trial: 100 Years of Sifting and Winnowing at the University of Wisconsin–Madison*, ed. W. Lee Hansen (Madison: Office of University Publications, University of Wisconsin–Madison, 1998), 94–95; W. Lee Hansen, "Introduction," in ibid., 3; Theron F. Schlabach, "An Aristocrat on Trial: The Case of Richard T. Ely," in ibid., 37–50; Dorothy Ross, "Socialism and American

Liberalism: Academic Social Thought in the 1880's," *Perspectives in American History* 11 (1977–78): 53.

15. Mary O. Furner, *Advocacy and Objectivity: A Crisis in the Professionalization of American Social Science, 1865–1905* (Lexington: University Press of Kentucky, 1975), 163–204.

16. Walter Metzger, *The Development of Academic Freedom in the United States: The Age of the University* (New York: Columbia University Press, 1955), 439.

17. Furner, *Advocacy and Objectivity*, 236–59.

18. "Report of the Committee of Inquiry on the Case of Professor Scott Nearing of the University of Pennsylvania," in *Professors on Guard: The First AAUP Investigations*, ed. Walter P. Metzger (New York: Arno Press, 1977), 38, 27, 40–41.

19. Scott Nearing, *The Making of a Radical: A Political Autobiography* (White River Junction, VT: Chelsea Green, 2000), 98–102.

20. Gruber, *Mars and Minerva*, 163–64.

21. Ibid., 165–69.

22. Ibid., 176–79.

23. Ibid., 196–202.

24. Ibid., 179–87, 203–5.

25. Ibid., 186.

26. Schrecker, *No Ivory Tower*, 144, 148.

27. Ibid., 104–12.

28. Sidney Hook, "Heresy—Yes, but Conspiracy—No," *New York Times Magazine*, July 9, 1950, 39.

29. Schrecker, *No Ivory Tower*, 111.

30. Wendell Furry, interview with the author, November 4, 1977.

31. Joseph McCarthy to Nathan Pusey, November 9, 1953, quoted in Dan Gillmor, *Fear, the Accuser* (New York: Abelard-Schuman, 1954), 146.

32. Association of American Universities, "The Rights and Responsibilities of Universities and their Faculties," March 24, 1953 (pamphlet published by Princeton University Press).

33. Bentley Glass et al., "Academic Freedom and Tenure in the Quest for National Security," *AAUP Bulletin* 42, no. 1 (Spring 1956): 81–83.

34. John Earl Haynes, Harvey Klehr, and Alexander Vassiliev, *Spies: The Rise and Fall of the KGB in America* (New Haven, CT: Yale University Press, 2009), 51, 81–87.

35. Fred Richard Zimring, "Academic Freedom and the Cold War: The Dismissal of Barrows Dunham from Temple University: A Case Study," Ed.D. diss., Columbia University Teachers College, 1981.

36. "Reed College," *AAUP Bulletin* 44, no. 1 (Spring 1958): 114.

37. David P. Gardner, *The California Oath Controversy* (Berkeley: University of California Press, 1967); Bob Blauner, *Resisting McCarthyism: To Sign or Not to Sign California's Loyalty Oath* (Stanford, CA: Stanford University Press, 2009).

38. Peter Novick, *That Noble Dream: The "Objectivity Question" and the American Historical Profession* (New York: Cambridge University Press, 1988); David H. Price, *Threatening Anthropology: The FBI's Surveillance and Repression of Activist Anthropologists* (Durham, NC: Duke University Press, 2004); John McCumber, *Time*

in the Ditch: American Philosophy and the McCarthy Era (Evanston, IL: Northwestern University Press, 2001).

39. Schrecker, *No Ivory Tower*, 314–35.

Chapter 3: "Part of the Struggle": Faculties Confront the 1960s

1. Dorothy Ansart and Judith Grier, "Inventory to the Records of the Office of Public Information on the Vietnam War Teach-Ins, 1965–1966," April 27, 1992, Special Collections and University Archives, Rutgers University Libraries, http://www2.scc.rutgers.edu/ead/uarchives/teachinsb.html (accessed May 5, 2008); "The Ninth Alexander Meiklejohn Award," *American Association of University Professors Bulletin* 52, no. 2 (June 1966): 211–13 (hereafter *AAUP Bulletin*); Richard M. Nixon, "Professor Genovese and Academic Freedom," in *Teach-Ins: U.S.A. Reports, Opinions, Documents*, ed. Louis Menashe and Ronald Radosh (New York: Praeger, 1967), 234.

2. "The Ninth Alexander Meiklejohn Award," 212; Ronald Sullivan, "Kennedy Defends Academic Liberty," *New York Times*, October 15, 1965 (hereafter *NYT*).

3. William V. Musto and Douglas E. Gimson, "Report on the 'Genovese Case,' " in *Teach-Ins: U.S.A.*, ed. Menashe and Radosh, 232–33; Ansart and Greer, "Inventory."

4. Jonathan M. Wiener, "Radical Historians and the Crisis in American History, 1959–1980," *Journal of American History* 76, no. 2 (September 1989): 416.

5. Clark Kerr, oral history interview, January 26, 1967, in Kerr, Personal and Professional Papers, CU 302 Carton 26, Folder 15, Bancroft Library, University of California–Berkeley.

6. George R. Stewart, "On University Government," *AAUP Bulletin* 47, no. 1 (Spring 1961): 60.

7. Clark Kerr, interview, June 19, 1967, in Kerr, Personal and Professional Papers, CU 302 Carton 26, Folder 18; Robert Cohen, "The Many Meanings of the FSM," in *The Free Speech Movement: Reflections on Berkeley in the 1960s*, ed. Robert Cohen and Reginald E. Zelnik (Berkeley: University of California Press, 2002), 15–16.

8. "The Ninth Alexander Meiklejohn Award," 213.

9. Bertram H. Davis, "From the General Secretary," *AAUP Bulletin* 54, no. 3 (September 1968): 292; Edward E. Ericson Jr., *Radicals in the University* (Stanford: CA Hoover Institution Press, 1975), 103.

10. Christopher J. Lucas, *Crisis in the Academy: Rethinking Higher Education in America* (New York: St. Martin's Press, 1996), 12; Everett Carll Ladd Jr. and Seymour Martin Lipset, *The Divided Academy: Professors and Politics* (New York: McGraw-Hill, 1975), 1–2.

11. Mason Gross, quoted in Arnold Beichman, "Study in Academic Freedom," in *Teach-Ins, U.S.A.*, ed. Menashe and Radosh, 242.

12. William G. Bowen, quoted in Eileen E. Schell, *Gypsy Academics and Mother-Teachers: Gender, Contingent Labor, and Writing Instruction* (Portsmouth, NH: Boynton/Cook, 1998), 33.

13. Paul Lauter, interview with the author, April 13, 2008; *NUC Newsletter*, 3, no. 10 (January 15, 1970), in New University Conference Papers, Tamiment Library, New York University.

14. Kenneth J. Heineman, *Campus Wars: The Peace Movement at American State Universities in the Vietnam Era* (New York: New York University Press, 1993), 44.

15. On the isolation of radical faculty members, see Heineman, *Campus Wars*, 42–75; Lauter, interview; Marvin Gettleman, interview with the author, June 5, 2008. Some administrations also supported the formation of SDS chapters in order to give their campuses a "with-it" image. Jack Nusan Porter, *Student Protest and the Technocratic Society: The Case of ROTC* (Chicago: Adams Press, 1971, 1973), 47–48.

16. "Academic Freedom and Tenure: Allen University and Benedict College," *AAUP Bulletin* 46, no. 1 (Spring 1960): 103; Jeff Woods, *Black Struggle, Red Scare: Segregation and Anti-Communism in the South, 1948–1968* (Baton Rouge: Louisiana State University Press, 2004), 114.

17. "Academic Freedom and Tenure: Alabama State College," *AAUP Bulletin* 47, no. 4 (December 1961) 303–9; Ralph F. Fuchs, "The Association and the Desegregation Controversy," March 30, 1962, *AAUP Bulletin* 48, no. 2 (June 1962): 167–69; "Academic Freedom and Tenure: Sam Houston State Teachers College," *AAUP Bulletin* 49, no. 1 (March 1963): 44–51; Carol Polsgrove, *Divided Minds: Intellectuals and the Civil Rights Movement* (New York: W.W. Norton, 2001), 106–10; Joy Williamson-Lott, "Academic Freedom as an Instrumentality of Treason: Faculty in Southern Colleges During the Civil Rights Movement," paper presented at the History of Education Society Conference, Philadelphia, PA, October 2009.

18. Woods, *Black Struggle, Red Scare*, 50–84; "Aid to the Arkansas Professors," *AAUP Bulletin* 46, no. 1 (March 1960): 50; *Shelton v. Tucker*, 364 U.S. 479 (1960).

19. Fuchs, "The Association and the Desegregation Controversy," 169.

20. "Academic Freedom in Mississippi: A Report of a Special Committee," *AAUP Bulletin* 51, no. 3 (September 1965): 341–56.

21. Woods, *Black Struggle, Red Scare*, 201–3; John Dittmer, *Local People: The Struggle for Civil Rights in Mississippi* (Urbana: University of Illinois Press. 1994), 234–36.

22. Dittmer estimates that there were 650 students in the project. *Local People*, 244.

23. Ladd and Lipset, *Divided Academy*, 108, 122.

24. For a good overview of the Berkeley Free Speech movement, see the collected essays in *Free Speech Movement*, ed. Cohen and Zelnik: for other schools, see Heineman, *Campus Wars*, 84.

25. David A. Hollinger, "A View from the Margins," in *Free Speech Movement*, ed. Cohen and Zelnick, 183.

26. William Kornhauser, "The Politics of Confrontation: Crisis of Authority," in *The New American Revolution*, ed. Roderick Aya and Norman Mills (New York: The Free Press, 1971), 271.

27. Ladd and Lipset, *Divided Academy*, 4, 26.

28. For an overview of the various teach-ins, see *Teach-Ins: U.S.A.*, ed. Menashe and Radosh.

29. Ibid., 25.

30. Ibid., 21.

31. Ibid., 29, 106, 104.

32. Heineman, *Campus Wars*, 141, 159, 233.

33. Ladd and Lipset, *Divided Academy*, 208–10.

34. Ibid., 115, 96–97: T.R. McConnell, "Faculty Interests in Value Change and Power Conflicts," *AAUP Bulletin* 55, no. 3 (September 1969): 346.

35. "A Statement of the Association's Special Committee on Challenge and Change," *AAUP Bulletin* 55, no. 4 (December 1969): 461–62.

36. Heineman, *Campus Wars*, 44.

37. Porter, *Student Protest*, 64–65.

38. Heineman, *Campus Wars*, 134.

39. Joanne Grant, *Confrontation on Campus: The Columbia Pattern for the New Protest* (New York: New American Library, 1969), 35.

40. Heineman, *Campus Wars*, 166.

41. Ibid., 167.

42. Ibid., 218.

43. Porter, *Student Protest*, 57–61.

44. "U. of Pittsburgh to Drop Credits for the ROTC," *NYT*, December 8, 1968, in personal files of Paul Lauter, Trinity College, Hartford, CT.

45. Porter, *Student Protest*, 101, 125–28.

46. Heineman, *Campus Wars*, 174.

47. Paul Forman, "Beyond Quantum Electronics: National Security as Basis for Physical Research in the United States, 1940–1960," *Historical Studies in the Physical and Biological Sciences* 18, no. 1 (1987): 207; Heineman, *Campus Wars*, 201.

48. McConnell, "Faculty Interests in Value Change and Power Conflicts," 343.

49. Heineman, *Campus Wars*, 13.

50. Grant, *Confrontation on Campus*, 35–36.

51. Heineman, *Campus Wars*, 13–18, 214–17; Roger L. Geiger, *Research and Relevant Knowledge: American Research Universities Since World War II* (New York: Oxford University Press, 1993), 194.

52. Edward S. Herman and Robert J. Rutman, "University of Pennsylvania's CB Warfare Controversy," *BioScience* 17, no. 8 (August 1967): 526–29; New York University Chapter, NUC, "A Rational Inquiry into the Roles Played by Dr. Ivan L. Bennett, Jr. and New York University in the Utilization and Development of Technical and Human Resources for the U.S. Government's Chemical Biological Weapons Program and Military Policies," 1970, NUC Papers, Tamiment.

53. Carol Brightman, "The Weed Killers: Chemical and Biological Warfare in V'nam," *Viet-Report*, June/July 1966, 9–14, http://members.aol.com/warlibrary/vwsr10.htm (accessed July 16, 2008).

54. Herman and Rutman, "University of Pennsylvania's CB Warfare Controversy," 526–27; Heineman, *Campus Wars*, 33, 44, 59–60, 65; Charles V. Kidd, "The Implications of Research Funds for Academic Freedom," *Law and Contemporary Problems* 28 (1963): 614.

55. Howard Brick, *Age of Contradiction: American Thought and Culture in the 1960s* (New York: Twayne, 1998), 28–33.

56. Lauter, interview.

57. Heineman, *Campus Wars*, 65; Porter, *Student Protest*, 58; Committee Against Academic Repression, *Counter-Attack*, no. 1 (September 1969), Lauter files.

58. "NUC Office Staff to Brother or Sister," October 17, 1969; John McDermott, "NUC as Cadre," *NUC Newsletter* 3, no. 3 (January 20, 1970), both in Lauter files.

59. "Interim Committee—New University Conference Statement, Draft #2," October 1968, NUC Papers, Tamiment.

60. Ericson, *Radicals in the University*, 65; Rich Rothstein to "Comrades," January 20, 1970; Memo to "All NUC Chapter Contacts, Executive Committee, 1970–71 Staff," April 12, 1970; Chris Bose and others to "Comrades," April 1973, all in Lauter files; Lauter, interview.

61. Rich Rothstein to NUC Exec. Comm., December 5, 1969; Richie to NUC Exec. Comm., March 16, 1970; Rich to NUC Exec. Comm., February 5, 1970; press release, February 9, 1970, all in Lauter files; John McDermott, interview with the author, May 3, 2008.

62. Barbara Andrews "Problems of NUC," NUC Papers, Tamiment.

63. McDermott, interview.

64. Lauter to Grover Furr, February 3, 1968 (or 1969), Lauter files; "Executive Committee Report," June 1970; "Open Admissions: Toward a Radical Perspective," 1970; Robert Klawitter, "Degrading Education," n.d., NUC Papers, Tamiment; Lauter, interview.

65. "Free University—Liberation School" at NYU, n.d., c. 1970; "Internal Education," n.d., both in NUC Papers, Tamiment.

66. Grant, *Confrontation on Campus*, 138–39.

67. Porter, *Student Protest*, 80.

68. Heineman, *Campus Wars*, 53.

69. Bart Meyers, interview with the author, April 14, 2008.

70. Heineman, *Campus Wars*, 52–53, 57–61.

71. Staughton Lynd, "Restructuring the University," 1969, NUC Papers, Tamiment; Heineman, *Campus Wars*, 140–41.

72. "Political Repression, Workshop Draft" n.d., probably summer 1968 or 1969, Lauter files.

73. Neil Resnikoff, "Progress Report from the Chairman of the National Committee's Subcommittee on Professional Organizing," Jan. 30, 1970, Lauter files; Lauter, interview.

74. Resnikoff, "Progress Report"; Walter Sullivan, "Strike to Protest 'Misuse' of Science," *NYT*, February 6, 1969, Lauter files.

75. Dick Flacks, " 'Radical Caucuses' Shake the Disciplines," Lauter files.

76. Martin Nicolaus, "Fat-Cat Sociology: Remarks at the American Sociological Association Convention," August 1968, NUC Papers, Tamiment; Flacks, " 'Radical Caucuses' Shake the Disciplines."

77. Peter Novick, *That Noble Dream: The "Objectivity Question" and the American Historical Profession* (New York: Cambridge University Press, 1988), 435.

78. Richard Ohmann, *English in America: A Radical View of the Profession* (1976; Middleton, CT: Wesleyan University Press, 1996), 28–32; New University Conference

of the Modern Language Association, Newsletter #1, January 1969; Howe, Lauter, Ohmann, Kampf to A.H. Raskin, January 1, 1969, Lauter files; Lauter, interview.

79. Heineman, *Campus Wars*, 45, 65, 72.

80. Ohmann, *English in America*, xxiii, 5.

81. William L. Van Deburg, *New Day in Babylon: The Black Power Movement and American Culture, 1965–1975* (Chicago: University of Chicago Press, 1992), 64–81; Donald Alexander Downs, *Cornell '69: Liberalism and the Crisis of the American University* (Ithaca, NY: Cornell University Press, 1999), 65.

82. Stephen Lythcott, "Black Studies at Antioch," in *New Perspectives on Black Studies*, ed. John W. Blassingame, (Urbana: University of Illinois Press, 1971), 128.

83. Manning Marable, "Black Studies and the Racial Mountain," *Souls* 2 (Summer 2000): 18–19.

84. Michele Russell, "Erased, Debased, and Encased: The Dynamics of African Educational Colonization in America," in *New Perspectives on Black Studies*, ed. Blassingame, 44.

85. June Jordan, "Black Studies: Bringing Back the Person," in *New Perspectives on Black Studies*, ed. Blassingame, 37.

86. Ibid., 35–36.

87. Novick, *That Noble Dream*, 477.

88. Lythcott, "Black Studies at Antioch," 126; Roger A. Fischer, "Ghetto and Gown: The Birth of Black Studies," in *New Perspectives on Black Studies*, ed. Blassingame, 23.

89. Downs, *Cornell '69*, 83.

90. Catharine R. Stimpson, "Black Culture/White Teacher," in *New Perspectives on Black Studies*, ed. Blassingame, 170–79; Marable, "Black Studies and the Racial Mountain," 24–25.

91. Van Deburg, *New Day in Babylon*, 74.

92. John Blassingame, "Introduction," in *New Perspectives on Black Studies*, ed. Blassingame, xvii–xviii; Van Deburg, *New Day in Babylon*, 74–75.

93. Van Deburg, *New Day in Babylon*, 75; Downs, *Cornell '69*, 129.

94. Van Deburg, *New Day in Babylon*, 74–75.

95. Marable, "Black Studies and the Racial Mountain," 22–26.

96. Blassingame, "Introduction," xiii–xix; Downs, *Cornell '69*, 129; Allan Bloom, *The Closing of the American Mind: How Higher Education Has Failed Democracy and Impoverished the Souls of Today's Students* (New York: Simon & Schuster, 1987), 95.

97. Accurate statistics on the numbers of black studies programs are hard to come by. For an assessment, see Marable, "Black Studies and the Racial Mountain," 24; Nellie Y. McKay, "Charting a Personal Journey: A Road to Women's Studies," in *The Politics of Women's Studies: Testimony from Thirty Founding Mothers*, ed. Florence Howe (New York: The Feminist Press, 2000), 211; Novick, *That Noble Dream*, 477.

98. Sundiata Keita Cha-Jua, "Black Studies in the New Millennium: Resurrecting Ghosts of the Past," *Souls* 2 (Summer 2000): 44.

99. Judith Jarvis Thompson, "Ideology and Faculty Selection," *Law and Contemporary Problems* (1990): 155–76.

100. For testimony about the problems of establishing the field, see the selections in *Politics of Women's Studies*, ed. Howe.

101. Mary Jo Buhle, "Introduction," Marilyn Jacoby Boxer, "Modern Woman Not Lost," and Elizabeth Lapovsky Kennedy, "Dream of Social Justice: Building Women's Studies at the State University of New York, Buffalo," in *Politics of Women's Studies*, ed. Howe, xv, xxii–xxiii, 238, 248; Marilyn Jacoby Boxer, *When Women Ask the Questions: Creating Women's Studies in America* (Baltimore: Johns Hopkins University Press, 1998), 2.

102. Buhle, "Introduction," xx.

103. Boxer, *When Women Ask the Questions*, 13–14.

104. Buhle, "Introduction," xxv; Ellen Carol DuBois, Gail Paradise Kelly, Elizabeth Lapovsky Kennedy, Carolyn W. Korsmeyer, and Lillian S. Robinson, *Feminist Scholarship: Kindling in the Groves of Academe* (Urbana: University of Illinois Press, 1985), 21–24.

105. Myra Dinnerstein, "A Political Education," in *Politics of Women's Studies*, ed. Howe, 294.

106. Buhle, "Introduction," xxv.

107. DuBois et al., *Feminist Scholarship*, 3.

108. Boxer, *When Women Ask the Questions*, 193.

109. Marvin Gettleman, interview, July 8, 2008; Margaret Strobel, "The Academy and the Activist," in *Politics of Women's Studies*, ed. Howe, 159.

110. Boxer, *When Women Ask the Questions*, 7–8; Nancy Topping Bazin, "The Gender Revolution," and Barbara W. Gerber, "Moving from the Periphery to the Center," both in *Politics of Women's Studies*, ed. Howe, 65, 77.

111. Annette Kolodny, "A Sense of Discovery, Mixed with a Sense of Justice," in *Politics of Women's Studies*, ed. Howe, 285.

112. Josephine Donovan, "A Cause of Our Own." in *Politics of Women's Studies*, ed. Howe, 98–99; Boxer, *When Women Ask the Questions*, 66; Michael Nash, interview, December 8, 2009.

113. Bazin "The Gender Revolution," and Annis Pratt, "Imploding Marginality," both in *Politics of Women's Studies*, ed. Howe, 65, 87.

114. Donovan, "A Cause of Our Own," 101.

115. Gerber, "Moving from the Periphery to the Center," Pratt, "Imploding Marginality," and Mary Anne Ferguson, "Awakening," all in *Politics of Women's Studies*, ed. Howe, 70, 82, 172.

116. Boxer, *When Women Ask the Questions*, 25–26, 12.

117. Sheila Tobias, "Beginning in the 1960s," in *Politics of Women's Studies*, ed. Howe, 36.

118. Boxer, *When Women Ask the Questions*, 37–43.

119. DuBois et al., *Feminist Scholarship*, 2.

120. Boxer, *When Women Ask the Questions*, xv.

121. DuBois et al., *Feminist Scholarship*, 16.

122. Boxer, *When Women Ask the Questions*, 15, 18, 20.

123. Buhle, "Introduction," xi.

124. Ibid., xxvi; Boxer, *When Women Ask the Questions*, 49–50, 74–76.

125. Buhle, "Introduction," xxiv.

126. Strobel, "The Academy and the Activist," 252–56.

127. Inez Martinez, "An Odyssey," in *Politics of Women's Studies*, ed. Howe, 110.

128. Donovan, "A Cause of Our Own," 97–98; Boxer, *When Women Ask the Questions*, 81–92, 201–2.

129. "Collective Bargaining and the Structure and Functioning of the Association," a Report by the Executive Committee for the Council, October 1971 (hereafter AAUP 1971 Report).

130. Tom Hecht, "The Spring National Committee Meeting: An Overview," 1972, NUC Papers, Tamiment.

131. NUC, Subcommittee on Labor, "Radicals and Education Unions," n.d., c. 1971, NUC Papers, Tamiment.

132. NUC, Subcommittee on Labor, "Radicals and Education Unions."

133. Judith Wagner DeCew, *Unionization in the Academy: Visions and Realities* (Lanham, MD: Rowman & Littlefield, 2003), 13.

134. Ibid., 12–16.

135. Ralph S. Brown Jr., "Representation of Economic Interests: Report of a Conference," *AAUP Bulletin* 51, no. 3 (September 1965): 374–77; AAUP 1971 Report.

Chapter 4: "A Long-Range and Difficult Project": The Backlash Against the 1960s

1. Donald Alexander Downs, *Cornell '69: Liberalism and the Crisis of the American University* (Ithaca, NY: Cornell University Press, 1999), 245.

2. Ibid., 236–45.

3. Ibid., 271–74.

4. Allan Bloom, *The Closing of the American Mind: How Higher Education Has Failed Democracy and Impoverished the Souls of Today's Students* (New York: Simon & Schuster, 1987), 320; Bruce Fellman, "Lion in Winter," *Yale Alumni Magazine*, April 2002, http://www.yalealumnimagazine.com/issues/02_04/kagan.html (accessed October 7, 2008).

5. Todd Gitlin, *The Whole World Is Watching: Mass Media in the Making and Unmaking of the New Left* (Berkeley: University of California Press, 1980), 48.

6. Robert Cohen, "The Many Meanings of the FSM," in *The Free Speech Movement: Reflections on Berkeley in the 1960s*, ed. Robert Cohen and Reginald E. Zelnik (Berkeley: University of California Press, 2002), 24–26. For a fuller discussion of the media's response to the student movement, see Gitlin, *Whole World Is Watching.*

7. See for example, "Professors Hold Vietnam Protest," *NYT*, March 25, 1965, 9; Mitchel Levitas, "Vietnam Comes to Oregon U.," *New York Times Magazine*, May 9, 1965, 24; "Excerpts from National Teach-In on Vietnam Policy," *NYT*, May 17, 1965, 30; James Reston, "The Decline of Serious Debate," *NYT*, April 21, 1965, 44.

8. "Freedom on the Campus," editorial, *NYT*, November 1, 1967.

9. Downs, *Cornell '69*, 282–83; Homer Bigart, "Cornell Faculty Reverses Itself on Negroes," *NYT*, April 24, 1969, 1; Bigart, "Faculty Revolt Upsets Cornell," *NYT*, April 25, 1969.

10. "Reform by Bully," editorial, *NYT*, April 26, 1969, 36; "Campus Totalitarians," editorial, *NYT*, May 20, 1969, 46.

11. *Chicago Tribune*, quoted in Rick Perlstein, *Nixonland: The Rise of a President and the Fracturing of America* (New York: Scribner, 2008), 258.

12. Sidney Hook, *Academic Freedom and Academic Anarchy* (New York: Cowles, 1970), 233; Steven V. Roberts, "Reagan Reaps Political Profit from Student Revolts on Coast," *NYT*, February 10, 1969.

13. Everett Carll Ladd Jr. and Seymour Martin Lipset, *The Divided Academy: Professors and Politics* (New York: McGraw-Hill, 1975), 35.

14. "Red Infiltration Alleged," *NYT*, October 15, 1965, 3; "Trial by Investigation," *NYT*, November 3, 1965, 38.

15. Ronald Reagan, speech, May 22, 1966, quoted in Perlstein, *Nixonland*, 83; W.J. Rorabaugh, *Berkeley at War: The 1960s* (New York: Oxford University Press, 1989), 109.

16. Gerald J. De Groot, "Ronald Reagan and Student Unrest, 1966–1970," *Pacific Historical Review* 65, no. 1 (February 1996): 107–9.

17. Ibid., 125.

18. Lawrence E. Davies, "Reagan Promises to Rid Campuses of 'Anarchists,'" *NYT*, January 8, 1969; Perlstein, *Nixonland*, 91; De Groot, "Reagan and Student Unrest," 122.

19. De Groot, "Reagan and Student Unrest," 121.

20. Perlstein, *Nixonland*, 202.

21. Ibid., 224.

22. James Calhoun, ed., *The Real Spiro Agnew: Commonsense Quotations of a Household Word* (Gretna, LA: Pelican, 1970), 40, 41.

23. Ibid., 41.

24. Ibid., 109.

25. Ibid., 107.

26. Ibid., 113.

27. Hook, *Academic Freedom and Academic Anarchy*, 233; Donald Janson, "Afro-American Center Is Burned at the University of Wisconsin," *NYT*, February 20, 1969; F.M.H. (Fred M. Hechinger?), "A Counterrevolution Against the Radicals," *NYT*, February 16, 1969; Downs, *Cornell: '69*, 283.

28. David Landes, "Letter to the Editor," *NYT*, December 29, 1964.

29. Sidney Hook, "Freedom to Learn, but Not to Riot," *New York Times Magazine*, January 3, 1965, 18.

30. Hook, *Academic Freedom and Academic Anarchy*, 183, 212, 216–17.

31. Ladd and Lipset, *Divided Academy*, 96–97, 203–18.

32. T.R. McConnell, "Faculty Interests in Value Change and Power Conflicts," *AAUP Bulletin* 55, no. 3 (September 1969): 346.

33. Bertram Davis, "From the General Secretary," 49; "The Fifty-Fifth Annual Meeting," 152; "Challenge and Change Forum," 276, all in *AAUP Bulletin* 55, no. 2 (June 1969).

34. Donald N. Koster, "On Institutional Neutrality," *AAUP Bulletin* 56, no. 1 (Spring 1970): 11–13.

35. Winton U. Solberg, "On Institutional Neutrality," *AAUP Bulletin* 56, no. 1 (Spring 1970): 11–13.

36. Russell Kirk, "The Scholar Is Not a Lion or a Fox," *NYT*, May 1, 1966.

37. Hook, *Academic Freedom and Academic Anarchy*, 171–72.

38. Rorabaugh, *Berkeley at War*, 168.

39. Downs, *Cornell '69*, 136–37; Steve Weissman, "Endgame, How the Berkeley Grads Organized to Win," in *Free Speech Movement*, ed. Cohen and Zelnick, 177.

40. Rorabaugh, *Berkeley at War*, 161.

41. Ladd and Lipset, *Divided Academy*, 205–10; Leon Wofsy, "When the FSM Disturbed the Faculty Peace," in *Free Speech Movement*, ed. Cohen and Zelnick, 354.

42. Joanne Grant, *Confrontation on Campus: The Columbia Pattern for the New Protest* (New York: New American Library, 1969), 124.

43. Ibid., 76.

44. Downs, *Cornell '69*, 91.

45. "1915 Declaration of Principles on Academic Freedom and Academic Tenure," in American Association of University Professors, *Policy Documents and Reports*, 9th ed. (Washington, DC: American Association of University Professors, 2001), 295.

46. Clark Kerr, *The Uses of the University* (Cambridge, MA: Harvard University Press, 1963), 18.

47. Richard F. Schier, "The Problem of the Lumpenprofessoriat," *AAUP Bulletin*, 56, no. 4 (December 1970): 362–63.

48. Fredson Bowers, "On a Future for Graduate Studies," *AAUP Bulletin* 56, no. 4 (December 1970): 367.

49. Frank R. Kemerer and J. Victor Baldridge, *Unions on Campus* (San Francisco: Jossey-Bass, 1975), 12; Julius Getman, *In the Company of Scholars: The Struggle for the Soul of Higher Education* (Austin: University of Texas Press, 1992), 103.

50. Jacques Barzun and Eric Hoffer testimony to Congress, May 9, 1969, cited in De Groot, "Reagan and Student Unrest," 120n.

51. See, for example, Bloom, *Closing of the American Mind*, 49–51, 322.

52. David Vogel, *Fluctuating Fortunes: The Political Power of Business in America* (New York: Basic Books, 1989), 221; John J. Miller, *A Gift of Freedom: How the John M. Olin Foundation Changed America* (San Francisco: Encounter Books, 2006), 37.

53. Lewis F. Powell, "Attack on American Free Enterprise System," August 23, 1971, copy in the author's possession, courtesy of David Hollinger.

54. John J. Miller, "Foundation's End: The Last Days of John M. Olin's Conservative Fortune," *National Review* online, April 6, 2005, http://article.nationalreview.com/?q=MzU5OTU2ZWV1OGRhMzA1NmMyNjM3MzAzMDNiNWEyNzA=, (accessed November 29, 2008).

55. Vogel, *Fluctuating Fortunes*, 222.

56. Ellen Messer-Davidow, "Manufacturing the Attack on Liberalized Higher Education," *Social Text*, no. 36 (Autumn 1993): 40–80.

57. Messer-Davidow, "Manufacturing the Attack," 61.

58. Lawrence C. Soley, *Leasing the Ivory Tower: The Corporate Takeover of Academia* (Boston: South End Press, 1995), 133.

59. Soley, *Leasing the Ivory Tower*, 110–14, 138–39; Daniel Rodgers, lecture, University Seminar, Columbia University, September 21, 2000; Miller, *Gift of Freedom*, 71–79.

60. William E. Simon, "To Reopen the American Mind," *Academic Questions* 1, no. 4 (Fall 1988): 74.

61. Lawrence J. Delaney Jr. and Leslie Lenkowsky, "The New Voice on Campus: 'Alternative Student Journalism,'" *Academic Questions* 1, no. 2 (Spring 1988): 32–41; Vogel, *Fluctuating Fortunes*, 222; Sara Diamond, "The Funding of the NAS," in *Beyond PC: Toward a Politics of Understanding*, ed. Patricia Aufderheide (St. Paul, MN: Graywolf Press, 1992), 89.

62. Herbert London, "A Call to the Academy," *Academic Questions* 1, no. 1 (Winter 1987–88): 3–4.

63. National Association of Scholars, "The Wrong Way to Reduce Campus Tensions," in *Beyond PC*, ed. Aufderheide, 7–8.

64. Messer-Davidow, "Manufacturing the Attack," 64; Sara Diamond, "The Funding of the NAS," in *Beyond PC*, ed. Aufderheide, 96.

65. Jacob Weisberg, "NAS—Who Are These Guys, Anyway?" in *Beyond PC*, ed. Aufderheide, Donald A. Downs Jr., "Speech Codes and the Mission of the University," in *Academic Freedom on Trial: 100 Years of Sifting and Winnowing at the University of Wisoconsin–Madison*, ed. W. Lee Hansen (Madison: Office of University Publications, University of Wisconsin–Madison, 1998), 159; National Association of Scholars Web site home page, http://www.nas.org/who.cfm (accessed Nov. 29, 2008).

66. Messer-Davidow, "Manufacturing the Attack," 47.

67. Vogel, *Fluctuating Fortunes*, 227.

68. Carol Iannone, "Thought Reform and Education: A View from the University of Pennsylvania," *Academic Questions* 1, no. 4 (Fall 1988): 89; Stanley Rothman, "Tradition and Change: The University Under Stress," in *The Imperiled Academy*, ed. Howard Dickman (New Brunswick, NJ: Transaction Publishers, 1993), 27.

69. Miller, *Gift of Freedom*, 56.

70. Herbert I. London, "William Bennett in Perspective," *Academic Questions* 1, no. 4 (Fall 1988): 3–4; William J. Bennett, *To Reclaim a Legacy: A Report on the Humanities in Higher Education* (Washington, DC: National Endowment for the Humanities, 1984), 2, 16, 20.

71. Paul Berman, "Introduction," in *Debating P.C.: The Controversy over Political Correctness on College Campuses*, ed. Paul Berman (New York: Dell, 1992).

72. Bloom, *Closing of the American Mind*, 314.

73. Ibid., 51.

74. Ibid., 96.

75. Ibid., 341, 272, 261.

76. Roger Kimball, *Tenured Radicals: How Politics Has Corrupted Our Higher Education* (New York: Harper & Row, 1990), 4.

77. John Searle, "The Storm over the University," in *Debating P.C.*, ed. Berman, 86.

78. Ronald Sullivan, "A Sweep in Jersey," *NYT*, November 3, 1965, 1.

79. George H.W. Bush, speech, University of Michigan, May 5, 1991, http://www.umich.edu/whitehouse/presidents/ghwbush.html (accessed November 5, 2009).

80. Jon Wiener, *Historians in Trouble: Plagiarism, Fraud, and Politics in the Ivory Tower* (New York: The New Press, 2004), 63–69.

81. Getman, *In the Company of Scholars*, 181–90.

82. *Hopwood v. Texas*, 78 F.3d 932 (5th Cir. 1996).

83. Charles R. Lawrence III, "If He Hollers Let Him Go: Regulating Racist Speech on Campus," *Duke Law Journal* 1990, no. 3 (June 1990): 452.

84. Lawrence, "If He Hollers Let Him Go," 431–83; Mari J. Matsuda, "Public Response to Racist Speech: Considering the Victim's Story," *Michigan Law Review* 87, no. 8 (August 1989): 2320–81; Patricia J. Williams, "Defending the Gains," in *Beyond PC*, ed. Aufderheide, 194; Alan Charles Kors and Harvey A. Silverglate, *The Shadow University: The Betrayal of Liberty on America's Campuses* (New York: The Free Press, 1998), 158, 167.

85. *R.A.V. v. St. Paul*, 505 U.S. 377 (1992).

86. Williams, "Defending the Gains," 199–200.

87. Downs, "Speech Codes," 57.

88. *Levin v. Harleston*, 966 F.2d 85 (2nd Cir. 1992); Neil W. Hamilton, *Zealotry and Academic Freedom: A Legal and Historical Perspective* (New Brunswick, NJ: Transaction Publishers, 1995), 81; Kors and Silverglate, *Shadow University*, 133–34.

89. C. Vann Woodward, "Freedom and the Universities," in *Beyond PC*, ed. Aufderheide, 41; Downs, "Speech Codes," 167; *Doe v. University of Michigan*, 721 F. Supp. 852 (E.D. Mich. 1989).

90. Downs, "Speech Codes," 168; Nat Hentoff, "Academic Freedom: The Indivisibility of Due Process," in *Academic Freedom on Trial*, ed. Hansen, 220.

91. Kors and Silverglate, *Shadow University*, 154, 147, 159, 152–53.

92. John K. Wilson, *The Myth of Political Correctness: The Conservative Attack on Higher Education* (Durham, NC: Duke University Press, 1995), 99.

93. Kors and Silverglate, *Shadow University*, 265–88; Ted Finman, "Hate Speech Codes in Theory and Practice," in *Academic Freedom on Trial*, ed. Hansen, 193–97; Hentoff, "Academic Freedom," 221; National Association of Scholars, "The Wrong Way to Reduce Campus Tensions," in *Beyond PC*, ed. Aufderheide, 7–9.

94. Kors and Silverglate, *Shadow University*, 148, 175, 181, 233, 251–60.

95. Ibid., 86–87.

96. Though there are discussions of the Silva case in the secondary literature, I have based my account of it on *Silva v. University of New Hampshire*, 888 F. Supp. 293 (D.N.H. 1994). See also Richard J. Bernstein, "Guilty If Charged," *New York Review of Books*, January 13, 1994; Kors and Silverglate, *Shadow University*, 118–20; and Hamilton, *Zealotry and Academic Freedom*, 82–83.

97. Hamilton, *Zealotry and Academic Freedom*, 83; Craig R. Smith, "Academic Freedom vs. Civil Rights: A Special Report of the Center for First Amendment Studies," California State University, Long Beach, 2004.

98. *Silva v. University of New Hampshire.*

99. Kors and Silverglate, *Shadow University*, 115–16.

100. Ibid., 99, 121–27.

101. Ibid., 141.

102. AAUP, *Policy Documents and Reports*, 10th ed. (Washington, DC: American Association of University Professors, 2006), 37–38.

103. Bennett, *To Reclaim a Legacy*, 31.

104. Katha Pollitt, "Why Do We Read?" in *Debating P.C.*, ed. Berman, 201–11; Benjamin Johnson, Patrick Kavanagh, and Kevin Mattson, eds., *Steal This University: The Rise of the Corporate University and the Academic Labor Movement* (New York: Routledge, 2003), 232.

105. Bennett, *To Reclaim a Legacy*, 2; Francis Oakley, "Ignorant Armies and Nighttime Clashes: Changes in the Humanities Classroom, 1970–1995," in *What's Happened to the Humanities?* ed. Alvin Kernan (Princeton, NJ: Princeton University Press, 1997), 65–74; Kernan, "Change in the Humanities and Higher Education" in *What's Happened to the Humanities*? ed. Kernan, 7.

106. Stanley Aronowitz, *The Knowledge Factory: Dismantling the Corporate University and Creating True Higher Learning* (Boston: Beacon Press, 2000), 169.

107. Arthur M. Schlesinger Jr., *The Disuniting of America: Reflections on a Multicultural Society*, 2nd ed. (New York: W.W. Norton, 1991), 17, 25.

108. Edward W. Said, "The Politics of Knowledge," in *Debating P.C.*, ed. Berman, 188–89.

109. Michael Berubé, "Public Image Limited: Political Correctness and the Media's Big Lie," in *Debating P.C.*, ed. Berman, 146; Marilyn Jacoby Boxer, *When Women Ask the Questions: Creating Women's Studies in America* (Baltimore: Johns Hopkins University Press, 1998), 2, 38, 195.

110. Thomas Short, " 'Diversity' and 'Breaking the Disciplines': Two New Assaults on the Curriculum," *Academic Questions* 1, no. 3 (Summer 1988): 15; Wilson, *Myth of Political Correctness*, 85.

111. Donald Kennedy, *Academic Duty* (Cambridge, MA: Harvard University Press, 1997), 8–9; Searle, "The Storm over the University," 107–8; Raoul V. Mowatt, "What Revolution at Stanford?" in *Beyond PC*, ed. Aufderheide, 129–32.

112. Dinesh D'Souza, *Illiberal Education: The Politics of Race and Sex on Campus* (New York: The Free Press, 1991); Wilson, *Myth of Political Correctness*, 64–72.

113. Linda Brodkey, "Writing Permitted in Designated Areas Only," in *Higher Education Under Fire*, ed. Michael Berubé and Cary Nelson (New York: Routledge, 1995), 229.

114. Alan Gribben quoted in Lynne V. Cheney, *Telling the Truth: A Report on the State of the Humanities in Higher Education* (Washington, DC: National Endowment for the Humanities, 1992), 31; Getman, *In the Company of Scholars*, 137–49; Linda Brodkey and Shelli Fowler, "What Happened to English 306," in *Beyond PC*, ed. Aufderheide, 113–17.

115. Alan Gribben, "English Departments: Salvaging What Remains," *Academic Questions* 2, no. 4 (Fall 1989): 90.

116. Gates, "Whose Canon Is It, Anyway?" in *Debating P.C.*, ed. Berman, 193.

117. See, for example, Russell Jacoby, *The Last Intellectuals: American Culture in the Age of Academe* (New York: Basic Books, 1987).

118. Paul Hollander, "From Iconoclasm to Conventional Wisdom: The Sixties in the Eighties," *Academic Questions* 2, no. 4 (Fall 1989): 37; Bennett, *To Reclaim a Legacy*, 16; Simon, "To Reopen the American Mind," 73.

119. Cheney, *Telling the Truth*, 6–7.

120. Bloom, *Closing of the American Mind*, 39, 314, 379.

121. Cheney, *Telling the Truth*, 39.

122. Ibid., 20; Kimball, *Tenured Radicals*, 96–115; Paul Berman, "Introduction," in *Debating P.C.*, ed. Berman, 23, 16–17.

123. Berman, "Introduction," 23–24.

124. D'Souza, *Illiberal Education*, 157–58.

125. Ibid., 157–62; Roger Kimball, *Tenured Radicals*; Kimball, "The Periphery v. the Center: The MLA in Chicago," in Berman, *Debating P.C.*, 67–73.

126. Schlesinger, *Disuniting of America*, 74.

127. Cary Nelson, *Manifesto of a Tenured Radical* (New York: New York University Press, 1997), 55–74; Berubé, "Public Image Limited," 127.

128. Boxer, *When Women Ask the Questions*, 209; Iannone, "Thought Reform and Education," 82.

129. Schlesinger, *Disuniting of America*, 70; "Paradise Lost at San Francisco State," Stanley Bailis, Donald S. Barnhart, Arthur B. Chandler, and Stuart C. Miller, interviewed by Carol Iannone, *Academic Questions* 2, no. 2 (Spring 1989): 48–63.

130. Kimball, *Tenured Radicals*, 15; Brigitte Berger, "Academic Feminism and the Left," *Academic Questions* 1, no. 2 (Spring 1988): 15, 6, 13.

131. Kimball, "The Periphery v. the Center," 67–73.

132. Thomas Short, "What Shall We Defend?" *Academic Questions* 4, no. 4 (Fall 1991): 21.

133. Jonathan M. Wiener, "Radical Historians and the Crisis in American History, 1959–1980," *Journal of American History* 76, no. 2. (September 1989): 434.

134. Gary B. Nash, Charlotte Crabtree, and Ross E. Dunn, *History on Trial: Culture Wars and the Teaching of the Past* (New York: Alfred A. Knopf, 1997), 198.

135. Mike Wallace, "The Battle of the *Enola Gay*," in *Hiroshima's Shadow*, ed. Kai Bird and Lawrence Lifschultz (Stony Creek, CT: Pamphleteer's Press, 1998), 332.

136. Nash et al., *History on Trial*, 232.

137. Kai Bird and Lawrence Lifschutz, "Introduction," in *Hiroshima's Shadow*, ed. Bird and Lifschutz, xliv.

Chapter 5: "Patterns of Misconduct": Ward Churchill and Academic Freedom After 9/11

1. Stephanie Olsen, " 'Got Ward?' " *Colorado Daily*, March 3, 2005; Elizabeth Mattern Clark, "Academic Freedom on Trial," *Daily Camera*, March 4, 2005. Much of the material on which this chapter is based comes from a collection of clippings and documents in the personal possession of Evelyn Hu-DeHart, the former chair of the Department of Ethnic Studies at the University of Colorado (hereafter Hu-DeHart papers).

2. Scott Smallwood, "Inside a Free-Speech Firestorm," *Chronicle of Higher Education* (hereafter *CHE*), February 18, 2005, Hu-DeHart papers.

3. Joan Hinde Stewart, statement, January 30, 2005, http://www.hamilton.edu/news/more_news/display.cfm?ID=9011 (accessed January 3, 2008).

4. Joan Hinde Stewart, statement, February 1, 2005, http://www.hamilton.edu/news/more_news/display.cfm?ID=9020 (accessed January 3, 2008).

5. Joseph Thomas, "Safety vs. Free Speech," *Colorado Daily*, February 7, 2005, Hu-DeHart papers.

6. Joseph Thomas, "Academic Freedom Under Fire?" *Colorado Daily*, February 2, 2005, Hu-DeHart papers.

7. "Report on Conclusion of Preliminary Review in the Matter of Professor Ward Churchill," http://www.colorado.edu/new/reports/churchill/report.html.

8. Brittany Anas, "Hoffman Tells Faculty Group She Supports Their Rights," *Daily Camera*, March 4, 2005, Hu-DeHart papers.

9. Jon Sarche, "CU President Hoffman Resigns," *Rocky Mountain News*, March 7, 2005; Hu-DeHart, handwritten memo, n.d., Hu-DeHart papers; John Aguilar, "Betsy Hoffman Testifies via Video at Churchill Trial," *Daily Camera*, March 13, 2009, http://www.dailycamera.com/news/2009/mar/13/betsy-hoffman-ward-churchill-trial-free-speech (accessed June 15, 2009).

10. For some examples of the hostility toward Churchill on the part of the American Indian Movement, see its Web site, http://www.aimovement.org.

11. Robert A. Williams Jr., statement, in Natsu Saito to "Dear Friends and Colleagues," March 21, 2005, Hu-DeHart papers.

12. "Controversial Professor Landed Tenure Without Usual Review Process," *Daily Camera*, February 16, 2005; Jefferson Dodge, "Churchill's Personnel Files Released by CU-Boulder," February 24, 2005, http://newmedia.colorado.edu/silverandgold/messages/4218.html; Michael Pacanowsky to John Waite Bowers et al., January 10, 1991, all in Hu-DeHart papers.

13. Kevin Flynn, "Churchill's 'Indian' Claim to Be Probed," *Rocky Mountain News*, March 25, 2005, Hu-DeHart papers.

14. Dodge, "Churchill's Personnel Files"; Charlie Brennan, "Ward Churchill: A Contentious Life," *Rocky Mountain News*, March 26, 2005, Hu-DeHart papers.

15. Kim Castleberry, "Department Familiar with Conflict," *Daily Camera*, February 19, 2005, Hu-DeHart papers.

16. Andrea O'Reilly Herrera and Abby Ferber to Pres. Hoffman and Interim Chancellor DiStefano, February 11, 2005. See also "An Open Letter from the Department of Ethnic Studies, University of Colorado at Boulder to the Board of Regents, President Betsy Hoffman and Interim Chancellor Phil DiStefano," April 25, 2005, both in Hu-DeHart papers.

17. "An Open Letter from the Department of Ethnic Studies"; Arturo Aldama et al., "Dear Colleagues and Comrades," July 31, 2006, both in Hu-DeHart papers.

18. Carlos Munoz Jr. to "Dear Friends and Colleagues," March 17, 2005, Hu-DeHart papers.

19. Anne D. Neal, "Foreword," in American Council of Trustees and Administrators (ACTA), "How Many Ward Churchills?" May 2006, http://www.goacta.org/publications/Reports/Churchill%20Final.pdf (accessed January 5, 2008).

20. ACTA, "How Many Ward Churchills?"

21. Phyllis Schlafly, "College Faculties: Farm Teams for the Radical Left," March 24, 2005, Human Events Online, Hu-DeHart papers.

22. Thomas Ryan and Steven Vincent, "Where Ward Left Off . . . ," Front PageMagazine.com, March 9, 2005, Hu-DeHart papers.

23. Schlafly, "College Faculties."

24. Patricia Hayes, quoted in Elizabeth Mattern Clark, "Regents to Take Close Look at Tenure Process," *Daily Camera*, February 17, 2005, Hu-DeHart papers.

25. Berny Morson, "Probe of Tenure Decision Awaiting on Back Burner," *Rocky Mountain News*, March 14, 2005; Jefferson Dodge, "Faculty, Regents Launch Tenure Review," *Silver and Gold*, March 31, 2005, Hu-DeHart papers.

26. Piper Fogg, "All Eyes on Tenure," *CHE*, January 6, 2006, http://chronicle.com/weekly/v52/i18/18a02201.htm (accessed January 4, 2006); Berny Morson, "Regents Approve Faster Prof Firing," *Rocky Mountain News*, March 23, 2007.

27. Fred Anderson, interview, January 9, 2008; Christine Yoshinaga-Itano to Hu-DeHart, February 10, 2005, in Hu-DeHart papers.

28. "Remarks by Chancellor Phil DiStefano at the CU Board of Regents Special Meeting Feb. 3, 2005," http://www.colorado.edu/news/releases/2005/49.html (accessed January 6, 2008).

29. "Report on Conclusion of Preliminary Review in the Matter of Professor Ward Churchill, March 24, 2005," http://www.colorado.edu/news/reports/churchill/report.html (accessed January 7, 2008) (hereafter Preliminary Review).

30. "Report of the Investigative Committee of the Standing Committee on Research Misconduct at the University of Colorado at Boulder Concerning Allegations of Academic Misconduct Against Professor Ward Churchill," May 16, 2006, 100, http://www.colorado.edu/news/reports/churchill/download/WardChurchillReport.pdf (accessed January 7, 2008) (hereafter, Investigative Committee Report). For a useful précis of the case from one of Churchill's supporters, see Eric Cheyfitz, "Framing Ward Churchill: The Political Construction of Research Misconduct," *Works and Days*, 51/52, 53/54 (2008–9), digital copy in the author's possession, courtesy of Ward Churchill.

31. Preliminary Review.

32. Natsu Saito to "Dear Friends and Colleagues," March 21, 2005.

33. Jefferson Dodge, "DiStefano: Churchill Case to Go to Standing Committee," March 31, 2005, http://newmedia.colorado.edu/silverandgold/messages/4325.html, Hu-DeHart papers; University of Colorado, Faculty Senate Committee on Privilege and Tenure, "Panel Report Regarding Dismissal for Cause of Ward Churchill and the Issue of Selective Enforcement," April 11, 2007, 8, 11, http://wardchurchill.net/files/PT_panel_report_041107.pdf (accessed January 9, 2008) (hereafter, PT Panel Report).

34. Pauline Hale, "Statement Regarding Decision of Standing Committee on Research Misconduct," September 9, 2005, http://www.colorado.edu/news/reports/churchill/standingcommittee.html (accessed January 7, 2008).

35. Defend Dissent and Critical Thinking on Campus, http://www.defendcritical thinking.org/CU%20%20President%call (accessed July 29, 2007).

36. PT Panel Report, 22–24; Bruce E. Johansen, "Parting Words from Member of Churchill Probe Panel," *Rocky Mountain News*, November 10, 2005, Hu-DeHart papers.

37. Investigative Committee Report, 4.

38. Fred Anderson, interview, January 9, 2007.

39. Investigative Committee Report, 4.

40. Jefferson Dodge, "Debate over Churchill Case Persists," *Silver and Gold*, March 29, 2007, Hu-DeHart papers.

41. Investigative Committee Report, 27.

42. "A Filing of Research Misconduct Charges Against the Churchill Investigating Committee," Vijay Gupta et al. to Hank Brown et al., May 10, 2007, Hu-DeHart papers, also accessible at http://wardchurchill.net/files/misconduct_charges_letter_and_supporting_docs.doc (accessed January 9, 2007).

43. Investigative Committee Report, 81.

44. Ibid., 89.

45. Ibid., 93; Tom Mayer, "The Plagiarism Charges Against Ward Churchill," http://wardchurchill.net/files/mayer_on_plagiarism_charges_0607.pdf (accessed January 9, 2008).

46. Investigative Committee Report, 96.

47. Ibid., 97.

48. Ibid., 98.

49. Ibid., 102.

50. "Report and Recommendations of the Standing Committee on Research Misconduct Concerning Allegations of Research Misconduct by Professor Ward Churchill," June 13, 2006, 10–11, http://www.colorado.edu/news/reports/churchill/download/ChurchillStandingCmteReport.pdf (accessed January 9, 2008).

51. Ibid., 11–12.

52. Ibid., 16.

53. "Recommendation of Interim Chancellor Phil DiStefano with Regard to Investigation of Research Misconduct," June 26, 2006, http://www.colorado.edu/news/reports/churchill/distefano062606.html (accessed January 9, 2008).

54. PT Panel Report, 6.

55. Ibid., 11–12.

56. Ibid., 19.

57. Ibid., 32.

58. Ibid., 38, 45–46.

59. Ibid., 38, 65–66, 70.

60. Ibid., 76.

61. Scott Jaschik, "The Ward Churchill Endgame," *Inside Higher Education*, May 30, 2007, http://www.insidehighered.com/news/2007/05/29/churchill (accessed January 13, 2010) (hereafter *IHE*).

62. Statement from University of Colorado Board of Regents, https://www.cusys.edu/regents/communique/churchill-reg-stmt.html (accessed January 11, 2008).

63. Hank Brown, "Inside Higher Ed, July 30, 2007," https://www.cu.edu/content/inside-higher-ed-july-30-2007 (accessed Jan. 11, 2008).

64. Statement from University of Colorado Board of Regents, https://www.cusys.edu/regents/communique/churchill-reg-stmt.html (accessed January 11, 2008); Hank Brown, "Statement," n.d., https://www.cusys.edu/regents/communique/churchill-brown-stmt.html (accessed January 11, 2008).

65. Hank Brown, "Statement," July 25, 2007, https://www.cu.edu/content/rocky-mountain-news-july-25-2007 (accessed January 11, 2008).

66. Anderson interview.

67. Berny Morson, "Suit Futile, Experts Say," *Rocky Mountain News*, June 27, 2006, Hu-DeHart papers.

68. "Ward Churchill's $1 Damage Award Said to Have Been Product of Jury Compromise," *CHE*, April 3, 2009, http://chronicle.com/news/index.php?id=6250&utm_source=pm&utm_medium=en (accessed April 7, 2009).

69. Peter Schmidt, "Judge Rejects Ward Churchill's Plea for Reinstatement, Vacates Verdict in His Favor," *CHE*, July 8, 2009, http://chronicle.com/daily/2009/07/21690n.htm (accessed July 8, 2009).

70. "EH.T: Plagiarism vs. Intentional Fraud," August 11, 1996, http://eh.net/pipermail/eh.teach/1996-August/000104.html (accessed January 13, 2010); John K. Wilson, "Further Thoughts on Plagiarism," in Wilson, "The Footnote Police vs. Ward Churchill," *IHE*, May 19, 2006, http://www.insidehighered.com/views/2006/05/19/wilson#Comments (accessed January 13, 2010).

71. Jon Wiener, *Historians in Trouble: Plagiarism, Fraud, and Politics in the Ivory Tower* (New York: The New Press, 2004), 172–77; Ron Robin, *Scandals and Scoundrels: Seven Cases That Shook the Academy* (Berkeley: University of California Press, 2004), 88.

72. Scott Smallwood, "U. of South Florida Fires Professor Accused of Terrorism," *CHE*, March 7, 2003, http://chronicle.com/article/U-of-South-Florida-Fires-P/20485 (accessed January 13, 2010).

73. Scott Jaschik, "Furor over Norm Finkelstein," *IHE*, April 4, 2007, http://www.normanfinkelstein.com/article.php?pg=11&ar=960 (accessed February 3, 2008).

74. Dennis H. Holtschneider to Norman Finkelstein, June 8, 2007, http://www.normanfinkelstein.com/pdf/tenuredenial/Finkelstein.Norman06.08.2007.pdf (accessed February 3, 2008).

75. "DePaul University Statement on the Tenure and Promotion Decision Concerning Professor Norman Finkelstein," June 8, 2007, http://www.normanfinkelstein.com/article.php?pg=11&ar=1070 (accessed February 3, 2008).

76. Scott Jaschik, "DePaul Rejects Finkelstein," *IHE*, June 11, 2007, http://www.normanfinkelstein.com/article.php?pg=11&ar=1082 (accessed February 3, 2008); "On Collegiality as a Criterion for Faculty Evaluation," in American Association of University Professors, *Policy Documents and Reports*, 9th ed. (Washington, DC: AAUP, 2001), 39–40.

77. "Report of the AAUP Special Committee on Academic Freedom and National Security in a Time of Crisis," October 2003, http://www.aaup.org/AAUP/comm/rep/crisistime.htm (accessed February 3, 2008) (hereafter AAUP Special Committee).

78. "North Carolina Teacher Fired for Antiwar Remarks," e-mail communication from Ito Defense Coalition, itodefense@hotmail.com, to elizabethito@hotmail.com (accessed September 16, 2003); Scott Jaschik, "Casualty of Anti-War Activism," *IHE*, December 2, 2005, http://insidehighered.com/news/2005/12/02/suit (accessed December 2, 2005).

79. Associated Press, "9/11 Conspiracy Theorist to Leave Brigham Young," *Washington Post*, October 22, 2006; Associated Press, "University Instructor Likens Bush to Hitler," CNN.com, October 11, 2006 (accessed October 12, 2006).

80. AAUP Special Committee.

81. Scott Jaschik, "Are You Now or Have You Ever . . . ," *IHE*, August 15, 2006, http://www.insidehighered.com/news/2006/08/15/oath (accessed January 12, 2008).

82. Anas, "Hoffman Tells Faculty Group She Supports Their Rights"; Phil DeStefano to Boulder Campus Teaching Faculty et al., February 21, 2005; S.S. Rajgopal to "Dear DES Friends," February 26, 2005; Jefferson Dodge, "DiStefano: Churchill Case to Go to Standing Committee," March 31, 2005, all in Hu-DeHart papers.

83. Scott Jaschik, "A Loyalty Oath Firing in 2008," *IHE*, March 30, 2008, http://insidehighered.com/news/2008/03/03/loyalty (accessed March 30, 2008); Scott Jaschik, "Loyalty Oath Compromise," *IHE*, June 3, 2008, http://www.insidehighered.com/news/2008/06/03/oaths (accessed January 12, 2009); Richard Byrne, "Cal State-Fullerton and Lecturer Reach Agreement Over State Loyalty Oath," *CHE*, June 3, 2008, http://chronicle.com/daily/2008/06/3085n.htm (accessed June 3, 2008).

84. Anna Weggel, "A Minnesota University's Decision Not to Invite Archbishop Tutu as a Speaker Brings Disappointment," *CHE*, October 4, 2007; Anna Weggel, "Minnesota University Regrets Its Failure to Invite Archbishop Tutu to Campus," *CHE*, October 11, 2007.

85. Scott Jaschik, "The Speech That Wasn't," *IHE*, September 22, 2006, http://www.insidehighered.com/news/2006/09/22/columbia (accessed January 13, 2010); Lee C. Bollinger, "Introductory Remarks at SIPA–World Leaders Forum with President of Iran Mahmoud Ahmadinejad," September 24, 2007, http://www.columbia.edu/cu/news/07/09/lcbopeningremarks.html (accessed September 25, 2007).

86. Rob Lipton, "Free Speech and the Israel Lobby," February 14, 2008, http://feedblitz.com/r.asp?l=26657202&f=150615&u=2461311 (accessed February 15, 2008).

87. Elia Powers, "A Speech and Its Aftermath," *CHE*, January 25, 2007.

88. Peter Schmidt, "Georgia Southern University Rescinds Speaking Engagement to William Ayers," *CHE*, February 12, 2009, http://chronicle.com/news/article/5973/georgia-southern-u-rescinds-speaking-invitation-to-william-ayers?utm_source=at&utm_medium=en (accessed February 13, 2009); Scott Jaschik, "Banned in Boston," *IHE*, March 30, 2009, http://www.insidehighered.com/news/2009/03/30/ayers#Comments (accessed March 30, 2009); Dave Pidgeon, "GOP Targets Ayers Reps Press Millersville University to KO Speech," *Intelligencer Journal* (Lancaster, PA), February 28, 2009, http://articles.lancasteronline.com/local/4/234427 (accessed March 2, 2009).

89. AAUP, Special Committee; Matthew W. Finkin and Robert C. Post, *For the Common Good: Principles of American Academic Freedom* (New Haven, CT: Yale University Press, 2009), 2–4.

90. Scott Jaschik, "Retractions from David Horowitz," *IHE*, January 11, 2006, http://insidehighered.com/news/2006/01/11/retract (accessed January 11, 2006); Jennifer Jacobson, "Pa. House Committee Hears More Testimony on Liberal Views of State's Professors," *CHE*, January 11, 2006, http://chronicle.com/daily/2006/01/2006011105n.htm (accessed January 11, 2006).

91. David Horowitz, *The Professors: The 101 Most Dangerous Academics in America* (Lanham, MD: Regnery, 2006).

92. Zachary Lockman, "Behind the Battles over US Middle East Studies," January 2004, http://www.merip.org/mero/interventions/lockman_interv.html#_ftn3 (accessed November 13, 2009).

93. Alisa Solomon, "Terror Hysteria Gone Absurdist," *The Nation* online, August 1, 2005. For the best information about the Kurtz case, see the Critical Art Ensemble Defense Fund Web site, http://www.caedefensefund.org.

94. The story of Thomas Butler comes from a seven-part series written by a reporter for the *Cleveland Plain Dealer*: John Mangels, "Plagued by Fear," *Cleveland Plain Dealer*, March 26–April 2, 2006, http://www.cleveland.com/plague/plaindealer/index.ssf?/plague/more/114371120197520.html (accessed February 5, 2008).

95. Barbara E. Murray et al., "Destroying the Life and Career of a Valued Physician-Scientist Who Tried to Protect Us from Plague: Was It Really Necessary?" *Clinical Infectious Diseases* 40, no. 11 (June 2005): 1644–48, http://www.fas.org/butler/cid060105.pdf (accessed February 7, 2008).

96. Mangels, "Plagued by Fear."

97. Tania Simoncelly with Jay Stanley, *Science Under Siege: The Bush Administration's Assault on Academic Freedom and Scientific Inquiry* (New York: American Civil Liberties Union, 2005), http://www.aclu.org/FilesPDFs/sciundersiege.pdf (accessed February 5, 2008).

98. AAUP Special Committee.

99. Ibid.

100. Ibid.

101. National Research Council, Committee on a New Government-University Partnership for Science and Security, Committee on Science, Technology, and Law, *Science and Security in a Post 9/11 World: A Report Based on Regional Discussions Between the Science and Security Communities* (Washington, DC: National Academies Press, 2007).

102. "Quick Takes," *IHE*, September 9, 2009, http://www.insidehighered.com/news/2009/09/09/qt#207780 (accessed September 9, 2009).

103. AAUP Special Committee.

104. Gwendolyn Bradley, "Scholars Excluded from the United States," *Academe* online, September–October 2007, http://www.aaup.org/AAUP/pubsres/academe/2007/SO/NB/excluded.htm (accessed January 12, 2009).

105. AAUP Special Committee.

Chapter 6: "Tough Choices": The Changing Structure of Higher Education

1. Ken McKinnon, quoted in Jan Currie and Lesley Vidovich, "Micro-Economic Reform Through Managerialism in American and Australian Universities," in *Universities and Globalization: Critical Perspectives*, ed. Jan Currie and Janice Newson (Thousand Oaks, CA: Sage Publications, 1998), 170.

2. Clark Kerr, *The Uses of the University* (Cambridge, MA: Harvard University Press, 1963).

3. Donald Kennedy, *Academic Duty* (Cambridge, MA: Harvard University Press, 1997), 3.

4. For a thoughtful discussion of the credentialing craze, see David F. Labaree, *How to Succeed in School Without Really Learning: The Credentials Race in American Education* (New Haven, CT: Yale University Press, 1997), especially chapters 1 and 8.

5. Roger L. Geiger, *To Advance Knowledge: The Growth of American Research Universities, 1900–1940* (New York: Oxford University Press, 1986), 50.

6. Roger L. Geiger, *Research and Relevant Knowledge: American Research Universities Since World War II* (1993; New Brunswick, NJ: Transaction, 2004), 40–41.

7. Christopher J. Lucas, *Crisis in the Academy: Rethinking Higher Education in America* (New York: St. Martin's Press, 1996), 12; David W. Breneman, "Liberal Arts Colleges: What Price Survival?" in *Higher Learning in America 1980–2000*, ed. Arthur Levine (Baltimore: Johns Hopkins University Press, 1993), 91.

8. Geiger, *Research and Relevant Knowledge*, 138.

9. The figures come from the Web site of the National Center for Educational Statistics (hereafter NCES), "Table SA-1. Number of Degree-Granting Institutions, by Control and Type of Institution: Academic Years 1974–75 Through 2006–07," in "Special Analysis 2008: Community Colleges," http://nces.ed.gov/programs/coe/2008/analysis/sa_table.asp?tableID=1053.

10. NCES, "Table 177. Enrollment, Staff, and Degrees Conferred in Postsecondary Institutions Participating in Title IV Programs, by Level and Control of Institution, Sex of Student, and Type of Degree: Fall 2005 and 2005–06," *Digest of Education Statistics*, August 2007, http://nces.ed.gov/programs/digest/d07/tables/dt07_177.asp.

11. For a recent discussion of the inequities in higher education, see Andrew Delbanco, "The Universities in Trouble," *New York Review of Books*, May 14, 2009.

12. Stephen M. Stigler, "Competition and the Research Universities," in *The Research University in a Time of Discontent*, ed. Jonathan R. Cole, Elinor G. Barger, and Stephen R. Graubard (Baltimore: Johns Hopkins University Press, 1994), 133–35; Kennedy, *Academic Duty*, 148.

13. Sheila Slaughter and Larry L. Leslie, *Academic Capitalism: Politics, Policies, and the Entrepreneurial University* (Baltimore: Johns Hopkins University Press, 1998), 57.

14. William G. Tierney and Estela Mara Bensimon, *Promotion and Tenure: Community and Socialization in Academe* (Albany: State University of New York Press,

1996), especially chapter 3. See also Geiger, *Research and Relevant Knowledge*, 210; Kennedy, *Academic Duty*, 147.

15. Slaughter and Leslie, *Academic Capitalism*, 17.

16. For an excellent study of Stanford's transformation, see Rebecca S. Lowen, *Creating the Cold War University: The Transformation of Stanford* (Berkeley: University of California Press, 1997); see also Geiger, *Research and Relevant Knowledge*, 74–5, 80, 125.

17. Slaughter and Leslie, *Academic Capitalism*, 11, 152.

18. George Keller, *Academic Strategy: The Management Revolution in American Higher Education* (Baltimore: Johns Hopkins University Press, 1983), 48.

19. Ibid., 3, 13; Margaret Gordon, "The Economy and Higher Education," in *Higher Learning*, ed. Levine, 21.

20. Geiger, *Research and Relevant Knowledge*, 243; Keller, *Academic Strategy*, 11, 4.

21. Newt Davidson Collective, *Crisis at CUNY* (New York: Newt Davidson Collective, 1974), 22.

22. Keller, *Academic Strategy*, 5.

23. Geiger, *Research and Relevant Knowledge*, 247.

24. Ibid., 248, 115.

25. Slaughter and Leslie, *Academic Capitalism*, 8. Almost every source I've consulted has produced different sets of figures for the percentages of higher education budgets supplied by state legislatures. The figures I've used are thus meant to be illustrative of general trends, rather than any definitive accounting.

26. James J. Duderstadt and Farris W. Womack, *The Future of the Public University in America: Beyond the Crossroads* (Baltimore: Johns Hopkins University Press, 2003), 27; Ami Zusman, "Challenges Facing Higher Education in the Twenty-First Century," in *American Higher Education in the Twenty-First Century: Social, Political, and Economic Challenges*, ed. Philip G. Altbach, Robert O. Berdahl, and Patricia J. Gumport, 2nd ed. (1999; Baltimore: Johns Hopkins University Press, 2005), 117.

27. Zusman, "Challenges," 119.

28. Sam Dillon, "At Public Universities, Warnings of Privatization," *NYT*, October 16, 2005; David L. Kirp, *Shakespeare, Einstein, and the Bottom Line: The Marketing of Higher Education* (Cambridge, MA: Harvard University Press, 2003), 135.

29. Kirp, *Shakespeare, Einstein, and the Bottom Line*, 125.

30. Aims C. McGuinness Jr., "The States and Higher Education," in *American Higher Education*, ed. Altbach et al., 202; Slaughter and Leslie, *Academic Capitalism*, 75; Patrick M. Callan, "Government and Higher Education," in *Higher Learning*, ed. Levine, 11–12, 16; Lawrence E. Gladieux, Jacqueline E. King, and Melanie E. Corrigan, "The Federal Government and Higher Education," in *American Higher Education*, ed. Altbach et al., 180.

31. Slaughter and Leslie, *Academic Capitalism*, 72–73.

32. Geiger, *Research and Relevant Knowledge*, 249–50.

33. Gladieux et al., "The Federal Government," 180.

34. Ibid., 178–80; Gordon, "The Economy and Higher Education," 30; Sheila Slaughter and Gary Rhoades, "Markets in Higher Education: Students in the Seventies, Patents in the Eighties, Copyrights in the Nineties," in *American Higher Education*, ed.

Altbach et al., 488–93; Paul Basken, "Replacing Student Loans with Grants Appears to Encourage More Graduates to Choose Public-Service Work," *CHE*, May 31, 2007, http://chronicle.com/daily/2007/05/2007053104n.htm; D. Bruce Johnstone, "Financing Higher Education: Who Should Pay?" in *American Higher Education*, ed. Altbach et al., 383.

35. NCES, http://nces.ed.gov/fastfacts/display.asp?id=76 (accessed February 12, 2010); CUNY Web site, http://www.cuny.edu/admissions/undergraduate/tuition-fees.html (accessed February 12, 2010).

36. John G. Cross and Edie N. Goldenberg, *Off-Track Profs: Nontenured Teachers in Higher Education* (Cambridge, MA: MIT Press, 2009), 61.

37. For a devastating look at the way in which colleges and universities market themselves, see Kirp, *Shakespeare, Einstein, and the Bottom Line*, 11–32; Tamar Lewin, "Public Universities Chase Excellence, at a Price," *NYT*, December 20, 2006, http://www.nytimes.com/2006/12/20/education/20colleges.html?_r=1&oref=s (accessed December 21, 2006).

38. Cross and Goldenberg, *Off-Track Profs*, 61.

39. American Council of Trustees and Alumni, Institute for Effective Governance, "Measuring Up: The Problem of Grade Inflation and What Trustees Can Do," July 2009, https://www.goacta.org/publications/downloads/MeasuringUp.pdf (accessed July 23, 2009).

40. Eric L. Dey and Sylvia Hurtado, "College Students in Changing Contexts," in *American Higher Education*, ed. Altbach et al., 333.

41. Elizabeth F. Farrell, "Freshmen Put High Value on How Well College Prepares Them for a Profession, Survey Finds," *CHE*, December 12, 2006, http://chronicle.com/daily/2006/12/2006121202n.htm (accessed December 12, 2006); Philip G. Altbach, "Harsh Realities: The Professoriate Faces a New Century," in *American Higher Education*, ed. Altbach et al., 288.

42. Alvin Kernan, "Change in the Humanities and Higher Education," in *What's Happened to the Humanities?* ed. Alvin Kernan, (Princeton, NJ: Princeton University Press, 1997), 6; Francis Oakley, "Ignorant Armies and Nighttime Clashes: Changes in the Humanities Classroom, 1970–1995," in *What's Happened to the Humanities?* ed. Kernan, 67; Breneman, "Liberal Arts Colleges," in *Higher Learning*, ed. Levine, 95–96.

43. Dey and Hurtado, "College Students," 330; Oakley, "Ignorant Armies," 67.

44. Jack Hammond to the author, December 12, 2009.

45. See Kirp, *Shakespeare, Einstein, and the Bottom Line*, 221–54.

46. National Science Foundation Web site, http://www.nsf.gov/statistics/nsf09303/pdf/tab1.pdf.

47. For a good discussion of the controversy about "best science," see Daniel Kevles, *The Physicists: The History of a Scientific Community in Modern America* (Cambridge, MA: Harvard University Press, 1995).

48. Geiger, *Research and Relevant Knowledge*, 175.

49. For a particularly useful discussion of the impact of national security and defense spending on scientific research, see Paul Forman, "Beyond Quantum Electronics: National Security as Basis for Physical Research in the United States,

1940–1960," *Historical Studies in the Physical and Biological Sciences* 18, no. 1 (1987): 149–229. Quote is on p. 221.

50. Lowen, *Creating the Cold War University*, 109–13, 137–46; Geiger, *Research and Relevant Knowledge*, 119–34.

51. Martin Trow, "Federalism in American Higher Education," in *Higher Learning*, ed. Levine, 62.

52. Gladieux et al., "The Federal Government," 170; Richard J. Bennoff, "Federal S&E Obligations to Academic Institutions Reach New Highs in FY but Fail to Keep Up with Inflation," National Science Foundation Web site, October 2008, http://www.nsf.gov/statistics/infbrief/nsf08316.

53. Kennedy, *Academic Duty*, 153.

54. Geiger, *Research and Relevant Knowledge*, 185, 195.

55. Ibid., 189–94.

56. Rodney W. Nichols, "Federal Science Policy and Universities: Consequences of Success," in *Research University*, ed. Cole et al., 276.

57. Kennedy, *Academic Duty*, 11.

58. Ibid., 154; Stigler, "Competition," 145–47; Tierney and Bensimon, *Promotion and Tenure*, 66.

59. Walter E. Massey, "Can the Research University Adapt to a Changing Future?" in *Research University*, ed. Cole et al., 196.

60. Jennifer Washburn, *University Inc.: The Corporate Corruption of Higher Education* (New York: Basic Books, 2005), 36.

61. "Table 1. R&D Expenditures at Universities and Colleges, by Source of Funds: FY 1953–2007," in "Academic Research and Development Expenditures," National Science Foundation Web site, March 2009, http://www.nsf.gov/statistics/nsf09303/pdf/tab1.pdf (accessed March 15, 2009).

62. Slaughter and Leslie, *Academic Capitalism*, 59–60.

63. Washburn, *University, Inc.*, 49–72; Sheldon Krimsky, *Science in the Private Interest: Has the Lure of Profits Corrupted Biomedical Research?* (Lanham, MD: Rowman & Littlefield, 2003), 30–32; *Diamond v. Chakrabarty*, 447 U.S. 303 (1980).

64. Henry Etzkowitz and Andrew Webster, "Entrepreneurial Science: The Second Academic Revolution," in *Capitalizing Knowledge: New Intersections of Industry and Academia*, ed. Henry Etzkowitz, Andrew Webster, and Peter Healey, (Albany: State University of New York Press, 1998), 43; Slaughter and Leslie, *Academic Capitalism*, 6–7.

65. Krimsky, *Science in the Private Interest*, 82–85; Washburn, *University, Inc.*, 73–75.

66. Slaughter and Leslie, *Academic Capitalism*, 134, 166–68; Washburn, *University, Inc.*, 86; Karen Seashore Louis and Melissa S. Anderson, "The Changing Context of Science and University-Industry Relations," in *Capitalizing Knowledge*, ed. Etzkowitz et al., 82–83.

67. Donald G. Stein, "A Personal Perspective on the Selling of Academia," in *Buying In or Selling Out? The Commercialization of the American Research University*, ed. Donald G. Stein (New Brunswick, NJ: Rutgers University Press, 2004), 7; Krimsky, *Science in the Private Interest*, 76; Washburn, *University, Inc.*, 146.

68. Krimsky, *Science in the Private Interest*, 67.

69. Ibid., 181, 223.

70. Slaughter and Leslie, *Academic Capitalism*, 145, 151.

71. Sheila Slaughter and Gary Rhoades, *Academic Capitalism and the New Economy: Markets, State, and Higher Education* (Baltimore: Johns Hopkins University Press, 2004), 187; Lawrence Busch, et al., *External Review of the Collaborative Research Agreement between Novartis Agricultural Discovery Institute, Inc. and the Regents of the University of California* (East Lansing, MI: Institute for Food and Agricultural Standards, Michigan State University, 2004); Washburn, *University, Inc.*, 14; Slaughter and Leslie, *Academic Capitalism*, 166, 194–95.

72. Slaughter and Rhoades, *Academic Capitalism and the New Economy*, 115–16.

73. Slaughter and Leslie, *Academic Capitalism*, 20, 167–69.

74. Washburn, *University, Inc.*, 192.

75. Ibid., 164–67.

76. Krimsky, *Science in the Private Interest*, 134; Washburn, *University, Inc.*, 125–27.

77. Richard Monastersky, "Conflict-of-Interest Concerns Halt NIH Project at Emory U.," *CHE*, October 15, 2008, http://chronicle.com/daily/2008/10/5114n.htm (accessed November 2, 2008).

78. Krimsky, *Science in the Private Interest*, 172, 96.

79. Katherine Mangan, "Survey Finds Extensive Ties Between Industry and Medical-School Department Chairs," *CHE*, October 17, 2007, http://chronicle.com/daily/2007/10/391n.htm (accessed October 17, 2007).

80. Washburn, *University, Inc.*, 110–11; Lila Gutterman, "Scientists May Be Putting Their Own Names on Papers Written by Companies," *CHE*, April 16, 2008, http://chronicle.com/daily/2008/04/2516n.htm (accessed April 26, 2008).

81. Marcia Angell, cited by Krimsky, *Science in the Private Interest*, 158.

82. Washburn, *University, Inc.*, 110–11; Marcia Angell, "The Clinical Trials Business: Who Gains?" in *Buying In or Selling Out?* ed. Stein, 130.

83. Washburn, *University, Inc.*, 127.

84. Ibid., 112–17.

85. Ibid., 19–20: Krimsky, *Science in the Private Interest*, 15–18.

86. Krimsky, *Science in the Private Interest*, 44–47.

87. Sheldon Krimsky, "Reforming Research Ethics in an Age of Multivested Science," in *Buying In or Selling Out?*, ed. Stein, 148; Doug Lederman, "Call for Crackdown on Research," *Inside Higher Ed*, January 21, 2008, http://insidehighered.com/news/2008/01/21/conflicts (accessed January 21, 2008), (hereafter *IHE*).

88. Krimsky, *Science in the Private Interest*, 92–97; Jeffrey Brainard, "NIH Doesn't Check Academics on Financial Conflicts of Interest, Auditors Say," *CHE*, January 21, 2008, http://chronicle.com/daily/2008/01/1308n.htm (accessed January 21, 2008).

89. Krimsky, *Science in the Private Interest*, 47–49.

90. Krimsky, "Reforming Research Ethics," 138, 148; Krimsky, *Science in the Private Interest*, 172.

91. Brainard, "NIH Doesn't Check Academics."

92. Krimsky, *Science in the Private Interest*, 199; Krimsky, "Reforming Research Ethics," 138; Angell, "The Clinical Trials Business," 132.

93. Kate Maternowski, "Conflict with My Interests," *IHE*, July 10, 2009, http://www.insidehighered.com/news/2009/07/10/acre (accessed July 10, 2009).

94. Washburn, *University, Inc.*, 170–97; Mary Lindenstein Walshok, "Expanding Roles for Research Universities in Regional Economic Development," in *The University's Role in Economic Development: From Research to Outreach*, ed. James P. Pappas (San Francisco: Jossey-Bass, 1997), 17–27; Etzkowitz and Webster, "Entrepreneurial Science," 31–33; James S. Fairweather, *Faculty Work and Public Trust: Restoring the Value of Teaching and Public Service in American Academic Life* (Boston: Allyn and Bacon, 1996), 123–24.

95. Washburn, *University, Inc.*, 141.

96. Ibid., 171–97.

97. Etzkowitz and Webster, "Entrepreneurial Science," 29–30; Andrew Webster, "Strategic Research Alliances: Testing the Collaborative Limits?" in *Capitalizing Knowledge*, ed. Etzkowitz et al., 97.

98. Busch et al., *External Review*, 53, 31–35.

99. Ibid., 111, 12, 38; Goldie Blumenstyk, "Berkeley's Pact with BP for Research Institute Gives Company Favorable Terms on Intellectual Property," *CHE*, November 15, 2007, http://chronicle.com/daily/2007/11/715n.htm (accessed November 15, 2007).

100. Blumenstyck, "Berkeley's Pact."

101. Callan, "Government and Higher Education," 12; Scott Jaschik, "The Shrinking Professoriate," *IHE*, March 12, 2008, http://www.insidehighered.com/news/2008/03/12/jobs (accessed March 12, 2008).

102. Robert M. Rosenzweig, "Governing the Modern University," in *Research University*, ed. Cole et al., 302–3; Donald Kennedy, "Making Choices in the Research University," in *Research University*, ed. Cole et al., 106; Doug Lederman, "Politicians Praise and Pressure Colleges," *IHE*, February 10, 2009, http://insidehighered.com/news/2009/02/10/ace (accessed February 10, 2009).

103. Gladieux, "The Federal Government," 193–94; Kennedy, "Making Choices," 106; Trow, "Federalism in American Higher Education," 63; Geiger, *Research and Relevant Knowledge*, 258–59.

104. Office of the General Counsel, "About Us," Yeshiva University Web site, http://www.yu.edu/ogc/index.aspx?id=24128&ekmensel=51b41ad4_2240_0_24128_1.

105. Etzkowitz and Webster, "Entrepreneurial Science," 37.

106. Washburn, *University, Inc.*, 168.

107. Steven Muller "Presidential Leadership," in *Research University*, ed. Cole et al., 123–24; Robert M. Rosenzweig, "Governing the Modern University," in *Research University*, ed. Cole et al., 303–4.

108. Duderstadt and Womack, *Future of the Public University*, 99.

109. Keller, *Academic Strategy*, 88.

110. Kennedy, "Making Choices," 97; Paul Fain, "Conservative Trustee Group Takes on the Academy During Annual Meeting," *CHE*, October 9, 2006, http://chronicle.com/daily/2006/10/2006100903n.htm (accessed October 9, 2006); Scott

Jaschik, "Us vs. Them in Academe," *IHE*, August 6, 2008, http://insidehighered.com/news/2008/08/04/divided (accessed August 6, 2008).

111. Susanne Lohmann, "Darwinian Medicine for the University," in *Governing Academia*, ed. Ronald G. Ehrenberg, (Ithaca, NY: Cornell University Press, 2004), 72–87.

112. Slaughter and Leslie, *Academic Capitalism*, 152–59, 232.

113. Gabriel E. Kaplan, "How Academic Ships Actually Navigate," in *Governing Academia*, ed. Ehrenberg, 168–75, 201.

114. Scott Jaschik, "Academic Freedom Violations Found at Hunter," *IHE*, May 13, 2008, http://insidehighered.com/news/2008/05/13/hunter (accessed May 13, 2008).

115. Slaughter and Rhoades, *Academic Capitalism in the New Economy*, 153n; Fathom Archive Web site, http://www.fathom.com/pop_up/archive.html (accessed July 9, 2009).

116. Steve Kolowich, "What Doomed Global Campus?" *IHE*, September 3, 2009, http://www.insidehighered.com/news/2009/09/03/globalcampus (accessed September 18, 2009).

117. Scott Jaschik, "International Campuses on the Rise," *IHE*, September 18, 2009, http://www.insidehighered.com/news/2009/09/03/branch (accessed September 18, 2009).

118. Michael A. Olivas, "Colleges Should Think Twice About Exporting Their Programs," *CHE*, November 7, 2008, http://chronicle.com/weekly/v55/i11/11a04601.htm (accessed November 3, 2008); C.L. Max Nikias, "Attracting Foreign Students to America Offers More Advantages," *CHE*, November 7, 2008, http://chronicle.com/weekly/v55/i11/11a04602.htm (accessed November 7, 2008).

119. Andrew Ross, "Global U," in *The University Against Itself: The NYU Strike and the Future of the Academic Workplace*, ed. Monika Krause, Mary Nolan, Michael Palm, and Andrew Ross (Philadelphia: Temple University Press, 2008), 212–17.

120. Andrew Mills, "George Mason U. Will Close Its Campus in the Persian Gulf," *CHE*, February 27, 2009, http://chronicle.com/daily/2009/02/12575n.htm (accessed February 27, 2009); Mills, "Economic Crisis in Dubai Hits American Branch Campuses," *CHE*, December 14, 2009, http://chronicle.com/article/Economic-Crisis-in-Dubai-Hits/49489/?sid=at&utm_source=at&utm_medium=en (accessed January 13, 2010).

121. Adam Green, "The High Cost of Learning: Tuition, Educational Aid and the New Economics of Prestige in Higher Education," in *University Against Itself*, ed. Krause et al., 84.

122. "The College Cost Crisis Report: Are Institutions Accountable Enough to Students and Parents?" hearing before the Subcommittee on 21st Century Competitiveness of the Committee on Education and the Workforce, U.S. House of Representatives, 108th Congress, 1st Session, September 23, 2003.

123. Zusman, "Challenges Facing Higher Education," 73.

124. Doug Lederman, "Dropping a Bomb on Accreditation," *IHE*, April 2, 2006, http://www.insidehighered.com/news/2006/03/31/accredit (accessed April 2, 2006).

125. Sara Hebel, "Many Colleges Assess Learning but May Not Use Data to Improve, Survey Finds," *CHE*, July 15, 2009, http://chronicle.com/news/article/6791/

many-colleges-assess-learning-but-may-not-use-data-to-improve-survey-finds?utm_source=at&utm_medium=en (accessed July 16, 2009).

126. Doug Lederman, "AAU Gets on Board," *IHE*, May 7, 2007, http://www.insidehighered.com/news/2007/05/07/aau (accessed January 13, 2010); Doug Lederman, "No College Left Behind," *IHE*, February 15, 2006, http://www.insidehighered.com/news/2006/02/15/testing (accessed January 13, 2010).

127. Hebel, "Many Colleges Assess Learning."

128. Jack Hammond to the author, December 12, 2009.

129. Gaye Tuchman, *Wannabe U: Inside the Corporate University* (Chicago: University of Chicago Press, 2009), 45.

130. Diane Auer Jones, "Are Graduation and Retention Rates the Right Measures?" *CHE*, August 24, 2009, http://chronicle.com/blogPost/Are-GraduationRetention/7774/?sid=at&utm_source=at&utm_medium=en (accessed August 21, 2009); Andrew David Moltz, "Could the Wrong Assessment Kill the Liberal Arts?" *IHE*, July 21, 2008, http://insidehighered.com/news/2008/07/21/assessments (accessed July 21, 2008); Doug Lederman, "Foreseeing the Future of Accreditation," *IHE*, July 3, 2008, http://insidehighered.com/news/2008/06/30/accredit (accessed July 3, 2008).

Chapter 7: "Under Our Noses": Restructuring the Academic Profession

1. Ernest L. Boyer, *Scholarship Reconsidered: Priorities of the Professoriate* (Princeton, NJ: Carnegie Foundation for the Advancement of Teaching, 1990).

2. MLA Task Force on Evaluating Scholarship for Tenure and Promotion, "Report of the MLA Task Force on Evaluating Scholarship for Tenure and Promotion," December 2006, 22–23, http://www.mla.org/pdf/taskforcereport0608.pdf (accessed July 1, 2009) (hereafter MLA, "Task Force").

3. Jennifer Washburn, *University Inc.: The Corporate Corruption of Higher Education* (New York: Basic Books, 2005), 84; Ami Zusman, "Challenges Facing Higher Education in the Twenty-First Century," in *American Higher Education in the Twenty-First Century: Social, Political, and Economic Challenges*, ed. Philip G. Altbach, Robert O. Berdahl, and Patricia J. Gumport (Baltimore: Johns Hopkins University Press, 1999), 126; William G. Tierney, "Faculty Productivity and Academic Culture," in *Faculty Productivity: Facts, Fictions, and Issues*, ed. William G. Tierney (New York: Falmer Press, 1999), 44; James J. Duderstadt and Farris W. Womack, *The Future of the Public University in America: Beyond the Crossroads* (Baltimore: Johns Hopkins University Press, 2003), 55.

4. James S. Fairweather, "The Highly Productive Faculty Member: Confronting the Mythologies of Faculty Work," in *Faculty Productivity*, ed. Tierney, 57–58; Sheila Slaughter and Gary Rhoades, *Academic Capitalism and the New Economy: Markets, State, and Higher Education* (Baltimore: Johns Hopkins University Press, 2004), 312; Julius Getman, *In the Company of Scholars: The Struggle for the Soul of Higher Education* (Austin: University of Texas Press, 1992), 40–44; John Thelin, *A History of American Higher Education* (Baltimore: Johns Hopkins University Press, 2004), 356.

5. James S. Fairweather, *Faculty Work and Public Trust: Restoring the Value of Teaching and Public Service in American Academic Life* (Boston: Allyn and Bacon, 1996), 55–66.

6. Donald G. Stein, "A Personal Perspective on the Selling of Academia," in *Buying In or Selling Out? The Commercialization of the American Research University*, ed. Donald G. Stein (New Brunswick, NJ: Rutgers University Press, 2004), 5.

7. Louis Menand, "The Demise of Disciplinary Authority," in *What's Happened to the Humanities?* ed. Alvin Kernan (Princeton, NJ: Princeton University Press, 1997), 214.

8. Aims C. McGuinness Jr., "The States and Higher Education," in *American Higher Education in the Twenty-first Century: Social, Political, and Economic Challenges*, ed. Philip G. Altbach, Robert O. Berdahl, and Patricia J. Gumport, 2nd ed. (Baltimore: Johns Hopkins University Press, 1999, 2005), 217.

9. Derek Bok quoted in Fairweather, *Faculty Work and Public Trust*, 185–86.

10. Zusman, "Challenges," 127; Robert Iosue, "College Costs: The High Price of Declining Productivity," *Academic Questions* 1, no. 2 (Spring 1988): 46–48.

11. Stein, "A Personal Perspective," 2–5; Benjamin Johnson, "The Drain-O of Higher Education: Casual Labor and University Teaching," in *Steal This University: The Rise of the Corporate University and the Academic Labor Movement*, ed. Benjamin Johnson, Patrick Kavanagh, and Kevin Mattson (New York: Routledge, 2003), 65; Thelin, *History of American Higher Education*, 331; David L. Kirp, *Shakespeare, Einstein, and the Bottom Line: The Marketing of Higher Education* (Cambridge, MA: Harvard University Press, 2003), 40.

12. Philip G. Altbach, "Harsh Realities: The Professoriate Faces a New Century," in *American Higher Education*, ed. Altbach et al., 2nd ed., 299; Washburn, *University, Inc.*, 183–85.

13. Richard J. Benoff, "Federal R&D Obligations to Universities and Colleges Totaled $25 Billion in FY 2007," National Science Foundation Web site, September 2009, http://www.nsf.gov/statistics/infbrief/nsf09313 (accessed July 15, 2009).

14. Paul Basken, "U.S. May Need to Prune Number of Research Universities, Lobby Group Says," *CHE*, June 26, 2009, http://chronicle.com/daily/2009/06/20810n.htm (accessed June 29, 2009); Walter E. Massey, "Can the Research University Adapt to a Changing Future?" in *The Research University in a Time of Discontent*, ed. Jonathan R. Cole, Elinor G. Barger, and Stephen R. Graubard (Baltimore: Johns Hopkins University Press, 1994), 196.

15. Daniel T. Layzell, "Higher Education's Changing Environment: Faculty Productivity and the Reward Structure," in *Faculty Productivity*, ed. Tierney, 19; Denise Marie Tanguay, "Inefficient Efficiency: A Critique of Merit Pay," in *Steal This University*, ed. Johnson et al., 51–52. For an extended discussion of the complex issues involved with the assessment of quality in faculty work, see Larry A. Braskamp and John C. Ory, *Assessing Faculty Work: Enhancing Individual and Institutional Performance* (San Francisco: Jossey-Bass, 1994).

16. Zusman, "Challenges," 127; Roger L. Geiger, *Research and Relevant Knowledge: American Research Universities Since World War II* (New York: Oxford University Press, 1993), 324; William G. Tierney and Estela Mara Bensimon, *Promotion and Tenure:*

Community and Socialization in Academe (Albany: State University of New York Press, 1996), 66.

17. Donald Kennedy, *Academic Duty* (Cambridge, MA: Harvard University Press, 1997), 200, 194.

18. MLA, "Task Force," 38, 21.

19. Comments of J.P. Craig in Scott Jaschik, "6-6 Course Loads and No Benefits," *IHE*, November 12, 2008, http://insidehighered.com/news/2008/11/12/adjunct (accessed November 12, 2008).

20. Altbach, "Harsh Realities," 300; Slaughter and Rhoades, *Academic Capitalism and the New Economy*, 200–1; Michèle Lamont, *How Professors Think: Inside the Curious World of Academic Judgment* (Cambridge, MA: Harvard University Press, 2009), 55.

21. Slaughter and Rhoades, *Academic Capitalism and the New Economy*, 201.

22. Carnegie Commission on Higher Education, *The More Effective Use of Resources: An Imperative for Higher Education* (New York: McGraw-Hill, 1972), 70–71; Fairweather, *Faculty Work and Public Trust*, 27.

23. Kennedy, *Academic Duty*, 62.

24. Tierney and Bensimon, *Promotion and Tenure*, 60–62.

25. Zusman, "Challenges," 127.

26. Kennedy, *Academic Duty*, 18; Stein, "A Personal Perspective," 6.

27. MLA, "Task Force," 36.

28. Ibid., 10, 30–31.

29. Ibid., 20; Association of American University Presses, "Titles Published—Survey 2005," http://www.aaupnet.org/programs/2005TitlesPublished.pdf (accessed May 20, 2009).

30. MLA, "Task Force," 66.

31. Getman, *In the Company of Scholars*, 47; Jennifer Howard, "Scholarly Publishers Discuss How They're Adapting to Changing Realities," *CHE*, June 30, 2009, http://chronicle.com/daily/2008/06/3597n.htm (accessed July 3, 2009).

32. Duderstadt and Womack, *The Future of the Public University*, 71.

33. Patricia J. Gumport and Marc Chun, "Technology and Higher Education: Opportunities and Challenges for the New Era," in *American Higher Education*, ed. Altbach et al., 2nd ed., 413–17; Charles M. Vest, "Research Universities: Overextended, Underfocused; Overstressed, Underfunded," in *The American University: National Treasure or Endangered Species?* ed. Ronald G. Ehrenberg (Ithaca, NY: Cornell University Press, 1997), 41.

34. John G. Cross and Edie N. Goldenberg, *Off-Track Profs: Nontenured Teachers in Higher Education* (Cambridge, MA: MIT Press, 2009), 141.

35. Francis Oakley, "Ignorant Armies and Nighttime Clashes: Changes in the Humanities Classroom, 1970–1995," in *What's Happened to the Humanities?* ed. Kernan, 63; Gumport and Chun, "Technology and Higher Education," 417.

36. Robert A. Gorman, "Intellectual Property: The Rights of Faculty as Creators and Users," *Academe* 84, no. 3 (May/June 1998); Gary Rhoades, *Managed Professionals: Unionized Faculty and Restructuring Academic Labor* (Albany: State University of New York Press, 1998), 175–92.

37. MLA. "Task Force," 11; Rhoades, *Managed Professionals*, 176; Karen A. Holbrook and Eric C. Dahl, "Conflicting Goals and Values: When Commercialization Enters into Tenure and Promotion Decisions," in *Buying In, Selling Out*, ed. Stein, 95–96.

38. Cross and Goldenberg, *Off-Track Profs*, 123; John A. Centra, *Determining Faculty Effectiveness* (San Francisco: Jossey-Bass, 1979); Braskamp and Ory, *Assessing Faculty Work*.

39. Tierney and Bensimon, *Promotion and Tenure*, 64–65.

40. J.M., response to Sara Hebel, "Many Colleges Assess Learning but May Not Use Data to Improve, Survey Finds," *CHE*, July 15, 2009, http://chronicle.com/news/article/6791/many-colleges-assess-learning-but-may-not-use-data-to-improve-survey-finds?utm_source=at&utm_medium=en (accessed July 16, 2009).

41. Tierney and Bensimon, *Promotion and Tenure*, 62.

42. Scott Jaschik, "Changing the Tenure Rules—Without Telling Anyone?" *IHE*, April 1, 2008, http://insidehighered.com/news/2008/04/01/baylor (accessed April 1, 2008).

43. MLA, "Task Force," 10, 33, 66.

44. Ibid., 10.

45. Eileen E. Schell, *Gypsy Academics and Mother-Teachers: Gender, Contingent Labor, and Writing Instruction* (Portsmouth, NH: Boynton/Cook Publishers, Inc., 1998), 48; Mary Ann Mason, "Balancing Act: Rethinking the Tenure Clock," *CHE*, May 20, 2009, http://chronicle.com/jobs/news/2009/05/2009052001c.htm (accessed May 20, 2009).

46. MLA, "Task Force," 10.

47. Emily K. Abel, *Terminal Degrees: The Job Crisis in Higher Education* (New York: Praeger, 1984), 2–3; Patricia J. Gumport, "Graduate Education and Research: Interdependence and Strain," in *American Higher Education*, ed. Altbach et al., 2nd ed., 440; Carnegie Commission, *More Effective Use of Resources*, 2.

48. Geiger, *Research and Relevant Knowledge*, 222–23; Gumport, "Graduate Education and Research," 427.

49. Geiger, *Research and Relevant Knowledge*, 249–50.

50. Abel, *Terminal Degrees*, 3; Carnegie Commission, *More Effective Use of Resources*, 20.

51. Abel, *Terminal Degrees*, 4–6, Marc Bousquet, *How the University Works: Higher Education and the Low-Wage Nation* (New York: New York University Press, 2008), 191; Joe Berry, *Reclaiming the Ivory Tower: Organizing Adjuncts to Change Higher Education* (New York: Monthly Review Press, 2005), 5.

52. Gumport, "Graduate Education and Research," 444–45; Thelin, *History of American Higher Education*.

53. William G. Bowen and Julie Ann Sosa, *Prospects for Faculty in the Arts and Sciences: A Study of Factors Affecting Demand and Supply* (Princeton, NJ: Princeton University Press, 1989), 14, 7–8; Johnson, "The Drain-O of Higher Education," 68; Susan Meisenhelder with Kevin Mattson, "Renewing Academic Unions and Democracy at the Same Time: The Case of the California Faculty Association," in *Steal This University*, ed. Johnson et al., 226.

54. Gappa and Leslie, *Invisible Faculty*, 92; Bousquet, *How the University Works*, 198.

55. Rhoades, *Managed Professionals*, 135.

56. AAUP, "Trends in Faculty Status, 1975–2007," http://www.aaup.org/NR/rdonlyres/7D01E0C7-C255-41F1-9F11-E27D0028CB2A/0/TrendsinFacultyStatus2007.pdf (accessed August 11, 2009).

57. Benjamin Johnson, "The Drain-O of Higher Education," 62; Berry, *Reclaiming the Ivory Tower*, 4.

58. Gappa and Leslie, *Invisible Faculty*, 133.

59. Cross and Goldenberg, *Off-Track Profs*, 5, 27.

60. Gappa and Leslie, *Invisible Faculty*, 93–100, 110, 133.

61. Ibid., 51–53.

62. Rhoades, *Managed Professionals*, 170; Gappa and Leslie, *Invisible Faculty*, 111, 118; Marc Bousquet, "Composition as Management Science," in *Tenured Bosses and Disposable Teachers: Writing Instruction in the Managed University*, ed. Marc Bousquet, Tony Scott, and Leo Parascondola (Carbondale: Southern Illinois University Press, 2004), 21; Tony Scott, "Managing Labor and Literacy in the Future of Composition Studies," in *Tenured Bosses*, ed. Bousquet et al., 154; Sharon Crowley, "Preface," in Schell, *Gypsy Academics*, x.

63. Richard Monastersky, "America's Science Test: The Real Science Crisis: Bleak Prospects for Young Researchers," *CHE*, September 21, 2007, http://chronicle.com/weekly/v54/i04/04a00102.htm (accessed September 21, 2007).

64. Bousquet, "Composition as Management Studies," 1.

65. Abel, *Terminal Degrees*, 84.

66. Ibid., 50; Berry, *Reclaiming the Ivory Tower*, 13; Schell, *Gypsy Academics*, 44.

67. Bousquet, *How the University Works*, 23–26; Berry, *Reclaiming the Ivory Tower*, 10.

68. Gappa and Leslie, *Invisible Faculty*, 24–31; Johnson, "The Drain-O of Higher Education," 73; Schell, *Gypsy Academics*, 5, 44.

69. Gappa and Leslie, *Invisible Faculty*, 4–5, 9; Johnson, "The Drain-O of Higher Education," 63; Cross and Goldenberg, *Off-Track Profs*, 22–23.

70. Schell, *Gypsy Academics*, 54.

71. Bousquet, *How the University Works*, 3.

72. Berry, *Reclaiming the Ivory Tower*, 7; Audrey William June, "Nearly Half of Undergraduate Courses Are Taught by Non-Tenure-Track Instructors," *CHE*, December 3, 2008, http://chronicle.com/daily/2008/12/7951n.htm (accessed December 3, 2008); Eric Marshall, "Teaching Writing in a Managed Environment," in *Tenured Bosses*, ed. Bousquet et al., 115; Scott Jaschik, "6-6 Course Loads and No Benefits," *IHE*, November 12, 2008, http://insidehighered.com/news/2008/11/12/adjunct (accessed November 12, 2008); Audrey Williams June, "A Philosopher Stirs Up the World of Adjuncts," *CHE*, May 23, 2008, http://chronicle.com/weekly/v54/i37/37a00102.htm (accessed May 22, 2008).

73. M. Elizabeth Wallace, ed., *Part-Time Academic Employment in the Humanities* (New York: Modern Language Association of America, 1984), 17; Gappa and Leslie, *Invisible Faculty*, 59.

74. Gappa and Leslie, *Invisible Faculty*, 59.

75. Alexis Moore, "The Art of Work in the Age of the Adjunct," *in Steal This University*, ed. Johnson et al., 101.

76. Kevin Mattson, "How I Became a Worker," in *Steal This University*, ed. Johnson et al., 88.

77. Abel, *Terminal Degrees*, 119.

78. Schell, *Gypsy Academics*, 60–61; Moore, "The Art of Work in the Age of the Adjunct," 101; Marshall, "Teaching Writing in a Managed Environment," 115; Berry, *Reclaiming the Ivory Tower*, 11; Gappa and Leslie, *Invisible Faculty*, 104.

79. Wallace, *Part-Time Academic Employment*, 14–15; Gappa and Leslie, *Invisible Faculty*, 56.

80. Johnson, "The Drain-O of Higher Education," 76; Abel, *Terminal Degrees*, 35–38, 114; G. James Jason, "Roadblock to Research: One Part-Timer's View," in *Part-Time Academic Employment*, ed. Wallace, 66–68.

81. Gappa and Leslie, *Invisible Faculty*, 12.

82. Scott, "Managing Labor and Literacy," 154; Wallace, *Part-Time Academic Employment*, 7.

83. Bousquet, *How the University Works*, 70; Cross and Goldenberg, *Off-Track Profs*, 35–36, 44; Gappa and Leslie, *Invisible Faculty*, 42, 55; Ruth Kiefson, "The Politics and Economics of the Super-Exploitation of Adjuncts," in *Tenured Bosses*, ed. Bousquet et al., 148.

84. Abel, *Terminal Degrees*, 73.

85. Gappa and Leslie, *Invisible Faculty*, 43; Cross and Goldenberg, *Off-Track Profs*, 14.

86. Abel, *Terminal Degrees*, 86; Gappa and Leslie, *Invisible Faculty*, 42.

87. Cross and Goldenberg, *Off-Track Profs*, 21; Johnson, "The Drain-O of Higher Education," 78.

88. Gappa and Leslie, *Invisible Faculty*, 22–23.

89. Schell, *Gypsy Academics*, 68.

90. Deborah Foreman, "We're Not Your Colleagues," *CHE*, July 22, 2008, http://chronicle.com/jobs/news/2008/07/2008072101c.htm (accessed July 22, 2008); Wallace, *Part-Time Academic Employment*, 65.

91. Berry, *Reclaiming the Ivory Tower*, x.

92. Schell, *Gypsy Academics*, 62.

93. Ibid., 64.

94. Scott Jaschik, "Presidential 'Pabulum' and a Professor's Punishment," *IHE*, August 14, 2008, http://insidehighered.com/news/2008/08/11/rpi (accessed August 14, 2008).

95. Wallace, *Part-Time Academic Employment*, 28–29, 26; Rhoades, *Managed Professionals*, 161; Cross and Goldenberg, *Off-Track Profs*, 133–35.

96. Rhoades, *Managed Professionals*, 163; Abel, *Terminal Degrees*, 122; William H. Thelin and Leann Bertoncini, "When Critical Pedagogy Becomes Bad Teaching: Blunders in Adjunct Review," in *Tenured Bosses*, ed. Bousquet et al., 135–36; Scott Jaschik, "Out of Work for Doing Extra Work?" *IHE*, July 23, 2008, http://insidehighered.com/news/2008/07/23/ivytech (accessed July 23, 2008).

97. Berry, *Reclaiming the Ivory Tower*, 28.

98. Cross and Goldenberg, *Off-Track Profs*, 128.

99. Gappa and Leslie, *Invisible Faculty*, 6, 120–27.

100. Meisenhelder, "Renewing Academic Unions and Democracy," 226; Berry, *Reclaiming the Ivory Tower*, 15; David Glenn, " 'Gatekeeper' Courses Should Not Be Assigned to Part-Time Instructors, Research Suggests," *CHE*, March 27, 2008, http://chronicle.com/daily/2008/03/2276n.htm (accessed March 27, 2008); Scott Jaschik, "Adjuncts and Graduation Rates," *IHE*, October 16, 2006.

101. Washburn, *University, Inc.*, 204; Johnson, "The Drain-O of Higher Education," 76.

102. AAUP, "Academic Freedom and Tenure: Nicholls State University," 2008, http://www.aaup.org/AAUP/protect/academicfreedom/investrep/2008/Nicholls.htm (accessed December 20, 2009).

103. Rhoades, *Managed Professionals*, 166: Cross and Goldenberg, *Off-Track Profs*, 11, 16.

104. Douglas Giles, "Temperature Rising: Global to Local Threats Against Academic Freedom," Presentation at COCAL VII, Vancouver, BC, August 13, 2006, in Jane Buck, e-mail to the author, August 2006.

105. Scott Jaschik, "Freedom to Discuss Virginia Tech?" *IHE*, May 3, 2007, http://www.insidehighered.com/news/2007/04/24/winset (accessed December 20, 2009).

106. Elia Powers, "Column on Gay Marriage Prompts Dismissal," *IHE*, June 15, 2006, http://www.insidehighered.com/news/2006/06/15/byu (accessed December 20, 2009).

107. Scott Jaschik, "Adjuncts and God: Why Are 2 Instructors Out of Jobs?" *IHE*, September 24, 2007, http://www.insidehighered.com/news/2007/09/24/adjuncts (accessed December 20, 2009); Robin Wilson, "Adjuncts Fight Back over Academic Freedom," *CHE*, October 3, 2008, http://chronicle.com/weekly/v55/i06/06a00102.htm (accessed October 1, 2008).

108. Wilson, "Adjuncts Fight Back."

109. Scott Jaschik, "Vigilante Justice on Plagiarism," *IHE*, November 14, 2008, http://www.insidehighered.com/news/2008/11/13/tamiu (accessed November 14, 2008); Jaschik, "Out of Work for Doing Extra Work?"; Berry, *Reclaiming the Ivory Tower*, 76–78.

110. Abel, *Terminal Degrees*, 78; Thelin and Bertoncini, "When Critical Pedagogy Becomes Bad Teaching," 132–42; Schell, *Gypsy Academics*, 4.

111. Schell, "Toward a New Labor Movement," 101.

112. Schell, *Gypsy Academics*, 42; Micki McGee, "Blue Team, Gray Team: Some Varieties of the Contingent Faculty Experience," in *The University Against Itself: The NYU Strike and the Future of the Academic Workplace*, ed. Monika Krause, Mary Nolan, Michael Palm, and Andrew Ross (Philadelphia: Temple University Press, 2008), 97; Gappa and Leslie, *Invisible Faculty*, 5, 46–47, 85–90.

113. Gappa and Leslie, *Invisible Faculty*, 73–77; June, "A Philosopher Stirs Up the World of Adjuncts."

114. AAUP, "Conversion of Appointments to the Tenure Track," 2009, http://www.aaup.org/AAUP/comm/rep/conversion.htm (accessed December 20, 2009).

115. Scott Jaschik, "Conversion Experience," *IHE*, December 12, 2006, http://www.insidehighered.com/news/2006/12/12/gsu (accessed December 20, 2009).

116. Scott Jaschik, "Rethinking Work," *IHE*, December 31, 2007, http://insidehighered.com/news/2007/12/31/mlajobs (accessed December 31, 2007).

117. Bousquet, "Composition as Management Science," 30.

118. AAUP, "Conversion of Appointments."

119. Berry, *Reclaiming the Ivory Tower*, xiv.

120. Scott Jaschik, "The Union Impact and Non-Impact," *IHE*, June 3, 2008, http://insidehighered.com/news/2008/06/03/labor (accessed June 3, 2008).

121. Berry, *Reclaiming the Ivory Tower*, 75.

122. Meisenhelder, "Renewing Academic Unions and Democracy," 227; Berry, *Reclaiming the Ivory Tower*, 94–95; Bill Hendricks, "Making a Place for Labor: Composition and Unions," in *Tenured Bosses*, ed. Bousquet et al., 97.

123. Mattson, "How I Became a Worker," 92; Moore, "The Art of Work in the Age of the Adjunct," 102; Barbara Gottfried and Gary Zabel, "Social Movement Unionism and Adjunct Faculty Organizing in Boston," in *Steal This University*, ed. Johnson et al., 210.

124. Berry, *Reclaiming the Ivory Tower*, 76–78, 89; June, "A Philosopher Stirs Up the World of Adjuncts."

125. Berry, *Reclaiming the Ivory Tower*, 18, 26; Abel, *Terminal Degrees*, 123–24; Hendricks, "Making a Place for Labor," 92.

126. Schell, "Toward a New Labor Movement," 105; Gottfried and Zabel, "Social Movement Unionism," 212–13.

127. Hendricks, "Making a Place for Labor," 99.

128. Scott Jaschik, "Bargaining for More Tenure-Track Lines," *IHE*, August 27, 2007, http://www.insidehighered.com/news/2007/08/27/rutgers (accessed August 27, 2007).

129. Berry, *Reclaiming the Ivory Tower*, 85; Ashley Dawson and Penny Lewis, "New York: Academic Labor Town," in *University Against Itself*, ed. Krause et al., 25.

130. Scott Jaschik, "Revolt in the Adjunct Ranks," *IHE*, August 5, 2008, http://insidehighered.com/news/2008/07/30/cuny (accessed August 5, 2008).

131. Gottfried and Zabel, "Social Movement Unionism," 212–13.

132. Frank R. Kemerer and J. Victor Baldridge, *Unions on Campus* (San Francisco: Jossey-Bass, 1975), 74.

133. Everett Carll Ladd Jr. and Seymour Martin Lipset, *Professors, Unions, and American Higher Education* (Berkeley: Carnegie Foundation for the Advancement of Teaching, 1973), 3, 29–32, 105; Kemerer and Baldridge, *Unions on Campus*, 4, 28–29, 39–46, 52–55: Mary Nolan, "A Leadership University for the Twenty-First Century? Corporate Administration, Contingent Labor, and the Erosion of Faculty Rights," in *University Against Itself*, ed. Krause et al., 53–54.

134. Philo A. Hutcheson, *A Professional Professoriate: Unionization, Bureaucratization, and the AAUP* (Nashville, TN: Vanderbilt University Press, 2000), 62.

135. Ralph S. Brown Jr., "Representation of Economic Interests: Report of a Conference," *Bulletin of the American Association of University Professors* 51, no. 3 (September 1965): 377.

136. Fritz Machlup and Robert Bierstedt, "Dissent" to "Representation of Economic Interests," *AAUP Bulletin* 52, no. 2 (June 1966): 233.

137. Robert K. Webb, "Statement," in "Collective Bargaining and the Structure and Functioning of the Association," report by the Executive Committee for the Council, October 1971, *AAUP Bulletin*.

138. Ladd and Lipset, *Professors, Unions, and American Higher Education*, 6; Hutcheson, *Professional Professoriate*, 153–58.

139. For an excellent assessment of the *Yeshiva* decision and its implications, see David M. Rabban, "Distinguishing Excluded Managers from Covered Professionals Under the NLRA," *Columbia Law Review* 89, no. 8 (December 1989): 1775–860.

140. Joan Moriarity and Michelle Savarese, *Directory of Faculty Contracts and Bargaining Agents in Institutions of Higher Education* (New York: National Center for the Study of Collective Bargaining in Higher Education and the Professions, 2006), 85.

141. Rhoades, *Managed Professionals*, 133.

142. Johnson, "The Drain-O of Higher Education," 79.

143. Bousquet, "Composition as Management Science," 27; Bousquet, *How the University Works*, 33–40; Christopher Newfield and Greg Grandin, "Building a Statue of Smoke: Finance Culture and the NYU Trustees," in *University Against Itself*, ed. Krause et al., 68; Susan Valentine, "The Administration Strikes Back: Union Busting at NYU," in *University Against Itself*, ed. Krause et al. 123–26.

144. Nolan, "A Leadership University," 48.

145. McGee, "Blue Team, Gray Team," 116–21; Jeff Goodwin, "Which Side Are We On? NYU's Full-Time Faculty and the GSOC Strike," in *University Against Itself*, ed. Krause et al., 162–68.

146. Corey Robin, "Blacklisted and Blue: On Theory and Practice at Yale," in *Steal This University*, ed. Johnson et al., 108.

147. Kennedy, *Academic Duty*, 286–87.

Epilogue: "Everything Is on the Table": The Academy's Response to the Great Recession

1. Nina Munk, "Rich Harvard, Poor Harvard," *Vanity Fair*, August 2009, http://www.vanityfair.com/politics/features/2009/08/harvard200908 (accessed July 27, 2009); Paul Fain, "Budget Cuts Cast Shadow over Florida's Universities," *CHE*, May 29, 2009, http://chronicle.com/weekly/v55/i38/38a00101.htm (accessed May 27, 2009).

2. Josh Keller, "Pacific West: States' Public Focus Collides with Budget Reality," *CHE*, August 24, 2009, http://chronicle.com/article/Pacific-West-States-Public/48148 (accessed August 24, 2009); Fain, "Budget Cuts"; Jack Stripling, "Insult to Injury," *CHE*, November 2, 2009, http://www.insidehighered.com/news/2009/11/02/cuts (accessed November 3, 2009); Josh Keller, "In California Budget Deal, Bad News for Colleges in 2010," *CHE*, July 21, 2009, http://chronicle.com/daily/2009/07/22372n.htm (accessed July 21, 2009); Robin Wilson, "Downturn Threatens the Faculty's Role in Running

Colleges," *CHE*, February 6, 2009, http://chronicle.com/weekly/v55/i22/22a00102.htm (accessed February 2, 2009).

3. Keller, "In California Budget Deal, Bad News for Colleges in 2010"; Stripling, "Insult to Injury"; Howard Bunsis, "Analysis of the Financial Condition of the University of Illinois System," January 2010, http://www.uigeo.org/wp-content/uploads/2010/03/Bunsis-analysis-of-UIC-financial-condition-Afternoon-29-January-2010.pdf (accessed March 25, 2010).

4. Jack Stripling, "Revenue Dip for Private Colleges," *IHE* November 3, 2009, http://www.insidehighered.com/news/2009/11/03/moodys (accessed November 3, 2009); Tamar Lewin, "Investment Losses Cause Steep Dip in University Endowments, Study Finds," *NYT*, January 28, 2010; Munk, "Rich Harvard, Poor Harvard"; David Shieh, "Johns Hopkins Freezes Hiring and Salaries, and Will Cut Top Administrators' Pay," *CHE*, February 13, 2009, http://chronicle.com/news/article/5977/johns-hopkins-freezes-hiring-and-salaries-and-will-cut-top-administrators-pay (accessed February 13, 2009); Goldie Blumenstyk, "In a Time of Uncertainty, Colleges Hold Fast to the Status Quo," *CHE*, October 25, 2009, http://chronicle.com/article/In-a-Time-of-Uncertainty/48911/?sid=at&utm_source=at&utm_medium=en (accessed October 27, 2009).

5. Doug Lederman, "The Economy's Large Shadow," *IHE*, June 29, 2009, http://www.insidehighered.com/news/2009/06/29/nacua#Comments (accessed June 29, 2009); Eric Hoover and Beckie Supiano, "Marketing Consultants Offer Advice on Making the Most of the Recession," *CHE*, February 2, 2009, http://chronicle.com/daily/2009/02/10870n.htm (accessed February 4, 2009); James Tracy, "Envisioning Faculty Layoffs," n.d., UFF-FAU, Blog Archive, http://www.uff-fau.org/?p=279 (accessed January 24, 2010); Blumenstyk, "In a Time of Uncertainty."

6. Doug Lederman, "Performance (De-)Funding," *IHE*, December 29, 2009, http://www.insidehighered.com/news/2009/12/28/indiana (accessed December 29, 2009); Chas Sisk, "Tennessee Lawmakers Pass Higher-Education Bill," *Tennessean*, January 22, 2010, http://www.tennessean.com/article/20100122/NEWS0201/1220326/1009/NEWS02 (accessed January 22, 2010).

7. Stripling, "Insult to Injury"; Eric Kelderman, "U. of Washington Cuts Hundreds of Jobs," *CHE*, April 30, 2009, http://chronicle.com/news/article/6407/u-of-washington-cuts-hundreds-of-jobs?utm_source=at&utm_medium=en (accessed May 1, 2009); "Proposed MSU Cuts Upset Staff, Students," *Lansing State Journal*, http://www.lansingstatejournal.com/apps/pbcs.dll/article?AID=2009310310004 (accessed November 3, 2009); Nate Holdren to H-Labor, August 1, 2009, http://h-net.msu.edu/cgi-bin/logbrowse.pl?trx=vx&list=h-labor&month=0908&week=a&msg=WcrJ7s419sOSPPHZgzGx8Q&user=&pw= (accessed March 20, 2010); Mark G. Yudof, "Why the U. of California Has to Raise Tuition," *CHE*, October 6, 2009, http://chronicle.com/article/Why-the-U-of-California-Has/48636/?sid=at&utm_source=at&utm_medium=en (accessed October 6, 2009); "U. System of Maryland to Cut 175 Jobs, Including Some Faculty Positions," *CHE*, August 2, 2009, http://chronicle.com/blogPost/U-System-of-Maryland-to-Cut/7556/?utm_source=at&utm_medium=en (August 24, 2009); Blumenstyk, "In a Time of Uncertainty"; Erica Hendry, "Faculty Members and Union Protest Staff Layoffs at Temple U. as 'Cruel,'" *CHE*,

May 29, 2009, http://chronicle.com/blogPost/Faculty-MembersUnion-P/7342/ (accessed June 1, 2009).

8. "Academic Freedom and Tenure: Clark Atlanta University," http://www.aaup.org/AAUP/protect/academicfreedom/investrep/2010/clarkatlanta.htm (accessed January 23, 2010).

9. Elizabeth Redden, "Broken Covenant," *IHE*, April 15, 2009, http://www.insidehighered.com/news/2009/04/15/covenant (accessed April 15, 2009); Robin Wilson, "In Hard Times, Colleges Search for Ways to Trim the Faculty," *CHE*, June 26, 2009, http://chronicle.com/weekly/v55/i40/40a00103.htm (accessed June 22, 2009); Eric Kelderman, "Pa. State System Considers Consolidating Programs amid Financial Squeeze," *CHE*, September 14, 2009, http://chronicle.com/article/Pa-State-System-Considers/48361/?sid=at&utm_source=at&utm_medium=en (accessed September 14, 2009); Jack Stripling, "Cruel Irony," August 14, 2009, *IHE*, http://www.insidehighered.com/news/2009/08/14/economics (accessed August 14, 2009); "Proposed MSU Cuts Upset Staff, Students"; "Baker U. Eliminates 5 Majors," *IHE*, February 11, 2010, http://www.insidehighered.com/news/2010/02/11/qt#219910 (accessed February 11, 2010).

10. David Moltz, "So Sue Me," *IHE*, July 6, 2009, http://www.insidehighered.com/news/2009/07/06/edison (accessed July 6, 2009).

11. "U. System of Maryland to Cut 175 Jobs"; Mike Fekula to H-Labor, August 3, 2009, http://h-net.msu.edu/cgi-bin/logbrowse.pl?trx=vx&list=h-labor&month=0908&week=a&msg=AIBPNJOtJr5EAEBn%2bTyEdg&user=&pw= (accessed March 20, 2010); Gary A. Olson, "The Unkindest Cut of All," *CHE*, October 5, 2009, http://chronicle.com/article/The-Unkindest-Cut-of-All/48694/?sid=at&utm_source=at&utm_medium=en (accessed October 6, 2009); Jack Hammond, e-mail to the author, January 26, 2010; Gary Rhoades, e-mail to the author, January 29, 2010.

12. Blumenstyk, "In a Time of Uncertainty"; Shieh, "Johns Hopkins Freezes Hiring and Salaries"; Kathryn Masterson, "2 Ivy League Universities, Hit by Financial Crisis, Announce Hiring Freezes," *CHE*, November 5, 2008, http://chronicle.com/news/index.php?id=5444 (accessed November 5, 2008); Sara Hebel, "Midwest: States Turn to Colleges to Help Reinvent Economies and Retool Workers," *CHE*, August 24, 2009, http://chronicle.com/article/Midwest-States-Turn-to-Col/48146/ (accessed August 26, 2009); Robert Townsend, "A Grim Year on the Academic Job Market for Historians," *Perspectives on History*, January 2010, http://www.historians.org/Perspectives/issues/2010/1001/1001new1.cfm (accessed January 26, 2010).

13. Townsend, "A Grim Year"; Scott Jaschik, "Disappearing Jobs," *IHE*, December 17, 2009, http://www.insidehighered.com/news/2009/12/17/mla (accessed December 17, 2009); Jaschik, "The Job Crisis for Faculty Jobs—Especially for New Ph.D.'s Looking for Tenure-Track Jobs—Is Spreading," *IHE*, January 4, 2010, http://www.insidehighered.com/news/2010/01/04/nojobs#Comments (accessed January 4, 2010).

14. Paul Fain, "Private Colleges Freeze Salaries and Slash Benefits, Survey Finds," *CHE*, August 12, 2009, http://chronicle.com/article/Private-Colleges-Freeze/47984/?sid=at&utm_source=at&utm_medium=en (accessed August 13, 2009); Sara Hebel, "Midwest: States Turn to Colleges"; Audrey Williams June, "Contract Fight at

U. of Hawaii Knocks Down Faculty Morale," *CHE*, January 11, 2010, http://chronicle.com/article/Contract-Fight-at-U-of-Hawaii/63466/?sid=at&utm_source=at&utm_medium=en (accessed January 11, 2010); "Greensboro College Cuts Salaries 20%," *IHE*, April 20, 2009, http://www.insidehighered.com/news/2009/04/20/qt#196770 (accessed April 29, 2009); Thomas Bartlett, "For Most, a Furlough Is No Day at the Beach," *CHE*, April 10, 2009, http://chronicle.com/weekly/v55/i31/31a00104.htm (accessed April 10, 2009); "Georgia Regents Approve 6 Furlough Days for Public-University Employees," *CHE*, August 12, 2009, http://chronicle.com/blogPost/Georgia-Regents-Approve-6-F/7653 (accessed August 12, 2009); Doug Lederman, "A Tradeoff Worth Making," *IHE*, June 2, 2009, http://www.insidehighered.com/news/2009/06/02/matc (accessed June 2, 2009).

15. Nanette Asimov, "College Seeks Sponsors to Save Courses," *San Francisco Chronicle*, June 21, 2009, http://www.sfgate.com/cgi-bin/article.cgi?f=/c/a/2009/06/21/BA7N18930O.DTL (accessed June 22, 2009); Blumenstyk, "In a Time of Uncertainty"; Stripling, "Tarnished Jewel."

16. Josh Keller, "Pacific West: States' Public Focus Collides with Budget Reality," *CHE*, August 24, 2009, http://chronicle.com/article/Pacific-West-States-Public/48148 (accessed August 24, 2009); Josh Keller, "At Transfer Time in California, Thousands of Students Hit a Dead End," *CHE*, October 5, 2009, http://chronicle.com/article/At-Transfer-Time-Thousands-of/48678/?sid=at&utm_source=at&utm_medium=en (accessed October 6, 2009).

17. Eric Kelderman, "U. of Washington Cuts Hundreds of Jobs," *CHE*, April 30, 2009, http://chronicle.com/news/article/6407/u-of-washington-cuts-hundreds-of-jobs?utm_source=at&utm_medium=en (accessed May 1, 2009); Stripling, "Insult to Injury"; Keller, "Pacific West: States Public Focus Collides with Budget Reality"; Goldie Blumenstyk, "Nacubo Meeting Attendees Say Economic Downturn Is Not All Bad News," *CHE*, June 30, 2009, http://chronicle.com/daily/2009/06/21032n.htm (accessed June 30, 2009); Scott Jaschik, "Tuition Is Up, Loans Are Shifting," *IHE*, October 21, 2009, http://www.insidehighered.com/news/2009/10/21/tuition (accessed October 22, 2009); Jack Stripling, "Revenue Dip for Private Colleges," *IHE*, November 3, 2009, http://www.insidehighered.com/news/2009/11/03/moodys (accessed November 3, 2009).

18. "65 Demonstrators Arrested at Berkeley as Protests Continue," *CHE*, December 11, 2009, http://chronicle.com/blogPost/65-Demonstrators-Arrested-at/9180/?sid=pm&utm_source=pm&utm_medium=en (accessed December 13, 2009); Jennifer Epstein, "New Wave of Student Activism," *IHE*, December 3, 2009, http://www.insidehighered.com/news/2009/12/03/activism (accessed December 3, 2009); Meredith Kolodner, "CUNY Bigs Get Pay Hike While Tuition Spikes," *Daily News*, January 7, 2010, http://www.nydailynews.com/ny_local/2010/01/07/2010-01-07_cuny_bigs_get_pay_hike_while_tuition_spikes.html#ixzz0cR1uXv5w (accessed January 7, 2010); John Thelin, "How to Bail Out Public Universities," *CHE*, October 18, 2009, http://chronicle.com/article/How-to-Bail-Out-Public/48818/?sid=at&utm_source=at&utm_medium=en (accessed October 22, 2009); Jaschik, "Tuition Is Up"; Christopher Newfield, "Militant Chairs," July 8, 2009, in EduFactory: Conflicts and Transformations of the University, http://www.edu-factory.org/edu15/index

.php?option=com_content&view=article&id=190:militant-chairs&catid=38:documentation&Itemid=56 (accessed January 19, 2010); Audrey Williams June, "Surge in Adjunct Activism Is Spurred by Bad Economy and Hungry Unions," *CHE*, December 14, 2009, http://chronicle.com/article/Surge-in-Adjunct-Activism-Is/49492/?sid=at&utm_source=at&utm_medium=en (accessed December 15, 2009).

19. "Collective Bargaining Agreement 2.0 Is Ratified," Akron-AAUP Web site, http://www.akronaaup.org/negotiations.html (accessed February 12, 2010).

20. Scott Jaschik, "The Economic Freeze on History," *IHE*, September 14, 2009, http://www.insidehighered.com/news/2009/09/14/history (accessed September 14, 2009).

INDEX